NAVAL BATTLES
FIRST WORLD WAR

Geoffrey Bennett served in the Royal Navy from 1923 until 1958, during which time he was for three years Naval Attaché in Moscow. As well as novels and children's books written under a *nom de plume*, he is the author of several distinguished books on the history of sea warfare, which include *The Battle of Jutland, Coronel and the Falklands,* and *Battle of the River Plate*.

GRAND STRATEGY

The books in this series show various developments in military science and tactics in their historical, political and strategic contexts. All are new editions of standard works, widely acclaimed for their authoritative approach, and complete with illustrations and maps. They will be revealing to the general reader, of marked interest to students of military history, and appealing to the growing numbers of war-gamers and military enthusiasts.

The painting *The Battle of the Dardanelles,* by Cull, is reproduced on the cover by kind permission of the National Maritime Museum, London.

Also available in this series

THE BOMBER OFFENSIVE
GALLIPOLI
GOOD-BYE DOLLY GRAY

Grand Strategy

NAVAL BATTLES OF THE FIRST WORLD WAR

GEOFFREY BENNETT

REVISED EDITION

PAN BOOKS LTD : LONDON

First published 1968 by B. T. Batsford Ltd
This revised edition published 1974 by Pan Books Ltd,
33 Tothill Street, London SW1

ISBN 0 330 23862 0

For Douglas and Chris

Printed in Great Britain by
Richard Clay (The Chaucer Press), Ltd, Bungay, Suffolk

Contents

List of Illustrations

Maps and Diagrams

Author's Acknowledgement

Since this book is derived, in part, from my two earlier works in this series, *Coronel and The Falklands* and *The Battle of Jutland*, my first duty must be to renew my thanks to all those whose help I then acknowledged. I am also grateful to the many readers who found both books of sufficient interest to offer constructive comments, of which I have taken advantage in this one.

I cannot express adequately my gratitude to Dr Douglas Robinson of Pennington, New Jersey, for the many hours which he spent in copying and translating German sources for me: this 'labour of love', together with his careful checking of my manuscript and proofs, have been of untold value.

I should be remiss if I did not also acknowledge the help which I have received from the work of another American friend of the Royal Navy, Professor Arthur Marder, whose four volumes titled *From the Dreadnought to Scapa Flow* are unlikely to be surpassed.

Historians who may make use of this book will wish to know that the quotations from contemporary documents and other sources are not always verbatim: for reasons of space I have abbreviated and edited without disfiguring them with ellipses and square brackets.

London, 1968 (Revised 1973)   *Geoffrey Bennett*

The Author and Publishers wish to thank the following for permission to reproduce the illustrations in this book: Captain A. D. Duckworth RN for figs 30 and 32; Associated Newspapers Ltd for fig 27; the Imperial War Museum for figs 1–3, 5–7, 8, 9, 11, 12, 14, 16, 17, 18, 20–26, 28–34, 36–41, 44–50 and 52–4; Süddeutscher Verlag, Munich for figs 4, 10, 19, 35 and 42; Verlag Ullstein, Berlin for figs 14, 43 and 51.

Notes

Abbreviations used in this book include:

AMC Armed merchant cruiser
BCS Battlecruiser Squadron
BS Battle Squadron (i.e. squadron of battleships)
CS Cruiser Squadron
DF Destroyer Flotilla (British) – each having a normal strength of 16 destroyers led by a light cruiser or flotilla leader
LCS Light Cruiser Squadron
RNAS Royal Naval Air Service
SG Scouting Group (German) (i.e. squadron of battlecruisers or light cruisers)
SMS *Seine Majestäts Schiffe* (His Majesty's Ship)
TBF Torpedoboat Flotilla (German) – each having a normal strength of 11 torpedoboats
W/T Wireless telegraphy

Battle Fleet (i.e. with initial capitals) is used to distinguish the main body of the British Grand Fleet or of the German High Seas Fleet (i.e. its battle squadrons *plus* its supporting cruiser squadrons and destroyer or torpedoboat flotillas) in contradistinction to *battle fleet* (i.e. with small initial letters) which refers only to each side's battle squadrons.

Destroyer is used for British vessels, *torpedoboat* for German, to facilitate distinction between the opposing flotillas and to emphasize the latter's superior torpedo armament in contrast to the former's greater gunpower.

Signal is used for messages transmitted by any means (flags, semaphore, light, W/T etc) although the Royal Navy was at this time accustomed to use *telegram* for those that went by cable or land line.

Bearings and courses are magnetic because most ships relied on this type of compass until after the First World War.

Times are given by the 24-hour clock, so as to avoid confusion between AM and PM. Where necessary they have been adjusted to agree with the zone time in use by the British ships concerned.

PROLOGUE

1

Operation 'ZZ'

The surrender of the German High Seas Fleet

Ever since that fateful 4 August 1914, I have remained
steadfast in my confidence that the Royal Navy would once
more prove the sure shield of the British Empire in the hour
of trial. Never in its history has the Royal Navy done
greater things for us, nor better sustained its old glories.

King George V, 21 November 1918

It is just fifty years – within the lifetime of some who will read these
words; for others, an age before they were born – since King
George V wrote in his diary: 'The great day has come, and we have
won the war'; to those who came through it the Great War, to us now
the First World War. Britain, France, Italy, the USA and the other
Allied Powers had granted Imperial Germany's request for an armistice: at 1100 on 11 November 1918, hostilities ceased on all fronts
after four and a half years of devastating conflict. And while London
mafficked, 'flag officers sang and danced with seamen and marines'
(according to *The Times*) on board the ships of the Grand Fleet as
they swung to their moorings off Rosyth – all, that is, except for the
commander of the 1st LCS. 'Why are you looking so sad?' asked a
brother officer. 'Nothing left to live for,' replied Rear-Admiral Walter
Cowan. 'He was,' reflected one of his captains, 'the only officer who
was sorry the war was over.'

Five weeks had elapsed since the German Chancellor, Prince Max
of Baden, had appealed to President Woodrow Wilson to bring about
this armistice. Obsessed with the need to destroy the armed might
with which Germany had all but conquered his country for a second
time within half a century, Marshal Foch, Generalissimo of the Allied
armies, drafted terms without naval conditions, lest they should
prejudice acceptance of his rigorous military ones. Admiral Sir David

Beatty, C-in-C of the Grand Fleet, protested. 'The Navy has swept the enemy from the seas and rendered secure the vast lines of communication of the Allies. Because ours was a passive victory, is no reason why we should not reap the fruits of that victory, the destruction of German sea power.' Knowing how near the unrestricted U-boat campaign had been to success before the Allied blockade brought Germany close to starvation, the First Sea Lord, Admiral Sir Rosslyn Wemyss, pressed Beatty's demand. As the German Army retreated from France and Belgium across the Rhine, the Supreme War Council revised the armistice terms: all U-boats must be surrendered and the enemy's surface fleet interned in an Allied harbour. 'Is it admissible that our Fleet should be given up without having been beaten?' queried the German delegates when these conditions were presented to them on 8 November. Fixing his adversaries with his monocle, Wemyss gave the frigid answer: 'It had only to come out.' Since their ships' companies had hoisted the red flag of mutiny when ordered to do just that as recently as 29 October, the Germans signed without further protest.

Nor was there delay in implementing these naval clauses. Forty-eight hours after the end of hostilities, the new light cruiser *Königsberg* sailed with 'the plenipotentiaries of the Workmen's and Soldiers' Councils of the German Fleet to meet representatives of the British Admiralty' (as a Berlin source expressed it). Fortunately, these six petty officers allowed their C-in-C, Admiral Franz von Hipper, to send Rear-Admiral Hugo Meurer with them; for when the *Königsberg* reached Inchkeith, whence the destroyer *Oak* conveyed the delegates to the Grand Fleet flagship at her berth above the Forth Bridge, Beatty made very clear that he would receive none but Meurer and his staff. Late next day, the evening of 16 November, the *Königsberg* returned to Germany with orders for the High Seas Fleet's submission. And as soon as the 20th, Rear-Admiral Sir Reginald Tyrwhitt, commanding the Harwich Force, received the surrender of the first 20 U-boats, which were followed by others on succeeding days until as many as 150 were berthed in the estuary of the Essex Stour.

On the 20th, too, King George V visited Rosyth, and was cheered by the Grand Fleet before, for the last time, it sailed as one mighty force in accordance with instructions appropriately titled *Operation ZZ*. Early on 21 November, whilst it was still dark, an awe-inspiring procession of ominous black shapes weighed anchor and began to move silently seawards. By daybreak, two squadrons of battle-cruisers, five squadrons of battleships and seven squadrons of cruisers were formed up in two columns six miles apart, each some 15 miles long, with Commodore Hugh Tweedie shepherding 150 destroyers ahead of them, all steaming eastwards at a sedate 12 knots. And as the rising sun showed its rim through a rift in the slate-grey clouds, bugles called their companies to action stations. The German ships they had come to meet had been ordered to sail with reduced crews and without ammunition, but a nation that had chosen humiliation rather than destruction might yet attempt some treachery against its conquerors.

But there was no fight in the Germans that day when they emerged like grey ghosts out of the white mist ahead of the Grand Fleet short-ly before 1000. The larger vessels were in a single column: five battle-cruisers, *Seydlitz*, *Moltke*, *Hindenburg*, *Derfflinger* and *Von der Tann*, preceded the *Friedrich der Grosse*, wearing the flag of Rear-Admiral von Reuter, and eight more dreadnoughts, the *Grosser Kurfürst*, *Prinzregent Luitpold*, *Markgraf*, *Bayern*, *Kaiserin*, *Kronprinz*, *Kaiser* and *König Albert*. Followed by seven light cruisers and 49 destroyers, these were led by Rear-Admiral Sir Edwin Alexander-Sinclair, in the light cruiser *Cardiff*, between the British lines until the *Queen Elizabeth*, flying the *Lion*'s shot-torn Jutland ensign, was abeam of the German flagship. Beatty's squadrons then wheeled outwards to-gether on to the westerly course being steered by their erstwhile foes. The column now to starboard comprised 19 battleships, five battlecruisers and four squadrons of cruisers; the port column 14 battleships, four battlecruisers, an aircraft-carrier and three squad-rons of cruisers. The flotillas followed this massive demonstration of maritime power which included more than one reminder that the Dominions and the Allies had made their contribution to the war at sea. The *Canada* and *Malaya* were among the battleships, the *Australia* and *New Zealand* among the battlecruisers. The 6th BS comprised five US dreadnoughts, headed by the *New York* fly-ing the flags of Admiral W. S. Sims and Rear-Admiral Hugh Rod-man. The cruiser *Amiral Aube* and two destroyers were of the French Navy.

To no louder sound than the swish of the sea, the hum of boiler room fans, and the whisper of the wind, captors and captives headed for Aberlady Bay, inside May Island, where the German ships dropped anchor. Not until then was the silence broken, the tension in the Grand Fleet relaxed. As each Allied ship passed to its berth higher up the Firth of Forth, officers and men saluted their victorious Com-mander-in-Chief with deep-throated cheers. 'The German flag will be hauled down at sunset today and will not be hoisted again without permission,' signalled Beatty before the Preparative fluttered down from the *Queen Elizabeth*'s masthead, and the bugles' sunset call was echoed by the Scottish hills across the sun-reddened waters of the Forth. 'It is my intention to hold a service of thanksgiving at 1800 today for the victory which Almighty God has vouchsafed to our arms,' signalled Beatty again – and when afterwards he addressed his flagship's crew, he ended with these all-sufficient words: 'Didn't I tell you they would have to come out?'

Next day the German ships were inspected to ensure that they carried no ammunition in their magazines, and that their guns had been rendered useless. Then they were escorted to Scapa Flow, to lie rusting at their anchors under the watchful eye of a British battle squadron. In the same week, an Allied deputation reached Kiel, charged with the task of sending the battleships *König* and *Baden*, the new light cruiser *Dresden*, and one more destroyer to Britain, to complete the numbers specified in the armistice terms; and to ensure that the handful of early dreadnoughts, obsolescent battleships and other warships that were allowed to remain in German ports, were disarmed and paid off. The curtain was thus rung down on one of the most momentous events in the long history of war: a great Navy had given three score of its best ships and all its submarines into ignominious captivity.

Many a good vessel has struck its flag in battle; many another has faced destruction rather than surrender; but the annals of naval warfare hold no parallel to 21 November 1918. 'The surrender of the German Fleet, accomplished without shock of battle, will remain for all time the example of the wonderful silence and sureness with which sea power attains its ends,' signalled the Admiralty. 'The world recognizes that this is due to the steadfastness with which the Navy has maintained its pressure on the enemy through more than four years of war, a pressure exerted no less insistently during the long months of waiting than in the rare opportunities of attack.' How that pressure was maintained is the subject of this book; and, if it highlights the 'rare opportunities of attack', 'the long months of waiting' should not be forgotten. First, however, a brief reminder of why, on 4 August 1914, Britain was required to meet such a vainglorious challenge by a haughty despot who, in the end, like Xerxes at Salamis, reaped the harvest

> *Of overweening pride, after full flower,*
> *Beneath a sheaf of doom, and garnered up*
> *A harvest all of tears.*

Of all the interlocking complex of causes which resulted in the First World War, one is not disputed; Kaiser Wilhelm II's determination to seize Britannia's trident. From her long struggle against Napoleon, Britain had emerged the predominant naval power: in 1815 her ships were without peer in both numbers and quality; their officers and men were skilled by twenty years of war at sea, and inspired by Nelson's three annihilating victories. But in the subsequent three-quarters of a century, Government parsimony – the Naval Estimates were consistently held below a paltry £10 million – cut the number of vessels fit to lie in the Royal Navy's line of battle from more than 100 wooden-hulled sailing ships, mounting broadside armaments of 60 to 120 guns, to as few as 27 steam-driven ironclads, with two or four turret-mounted guns, against which Britain's potential enemies, France and Russia, could match as many as 36. The dangerous extent to which Britain's naval strength had been eroded was revealed in 1885: when a Russian threat required the Admiralty to commission a squadron for service in the Baltic, they could assemble no more than a 'menagerie of unruly and curiously assorted ships', because the greater part of the Fleet was policing the Empire overseas. Persuaded by such naval Members as Captain Lord Charles Beresford, and by the press, led by W. T. Stead, Parliament passed the Naval Defence Act of 1889, which transformed Britain's battle fleet from an ineffective force of experimental ironclads into homogeneous squadrons that were the admiration of the world: in the next two decades more than 50 first-class battleships were built whilst France and Russia together completed only half this number.

By then, however – the first years of the new century – these two nations were no longer Britain's likely foes. Prince von Bismarck's unification of Germany (1866) had enabled the Prussian and other German armies to overwhelm France in less than six weeks (1870); and with the subsequent rapid growth of German industry and commerce, a new world Power was born. The Iron Chancellor might be content to dominate Europe with the military might of the Triple Alliance – Germany, Austria-Hungary and Italy – formed in 1882, and to rely on tactful diplomacy to avoid a conflict with British interests further afield; but Wilhelm II, who succeeded to the German throne in 1888, had very different ideas. This impulsive, power-hungry grandson of Queen Victoria determined to pursue an aggressive foreign policy. His first obstacle was soon removed: in 1890 von Bismarck resigned. Next, by making the Chiefs of the Imperial Naval Cabinet (*Marinekabinett*) and of the Naval Staff (*Admiralstab*) directly responsible to him, the Kaiser gained personal control of his Fleet. But to what avail so long as it numbered only four battle-ships? He needed 'a certain measure of naval power as a political factor against Britain', if Germany was to gain her rightful 'place in the sun'.

In Rear-Admiral Alfred Tirpitz the Kaiser found the man to over-come the Reichstag's refusal to vote funds for the Navy he had dreamed of building ever since his boyhood visits to Portsmouth Dockyard. Remembering how his ships had been ignominiously confined to Schillig Roads by the blockade of a superior enemy during the Franco-Prussian War, this able specialist in the mine and the torpedo was so obsessed with Germany's need for a powerful battle fleet that, within a year of being appointed State Secretary of the Imperial Naval Office in 1897, he had virtually tricked the Reich-stag into authorizing the construction of as many as 19 battleships. And when Britain responded to the Kaiser's open encouragement of the Boers by searching German merchant ships for arms off the South African coast, Tirpitz seized his chance to persuade an angry Reichstag to pass a second Navy Law that not only doubled the planned size of the *Hochseeflotte*, but made clear the purpose for which it was to be built: 'Germany must have a battle fleet so strong that, even for the strongest sea power, war against it would invite such dangers as to imperil its position in the world.'

Britain reacted to this challenge by abandoning Canning's cen-tury-old policy of 'splendid isolation' in favour of an alliance with Japan (1902), the *Entente Cordiale* with France (1904), and *rap-prochement* with Russia (1907) with whom France had formed a dual alliance in 1893; and by a decision that British supremacy at sea should be maintained by laying down four new battleships each year, twice the rate at which German yards could build them. But ships are not all; lacking the stimulus of a major naval war for the best part of a century, the Royal Navy had failed to tackle many of the problems arising out of the transformation from sail to steam and the introduction of new weapons. The Admiralty had no war plans because successive First Sea Lords had refused to allow the innova-tion of a Naval Staff: tactics had been neglected for want of fleets with which to practise them; and fighting efficiency was of smaller importance than spotless paint and polished brass. Fortunately, in 1900 Vice-Admiral Sir John Fisher hoisted his flag as C-in-C Medi-terranean, where he stimulated the study of tactics with realistic fleet exercises, and increased the range of gunnery practices from the point-blank 2,000 yards of Nelson's day to a realistic 6,000.

More important, in 1904 this 'veritable volcano' became First Sea Lord, in which office he was just in time to 'hoist the storm signal and beat all hands to quarters'.

For as long as France, with her Fleet divided between the Channel, Atlantic and Mediterranean, and Russia, with hers divided between the Baltic, Black Sea and Pacific, had been her potential enemies, Britain's battleships could be divided between the Mediterranean, Far East and Home waters. A growing German Fleet that threatened Britain's east coast from Kiel and Wilhelmshaven required the Royal Navy to be redeployed. The Anglo-Japanese alliance, and the destruction of the Russian Far East Fleet in 1905, allowed Fisher to withdraw Britain's battleships from those waters. Out of the *Entente* came in 1912 an agreement for France to base her Fleet on Toulon with responsibility for the Mediterranean, so that Britain could transfer her battleships from there to the North Sea. Elsewhere Fisher replaced the swarm of third-class cruisers and sloops, that were a relic of Palmerston's 'gunboat diplomacy', by a few squadrons of modern cruisers that could be quickly summoned anywhere by telegraph in peace, and in war would serve to protect the trade routes. With the men saved by the wholesale scrapping of ships that could 'neither fight nor run away', Fisher further increased Britain's readiness for war by giving nucleus crews to the more modern vessels lying in reserve so that they could be commissioned for sea at short notice.

These notable reforms were paralleled by another for which Fisher is much better known. The 'Majestic' and subsequent classes of battleship, built from 1893 onwards, mounted four 12-inch and ten or twelve 6-inch guns. At close range this dual-calibre armament combined the rapid fire of small weapons for devastating an enemy's superstructure, with the heavy shell of larger guns to pierce her armoured hull. But the increase in range that was needed after the turn of the century to counter the torpedo threat tipped the scales in favour of the bigger weapon; the armaments of the 'King Edward VII' class, completed 1905–6, and of the subsequent 'Lord Nelsons', were augmented with 9·2-inch guns. And when Togo's victory at Tsushima confirmed the decisive value of the big gun at long ranges, at which it was impossible to control a mixed armament because of the difficulty of distinguishing between the shell splashes, Fisher directed that Britain's next battleship should be armed only with ten 12-inch guns. She was, moreover, to be turbine-driven at 21 knots to give her the tactical advantage of 3–4 knots over earlier designs.

Because such radical changes would render previous vessels obsolete, and so wipe out Britain's superiority of 53 to Germany's 20, he completed HMS *Dreadnought* so quickly, and in such secrecy, that Admiral von Tirpitz, as he was now, did not know, until she was completed in 1906, that the German battle fleet would have to be designed anew. Indeed, Britain commissioned three more dreadnoughts before Germany had built her first two, armed with twelve 11-inch guns. Fisher likewise transformed the armoured cruiser, a hybrid type intended for the dual roles of scouting and fast wing to the battle line. To follow the 'Minotaur' class, which carried a mixed armament of 9·2-inch and 7·5-inch guns at 23 knots, he ordered battlecruisers with eight 12-inch guns and a speed of 25 knots, the three 'Invincibles' being completed in 1908, whereas Germany's *Von der Tann*, armed with eight 11-inch guns, was not commissioned until two years later.

At this point in time, Asquith's Cabinet, being bent on expensive social reforms, would have accepted the Kaiser's facile assurance that his Fleet was no challenge to Britain, and cut the Admiralty's building programme from four dreadnoughts to two. But Austria's sudden annexation of Bosnia and Herzegovina alarmed the British public into demanding, 'we want eight, we won't wait'. Since Australia and New Zealand also suffered the cost of two battlecruisers, and Malaya that of a battleship, Britain's impetus was maintained at five dreadnoughts a year until, by July 1914, when for the first time the Navy Estimates exceeded £50 million, 29 battleships and battlecruisers had been built, the latest with 13·5-inch guns. Moreover, although Germany had completed 20, many with 12-inch guns, she had only seven on the stocks, four of these with 15-inch guns, whereas Britain was building 20, half with weapons of this large calibre.

Eight years before 1914, von Metternich, German Ambassador in London, warned his Government that 'the real cause of political tension is not commercial rivalry but the growing importance of our Navy'; but the Kaiser preferred his Service attachés' reports that he had little to fear from Britain. The Foreign Secretary, Sir Edward Grey, declared: 'Our Navy is to us what the German Army is to them: if the German Navy were superior to ours, our independence, our very existence would be at stake'; but Wilhelm II told his Chancellor, Prince von Bülow: 'The English agitation about our new naval building programme is simply bluff for reasons of domestic policy.' Whitehall's pacific approaches were dismissed as 'groundless impertinence'. The Second Hague Conference of 1907 was torpedoed by Fisher's jingoistic utterances. Von Tirpitz and his supporters were angered by Churchill's comment: 'The British Navy is to us a necessity; the German Navy is in the nature of a luxury.' Above all, when France occupied Fez in 1911, the Kaiser ordered the gunboat *Panther* to support Germany's alleged, but *de facto* non-existent, interests in Agadir, when war was only averted by Britain's declared support for France, and by von Tirpitz's emphatic protests that the High Seas Fleet would be at a grave disadvantage until the Kiel Canal had been widened and deepened to allow dreadnoughts to pass quickly between the North Sea and the Baltic.

By the summer of 1914 most people had come to regard war as inevitable, but few realized its imminence. A British squadron was paying a friendly visit to Kiel, for the opening of the enlarged canal, when the heir to the Austro-Hungarian throne was assassinated on 28 June. Attributing this crime to Serbian intrigue, Vienna sent an ultimatum to Belgrade. But, though Serbia responded with an appeal for Russian support, Berlin saw so little danger in the situation that the High Seas Fleet was allowed to sail from Kiel on 7 July for Norwegian waters. With a like unconcern for the clouds on the international horizon, the Admiralty went ahead with a long-planned test mobilization of the Reserve Fleets, which joined the Home Fleet for a royal review at Spithead, then returned to Chatham, Portsmouth and Devonport to discharge their crews, clear evidence that the storm was expected to blow over before the August bank holiday.

If the First Sea Lord, now Admiral Prince Louis of Battenberg, shared this optimism, it vanished on Sunday 24 July, when he heard that Serbia's conciliatory reply to Austria's ultimatum had been rejected. He at once issued orders postponing the Home Fleet's summer leave, a decision that was fully justified next day by the news that Austria had declared war, and that the High Seas Fleet had been recalled to the Jade. Four tense days later the Tsar responded to Serbia's appeal by ordering general mobilization. Battenberg recognized this as the decisive moment: with the full support of Winston Churchill, a First Lord with the courage to act without waiting for the Cabinet to be recalled, he ordered the British Fleet to its war stations. In the words of Midshipman Prince Albert, later King George VI, who was serving in the *Collingwood*, one of the Home Fleet's dreadnoughts: 'We left Portland and steered west, then east, starting war routine at 1 pm. After dinner we went to night defence stations, all ready for a destroyer attack, and passed the Straits of Dover at midnight.' They reached Scapa Flow on 1 August, as the

Kaiser reacted to Russia's mobilization with a declaration of war, and sent an ultimatum to her ally, France. Remembering the latter's ready response to the suggestion that her Fleet should be concentrated in the Mediterranean, Grey declared: 'If the German Fleet undertakes hostile operations against French coasts or shipping, the British Fleet will give all the protection in its power.' But there was no call to fulfil this promise before the German Army's advance through the Ardennes obliged Britain to honour her guarantee of Belgium's neutrality. At 2300 on 4 August, the prologue to a drama that needed the whole world for its stage was ended. The British Fleet was ordered to 'commence hostilities against Germany'.

But before the curtain is lifted on the war at sea that followed Britain's ultimatum, a word must be said of another, fundamentally more important, aspect of this, the first conflict in all history that was to engulf most nations of the world before it ended four and a half years later. Germany's chief weapon was her incomparable and wholly professional Army. Born in the Napoleonic wars, nursed by Gneisenau and Scharnhorst, tutored by Roon and the elder Moltke, this had reached maturity at Sedan in 1870. And far from the least of its assets was a General Staff of officers whose military skills were matched by an arrogant confidence in their superiority over their countrymen, whose wholehearted devotion to the arts of war matched Wilhelm II's belief in his Army as the means of achieving German hegemony in Europe. The General Staff was, therefore, primarily responsible for leading Germany into war in 1914, a war that was to be fought chiefly *on land*.

Graf von Schlieffen, their chief from 1891 to 1906, conceived a plan by which 53 divisions would invade France through Belgium, then wheel to the left and surround Paris, to ensure a second triumphant defeat of their old enemy within a matter of weeks, during which the Russian Army could be held at bay by a mere nine divisions. And this lightning stroke all but succeeded in August 1914. It failed because the younger Moltke modified his predecessor's plan, weakening its thrust, and because the Russian Army mobilized and began its invasion of East Prussia sooner than was expected. By the time the stout resistance of the Belgians at Liège and Namur had been overcome, Berlin was compelled to transfer two corps from the west to the east, to enable von Hindenberg and Ludendorff to win the victory of Tannenberg (26-28 August) – and the British Expeditionary Force had gained its position on the French left wing. To the Kaiser, Field Marshal Sir John French's four divisions might be a 'contemptible little army', but they were instrumental in stemming von Falkenhayn's advance, first on the Marne (6 September), then on the Aisne (17 September) and finally at Ypres (31 October).

This ended the traditional war of movement, both sides lacking the men and the material to end the conflict by Christmas as many had confidently predicted. The Allies and their enemies were committed to the mud and blood of trench warfare along fronts that neither was able to break, though they deployed all the flower of their manhood in fresh armies, though they strained their industrial resources to provide guns and ammunition on a previously undreamed-of scale, though they devised armour in the form of tanks, and though Germany, in defiance of the Hague Convention of 1899, used gas and suffered retribution by the Allies.

The German failure to achieve an early victory on land also had another, ultimately fatal, consequence. It allowed time for sea power to play a decisive role. Though the war in the East was ended by the Bolshevik Revolution (1917) and though the titanic struggle on the Western Front dominated the strategy of the Allies, it was their Navies, of which the British was immeasurably the strongest, that in the end brought Germany to her knees. And this is the theme of all that follows – a drama to be played in three acts, the first between cruisers overseas, the second in Home waters between the opposing battle fleets, the third and last – for the first time in any war – under the sea.

ACT ONE

Overseas

2

A Curse on the Orient

The pursuit of SMS Goeben *and* Breslau – *The Dardanelles*

For the peoples of the Middle East SMS *Goeben* carried more slaughter, more misery and more ruin than has ever before been borne within the compass of a ship.

Winston Churchill

The initial setting for Act One was the Mediterranean on which the curtain was rung up early, several days before Britain's declaration of war. Here the Admiralty's plans to withdraw all their dreadnoughts to Home waters had gone awry. France had been slow to build such ships; by July 1914 she had completed no more than four, of which only one had been transferred from Brest to Toulon. Since Germany's partners in the Triple Alliance, Austria-Hungary and Italy, each had three dreadnoughts in the Mediterranean, the Admiralty had to leave a squadron of battlecruisers at Malta. The *Inflexible*, *Indefatigable* and *Indomitable*, with eight 12-inch guns and a designed speed of 25·5 knots, were supported by the 1st CS of four armoured cruisers, *Defence*, *Black Prince*, *Duke of Edinburgh* and *Warrior*, which bristled with 9·2-inch, 7·5-inch and 6-inch guns, but could go no faster than 23 knots.* These seven ships, together with four 25.5-knot, 6-inch-and 4-inch-gunned light cruisers of the 'Town' class and a flotilla of destroyers, came under the command of Admiral Sir Berkeley Milne, who owed his rank and his appointment more to his talents as a courtier than to his professional ability. As Fisher wrote to Churchill in 1912: 'In regard to what you have done in the appointment of Sir Berkeley Milne, you have betrayed the Navy. You are aware that he is unfitted to be the senior admiral afloat, as you have now made him.'

By 1914 the British C-in-C Mediterranean had more to contend with than Austria's and Italy's dreadnoughts. In Napoleon's words: 'Essentially the great question remains: who will hold Constan-

---

* Fuller details of these and other ships involved in this chapter will be found in Appendix A on p 35.

tinople?' As rival suitors for Sultan Mohammed V's favours, Britain had sent a mission headed by Rear-Admiral Arthur Limpus to train his Navy, and Germany had provided another led by General Liman von Sanders to train his Army. And to counter the influence wielded by Milne's fleet in the eastern Mediterranean the *Admiralstab* detached from their High Seas Fleet the battlecruiser *Goeben*, armed with ten 11-inch guns and with the same designed speed as the *Inflexible*, and the 28-knot, 4·1-inch-gunned light cruiser *Breslau*, whose junior officers included, incidentally, the future Grand Admiral Doenitz, of World War Two. However, by June 1914 the *Goeben* was in need of a refit, so that the Sarajevo assassination caught her in dockyard hands at Pola. But in Rear-Admiral Wilhelm Souchon the German ships had a commander whose initiative and determination were in sharp contrast to Milne's lack of these qualities. He had no intention of being trapped in the Adriatric if there was to be war, between the Triple Alliance and the Entente. In mid-July he cut short the *Goeben*'s repairs and, with the *Breslau* in company, headed south.

The bulk of Milne's fleet remained in the eastern Mediterranean until the Admiralty signalled on 27 July:

> European political situation makes war by no means impossible. Be prepared to shadow possible hostile men-of-war. Return to Malta at ordinary speed and remain there with all your ships completing with coal and stores.

This brought Milne back to Valetta where, on the 30th, he received this signal shortly after the Warning Telegram:

> It is important that your squadrons should not be seriously engaged with Austrian ships before we know what Italy will do. Your first task should be to aid the French in the transportation of their African army by covering and, if possible bringing to action, individual fast German ships, particularly *Goeben*, who may interfere with that transportation. You will be notified when you may consult with the French Admiral. Do not at this stage be brought to action against superior forces. The speed of your squadrons is sufficient to enable you to choose your moment. You must husband your force at the outset and we shall hope later to reinforce the Mediterranean.

These instructions focused Milne's attention on the French troop convoy routes from the Algerian ports to Marseilles. They contained no hint that the German ships might go *east*, even though the British Ambassador in Constantinople, Sir Louis Mallet, had warned that the scales of the Ottoman Empire were weighted in Germany's favour, because his colleague, von Wangenheim, had persuaded the Turkish War Minister, the ambitious 33-year-old Enver, to mobilize his Army under the direction of the dynamic von Sanders.

Not until the evening of 2 August was Milne authorized to get in touch with his potential ally and colleague, the French Vice-Admiral Lapeyrère. He tried to do so by W/T; when this failed he sailed the light cruiser *Dublin* to Bizerta with a letter. He did not know that the French Government was so anxious to avoid any movement that might precipitate hostilities, that they would not allow their fleet to leave Toulon until early on 3 August, with instructions 'to watch the *Goeben* and protect the transport of French troops', whose embarkation did not, therefore, begin until after Lapeyrère's arrival at Algiers on the 5th — by which time Souchon had struck the first blow. On 3 August Milne received new orders:

> *Goeben* must be shadowed by two battlecruisers. Approaches to Adriatic must be watched by cruisers and destroyers. Remain near Malta yourself.

Having no more recent news of the *Goeben* and *Breslau* than that they had coaled at Brindisi at the end of July, Milne sent the light cruiser *Chatham* to watch the Strait of Messina and ordered the *Indomitable* and *Indefatigable*, with the 1st CS, the light cruiser *Gloucester* and eight destroyers to the Strait of Otranto. This considerable force was under the command of a man who not only bore the honoured name of one of Nelson's captains, but whose reputation as a leader matched his robust physique. Rear-Admiral Ernest Troubridge, who flew his flag in the *Defence*, did not, however, enjoy the strong support of two battlecruisers for very long. When the *Chatham* reported Messina to be empty, the Admiralty became sufficiently concerned at the absence of any news of Souchon's ships, to decide that he must be heading for the Atlantic: Milne was ordered to divert the *Indefatigable* and *Indomitable* to Gibraltar.

The *Chatham* had missed the *Goeben* and *Breslau* by only a few hours. Knowing that his country was now at war with France, Souchon left Messina that morning, and set course at high speed to the west, intent on disrupting the embarkation of the French XIXth Army. At dawn on the 4th the German battlecruiser appeared off Philippeville, her consort off Bône, each to carry out a short unopposed bombardment, without doing much damage to either port. The two ships then rejoined and returned the way they had come, Berlin having signalled Souchon early that morning: 'Alliance concluded with Turkey. *Goeben* and *Breslau* to proceed immediately to Constantinople.' Souchon did not know that, in sending such orders, the wily von Tirpitz was 'jumping the gun': von Wangenheim's intrigues had not yet fully persuaded Enver that to side with Germany was in the best interests of the Young Turks who were so near to gaining effective control in their country. But such complications were not the Admiral's immediate concern: for such a voyage his ships must first refill their bunkers.

The Germans failed, however, to regain Messina unobserved. At 1030 on the 4th, not long after they had begun their retirement from Philippeville and Bône, they were sighted by the *Indomitable* and *Indefatigable* by the sheer chance that, on the previous evening, the two British battlecruisers had been detached from Troubridge's force and ordered to Gibraltar. They passed each other, these four ships whose countries were not yet at war, on opposite courses at a distance of only 8,000 yards, with their guns trained fore and aft. Moreover, Captain F. W. Kennedy, the British senior officer in the *Indomitable*, refrained from firing the customary salute to Souchon's flag lest this international courtesy should be misunderstood. Otherwise he knew his duty: he led the *Indomitable* and *Indefatigable* round to shadow the *Goeben* and *Breslau* from a discreet distance on each quarter. The news delighted Churchill: 'Very good. Hold her [*sic*]. War imminent', he answered from Whitehall, and wrote afterwards, with a greater sense of drama than accuracy of detail:

> Throughout this long summer afternoon three great ships, hunted and hunters, were cleaving the clear waters of the Mediterranean in tense and oppressive calm. At any moment the *Goeben* could have been smitten by sixteen 12-inch guns firing nearly treble her own weight of metal. At the Admiralty we suffered the tortures of Tantalus. At about 5 o'clock Prince Louis observed that there was still time to sink the *Goeben* before dark.

'I was unable to utter a word,' Churchill concluded, because the Cabinet would not sanction any such action before their ultimatum to Germany expired at midnight. But had it been otherwise, one doubts whether the *Goeben* would have been so easily disposed of. Whilst she maintained a speed of 22·5 knots, sometimes achieving as much as 24, despite boiler defects which there had been no time to remedy during her recent curtailed refit, the British battlecruisers did not do so well; they were longer out of dock, and they carried reduced peace-time complements for their stokeholds. By 1636

Souchon had so far outstripped his shadowers that Kennedy reported losing sight of his quarry. The faster *Dublin*, which had joined from Bizerta, held on for longer; but at 2100, when three hours still remained before Britain went to war, she too lost contact.

Judging that the German ships must be returning to the Adriatic, Kennedy would have continued eastwards and used his battle-cruisers to close the northern entrance to the Strait of Messina; but news that Italy had opted out of the Triple Alliance and declared her neutrality, coupled with a warning from Whitehall that her ban on belligerent warships approaching within six miles of her coast must be respected so as not to antagonize a possible ally, made this impossible. The *Indomitable* and *Indefatigable* were ordered to join the *Inflexible* and the light cruisers *Chatham* and *Weymouth* to the west of Sicily, where Milne established a patrol designed to prevent Souchon making a further more destructive foray to impede the passage of the French XIXth Army. The British C-in-C did not, however, disregard the possibility that the Germans might be less scrupulous in their respect for Italian neutrality: he ordered Troubridge to detach the light cruiser *Gloucester*, Captain Howard Kelly, to watch the southern entrance to Messina.

Souchon had the advantage of a signal from the German naval attaché in Rome: 'In spite of the Alliance Italy is neutral, but the naval authorities are ashamed of this and kindly disposed to us.' He did not, therefore, hesitate to take his two ships into Messina at 0500 on 5 August. Nor did the authorities object to them replenishing their bunkers from a German collier until 1700, when Souchon blithely agreed to respect the International Law forbidding a belligerent warship to remain in a neutral port for more than 24 hours, on the clear understanding that this period began from the time the notice was served, an interpretation with which the 'kindly disposed' Italians did not argue. So the *Goeben* and *Breslau* were able to remain in Messina for 36 hours, until 1700 on the 6th. Before this, however, the German Admiral had to face a more serious problem than ensuring that his ships were complete with fuel. Von Wangenheim deprecated von Tirpitz's attempt at persuading Enver to make a too hurried decision in Germany's favour by sending warships into Turkish waters. And this was enough for the *Admiralstab* to signal Souchon: 'For political reasons entry into Constantinople is not yet possible. You should proceed to Pola or the Atlantic.' But the possibility that Austria-Hungary, which had done so much to precipitate the crisis that had now reached the stark reality of war,

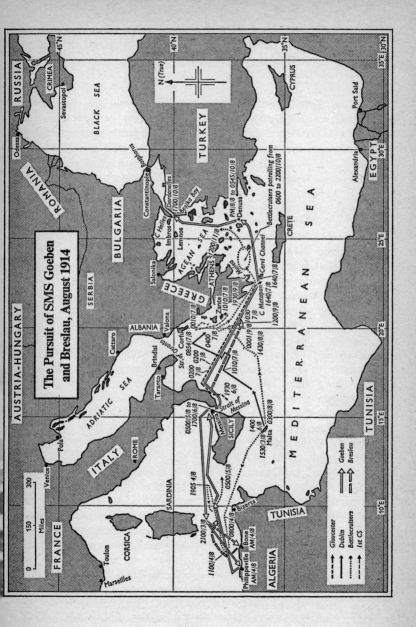

The Pursuit of SMS Goeben and Breslau, August 1914

might follow Italy's example and remain neutral, brought a modi-
fication to these orders: the *Goeben*'s and *Breslau*'s destination
was left to Souchon's discretion, albeit with the inference that the
easiest solution would be the Adriatic.

There are few better examples of the advantages of leaving
matters in the hands of the man on the spot. Believing that Austria
would remain true to the Alliance, and that no useful purpose
would be served by strengthening her small battle fleet in the confined waters of the Adriatic, the German Admiral calculated that
his country would gain far more from having Turkey as an ally than
from any damage the *Goeben* and *Breslau* might inflict on French
troop convoys in the Mediterranean, or on Allied trade in the
Atlantic. Clearing Messina in the first dog watch of 6 August, he
took his ships through the southern entrance of the Strait into
the eastern Mediterranean. They were sighted and reported almost
at once by Howard Kelly in the watching *Gloucester*. But Milne's
three battlecruisers were powerless to intercept, even though the
Admiralty hurriedly relaxed the ban on them passing through the
Strait of Messina. Two were 100 miles to the west; the third, HMS
Indomitable, was even further away because she had been detached
to Bizerta for coal. If Milne had had less of an eye for the French
transports (and if he had been able to establish effective cooperation with Lapeyrère), he would have ordered her to refuel at Malta,
whence she could have sailed to join Troubridge. As it was, only
the 1st CS and a flotilla of destroyers stood between Souchon and
his objective.

Because the German Admiral steered first towards the Adriatic,
Troubridge supposed he must be making for Pola: from his station
near Corfu, he took his four armoured cruisers north to intercept.
He did not realize that he was being deliberately misled: on the
contrary, when Howard Kelly reported that the *Goeben* and *Breslau*
had altered course towards Cape Matapan shortly after dark, he
supposed this to be a feint. Not until 0010, after the *Breslau* had
failed to fend off the *Gloucester*, whose Captain continued to report
the *Goeben* to be steering SE, did Troubridge realize his mistake
and alter to the south, when his destroyers' shortage of coal prevented him from sending them on ahead. There were, however, two
other destroyers more fortunately placed. These had left Malta at
1400 in company with the *Dublin*, which had been sent there for
coal before joining Troubridge. At 2030 Milne ordered these three
ships to attack the *Goeben* with torpedoes during this moonlit
night. Guided by the *Gloucester*'s reports, Howard Kelly's brother,

Captain John Kelly, led the *Dublin* and her two small consorts for a position on the enemy's bow. By 0330 they expected to sight their foe at any moment. 'Dammit, we must get her,' John Kelly declared. Alas, he saw nothing of the *Goeben*: forewarned by the *Breslau*, which glimpsed the *Dublin* without being sighted herself, Souchon turned his flagship away and passed unseen to starboard of the British ships whose crews were all looking expectantly to port.

Events on board the *Defence* took a very different turn during this middle watch, as she led the 1st CS to intercept the German vessels near Cape Matapan soon after dawn. At 0245, Flag Captain Fawcett Wray asked Troubridge whether he intended to engage the *Goeben*. 'Yes,' answered the Admiral, and explained a decision that ran counter to the Admiralty's orders not to engage a 'superior force' with the words: 'I know it is wrong, but I cannot have the name of the whole Mediterranean Squadron stink.' Three-quarters of an hour later, Wray told the Admiral that he did not like the prospect of a fight with such a powerful ship, and on receiving the reply, 'Neither do I', pressed his point: 'I don't see what you can do, sir. The *Goeben* can circle round us within range of her guns but outside ours. It seems likely to be the suicide of your squadron.' Troubridge answered, 'I cannot turn away now; think of my pride'; but Wray countered with: 'Has your pride got anything to do with it, sir? Surely it is your country's welfare which is at stake.' This was an argument that decided the fate of nations. Ten minutes later, at 0355, when the 1st CS was off Zante and still some 70 miles from the *Goeben*, Troubridge abandoned the chase. Wray commended his decision: 'This is the bravest thing you have ever done.' But the Admiral was in tears, already half-aware, perhaps, that he had allowed himself to be persuaded into making the greatest mistake of his life.

All hinged now on the *Gloucester* which was still relentlessly holding to her quarry. Early in the afternoon, Howard Kelly took the brave decision to engage the *Breslau* in the hope of delaying the *Goeben*'s flight. Turning the blind eye of a Nelson to Milne's signalled warning 'to drop astern and avoid capture', he closed the German light cruiser and, at 1335, opened fire at 11,500 yards. As he hoped, the *Goeben* turned back to drive him off with her 11-inch guns. And Howard Kelly would have done as much again, with a like disregard for Milne's ban on going east of Cape Matapan, if the coal in the *Gloucester*'s bunkers had allowed. As it was, no man was more disappointed than her Captain when, at 1640, shortage of

fuel compelled him to abandon pursuit of an enemy whom he had
so skilfully shadowed for 24 hours.

Milne had, meantime, taken his three battlecruisers into Malta
for fuel: knowing from Kennedy's experience that they would need
every knot of their speed for many hours if they were to outpace the
Goeben, he would not pursue Souchon until they had coaled. So
they did not sail for the eastern Mediterranean until 0030 on 8
August. Fourteen hours later, when they were halfway to Cape Matapan, fate played them a dirty trick. An Admiralty clerk, returning
early from lunch, saw a bunch of telegrams lying on a colleague's
desk ready for dispatch. Supposing that they had been uninten-
tionally forgotten, he sent them off. One was to Milne: 'Commence
hostilities against Austria.' At once he turned his battlecruisers
northwards to Troubridge's support against a sortie by the Austrian
Fleet. Four hours passed before he learned that it was a false alarm;
but because the Admiralty also warned him that the situation
vis-à-vis Austria remained critical, he maintained his resolve to go
to Troubridge's support. And it was not until 1230 next day, the
9th, that the Admiralty realized this and signalled: 'Not at war
with Austria. Continue chase of *Goeben*.'

By this time, 24 precious hours had been lost – a delay that
made all the difference. On the afternoon of the 8th Souchon's
ships stopped at the Aegean island of Denusa to replenish their
bunkers, whence they did not sail again until 0545 on the 10th.
Since this was the day Milne's battlecruisers entered the Aegean, it
is clear that, if they had not delayed to coal at Malta, or if there
had been no false alarm about Austria, they could have caught the
Goeben and *Breslau* as they left Denusa. As it was, Milne's force
was 40 miles north of the island by noon on the 11th, when he
received the sobering news that Souchon's ships had entered the
Dardanelles at 1700 the previous day. The German Admiral had
doubts about the welcome he would receive up to the last moment.
Berlin's final injunction, 'It is of great importance that *Goeben*
enters the Dardanelles as soon as possible', had been followed by
this from von Sanders: 'Come in, demand capitulation of fortress,
and take the mine barrage pilot.' So it was with some apprehension
that Souchon closed Cape Helles, his ships ready for action. But
they were not met by gunfire from the forts, only by a Turkish
picket boat which offered to lead them through the Narrows into
the Sea of Marmora. And when Milne sent the *Weymouth* to the
entrance to the Dardanelles next day to remind a neutral Turkey
that belligerent vessels might stay for only 24 hours, her captain

learned the realities of German cunning: the *Goeben* and *Breslau* had been 'sold' to Turkey whose flag now flew at their sterns instead of the German ensign.

'To think that it was the Navy that provided the first instance of failure,' groaned Beatty to his wife. 'God, it makes me sick.' But not even he realized the enormity of the snook which the Imperial German Navy had cocked at the Royal Navy at the very outset of the war. When Austria-Hungary finally opted for the side of the Alliance on 12 August, Milne was sufficiently convinced that Souchon would try to return to the Adriatic, to leave two of his battle-cruisers in Besika Bay while he himself returned to Britain in the *Inflexible*, in fulfilment of an agreement that Lapeyrère, who was his junior in rank, should be C-in-C of all Allied ships in the Mediterranean. And when Milne reached London, Churchill and Battenberg were sufficiently satisfied with what he told them, to publish on 30 August their formal approval of his 'conduct and dispositions', with which they coupled the complacent statement that he had been successful in 'preventing the Germans from carrying out their primary role of preventing French troops crossing from Africa'. Milne then went on leave well assured that, as had been announced in July, he would become C-in-C Nore in November.

Troubridge was not so fortunate. 'Not one of his excuses [for failing to engage the *Goeben*] can be accepted,' wrote Battenberg on reading his report, a verdict with which Churchill agreed. On 9 September Troubridge was ordered to return to England to give evidence at a Court of Inquiry on the 22nd. This echoed Battenberg's strictures: that the 1st CS had as many as twenty-two 9·2-inch, fourteen 7·5-inch and twenty 6-inch guns to the *Goeben*'s ten 11-inch and twelve 6-inch; that there was no significant difference between the range of 11-inch and 9·2-inch guns; and that superior speed in a single ship could be nullified by the proper tactical disposition of four units. Troubridge's 'failure to endeavour to engage was deplorable and contrary to the traditions of the British Navy', concluded Admirals Sir George Callaghan and Sir Hedworth Meux. Six weeks later he appeared before a court martial, comprised of nine flag officers and senior captains, which assembled at Portland on 5 November under the presidency of Admiral Sir George Egerton.

By this time feeling was running so high against Troubridge that the Prosecutor, Rear-Admiral Sydney Fremantle, was urged to charge him with the ignominy of cowardice; but the difficulty of proving such an accusation was enough for Fremantle to confine himself to one of 'negligence or through other default, did forbear to chase SMS *Goeben*, being an enemy then flying'. He made two main points: that Troubridge had definite orders that the *Goeben* was his objective, and that she was not a superior force. Troubridge answered that he had told Milne on 2 August that, 'I consider a battlecruiser a superior force to a cruiser squadron', and had received the reply, 'That question won't arise as you will have the *Indomitable* and *Indefatigable* with you'; and that immediately after this he had told his captains that he would not engage the *Goeben*, because of her marked superiority, unless he had the support of the battlecruisers.

The admiral's cabin in HMS *Bulwark* was cleared for the Court to consider its verdict on the fifth day of Troubridge's trial. When he was summoned to return he looked quickly at his sword lying on the table and, with ineffable relief, saw that the hilt, not the blade, was pointing towards him, before Egerton read this verdict:

> In view of the Admiralty's instructions to the C-in-C, repeated by him to the accused in his sailing orders, and also by signal on 4 August, the Court is of the opinion that the accused was justified in considering the *Goeben* a superior force to the 1st CS; that, although it might have been possible to bring the *Goeben* to action off Cape Malea or in the Cervi Channel, the Court considers that, in view of the accused's orders to keep a close watch on the Adriatic, he was justified in abandoning the chase, as he had no prospect of any force being sent to his assistance. The Court therefore finds the charge against the accused is not proved, and honourably acquits him of the same.

The Admiralty Board resented this implied criticism of their instructions. One Sea Lord argued that, since Troubridge was twice told that the *Goeben* was his objective, it should have been abundantly clear that she was not the superior force the Admiralty had in mind. Another observed that, if Troubridge considered pursuit of the *Goeben* incompatible with his instructions to watch the Adriatic, he should have pointed this out to Milne. And though the Board shrank from going so far as a *de facto* reversal of the court martial verdict by refusing Troubridge further employment, he had to swallow the bitter pill of never again receiving a sea command. Milne and Wray also suffered, without an opportunity to answer formal charges. The Board had second thoughts over the vindication of the C-in-C; on 19 November Churchill informed him that he would not, after

all, go to the Nore Command, nor to any other. Troubridge's Flag
Captain was ostracized by the Service for the advice which he had
given his Admiral and for commending his decision to abandon the
chase.

What is history's verdict? Early in 1915 Troubridge told Wray
that, but for his advice, he would have fought the *Goeben*. Wray
argued that his advice had been misunderstood, and that he 'was
astounded when Troubridge announced his intention of abandoning
the chase'. But the responsibility was never Wray's: it could only be
Troubridge's, whatever advice his subordinate gave him. That Milne
– and the Admiralty – placed the Rear-Admiral in a difficult position
none would deny: but so is it clear that, in deciding to return to
watching the Adriatic instead of trying to bring the *Goeben* to
action, he made a disastrous error of judgement. The Austrians were
not yet at war (nor, when they did come in, did their battle fleet
make any serious attempt to emerge from the Adriatic). On the
other hand, if Souchon had determined to fight, four armoured
cruisers could have engaged the *Goeben* from two different bearings,
compelling her to divide her armament, with every chance of inflicting damage which, if it had obliged Souchon to seek a refuge short
of his goal, would have been worth the loss of part of Troubridge's
squadron. Commodore Harwood's decision to use two 6-inch and
one 8-inch cruisers in this way against the 11-inch-gunned *Graf Spee*
in 1939 is the shining example that this can be done. Contrariwise,
had Souchon chosen flight, the *Goeben* might have expended all her
ammunition in a vain (except for some lucky hit) engagement at
maximum range that would have drawn her sting, just as von Spee
was to draw much of Vice-Admiral Sturdee's in December 1914, in
circumstances to be described in Chapter Six.

But if this be the just verdict on Troubridge, he was also right to
imply, as the Court accepted, that the Admiralty was at fault. They
fell into the trap, which the *Admiralstab* avoided, of supposing that
they should use – in fact, abuse – the advantages conferred by W/T
for direct control of naval operations overseas, instead of leaving
this to each C-in-C who, as the man on the spot, was in a better
position to exercise it. Secondly, because the Naval War Staff was a
recent innovation, neither the First Sea Lord nor the Chief of Staff
understood how to use it. Battenberg and Sturdee also had to contend with a dynamic First Lord who was not content to leave the
conduct of naval operations in professional hands. Moreover, all
three were burdened with so many problems of world-wide import
in these crucial early days of the war, that their decisions were some-

times ill-considered, and their signals so hurriedly written as to be ambiguous to their recipients. Both were cardinal errors, to which we shall return in subsequent chapters, for all that Churchill denied them in his *World Crisis* and elsewhere.

There remains Milne's share of the responsibility for the *Goeben's* escape. In simple terms, his first fault was in being one move behind his enemy; he continued looking west, to the protection of the French troop convoys, when Souchon was heading east. His second fault lay in passing on to his subordinates, and to Troubridge in particular, the Admiralty's ambiguous instructions without attempting to clarify them. But if he lacked the demanding qualities needed in a man filling a vital overseas command, he was not the only British C-in-C whose plans were confused by ill-conceived interventions from Whitehall, which in one case, to be told in Chapter Five, had results much more tragic for the admiral chiefly involved, even though they were not of such consequence as the escape of the *Goeben* and *Breslau* in prolonging the war.

The Admiralty did not have to wait until Troubridge's court martial to learn that the arrival of the *Goeben* and *Breslau* off Constantinople would lead to far greater consequences than the need to leave battlecruisers in the Mediterranean. In Churchill's words, 'the Curse descended irrevocably upon Turkey and the Middle East'. In mid-September he signalled Vice-Admiral S. H. Carden, whose talents for administration were better suited to the post of Superintendent of Malta Dockyard than command of a fleet:

> Assume command of squadron off Dardanelles. Your sole duty is to sink *Goeben* and *Breslau* if they come out no matter what flag they fly. We are not at war with Turkey but Admiral Souchon is now C-in-C Turkish Navy and Germans are largely controlling it.

But Souchon was after a much bigger fish than attempting to run the gauntlet of a powerful Allied force. In two months he did more to revive a moribund Turkish Fleet, whose three battleships were all of pre-1900 vintage, than Admiral Limpus had been able to achieve in as many years. He helped von Wangenheim and von Sanders to fan the flames of the Turks' anger at Churchill's seizure of their first two dreadnoughts in August 1914, when they were nearing completion in British shipyards, now renamed *Agincourt* and *Erin*. And, in the last week of October he forced their hesitant hands: in secret agreement with Enver, he led a Turkish squadron

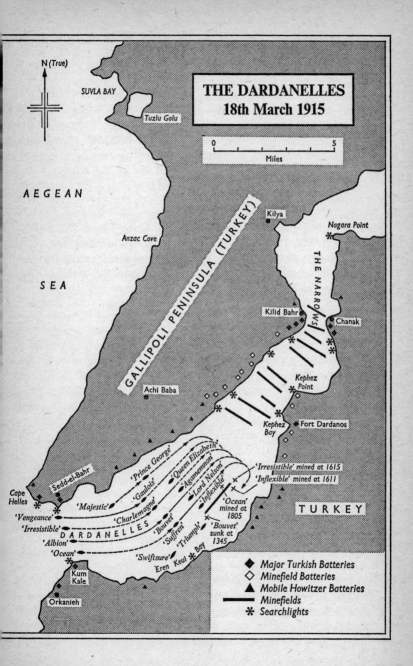

THE DARDANELLES
18th March 1915

N (True)

SUVLA BAY

Tuzlu Golu

0   Miles   5

A E G E A N

Kilya

Nagara Point

Anzac Cove

THE NARROWS

S E A

GALLIPOLI PENINSULA (TURKEY)

Kilid Bahr

Chanak

Achi Baba

Kephez
Point

Kephez
Bay

Fort Dardanos

'Prince George'

'Queen Elizabeth'

'Gaulois'

'Agamemnon'

'Lord Nelson'

'Irresistible' mined at 1615

'Inflexible' mined at 1611

Cape
Helles

Sedd-el-Bahr

'Majestic'

'Charlemagne'

'Inflexible'

'Ocean'
mined at
1805

T U R K E Y

'Vengeance'

'Bouvet'

'Irresistible'

DARDANELLES

'Suffren'

'Bouvet'
sunk at
1345

'Albion'

'Triumph'

'Ocean'

'Swiftsure'

'Eren Keui' Bay

Kum
Kale

Orkanieh

◆	Major Turkish Batteries
◇	Minefield Batteries
▲	Mobile Howitzer Batteries
▬	Minefields
✳	Searchlights

into the Black Sea, ostensibly for exercises, in reality for an act of aggression as naked as the Japanese attack on Port Arthur, or in a later age on Pearl Harbor. At dawn on the 30th the *Goeben* opened a devastating fire on Sevastopol, the *Breslau* at Novorossiisk, the cruiser *Hamidieh* at Odessa. Next morning the Russian Ambassador in Constantinople asked for his passports, closely followed by his British colleague.

The Admiralty reacted to Turkey's entry into the war on Germany's side with what Admiral Jellicoe was to classify as an 'unforgivable error', Admiral Bacon as 'an act of sheer lunacy'. For no purpose except to test 'what the effect of ships' guns would be on the outer forts' of the Dardanelles, Carden was ordered to carry out a brief bombardment. On 3 November the *Indefatigable* and *Indomitable*, together with the French pre-dreadnoughts *Suffren* and *Vérité*, fired seventy-six 12-inch shells at Kum Kale and Seddel-Bahr, of which one detonated the latter's magazine. This encouraged the Admiralty — and Carden — to suppose that, notwithstanding the lessons of history, warships could subdue the forts defending the Dardanelles. But it also warned the Turks to strengthen the defences of the Straits and gave them time to do this. For it was not until January 1915, when Russia appealed for an Allied 'demonstration' against Turkey to relieve the pressure on their armies in the Caucasus, that Churchill and Fisher (who had succeeded Battenberg in circumstances to be related in another chapter) signalled Carden: 'Do you think it is practicable to force the Dardanelles by ships alone?', to which they received the answer: 'I do not think they can be rushed, but they might be forced by extended operations with a large number of ships.'

Carden followed this with plans for, first reducing the entrance forts, then to knock out the inner forts up to Kephez Point, next to destroy the defences at the Narrows, and finally to clear a way through the minefields between Kephez and the Narrows into the Sea of Marmora, all to take about a month, if he was given a sufficient force of pre-dreadnoughts. Fisher was so impressed that he offered the newly-completed dreadnought *Queen Elizabeth*, giving Churchill a mental picture of Captain G. P. W. Hope using her eight 15-inch guns, first to blast the forts into powdered dust, then to sink the *Goeben* at anchor off the Golden Horn. The War Council settled that 'the Admiralty should prepare for a naval expedition in February to bombard and take the Gallipoli peninsula with Constantinople as its objective', no one — except Kitchener who warned that no troops were available — giving a thought to how a *naval* force could take a precipitous peninsula, and then *occupy* a capital city of a million people. However, no sooner had steps to provide Carden with the requisite ships been put in train than Fisher had serious misgivings, which he put to Churchill on 25 January. But when the War Council considered the plan again, Churchill's eloquence gained the day: if all went well the naval operations would 'cut the Turkish Empire in two, paralyse its capital, unite the Balkan States against our enemies, rescue Serbia, help the Grand Duke in the main operations of the war and, by shortening its duration, save countless lives'. Such enthusiasm, to which Kitchener gave his strong support because it required none of his precious troops, 'persuaded the First Sea Lord to give his reluctant consent to the Dardanelles bombardment as a great diplomatic and political necessity', although he thought it 'futile without troops. Naval opinion was unanimous. Churchill had them all on his side. I [Fisher] was the only rebel.'

Carden's fleet, which now comprised the *Queen Elizabeth, Inflexible*, 12 British pre-dreadnoughts, including the *Lord Nelson* and *Agamemnon*, and four French under Vice-Admiral Guépratte, plus a miscellany of other vessels based on Mudros, began the bombardment on 19 February. Starting at 1000, the heavy guns of the *Inflexible, Albion, Cornwallis, Triumph, Bouvet* and *Suffren* engaged the outer forts at 11,000 yards without reply from their 11-inch weapons until 1645, when the ships withdrew, having done negligible damage. Bad weather then intervened until the 25th when, taking advantage of the lessons learned from the first occasion, Allied naval gunfire was more effective, direct hits being scored on Forts Helles and Orkanieh. And by 1 March, the destruction of the outer defences had been completed by demolition parties landed from Carden's ships. So far so good – but thereafter things began to go awry. Bombardments of the intermediate defences on 2 and 3 March were indecisive, the few battleships employed meeting considerable opposition from the numerous mobile howitzers which the Turks had now deployed in support of their forts. Nonetheless Carden began the next phase, reduction of the defences of the Narrows, on the 5th; but not even the *Queen Elizabeth* could silence them, largely due to the inadequacy of the available spotting aircraft. More important, the minesweeping trawlers were prevented from making much progress with clearing the Straits of mines even though they did this at night: revealed in the glare of searchlights, their crews of untrained fishermen 'turned tail directly they were fired upon.'

On the 10th Carden had to admit that the attack had failed. Churchill and Fisher replied with an injunction to abandon his 'caution and deliberate methods', and to use all his force in 'a vigorous attempt to overwhelm the forts of the Narrows at decisive range', the operation being 'of such consequence as to justify the loss of ships and men'. Carden agreed but, when his minesweepers again failed him, came near to a nervous breakdown and resigned. His able second-in-command, Rear-Admiral John de Robeck, succeeded him on 15 March, and quickly fixed the 18th for the 'big push'. At 1125 that day the *Queen Elizabeth, Inflexible, Lord Nelson* and *Agamemnon* began bombarding forts mounting as many as 75 guns of calibres ranging from 6 inches up to 14 inches, at 14,000 yards from a position six miles inside the Straits, whilst the *Majestic, Prince George, Swiftsure* and *Triumph* engaged the intermediate mobile defences. By noon the latter, after scoring hits on the *Agamemnon* and *Inflexible* without doing significant damage, were silent. Guépratte's four battleships then advanced to within 8,000 yards of the Narrows, to fire on the forts with such effect that these were nearly silenced at no greater cost than damage to the *Gaulois*, which caused her to withdraw and beach on Rabbit Island.

Six British pre-dreadnoughts were moving up the Straits to continue this destructive fire when the first disaster occurred. At 1354, the retiring *Bouvet* was struck by a 14-inch shell which detonated a magazine, sinking her with Captain R. de la Touche and all 700 of her crew. This success put fresh life into the Turkish gunners, but they were soon silenced again by the British squadron. De Robeck then ordered his trawlers to clear a way through the Kephez minefield, so that his battleships might complete the destruction of the Narrows defences at point-blank range. But these failed him as badly as they had failed Carden: when they came under fire from the Turks' mobile batteries, their fishermen crews slipped their gear and fled. These two reverses were followed by the first of three more that were to be decisive. At 1611 the *Inflexible* struck a mine, one of 20 laid by the Turks on 8 March, in waters near the Asiatic shore already swept by the Allies and believed to be safe. Flooded with 2,000 tons of water, badly down by the bows, and with 29 men killed, Captain R. F. Phillimore managed to take her to Tenedos, and eventually to Malta for repairs. Only four minutes later, the *Irresistible* was trapped in the same fresh field, and had to be abandoned in a sinking condition after the removal of Captain D. L. Dent and his crew. Nor was she the last; when de Robeck

decided against hazarding his ships further, to what he supposed
to be mines floated down on the current, or torpedoes fired from
the shore, and ordered their withdrawal, the *Ocean* was caught in
the same fatal field at 1805, and foundered during the night.

Out of 16 Allied battleships and battlecruisers, three had been
sunk and three seriously damaged. For this steep price only two of
the Turks' numerous big guns and a handful of smaller ones had
been destroyed. But, as de Robeck realized, it was not the forts
that barred his way through the Narrows; the minefields were
the real obstacle: if only these could be cleared, the Allied fleet
could reach Constantinople as easily as Duckworth had done in
1807. With the comforting knowledge that five more pre-dreadnoughts were on their way to restore his strength, the Admiral
organized a more effective minesweeping force, using specially fitted
destroyers, for another all-out attempt on the Narrows. Simultaneously, however, he was subjected to another influence. As early
as Carden's admission of failure on the 15th, the War Council had
begun to consider using troops. Nothwithstanding Fisher's growing opposition, Churchill maintained that the Allies could strike a
near-mortal blow at Germany's soft underbelly through the Dardanelles; one which would not only force Turkey out of the war, but
end the threat to the Suez Canal, the campaigns in Mesopotamia
and the Caucasus, and open a way for the speedy supply of much-
needed arms to Russia. And Kitchener was so infected by his enthusiasm that he agreed to make available the Australian and New
Zealand (Anzac) Corps, the Naval Division and the 29th Division,
which the French brought up to a total of 81,000 men, all to
assemble on Lemnos under General Sir Ian Hamilton.

This changed de Robeck's mind: on 22 March 'he was now
quite clear he could not get through without the help of troops' –
and this was the end of the Navy's attempt to force the Straits
with ships alone. The tragedy is that it so nearly succeeded: as
Enver and von Sanders later admitted, by sunset on 18 March the
Turkish defenders were near to being demoralized, their ammunition exhausted. If Carden's attacks had been more vigorous, if de
Robeck had nerved himself to face further losses on the 19th, both
forts and mobile defences would have been silent by the 20th, when
the British minesweepers would have had little difficulty in clearing the way for an Allied force to enter the Sea of Marmora. As it
was, the Allies were committed to the Gallipoli campaign, for
which the 63-year-old, easy-going Hamilton could not have his
troops ready until 25 April. Their ships had first to be sent to

Alexandria to be restowed: no one at home had imagined that they would be required to make an opposed landing.

This delay was as fatal as that between Carden's trial bombardment in November and his first attempt to force the Straits in February. When de Robeck's fleet, strengthened to 18 battleships supported by 12 cruisers, landed the first 29,000 men on five beaches around Cape Helles and Gaba Tepe, using little more than these warships' picket boats and cutters, because no specialized landing craft were available, the brilliant 33-year-old Mustapha Kemal was as ready for them as the British generals were lacking in the skill and the will to win. (To quote only one example, Major-General Sir Alexander Godley, with almost unbelievable lack of tact, addressed his New Zealand Brigade as a 'handful of decrepit, homesick, thoroughly verminous and blasphemous fed-up scarecrows'.) Not then, nor in the eight months that followed, did Allied troops gain more than a precarious foothold on the toe of the peninsula. Their Navies gave them all the support they could, losing the *Goliath*, Captain T. L. Shelford, to torpedo attack by a Turkish destroyer on 13 May, and the *Triumph*, Captain M. S. Fitzmaurice, and the *Majestic*, Captain H. F. G. Talbot, to *U21*'s torpedoes near the end of the same month – but to no avail. Hamilton's troops never advanced as far inland as Carden's small marine demolition parties had been able to do without opposition in February.

All through the hot summer months the casualties mounted – they included a future Prime Minister, Major Clement Attlee, and the future Field-Marshal Lord Slim – until by November they exceeded 250,000, of whom more than 50,000 had been killed or died of wounds. By then it was clear that all their gallantry could not overcome the fierce resistance that Kemal inspired in the Turks, though they suffered even more grievous losses. Accepting the reality of one of the bloodiest defeats suffered by the Allies in the whole war, the War Council bowed to French pressure to open a new campaign in Salonika. In December the British Navy gave a final helping hand to its sister Service: on the night of 18–19 December the last troops were withdrawn from Suvla Bay and Anzac Cove, and three weeks later from the Helles beaches, in each case without the loss of a single man.

But there is little consolation in this. Churchill was right to press for an assault on the Dardanelles: success would have brought the Allies enormous benefits, not least a shortening of the war. Unfortunately, neither the Admiralty nor the War Office was prepared for this master stroke, nor had their leaders, Fisher and Kitchener, much heart for it. Yet, out of all these faults came ultimate good: the efficiency with which landings were planned and executed on a far greater scale in North Africa and Normandy, during the Second World War, was a direct consequence of the lessons learned by Britain and her Allies in 1915.

What, meantime, of the *Goeben* and *Breslau*? At the end of April 1915, the battlecruiser came into the Sea of Marmora intent on attacking the Allied transports off Gallipoli, but the mere sight of the *Queen Elizabeth* was enough to send her under the cover of the Narrows' cliffs. Otherwise Souchon was wholly concerned to counter the offensive operations of the Russian fleet in the Black Sea, under Vice-Admiral A. A. Eberhardt, with which both German ships were in action several times without decisive results, and by whose mines, laid off the entrance of the Bosphorus, the *Goeben* was damaged in December 1914, the *Breslau* in July 1915. Not until after the Russian threat to Constantinople was removed by the Bolsheviks' seizure of power in November 1917 did Vice-Admiral von Rebeur-Paschwitz, Souchon's successor, attempt a sortie into the Mediterranean, by which time the British had accepted this risk to the extent of reducing the Aegean squadron to the *Lord Nelson* and *Agamemnon*, and eight light cruisers, with a flotilla of old destroyers and a handful of small monitors.

Rear-Admiral A. Hayes-Sadler, who had been captain of the *Ocean* when she was sunk on 18 March 1915, and had just taken over from Rear-Admiral Sydney Fremantle, supposed that the German ships, if they sortied at all after such a long time, would make a dash for the Adriatic despite the fact that Italy had joined the Allies in August 1915. He expected, moreover, to receive ample warning of such a move because the enemy ships would first have to be swept through the Allied minefields to seaward of Sedd-el-Bahr, an operation which the British patrols in Kusu Bay (in the island of Tenedos) would be sure to see. He was wrong on both counts. Early on 19 January 1918, the *Goeben* and *Breslau* left the Bosphorus, intending only to destroy any British craft found off the Dardanelles and then to bombard the Allied base at Mudros. To gain the advantage of secrecy, the Germans ignored the mine danger, successfully clearing Sedd-el-Bahr early on the 20th with no more than slight damage to the *Goeben*. And at 0740 they surprised Commander Viscount Broome's 14-inch-gunned monitor *Raglan*, and the smaller *M28*, in Kusu Bay, quickly sinking both.

Hayes-Sadler received the alarm on board the *Lord Nelson* shortly before 0800, and sailed at once from Salonika; so did the *Agamemnon* and the light cruisers *Foresight*, *Lowestoft* and *Skirmisher* from Mudros as soon as they raised steam. But to no avail. Long before von Rebeur-Paschwitz reached Mudros, disaster all but overwhelmed his force. At 0830 the *Breslau* struck a mine off Cape Kephalo; and as the *Goeben* was manœuvring to take her in tow at 0855, she struck another in the same British field. A few minutes later, the drifting *Breslau* detonated four more mines and began settling fast. The *Goeben*'s captain managed to extricate his ship from this field and, leaving the *Breslau* to sink, to head back for the Straits. But he did not gain them safely: at 0948 the battlecruiser struck her third mine that day. Listing to port, she steamed as far as Nagara Point, where her Captain had the misfortune to give a wrong order to his helmsman. At 1130 the *Goeben* ran hard aground. There she was soon under attack by British aircraft, but this did no more than impede salvage operations: otherwise she was inaccessible except to a submarine. And the nearest available Allied boat was the British *E14*, at Corfu. By the time she entered the Straits a whole week later, her target had gone: the Turkish battleship *Turgut Reis* had towed her off the sandbank on the afternoon of the 25th.

The *Goeben* was, nonetheless, so severely damaged that she made only one more voyage before the war ended – to German-occupied Sevastopol for major repairs which were completed just in time for her to return to Constantinople in November 1918. But that was four years after she and the *Breslau* did yet more damage to the Allied cause than that which has been recorded here: in November 1914, as will be told in Chapter Five, these two ships contributed to a disaster suffered by the British Fleet half the world away from the Dardanelles.

Appendix A

Particulars of ships involved in the pursuit of SMS *Goeben* and *Breslau*

Type	Name	Year of Completion	Displacement (tons)	Main Armament		Designed speed (knots)	Notes
BRITISH Battlecruiser	Inflexible Indomitable	1908	17,250	8	12"	25·5	Flag of Admiral Sir Berkeley Milne
	Indefatigable	1911	18,750	8	12"	26	Captain F. W. Kennedy
Armoured cruiser	Defence	1908	14,600	4 10	9·2" 7·5"	23	Flag of Rear-Admiral E. Troubridge Captain F. Wray
	Black Prince Duke of Edinburgh	1906	13,550	6 10	9·2" 6"	23	
	Warrior	1907	13,550	6 4	9·2" 7·5"	23	
Light cruiser	Chatham Dublin	1912	5,400	8	6"	25·5	Captain John Kelly Captain Howard Kelly
	Gloucester	1911	4,800	2 10	6" 4"	26	
	Weymouth	1911	5,250	8	6"	25·5	
GERMAN Battlecruiser	Goeben	1912	22,980	10	11"	25·5	Flag of Rear-Admiral W. Souchon
Light cruiser	Breslau	1912	4,550	12	4·1"	28·5	

3

Lone Wolf

SMS Emden's *last cruise; her action with* HMAS Sydney

Captains, officers and crew of *Emden* appear to be entitled
to all the honours of war. Unless you know of any reason
to the contrary Captain and officers should be permitted
to retain their swords.
Admiralty to Commander-in-Chief China, 11 November 1914

Renamed *Yavuz*, the *Goeben* survived for much longer than the
First World War: at the time of writing she is still afloat
(1967). The *Breslau* remained a threat to the Allies' control of the
eastern Mediterranean for all but the last months of 1918. But the
other eight German cruisers that were overseas on 4 August 1914
had much shorter lives. Five of these — the armoured *Scharnhorst*
(flag) and *Gneisenau*, and the smaller *Emden*, *Leipzig* and *Nürnberg*
— comprised Vice-Admiral Maximilian Count von Spee's East Asiatic
Squadron. The others, also light cruisers, were the *Königsberg* in
East African waters, and the *Dresden* and *Karlsruhe* in the Caribbean. All were so employed, notwithstanding von Tirpitz's demand
for the largest possible fleet in Home waters, because there were
weighty reasons — colonies in Africa and the Pacific islands, and
substantial interests in China and Mexico — why Germany should be
represented in peace by more than a handful of gunboats.

However, in the event of war, these ships would have small chance
of running the gauntlet of the British Fleet in order to return to the
Fatherland. They were, therefore, 'to carry on cruiser warfare against
enemy merchant vessels and against contraband carried in neutral
vessels, raid the enemy's coasts, bombard military establishments,
and destroy cable and wireless stations', to all of which the British
Empire was vulnerable. Moreover, 'by engaging equal or inferior
enemy forces, the conduct of the war in Home waters would be as-
sisted by holding many of the enemy's forces overseas'. For all this
Germany made thorough preparations. Having few overseas bases,
plans were laid for her cruisers to replenish with coal and other

supplies in lonely anchorages. They were to be reinforced by passenger liners converted into AMCs. They were to be helped by an intelligence organization with tentacles in every neutral country. And, since the *Admiralstab* expected to have great difficulty in communicating with them once war had begun, each cruiser captain was instructed that he

> must make his own decisions, bearing in mind that his chief duty is to damage the enemy as severely as possible. His heavy responsibility will be increased by the isolated position of his ship; the situation will sometimes appear hopeless, but he must never show weakness. If he succeeds in winning an honourable place for his ship in the history of the German Fleet, he is assured of the Emperor's favour.

Von Spee was also given this order: 'The best means of affording relief to Tsingtau is for ships of the Cruiser Squadron to retain their freedom of movement for as long as possible.' He was not to repeat the mistake made by the Russians at Port Arthur, and allow his squadron to be blockaded in the north China port that Germany had turned into a fortified naval base, after occupying it on the flimsiest of excuses in 1897.

As a counter to the six German cruisers that were east of Suez in July 1914, Britain deployed three squadrons. On the China Station Vice-Admiral Sir Martyn Jerram commanded the armoured cruisers *Minotaur* (flag) and *Hampshire*, the light cruisers *Newcastle* and *Yarmouth* and, in reserve at Hongkong, the pre-dreadnought battleship *Triumph*. In the East Indies Rear-Admiral Sir Richard Pierse had the *Swiftsure* (sister-ship to the *Triumph*), the light cruiser *Dartmouth* and the obsolescent cruiser *Fox*. In Australian and New Zealand waters, were the battlecruiser *Australia* (flag), the light cruisers *Melbourne* and *Sydney* and the old cruisers *Encounter* and *Pioneer*, under Rear-Admiral Sir George Patey. If all these ships, which had a whole chain of supply bases and dockyards to support them – Colombo, Singapore, Hongkong, Sydney, Auckland and more – had been ordered to seek out and destroy von Spee's force, its life might have been a short one. But they were not so used: Pierse had to remember the *Königsberg*: Patey was directed to support expeditions to capture the German colonies of New Guinea, Yap, Nauru and Samoa, ripe plums whose collection could have waited until the more serious threat presented by von Spee's squadron had been disposed of. This left only Jerram's ships which, though of comparable strength to the Germans, were too few to bring them to

action in so vast an ocean, except by some fortuitous chance. Nor
could he expect much help from Britain's Allies; the French and
Russians had no more than one armoured and three light cruisers
between them in the Far East. The Japanese Fleet, of 12 capital
ships, 11 armoured cruisers and 12 light cruisers, was another matter – except that the Anglo-Japanese alliance did not require Japan
to come to Britain's support should she be involved in a war with
another European power.

Jerram received the Warning Telegram on 28 July. He at once
ordered the *Triumph* to be commissioned. Then, having ascertained
that the *Scharnhorst* was at Yap, the *Gneisenau* (incorrectly owing to
a cipher error) at Singapore, and the *Nürnberg* and *Leipzig* as far
away as the west coast of Mexico, so that the only German warship
in Chinese waters was the *Emden* at Tsingtau, he signalled the Admiralty on the 30th:

> *Minotaur* and *Hampshire* leave Wei-hai-wei today. *Newcastle*
> joins at sea tomorrow. *Yarmouth* should arrive Shanghai tonight
> and will remain until outbreak of war.* I am sailing to a rendez-
> vous north of Saddle Islands to prevent *Gneisenau* and *Scharnhorst*
> reaching Japan.

But the Admiralty had different ideas. With a Marlborough's zest
for war, Churchill was not content to leave naval operations in
Battenberg's hands. On 28 July the First Lord advised the First Sea
Lord that 'the *Triumph* should be quickly mobilized ready to close
the China flagship. Without her the margin of superiority is small.'
Battenberg reacted with a signal ordering the China Squadron to
concentrate at Hongkong. And though reluctant to comply because
this 'placed me almost 900 miles from my correct strategical position', Jerram 'assumed that Their Lordships had good reason for
sending me there'. He reached Hongkong on 4 August, to be reinforced by the French light cruiser *Dupleix* on the 8th.

The consequences of this interference with the judgement of the
man on the spot were serious. The *Scharnhorst* and *Gneisenau* had
left Tsingtau at the end of June for a three months' cruise in the
Pacific. They were to be joined at Samoa in August by the *Nürnberg*

---

* To receive and send signals by cable because the ship-shore range of W/T
was only a few hundred miles. Since this limitation had a considerable influence
on both British and German naval operations, the reader will find
Appendix B on p 95, which deals with this and other relevant aspects of
signal communications, of help to an understanding of this and the next two
chapters.

from the west coast of Mexico, whither the *Leipzig* had gone to relieve her. Captain Karl von Müller, of the *Emden*, remained as senior officer in Chinese waters. Von Spee was at Truk on 7 July, when Berlin warned him that the 'political situation is not entirely satisfactory'. He decided to await developments at Ponapé, and to order the *Emden* to postpone a projected cruise up the Yangtse. Three weeks later he was told:

> Strained relations between Dual Alliance and Triple Entente are possible. Samoan cruise will probably have to be abandoned. *Nürnberg* has been ordered to proceed to Tsingtau. Everything else is left to you.

His reaction was characteristically swift: believing that Japan would seize the opportunity presented by a European war to invest Tsingtau, he ordered the *Nürnberg* to join him at Ponapé, where she arrived on 5 August.

Von Müller already had his orders: 'In event of strained relations *Emden* is to protect colliers leaving Tsingtau, but must not allow herself to be blockaded there. Colliers are to proceed to Pagan [like Ponapé a German colony]. *Emden* will endeavour to join the squadron.' He acted accordingly when Berlin signalled on 1 August: 'Imminent danger of war with Great Britain, France and Russia'. Because the Admiralty had withdrawn Jerram's ships to Hongkong, the *Emden*, together with the AMCs *Prinz Eitel Friedrich* and *Yorck*, and eight colliers, escaped unobserved from Tsingtau and joined von Spee in the German Mariana Islands on the 12th, while Jerram took his squadron to destroy the German W/T station on Yap, – after detaching the *Yarmouth* and *Dupleix* to watch Tsingtau, when it was already too late.

On 11 August the Admiralty signalled fresh instructions to Jerram:

> Practically certain Japan declares war on 12th. You may now leave protection of British trade north of Hongkong to Japanese, concentrating your attention in concert with Australian Squadron on destroying German cruisers. Send one light cruiser to close *Rainbow* [a small obsolescent cruiser] at Vancouver.

So the *Newcastle* was ordered to the west coast of Canada, and the *Minotaur* and *Hampshire* returned to Hongkong, to remain there until the 23rd because Japan delayed making war until that date. Although Jerram was then required to allocate some of his ships, notably the *Triumph*, to assist a Japanese investment of Tsingtau, this port was no longer of value to Germany, and its fall could be taken as certain. (It surrendered on 7 November.) Moreover, with the Japanese Fleet available for operations against von Spee, there was no possibility that he would return to the north-west Pacific: the British, French and Russian cruisers were free to proceed to more southern waters.

Von Spee's initial plan was to use his squadron to attack Allied trade in East Asiatic waters in the hope of drawing Jerram's ships away from Tsingtau. But on 13 August he called his captains to a conference, Felix Schultz of the *Scharnhorst*, Maerker of the *Gneisenau*, Karl von Schönberg of the *Nürnberg* and von Müller of the *Emden*, to whom (according to the last of these) 'the Commander-in-Chief drew attention to the threatening attitude of Japan, and to the advantage of maintaining the squadron together and concealing its whereabouts as long as possible, thereby holding a large number of enemy ships. He had decided to take the squadron to the west coast of America.' But something else was also said that was to have more immediate consequences.

> When we commanding officers were asked for our opinion, I [von Müller] said I was afraid that the squadron would be able to do practically nothing during a long cruise in the Pacific, and questioned whether so much value should be attached to the 'fleet in being' theory. If coaling the whole squadron in East Asian, Australian and Indian waters presented too great difficulties, we might consider detaching one light cruiser to the Indian Ocean.

Again von Spee was quick with a decision: 'A single light cruiser which consumes far less coal and can, if necessary, coal from captured steamships, will be able to maintain herself longer than the whole squadron in the Indian Ocean, where there are great prizes to be won.' Early next morning, as his force headed east from Pagan, the *Emden*, with the collier *Markomannia* in company, turned away to the west. 'I thank Your Excellency for the confidence placed in me,' von Müller signalled as he parted company. He was to do much to justify it.

When the *Emden*, completed in 1908 and armed with nothing heavier than ten 4·1-inch guns, 'came down like a wolf on the fold', she earned greater fame than any other German warship in the First World War. The 41-year-old von Müller was born in the same mould as the French privateer captains of the eighteenth century. Tall, blond, with fine-drawn features and a quiet manner, he represented all that was best in the Prussian officer class, combining single-minded audacity with clear-headed skill, courage with chivalry. The 23 vessels which he captured in the course of 70 days is only one measure of his success. The *Emden* also bombarded British ports, compelled Whitehall to order shipping to stay in harbour with a significant effect on trade in the Indian Ocean, required the Allies to search for her at a time when their resources were strained by other needs and in other seas, and imposed the need to provide strong escorts for troop convoys from Australia and New Zealand.

Von Müller steamed first for the Palau Islands, where he coaled off Timor. Thence he took the *Emden* along the northern shores of the Sumbawa Islands. Disguised with a false fourth funnel to resemble the *Yarmouth*, she slipped between Bali and Lombok on 28 August. A week later she had her first narrow escape when she stopped to coal in an anchorage to the east of Simalur Island which had been searched by HMS *Hampshire* only 24 hours before. On 10 September the *Emden* began her marauding career in the Bay of Bengal.

> During the next few days our business flourished [wrote her First Lieutenant]. As soon as a steamer came our way she was stopped, and one officer and ten men were sent aboard to make her ready to be sunk. Then another masthead appeared on the horizon. At times we had five or six vessels collected at one spot. You could just see the top of the funnels of one, the next was under water right up to her decks, the next was still fairly normal – just rolling from side to side as she slowly filled.

Von Müller had rightly judged this area to be the richest and safest hunting ground in the Indian Ocean. The Admiralty did not learn that he was there until 14 September, when all vessels trading in the Bay of Bengal were detained in port, and traffic was stopped on the Colombo–Singapore route. This deprived von Müller of further prey, but he could not complain: he had eluded the Allies for a month, he had captured or sunk nine ships, and he had assured his coal supply for the dangerous days that lay ahead, now that the hunt was on.

This had its genesis in an appreciation made by Jerram after Japan's declaration of war:

> I was aware that the Australian and New Zealand Squadrons and the French armoured cruiser *Montcalm* were to the east of Australia escorting expeditions to Samoa and New Britain; that the best ships of the East Indies Squadron were escorting troops from

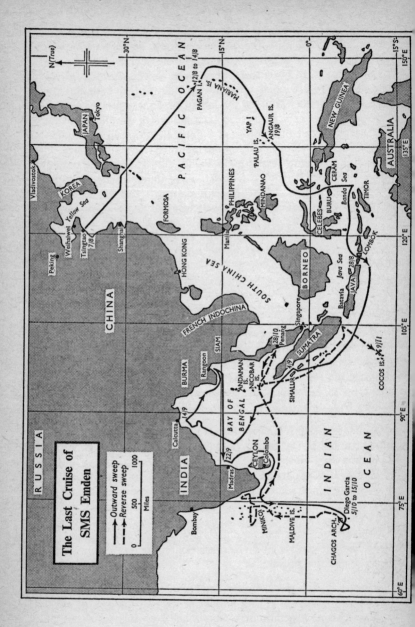

The Last Cruise of SMS Emden

India westwards; and that the only British force on the trade routes between Colombo, Singapore and Australia were the *Fox* and the *Espiègle* [sloop] near Colombo, and the *Pioneer* near Fremantle. With the possibility that the Germans might go to the Dutch East Indies, with disastrous results to our trade, the conclusion was irresistible, that a strong force was needed to work from Singapore.

Patey confirmed this decision by signalling that, though he believed the German squadron's destination to be South America, enemy AMCs could be expected to attack the shipping routes between China and Australia, where they would do much more damage than anything von Spee could do in the Pacific. The Admiralty also thought von Spee might be on his way to South America; the British consuls in Valparaiso and Buenos Aires reported German ships, laden with coal and provisions, sailing from Chilean waters and the Straits of Magellan. So Jerram was asked:

> How is China Squadron disposed? Destruction of *Scharnhorst* and *Gneisenau* is of first importance. Proceed on this service as soon as possible with *Minotaur*, *Hampshire* and *Dupleix*, keeping in communication with Patey who is engaged on same service.

It is difficult to know whether to be more astonished at the Admiralty's apparent ignorance of Jerram's dispositions; at the absence of any indication of *whither* he should 'proceed on this service'; or at their delusion that Patey was already searching for von Spee. Indeed, it is impossible to believe such a signal could have been drafted by the Naval War Staff. It bears the hallmark of an amateur; its phrasing is Churchillian: it must have been initiated by the First Lord. Although the consequences were not important, it is a further example of the unsatisfactory way in which the Admiralty attempted to control its forces overseas during the first months of the war.

Believing the German squadron to have gone to the Java Sea, Jerram went after it with the *Minotaur*, *Hampshire*, *Yarmouth*, *Dupleix*, the AMCs *Empress of Asia*, *Empress of Japan* and *Himalaya*, and the Japanese cruisers *Ibuki* and *Chikuma*. But a fortnight's search of the East Indies evoked this signal from him in the middle of September:

> There is absolutely no news of *Scharnhorst* and *Gneisenau*. I consider it probable they will next be heard of on South American coast. Only solution is to establish my headquarters ashore and send *Minotaur* and *Hampshire* to join Australian Squadron.

Jerram's intention to transfer his flag ashore, from where he could control his scattered force more easily than from a ship at sea which must keep W/T silence, was approved. But the *Hampshire* was ordered to Fremantle to augment the escort for the first troop convoy which was scheduled to leave for Europe on 22 September, and the movements of the *Minotaur* were to be decided later. Concluding from this that the Admiralty did not share his assessment of von Spee's intentions, Jerram sent the *Minotaur*, *Ibuki* and *Chikuma* to New Britain against the possibility of the East Asiatic Squadron threatening Australian waters whilst Patey was at Samoa. But another forty-eight hours brought first news of the *Emden*. Jerram immediately ordered the *Hampshire*, *Yarmouth*, *Dupleix* and *Chikuma* to search for her. Something more important happened very soon after this; the *Scharnhorst* and *Gneisenau* appeared off Apia in Samoa (already occupied by the New Zealand expedition), the news of which had many consequences. For the moment, however, we are concerned only with its effect on Jerram's ships: the *Minotaur* and *Ibuki* were sent south to take the *Hampshire*'s place in the troop convoy's escort.

Meantime, von Müller sighted nothing more after leaving the approaches to Calcutta until 18 September, when he found a Norwegian vessel off Rangoon. But there was no other prey for him there: moreover, intercepted chatter between shore W/T stations told him that the *Hampshire*, Captain H. W. Grant, was on his tail. He decided to leave the Rangoon area and strike against British interests in another way – whereby he just eluded Grant for the second time: at 0400 on 20 September the British armoured cruiser passed through the *Emden*'s noon position of the previous day. The half-million inhabitants of Madras were not worried by the inadequacies of that port's coast defences: six 6·3-inch muzzle-loading howitzers, six 15-pounders and two 4·7-inch quick-firers on carriages that required ten pairs of bullocks to bring them into action. They thought the war was a long way off – until this illusory sense of security was rudely shattered at 2130 on 22 September. From a range of 3,000 yards, the *Emden*'s searchlights settled on the Burmah Oil Company's tanks, to be followed by the sharp crack of gun salvoes and the louder detonation of exploding shells. Two of the tanks were ablaze before von Müller's ship had fired 30 rounds. A few stray shells out of 125 fell in the town and among bungalows near the tanks, but none caused casualties comparable with those in a merchant ship in the harbour, 26 of whose crew were wounded. The action lasted for only half an hour, by which time the shore batteries had begun to reply, but without effect. At 2200 von Müller turned his ship seawards and disappeared into the darkness.

'The *Emden* has had a momentous cruise,' wrote the London *Daily Chronicle*. 'The ship's company have proved their gallantry. We admire the sportsmanship of their exploits, as much as we heartily wish that the ship may soon be taken.' The need to find and destroy this dangerous marauder before she made a more destructive raid was urgent; but Jerram could spare only the *Hampshire*, *Yarmouth* and *Chikuma*; the rest of his ships had other tasks. Pierse could do no more: his war orders had specified patrols for five focal points on the trade routes, one by the island of Minikoi, to the west of Ceylon. But, like Jerram, his plans had been upset by unexpected Admiralty orders giving precedence to escorting convoys carrying the Indian Army to Egypt and France. He was left with nothing to protect the trade that von Müller made his next target. Missing, again by a matter of hours, a third encounter with the *Hampshire*, the *Emden* closed Colombo, only to be warned by the sweeping searchlights against attempting an attack such as she had made on Madras. Von Müller set course instead for Minikoi where, between 25 and 29 September, he disposed of six Allied ships before the alarm was raised. By the time the *Hampshire* and *Chikuma* reached this area, the *Emden* had withdrawn to a refuge in the Maldive Islands. And the *New York Times* wrote:

Her Commander is doing with luck and skill an appointed task fully legitimized by the laws of war. Our own Paul Jones did the same thing, and to this day is occasionally called a pirate by the British. They know, however, that he wasn't one, and no more is the Commander of the *Emden*.

Misled by an old chart into supposing that he might make a rich haul in the Chagos Archipelago, von Müller next steamed 600 miles to the south. A week later he anchored his ship off lonely Diego Garcia, where he was astute enough to support the few British inhabitants' ignorance of the outbreak of war to the extent of repairing their motorboat. If the *Emden* was to maintain her speed, her bottom had to be cleaned by heeling her, and her machinery must be overhauled. At the end of a valuable ten days spent doing this, intercepted W/T signals told von Müller that Allied shipping was again flowing freely east and west of Ceylon, and that the *Hampshire* and *Chikuma* had been augmented by nothing more than the *Empress of Asia*. He decided to make a second foray against the

Minikoi area. The results were more profitable than before: when the SS *Saint Egbert* put into Cochin on 20 October, to land von Müller's latest captives, she brought news that between the 16th and 19th the *Emden* had sunk seven more ships.

Once again sailings out of Colombo were suspended, and the *Hampshire* and *Empress of Asia* sailed in pursuit. Grant had already missed the *Emden* three times by the narrowest of margins: on the morning of 21 October, von Müller had the luck that only the brave deserve. The two British ships had spent the night steaming in single line ahead towards the Maldives, whither Grant believed the German cruiser would again retire. When dawn came he ordered the *Empress of Asia* to open to twenty miles on his starboard beam. She reached this position at 0800, and turned to the *Hampshire*'s course. At that hour the *Emden* and two colliers were only ten miles farther away – but rain squalls, and the chance that the two forces were steaming on almost opposite courses, allowed them to go their different ways without sighting each other.

The Allies now stirred themselves to more drastic action to counter the depredations of this Assyrian wolf. Merchant ships were sailed on diverse routes away from the regular tracks, and were darkened at night. The *Yarmouth* and the Russian cruiser *Askold* were released from escorting convoys to join the hunt. The *Chikuma* and the Russian cruiser *Zemchug* were ordered to patrol the east side of the Bay of Bengal, whither the Japanese sent the armoured cruisers *Tokiwa* and *Yakumo*. But none of these movements trapped the *Emden* before she coaled at a lonely anchorage in the Nicobar Islands, then proceeded to carry out the most audacious of von Müller's exploits.

Allied warships used the roadstead between the island of Penang and the Malayan mainland for coaling and servicing their engines. To be able to repel an attack from seaward, the *Yarmouth*, when she was there, anchored bow and stern across the northern entrance, so that she could be sure of bringing a broadside to bear. The *Zemchug*, which arrived on 26 October, was advised to take the same precaution; but at dawn on the 28th she was lying to the tide, with only two 4·7-inch guns available to defend the harbour. Of four smaller warships, all of them French, the destroyer *Mousquet* was patrolling to seaward, the destroyer *Pistolet* anchored in the roadstead with steam at one hour's notice, and the destroyer *Fronde* and gunboat *D'Iberville* berthed amongst the merchant shipping with their boilers cold. For all of these the awakening came at 0530; the Captain of the *D'Iberville* was roused by a deafening detonation resembling a clap of thunder, followed almost immediately by vigorous gunfire. Hurrying on deck I saw the *Zemchug* disappearing in a cloud of yellow smoke. To her right appeared the vague silhouette of a four-funnelled man-of-war making for the anchorage. My first impression was that the *Zemchug* had opened fire on an Allied ship, so I ordered boats away to help the victims of an inexplicable error. Then the unknown cruiser completed her turn towards the sea and showed that her foremost funnel was a dummy. Simultaneously we cried: 'It's the *Emden*', and went to action stations.

But neither the *D'Iberville*, nor the likewise immobile *Fronde*, was so unwise as to draw the enemy's fire; they left this to the *Pistolet* which slipped from her moorings an hour after the first salvo from the *Emden*, whose First Lieutenant wrote this account of the raid:

On the morning of 28 October, whilst it was still dark, we made for Penang at twenty knots, carrying four funnels, the fourth being of wood and canvas to give us the appearance of an English cruiser. [The launch patrolling the entrance was thus deceived into allowing the *Emden* to pass unchallenged. The early morning mist concealed her from the *Mousquet*.] As we approached the roadstead the sun was on the point of rising, and we could see a number of merchant ships, but no man-of-war. Then, in the midst of the trading vessels, a dark shape emerged, though we did not know she was the *Zemchug* until we had approached within half a mile. Everyone was asleep on board the Russian cruiser. Hoisting the German ensign we fired a torpedo into her port quarter [flooding the engine room]. Then there was much activity; we could see Russian officers running on deck and throwing themselves overboard. But our guns shelled the *Zemchug* until she looked like a sieve, with fires plainly visible through the holes. As we turned to go out again, we fired a second torpedo which struck her below the bridge, exploding the forward magazine. A huge black and white cloud of water, spars and splinters covered the whole ship. When it subsided, nothing could be seen except the top of one of her masts. [She lost 91 officers and men, with a further 108 wounded, out of a complement of 340. Sixty Chinese prostitutes were lost with them.]

We then observed the French gunboat *D'Iberville*, an ancient tub with two light guns, and were about to come to grips with her when a destroyer was reported coming in. We steamed towards her at high speed and opened fire, only to realize that she was a Government steamer [the patrol launch] when firing was immediately stopped. Next, a large ship, apparently a man-of-war, was reported out at sea. We expected one of the French armoured cruisers, but it turned out to be the destroyer *Mousquet*.

Having been deceived by the patrol launch into leaving the roadstead, von Müller decided against returning: instead he steered west to intercept the SS *Glenturret*. But before the *Emden*'s boarding party could complete their work, the *Mousquet* was sighted, and the *Glenturret* was allowed to proceed into Penang carrying von Müller's apologies for firing on the unarmed launch. Commander Théroinne's destroyer put up a gallant fight, but was overpowered and sank in ten minutes. 'All the *Emden*'s boats were lowered to save survivors. We fished up 33 men, who had the best of attention before they were transferred to a passing English steamer and landed at Sabang.' The *Pistolet*, which had slipped her moorings at 0635, chased the *Emden* until 1000, when an overheated bearing reduced her speed. The *Fronde*, having followed the *Pistolet* out of harbour an hour later, had even less success. And by the time the *D'Iberville* limped out on one engine at 1000, there was nothing she could do except search for survivors from the *Mousquet*. The *Emden* had vanished again, leaving the Allies to reflect that, having been caught so completely asleep that morning, they were fortunate to have lost no more than the *Zemchug* and the *Mousquet*. A subsequent court martial reduced the hapless Russian captain to the rank of common sailor.

There was, nonetheless, very little sand left in the upper segment of the *Emden*'s hour-glass. As, from Penang, she steamed for the Sunda Strait, yet more warships were being sent to hunt her down; the light cruiser *Gloucester* from the Mediterranean, the *Dartmouth* and *Weymouth* from East Africa, three more cruisers from Japan. These were not, however, to be needed, because for his next objective von Müller chose the Cocos Islands.

Apart from the damage the enemy would suffer by the destruction of this cable and wireless station, and the interruption of communications between Australia and England, I hoped to create the impression that the *Emden* was about to harry the steamer traffic south and west of Australia and so withdraw from the Indian Ocean some of the English cruisers that were hunting her there before I made for Socotra and the steamer route between Aden and Bombay.

But this was not the *Emden*'s destiny. 'The possibility of Cocos being seized by the *Emden* had been in my [Jerram's] mind, and since I could not station a ship there, I instructed the cable station to give immediate warning, in the event of attack, to all Allied ships in those waters.' So, when Superintendent Darcy Farrant of the Eastern Telegraph Company was informed that a four-funnelled warship was steaming towards Direction Island at 0550 on the morning of 9 November, he knew what to do.

Seeing that the fourth funnel was palpably of canvas, I found Mr La Nauze and instructed him to proceed immediately to the W/T hut, and put out a general call that there was a strange warship in our vicinity. After watching the *Emden* anchor about a mile off-shore and lower an armed launch and two heavily manned boats which headed for the jetty, I returned to the W/T hut where Mr Nauze informed me that the *Emden* and her collier were trying to jam him. I instructed him to continue the call, so as to force the two ships to use their strong Telefunken notes which would be treated as suspicious by our warships; and I remained with him in the hut until an officer and some half-dozen bluejackets ordered us to leave.

These came from an armed landing party, 50 strong, led by the *Emden*'s First Lieutenant, Hellmuth von Mücke, which quickly got to work.

I [wrote one of this party] and two wireless operators went to the W/T station, where calls for help were being sent out. We at once destroyed the electrical machinery, motor engine, switchboard, etc. Others did the same work in the telegraph house. Lieutenant-Commander von Mücke fished up the cable to Perth and cut it. The wireless mast was blown up, also a house with spare cables.

All this occupied some two and a half hours: then, before the other cables could be cut, the *Emden* blew her siren.

This was the signal to return with all speed. As the boats shoved off from the shore I [von Mücke] saw that she was already leaving the harbour. I steamed after her as fast as my pinnace would go, because I had no idea what she was doing. Then, suddenly, she opened fire.

La Nauze's alarm signals had been intercepted by HMAS *Melbourne*, Captain M. L. Silver, who was senior officer of the Australian troop convoy escort which, all unknown to von Müller, was only 55 miles to the north of Cocos on its way to Colombo at 0700 that morning. And he decided 'that it was in the interest of the safety of the convoy to get into touch with this cruiser, which could only be the *Emden* or the *Königsberg*. I therefore directed HMAS *Sydney* to raise steam for full speed and proceed to Cocos.' The result wholly justified his decision; but had it been otherwise — if the *Emden* had eluded the *Sydney* and attacked the convoy (together with the *Königsberg* for all that Silver knew) — he could have been accused of hazarding its safe and timely arrival, more especially since the *Minotaur*, now on her way to South Africa, was near enough to be diverted to the Cocos Islands.

I have the honour to report [wrote Captain John Glossop to the Admiralty] that whilst on convoy escort duty at 0630 on 9th November, a W/T message from Cocos was heard: 'Strange warship at entrance'. I was ordered to raise steam for full speed and proceed thither. I worked up to twenty knots and at 0915 sighted land ahead, and almost immediately smoke which proved to be SMS *Emden* coming towards me. At 0940 she fired the first shot at 9,500 yards. Her fire was very accurate and rapid to begin with, my foremost rangefinder being dismounted quite early and the after control put out of action by the third salvo, but it seemed to slacken quickly. I kept my distance to obtain the advantage of my heavier calibre, longer range guns. First the foremost funnel of the *Emden* went, secondly the foremast, and she was badly on fire aft. Then the second funnel went, and lastly the third; and I saw she was making for North Keeling Island, where she grounded at 1120. I gave her two more broadsides, then left to pursue a merchant ship which had come up during the action.

Although this duel lasted for an hour and a half, the result was never in doubt. The light cruiser *Sydney*, completed as recently as the previous year, opposed eight 6-inch guns to the Emden's ten 4·1-inch. As von Müller expressed it:

As soon as the *Sydney* got our range a good deal of damage was done to the *Emden*, and this increased quickly, the *Sydney* having fire superiority over us, as well as superior speed. About twenty minutes after beginning the fight, our steering gear went wrong. I ordered the hand gear to be manned, but its shafting had been jammed by a direct hit. Meanwhile, the ship had swung about eight points before she was checked by the screws. As the fire from our starboard guns had already weakened considerably,

I let the port battery come into action. But its fire soon weakened also, from serious casualties among the guns' crews. By this time the prospect of getting within torpedo range had become extremely small, though I did not wish to give up the attempt. But when the distance dropped to 4,900 yards, the *Sydney*, after making an unsuccessful attempt to torpedo us, swung sharply to starboard and stood away at high speed.

By 1045 the *Emden*'s upper bridge had been destroyed, the centre and after funnels knocked over, and the foremast was over the side. I wanted to make a second attempt to get within torpedo range, but was unable to pass the order, 'Stop starboard screw'. Our engines could only attain 19 knots, because two boilers had ceased functioning. A few minutes after 1100 our gun-fire ceased, so I swung away from the *Sydney*. Shortly afterwards I was informed that the torpedo room must be abandoned on account of flooding from a hit under water. Since it was now impossible for me to do further damage to my opponent, I decided to wreck my badly damaged ship on the weather side of North Keeling Island, rather than sacrifice needlessly the lives of those who still survived.

But the end of the *Emden* was not quite yet: the merchant ship sighted by Glossop was her collier, the captured British SS *Buresk*.

I pursued and overtook her at 1210, firing a gun across her bows to stop her. I sent an armed boat but she was already sinking, the Kingston having been damaged beyond repair. I took all onboard, fired four shells into her, and returned to the *Emden*, passing men swimming in the water for whom I left two boats. Since she still had her colours up, I enquired twice by signal: 'Will you surrender?' The German officer from the *Buresk* gave me to understand that her Captain would never surrender, so very reluctantly I again fired at her at 1630, ceasing at 1635 when she showed white flags and hauled down her ensign.

Glossop then sent a boat to the *Emden* with this letter for von Müller:

I have the honour to request in the name of humanity that you now surrender your ship to me. To show how much I appreciate your gallantry, I will recapitulate the position. You are ashore, three funnels and one mast down and most guns disabled. You cannot leave this island, and my ship is intact. In the event of your surrendering, in which I venture to remind you is no dis-

grace but rather your misfortune, I will endeavour to do all I can
for your sick and wounded and take them to a hospital.

The *Sydney*'s Captain would do no more for the stricken ship until
he had found out the condition of the cable and W/T station on
Direction Island. But on passage over he delayed to rescue a German sailor, so that it was too late to make a landing before dark.
He had to lie off and on all night until he could communicate with
the island next morning, when he had a disagreeable surprise. After
the *Emden*'s hurried departure, von Mücke had returned, 'hoisted
the German flag, and declared the island a German possession, putting all the Englishmen under martial law, and making arrangements
for the defence of the beach, installing machine guns and having
trenches dug'. The *Emden*'s First Lieutenant also watched his ship's
fight with the *Sydney* until, by the late afternoon,

> it was quite clear that my ship could not come back to help us.
> Since it was to be expected that an enemy cruiser would call on
> one of the following days, I gave orders to get the old sailing
> vessel *Ayesha* ready for sea. She was of 97 tons and formerly car-
> ried copra from Keeling to Batavia. The Englishmen on the island
> warned me against taking her as she was old and rotten.

Nonetheless, von Mücke pressed his plan with such vigour that the
Ayesha was away, with all the German landing party and their
weapons onboard, before dark – as Glossop found when he landed
next morning.*

Having learned that all on Direction Island were safe, he bor-
rowed their doctor and returned to the *Emden*, sending an officer
to see von Müller.

> In view of the large number of prisoners and wounded, and the
> impossibility of leaving them where they were, he agreed that, if
> I received them, they would cause no interference with ship or
> fittings, and would be amenable to discipline for such time as they
> remained in the *Sydney*. I then set to work to tranship them, a
> most difficult operation, the send alongside her being very heavy.
> The conditions in the *Emden* were indescribable. I received the
> last man from her at 1500, then had to go round to the lee side

---

* After a long and hazardous journey by way of Padang in the Dutch East
Indies, von Mücke and his men reached Hodeida in Turkish-occupied Yemen,
whence they travelled overland to Constantinople, to be welcomed there as
heroes by Admiral Souchon in June 1915.

of North Keeling Island to pick up twenty more who had managed to get ashore. Dark came on before this could be accomplished and we again stood off and on all night, resuming operations at 0500 on 11 November,

when the gallant von Müller was the last to leave his stricken ship. The *Sydney*

proceeded for Colombo at 1035. Her total casualties were three killed and 13 wounded, of whom one has since died. In the *Emden* I can only approximately state the killed as seven officers and 108 men. I had onboard 11 of her officers and 191 of her men, of whom three officers and 53 men were wounded. The damage to the *Sydney*'s hull was surprisingly small, although about ten hits were made. The *Sydney* fired one torpedo, but nothing is known of its behaviour, and expended 670 rounds of ammunition, the effect of which was appalling. I have great pleasure in stating that the behaviour of my ship's company was excellent in every way. The engines worked magnificently, and I cannot speak too highly of the medical staff, the ship being nothing but a hospital of the most painful description.

Such was the not inglorious end of the *Emden*, the first of von Spee's squadron to be destroyed. Chivalrous to the last, von Müller, who spent the rest of the war as a prisoner in Malta, merited the Iron Cross First Class that the Kaiser bestowed upon him. The Emperor's message to the city of Emden, 'a new and stronger *Emden* shall arise, on whose bow the Iron Cross shall be fixed', was well deserved. So, too, were newspaper tributes:

For three full months, under the most difficult conditions, the *Emden*, with tenacious courage and exemplary seamanship, has harried the enemy and caused them heavy losses. Finally, she had to succumb to the hunt organized for her by British, Russian, French and Japanese warships; but her name will live in the memory of the German people (*Norddeutsche Allgemeine Zeitung*).

The *Daily Telegraph* wrote:

It is almost in our heart to regret that the *Emden* has been destroyed. Von Müller has been enterprising, cool and daring in making war on our shipping, and has revealed a nice sense of humour. He has, moreover, shown every possible consideration to the crews of his prizes. There is not a survivor who does not speak well of this young German, the officers under him and the crew obedient to his orders. The war at sea will lose something of its piquancy, its humour and its interest now that the *Emden* has gone.

Such reflections do not, however, detract from the credit which is due to those who ensured the *Emden*'s destruction. This goes, above all, to Captain Glossop and the officers and men of the *Sydney* of the newly-fledged Australian Navy; but Admiral Jerram's foresight, Superintendent Farrant's presence of mind, and Captain Silver's bold decision should not be forgotten.

4

The Long Voyage

The search for von Spee's squadron

I am quite homeless. I cannot reach Germany. We possess no other secure harbour. I must plough the seas of the world doing as much mischief as I can, until my ammunition is exhausted, or a foe far superior in power succeeds in catching me.

Vice-Admiral Graf von Spee

Von Spee had just passed his fifty-third birthday when, on 13 August 1914, he detached the *Emden* to 'cry havoc' in the Indian Ocean. A gunnery specialist, he had reached flag rank in 1910. By the time Germany became engulfed in a war of her own making, he had been in command of the East Asiatic Squadron for the best part of two years; time enough for his ships to reach a high peak of efficiency; time enough for him to decide how they could best be used to blunt a prong of Britannia's trident. Tall, broad-shouldered, with a pointed beard and blue eyes, his keen intelligence, his fighting spirit, his strength of will and his willingness to take responsibility made him a dangerous adversary.

From Pagan in the Mariana Islands, he took the armoured cruisers *Scharnhorst* and *Gneisenau*, the light cruiser *Nürnberg*, the AMCs *Prinz Eitel Friedrich* and *Cormoran*, and a group of supply ships, eastwards across the Pacific Ocean, to call first at the German Marshall Islands. Here, from 19 to 22 August, the squadron coaled in Eniwetok Lagoon, secure in the knowledge, from intercepted W/T traffic, that the nearest enemy force, Patey's, was far to the south. The two AMCs were then ordered to raid trade in Australian waters, whilst the *Nürnberg* was sent to Honolulu with signals for Berlin which included this intention: 'I shall proceed to Chile arriving at Juan Fernandez on 15 October.' Since the Allies would know that the *Nürnberg* had recently left Mexican waters, a visit to Hawaii could not compromise the movements of von Spee's heavy ships as they steamed on to Majuro Atoll, at the south-eastern end of the Marshalls. He was there on 27 August when Japan declared war.

In the light of Whitehall's attempts to control the operations of its overseas forces, Berlin's very different attitude is of special interest. On 18 August the *Admiralstab* made this appreciation:

> It may be assumed that the Cruiser Squadron is in East Asiatic waters. Japan's impending entry into the war makes its position hopeless. It is impossible to judge whether the squadron will be able to choose against which enemy it will deal its dying blows. We are ignorant of the Commander-in-Chief's coal supplies, and, judging from his oft repeated utterances, it may be taken for granted that he will attempt to bring the enemy to action. Whether he engages the British or the Japanese must depend on their relative situations, and any interference on our part might be disastrous. The Commander-in-Chief must have complete liberty of action. If he succeeds in beating the British before the Japanese have time to come in, we should regard it as a great achievement. In view of the above it is better to send him no instructions.

So none were sent, least of all after Berlin received word of von Spee's intentions. There was only this signal from the Kaiser: 'God be with you in the impending stern struggle.' The Admiral was to justify this trust: in the words of the German historian, his 'was a brilliant achievement: cut off from home, he was entirely dependent on his own resources, and in drawing up his plans he had to consider what the situation might be in almost every part of the world'. On the other hand, to quote Churchill:

> He had no lack of objectives. He had only to hide and to strike. The vastness of the Pacific and its multitude of islands offered him their shelter and, once he had vanished, who should say where he would reappear. So long as he lived, all the Allies' enterprises lay under the shadow of a serious potential danger. We could not be strong enough every day everywhere to meet him.

From the Marshalls von Spee took his armoured cruisers and five supply ships to Christmas Island, where the *Nürnberg*, after a call at Fanning Island to cut the Fiji–Honolulu cable, rejoined with news that New Zealand troops had occupied Samoa. 'This force,' wrote von Spee, 'will need constant provisioning by steamers. An attack on ships at anchor might have good results.' Unfortunately, when the

Scharnhorst and *Gneisenau* approached Apia at dawn on 14 September, they found nothing but one small sailing vessel. Having insufficient men for a landing, and seeing no target worth the expenditure of irreplaceable ammunition, von Spee withdrew, steering initially to the NW so as to deceive the island's observers into supposing that his squadron was not crossing the Pacific – with what success will soon be seen. His next call was at the isolated British Suvorov Island. Since the swell prevented coaling here, he moved on to Bora Bora in the Society Islands. Thence the squadron headed for Tahiti, where von Spee intended 'to engage any enemy ships encountered and to requisition coal and provisions'. But the French were ready to resist a landing, when the German ships approached the island at dawn on 22 September. As the intruders opened fire on the fort and the old gunboat *Zelée*, the Governor ignited his coal stocks and blew up his storehouses. Von Spee's plan was finally thwarted by his discovery that the leading marks for entering Papeeté harbour had been removed. The German squadron resumed its eastward voyage, having achieved nothing at the expense of valuable ammunition – and of disclosing its movements: the Governor sent a steamer to Samoa with news of the attack that reached London on the 30th. But the Admiralty ignored this fresh evidence that von Spee was moving east: Patey was told:

It is very probable that *Gneisenau* and *Scharnhorst* may repeat attacks similar to one at Papeeté; they may be expected to return towards Samoa, Fiji and even New Zealand. Making Suva your base, search in these waters.

From 26 September to 3 October the German ships were at the Marquesas Islands, where they coaled and provisioned, whilst their crews had their first chance to stretch their sea legs ashore, because the few French inhabitants had no means of resistance, nor of reporting the enemy's presence to the outside world. Von Spee also detached two of his supply ships to Honolulu with signals to Berlin reporting that he would proceed by way of Easter Island and Juan Fernandez to Valparaiso, and to the German Consul at San Francisco stating his coal requirements at these places. As important, the *Scharnhorst* heard the *Leipzig*, Captain Haun, in W/T communication with the *Dresden*, whereby the German Admiral learned that both these light cruisers were off the west coast of South America.

At the beginning of August, Haun's ship was protecting German interests in Mexico. On the 2nd she left Mazatlan for Tsingtau; but

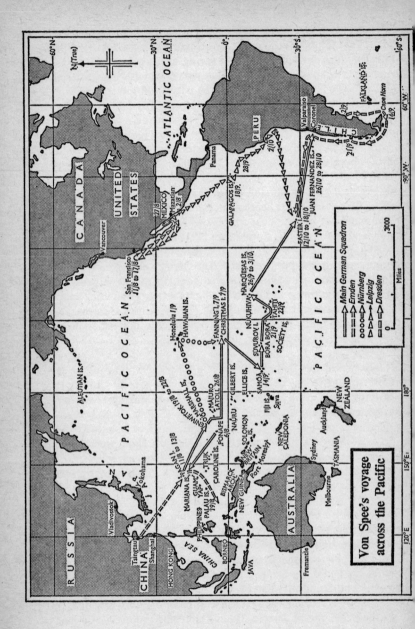

Von Spee's voyage across the Pacific

when war began two days later her Captain decided to operate off San Francisco. The *Leipzig* was to seaward of the Golden Gate from 11 to 18 August, but achieved nothing because, on orders from London, British merchant shipping remained in port. Meantime, the only British cruiser in the area, the obsolete *Rainbow*, not only eluded her but escorted two British sloops from Mexican waters to the safety of Vancouver. (It was the unanimous view of the *Shearwater*'s crew that the *Leipzig* deliberately allowed them to pass because all four ships had been working together for several months in which the British and German crews had become good friends.) Next, the American authorities placed such a strict interpretation on International Law that Haun could not obtain enough coal. Then came news that the *Newcastle* was on her way from Hongkong and that, if Japan entered the war, this British light cruiser would be reinforced by the armoured cruiser *Idzumo*. So the *Leipzig* went south: on the 18th she reached the Galapagos Islands; on the 25th she sank a ship with a cargo of sugar; by the 28th she was off the Peruvian coast. But there Haun found the trade routes devoid of Allied shipping.

He then received orders from Berlin to operate with the *Dresden*, so he headed for Easter Island. Since he had no news of von Spee's plans, this choice for a rendezvous was no more than coincidence; but that it was a wise one was confirmed on the night of 2–3 October when the *Dresden* signalled: 'My position Mas a Fuera Island. Intend to proceed to Easter Island to get in touch with the Cruiser Squadron.' And by establishing W/T communication with the *Dresden* on the night of 5–6 October, von Spee was able to coordinate the arrival of these welcome reinforcements, which brought his squadron up to two armoured and three light cruisers. They stayed at this remote Pacific outpost from 12 to 18 October, where they again coaled; and the German Admiral was reunited with both his sons, Otto who was a lieutenant in the *Nürnberg* and Heinrich who was serving in the *Gneisenau*. Another 1,500 miles brought the squadron to Mas a Fuera on 26 October, where it was joined unexpectedly by the *Prinz Eitel Friedrich*, which for want of coal had abandoned her attempts to attack trade in Australian waters. (The same reason compelled the *Cormoran* to seek internment at Guam.) But von Spee's supply ships could not fill this vessel's bunkers as well as his cruisers'; he had to detach her to Valparaiso when the squadron again sailed eastwards on the 28th. Two days later his officers and men were heartened by the sight of the snow-capped Andes rising above the horizon ahead of them.

Why had the *Dresden* moved from the Caribbean round into the Pacific? And what action had the Admiralty taken in response to warnings that the East Asiatic Squadron's likely destination was South America? Britain's war plans recognized the special importance of the Atlantic trade routes. On the assumption that the Grand Fleet, from its base at Scapa, would deter any units of the High Seas Fleet from breaking out of the North Sea, Allied merchant shipping proceeding to and from North and South America, South and West Africa, and the Mediterranean, was threatened on 4 August 1914 by no more than the *Dresden*, which had been watching German interests in Mexico, and the newer *Karlsruhe* which had, by chance, just arrived in the Caribbean to relieve her. Against these two light cruisers, plus the possibility that German liners might emerge from neutral ports secretly converted into AMCs, the Allies deployed five squadrons of cruisers. Rear-Admiral Sir Christopher Cradock, with the armoured *Suffolk*, *Berwick*, *Essex* and *Lancaster*, and the unarmoured *Bristol*, was in the West Indies, whither the French had sent the *Descartes* and *Condé*. A further light cruiser, HMS *Glasgow*, was on the east coast of South America. On mobilization, this peacetime force was augmented by the armoured cruisers *Carnarvon*, flagship of Rear-Admiral A. C. Stoddart, *Cornwall*, *Cumberland* and *Monmouth* in the Cape Verde area; by the 9th CS in the Azores; by the 11th CS to the west of Ireland; and by the 12th CS, plus a French force, in the South-Western Approaches.

The 52-year-old Cradock had proved his courage with the naval brigade in the Boxer rebellion; his skill as a seaman in the rescue of the Duke of Fife and the Princess Royal when the P & O liner *Delhi* was wrecked on the coast of Morocco; his wit and wisdom, his sense and sensibility, in his book *Whispers from the Fleet*. Fisher considered him 'one of our very best officers' to whom (wrote Archibald Hurd) 'the Navy was not a collection of ships, but a community of men with high purpose'. And his reaction to the Admiralty's first war warning on 27 July was swift and clear: since he could not be sure whether the *Karlsruhe* (at Havana) and the *Dresden* (at Port au Prince) would move towards the North or South Atlantic, he must cover both. From the *Suffolk* at Vera Cruz, he ordered the *Essex* and *Lancaster* to Halifax, the *Berwick* to Jamaica, the *Bristol* to join the *Glasgow* off Pernambuco. But, as with Jerram, Cradock's dispositions were modified by orders from Whitehall. Under the mistaken belief that the German liners which were in New York on 4 August would quickly emerge as AMCs to harry Allied trade off that port, the armoured cruiser *Good Hope* was detached from the

Grand Fleet to Halifax, and Stoddart was instructed to send the *Monmouth* to Pernambuco, so that the *Bristol* could go north to join the *Essex* and *Lancaster* off Sandy Hook, to which supposed danger area Cradock decided to take the *Suffolk* – with potentially fruitful consequences.

As soon as he knew that war was imminent, Captain Erich Köhler steamed the *Karlsruhe* to a deserted anchorage in the Bahamas. Thence he rendezvoused with the SS *Kronprinz Wilhelm* 120 miles north of Watling Island on 6 August, to transfer the guns needed to convert this 25,000-ton liner into an AMC. The *Karlsruhe* was so engaged at 1100 when the *Suffolk* appeared over the southern horizon. Hurriedly the German vessels parted company; before the British flagship could get within range, the *Karlsruhe* sped north, the *Kronprinz Wilhelm* NNE. And with the advantage of 27 knots to the *Suffolk*'s 23, the *Karlsruhe* left her opponent out of sight astern by nightfall. But the British Admiral had already wirelessed the north-bound *Bristol* to reverse course; at 2015 Captain B. H. Fanshawe took advantage of a full moon to open fire on the *Karlsruhe* at a range of six miles. Though taken by surprise, Köhler managed to turn his ship away to the east before she suffered damage; and spotting conditions were too poor for either side to achieve a hit before the German's greater speed allowed her to elude this new pursuer. The *Karlsruhe* had not, however, yet escaped from Cradock's trap: the *Suffolk* turned to intercept her again. But the luck that led Cradock to make contact so soon after the outbreak of war now eluded him. Shortly after 0800, the *Suffolk* crossed the *Karlsruhe*'s course just far enough astern for Köhler's ship to avoid being seen; and the *Berwick*, which had also been ordered to intercept, chanced to alter course away from her quarry when she, too, was near to sighting her. On 9 August, when only 12 tons of coal remained in her bunkers, the *Karlsruhe* reached the safety of Puerto Rico.

Off Sandy Hook, Cradock learned that, contrary to the Admiralty's belief, no German liner was likely to leave New York in the guise of an AMC: and on the 13th the *Karlsruhe* was reported at Curaçao, the *Dresden* off the mouth of the Amazon. This changed the picture; now there was no significant threat to Allied trade in the north-west Atlantic except, perhaps, from the *Kronprinz Wilhelm*. Leaving the northern part of his command in the *Suffolk*'s charge, Cradock transferred his flag to the *Good Hope* – after his failure to catch the *Karlsruhe* he favoured the latter's higher speed – and sailed to join the *Berwick*, *Bristol*, *Condé* and *Descartes* at St Lucia on 23 August.

Lüdecke was taking the *Dresden* down the coast of South America, to attack British shipping off Pernambuco, before proceeding to do likewise off the Plate. Köhler, having been deterred from venturing north, had also headed the *Karlsruhe* for Pernambuco. When both German cruisers were reported off the South American coast, the Admiralty knew that there was a major threat in an area covered only by the *Glasgow* and *Monmouth*: so the *Cornwall* and the AMCs *Otranto* and *Macedonia* were ordered to reinforce them. But the movement of the *Karlsruhe* and *Dresden* to the south was not the only reason why Cradock extended his operations beyond the limits of his own command into that for which Stoddart was responsible. On 3 September he signalled Whitehall:

> *Good Hope* arrived Fernando Noronha. *Cornwall* is proceeding south. *Glasgow* is proceeding with *Monmouth* and *Otranto* to Magellan Straits, where German colliers reported, and where concentration of German cruisers from China, Pacific and Atlantic appears possible. (*No 1*)*

The Admiralty approved, telling him 'to take charge of SE coast of America'. Cradock responded: '*Gneisenau* and *Scharnhorst* reported Caroline Islands 8th August. Is there any later information?' (*No 2*) Since the Admiralty could only tell him: 'Nothing since 8th August. Magellan Straits quite possible. Falkland Islands might be used' (*No 3*), Cradock ordered the *Good Hope, Cornwall* and *Bristol*, and the AMCs *Carmania* and *Macedonia* to operate between the Abrolhos Rocks and the Plate, and sent the *Glasgow* and *Monmouth* and the AMC *Otranto* to cover the Magellan Straits. Four days later, 14 September, the *Carmania* found the German AMC *Cap Trafalgar* coaling off the Brazilian island of Trinidada, and sank her after a spirited action lasting an hour and a half, in which the *Carmania* suffered sufficient damage to need the *Macedonia*'s escort to Gibraltar for repairs.

Neither Köhler nor Lüdecke had a tithe of von Müller's talent for cruiser warfare. The former, operating off Pernambuco, was so much concerned to avoid British cruisers that the *Karlsruhe* achieved little beyond being an elusive threat of which nothing was heard for many weeks. The latter, after sinking a couple of

* This and subsequent signals are numbered serially to facilitate further reference in later pages.

freighters off the Plate at the end of August, moved south to Caye-
tano Bay on the Patagonian coast, whence he arrived in Orange
Bay, in the Magellan Straits, on 4 September. There the supply ship
Santa Isabel gave him false news that British cruisers were off the
eastern entrance to the Straits. Coupled with an injunction from
Berlin, 'It is advisable to operate with the *Leipzig*', which Lüdecke
knew to be on the Pacific coast, this was enough to persuade him to
take the *Dresden* there on the 18th.

Four days before this the Admiralty signalled Cradock:

There is strong possibility of *Scharnhorst and Gneisenau* arriving
in Magellan Straits or on west coast of South America. Germans
have begun to carry on trade there. Leave sufficient force to deal
with *Dresden* and *Karlsruhe*. Concentrate a squadron strong
enough to meet *Scharnhorst* and *Gneisenau,* making Falkland
Islands your coaling base. *Canopus* is en route to Abrolhos;
Defence is joining you from Mediterranean. Until *Defence* joins,
keep at least *Canopus* and one 'County' class cruiser with your
flagship. As soon as you have superior force, search Magellan
Straits, being ready to return and cover Plate, or search north as
far as Valparaiso. Break up German trade and destroy German
cruisers. (*No 4*)

Two points emerge from these instructions. First, their confused
phrasing; could Cradock be sure he understood the Admiralty's
intentions? Second, he was told that the old cruisers *Good Hope*
and *Monmouth* plus the obsolescent battleship *Canopus* were an
adequate force to deal with von Spee's two modern armoured
cruisers. He could not know that an Admiralty memorandum of 7
September had recommended reinforcing him with *three* armoured
cruisers *and* a light cruiser from the Mediterranean. The activities
of the *Emden* and *Königsberg* prevented Battenberg and Vice-
Admiral Sir Doveton Sturdee, Chief of the War Staff, from accepting this: they proposed to send battlecruisers from the Grand Fleet;
but Churchill would not overrule Jellicoe's protests against any
reduction in his strength. So it was decided to send only the
armoured cruiser *Defence*: with four 9·2-inch and ten 7·5-inch
guns, she was a more powerful vessel than the *Canopus* or any other
ship under Cradock's command.

Any doubts Cradock may have had over these instructions were,
however, dissipated by von Spee's deceptive withdrawal from Apia
(see p 57) two days later. On 16 September the Admiralty signalled:

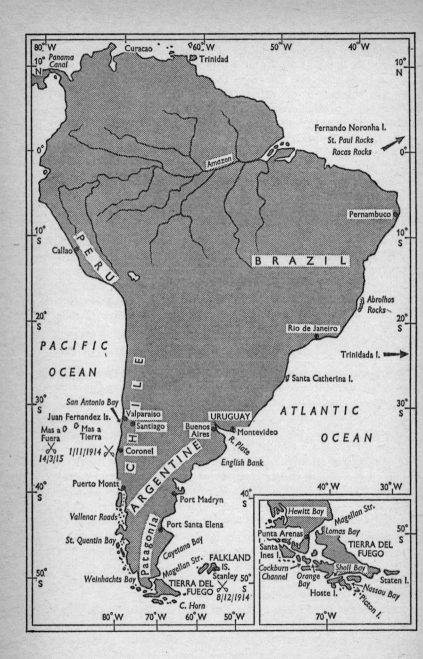

Scharnhorst and *Gneisenau* appeared off Samoa on 14th and left steering NW. German trade on west coast of America is to be attacked at once. Cruisers need not be concentrated. Two cruisers and an armed liner appear sufficient for Magellan Straits and west coast. Report what you propose about *Canopus*. (*No 5*)

Two days later Cradock replied from Montevideo:

Am proceeding with *Good Hope, Glasgow, Monmouth* and *Otranto* to sweep south and search Magellan Straits. *Glasgow* and *Monmouth* will continue to west coast to destroy trade. *Canopus* will be ordered to Rio de la Plata to guard trade and colliers. (*No 6*)

The instructions in *No 5* were of no great consequence to Cradock's future; but the Admiralty's simultaneous decision to order the *Defence* to remain at Malta was fatal, more especially since Cradock was not informed.

On 25 September Cradock had the good fortune to meet the homeward-bound British liner *Ortega*, from whom he heard that, whilst passing through the Magellan Straits a week before, she had been chased by a German light cruiser, escaping capture by entering neutral waters. Cradock at once set course for Punta Arenas where, on the 28th, the British Consul told him that the *Dresden* had been using Orange Bay. In the hope that she might still be there, he took his squadron round Cape Horn. But the 'battle of Orange Bay was rather a farce', wrote one of the *Glasgow's* officers, 'as the enemy didn't turn up'. With his ships in need of coal, Cradock ordered the *Otranto* back to Punta Arenas and took his cruisers to the Falklands. The *Monmouth* and *Glasgow* sailed again on 3 October to join with the *Otranto* in operating against German trade on the west coast of South America, whilst the *Good Hope* remained at the Falklands against the possibility of the *Dresden* returning to the east coast.

Two days later, however, German W/T messages, intercepted by the *Otranto* at Punta Arenas, led Cradock to leave the Falklands at high speed, after ordering the *Monmouth* and *Glasgow* to rejoin him for another descent on Orange Bay. But: 'Second battle of Orange Bay also a frost. Weather atrocious and it would have been quite impossible to fight our guns.' Nonetheless, a landing party from the *Good Hope* found evidence that the *Dresden* had been there from 9 to 11 September. So, whilst the *Monmouth* and *Glasgow* resumed their course to the west, the *Good Hope* returned to the

Falklands where Cradock received fresh news from the Admiralty on 7 October. The W/T station at Suva had intercepted a signal from the *Scharnhorst* on the 4th, to the effect that she was on the way from the Marquesas to Easter Island, from which

> it appears that *Scharnhorst* and *Gneisenau* are working across to South America. You must be prepared to meet them in company, possibly with a 'Dresden' scouting for them. *Canopus* should accompany *Glasgow*, *Monmouth* and *Otranto*, to search and protect trade in combination. If you propose *Good Hope* to go, leave *Monmouth* on east coast. (*No 7*)

Cradock replied:

> Indications show possibility of *Dresden*, *Leipzig*, *Nürnberg* joining *Gneisenau* and *Scharnhorst*. Have ordered *Canopus* to Falklands where I intend to concentrate and avoid division of forces. Have ordered *Glasgow*, *Monmouth* and *Otranto* not to go north of Valparaiso until German cruisers located. *Karlsruhe* apparently operating in South American waters: suggest *Essex* be detached to relieve *Cornwall*; *Cornwall* then proceeding south. When does *Defence* join my command? Do regulations of Panama Canal Company permit passage of belligerent ships? (*No 8*)

The Admiralty dealt with this signal at the same time as another sent by Cradock on the 11th:

> Without alarming, respectfully suggest that in event of enemy's heavy cruisers and others concentrating on west coast of South America, it is necessary to have a British force on each coast strong enough to bring them to action. Otherwise, should concentrated British force sent from south-east coast be evaded in Pacific, and get behind the enemy, latter could destroy Falklands, English Bank and Abrolhos coaling bases in turn, and with British ships unable to follow up owing to want of coal, enemy might reach West Indies. (*No 9*)

It is undeniable that *Nos 8* and *9* were both lacking in clarity. Did the first mean that Cradock was concentrating his whole force at the Falklands; or was he intending that the *Monmouth*, *Glasgow* and *Otranto* should operate on the west coast whilst the *Good Hope*, *Canopus*, *Cornwall*, and perhaps the *Defence*, constituted another force on the east coast? If the latter, the three first-named ships were no match for the Germans. On the other hand, in *No 9* he referred to a concentrated British force being evaded in the Pacific. Churchill minuted his copy:

> It would be best for the British ships to keep within supporting distance of one another, whether in the Straits or near the Falklands, and to postpone the cruise along the west coast until the present uncertainty about *Scharnhorst–Gneisenau* is cleared up. They and not the trade are our quarry for the moment.

Battenberg was satisfied that this was Cradock's intention; he annotated the First Lord's comment with the single word, 'Settled'.

However, after Churchill and the First Sea Lord had discussed the situation two days later, the former minuted:

> I understand that the dispositions you proposed for South Pacific and South Atlantic were as follows: (*a*) Cradock to concentrate at the Falklands *Canopus*, *Monmouth*, *Good Hope* and *Otranto*, (*b*) send *Glasgow* to look for *Leipzig* and attack and protect trade on west coast of South America as far north as Valparaiso, (*c*) *Defence* to join *Carnarvon* in forming a new squadron on the trade route from Rio. These arrangements have my full approval. I presume Cradock is aware of the possibility of *Scharnhorst* and *Gneisenau* arriving in his neighbourhood on or after the 17th; and that if not strong enough to attack, he will do his utmost to shadow them, pending the arrival of reinforcements.

But the reply that was sent to Cradock in answer to *Nos 8* and *9* said no more than this:

> Your concentration of *Good Hope*, *Canopus*, *Monmouth*, *Glasgow* and *Otranto* for combined operations concurred in. Stoddart in *Carnarvon* has been ordered to Montevideo. *Defence* ordered to join *Carnarvon*. He will also have *Cornwall*, *Bristol*, *Macedonia* and *Orama* under his orders. *Essex* remains in West Indies. (*No 10*)

whilst to Stoddart the Admiralty signalled:

> Proceed from Sierra Leone down trade route to Montevideo, calling at Pernambuco. *Defence* is following you from Gibraltar. *Cornwall*, *Bristol*, *Macedonia* and *Orama* will be under your orders. Keep sufficient force ready to concentrate in case German squadron escapes past Cradock who is in vicinity of Falkland Islands. (*No 11*)

In *No 10* the Admiralty referred to 'combined operations', but made no reference to Cradock concentrating his force in the Falklands. Unlike Churchill, the Naval War Staff assumed that this was implicit in Cradock's *No 8*, when he had, in fact, sent the *Monmouth*, *Glasgow* and *Otranto* round to the west coast, while the *Good Hope* waited for the *Canopus* to reach Port Stanley, capital of the Falklands. But when this pre-dreadnought arrived on 18 October, he was dismayed to hear from Captain H. S. Grant that she needed five days to repair machinery defects and clean boilers; and that, even then, her speed would be limited to 12 knots. He signalled the Admiralty:

> *Karlsruhe* not reported since 22nd September. Consider it possible she has been driven west of Cape Horn and is to join von Spee's force. I fear that speed of my squadron cannot exceed 12 knots owing to *Canopus*, but trust circumstances will enable me to force an action. (*No 12*)

The *Karlsruhe* was still operating, without much effect, off Pernambuco, but the Admiralty did not relieve one of Cradock's anxieties by telling him this, any more than they answered his question about belligerent warships passing through the newly opened Panama Canal, for which they had some excuse. The Foreign Office was having some difficulty in getting Washington to give a clear decision, though it seemed that they would agree to a maximum of three at any one time – enough for the *Scharnhorst* and *Gneisenau* to descend on the West Indies.

To Churchill, Cradock's *No 12* was confirmation that he understood that his force should be concentrated on the Falklands. If one believed that the *Canopus* gave the *Good Hope* and *Monmouth* the strength to deal with von Spee's two crack ships, all seemed well. But in a letter to the Governor of the Falklands, Cradock said:

> I shall not fail to let them know at home what I have seen and think of your gallant precautions for upholding our honour. I will give all warning I can if the German squadron eludes us; and only in case of my 'disappearance' will you send the letter to Meux. I mean to say, if my squadron disappears – and me too. I have no intention, after forty years at sea, of being an unheard victim.

The letter to Admiral Sir Hedworth Meux has disappeared, but one can surmise its contents: Troubridge had suffered for his decision not to engage the powerful *Goeben*; Cradock was not going to hazard his reputation by having to appear before a court martial on a charge that savoured of cowardice. As the Governor's ADC wrote:

> He knew what he was up against and asked for a fast cruiser with big guns to be added to his squadron, for he had nothing very powerful and nothing very fast, but the Admiralty said he'd have to go without. So old Cradock said, 'All right; we'll do without', and he slipped off early one morning, and left the *Canopus* to look after the colliers and transports, and picked up the *Glasgow* and the *Monmouth* and set out to look for these crack Germans.

On 22 October Cradock signalled:

> *Good Hope* left Port Stanley via Cape Horn. *Canopus* following on 23rd via Magellan Straits with three colliers for west coast of South America. (*No 13*)

This told the Admiralty that he was taking his whole force into the Pacific, but because they had good grounds for believing that both the *Good Hope* and *Canopus* were to join up with the *Glasgow*'s force, and because Stoddart's squadron was concentrating north of Montevideo where it could be used against von Spee should he enter the Atlantic, they saw no reason to intervene.

In fact, the *Good Hope* reached Vallenar Roads on 27 October, when the *Canopus* had progressed no further than Punta Arenas; and, whilst coaling, Cradock signalled:

> With reference to orders to search for enemy and our great desire for early success, consider it impracticable on account of *Canopus*' slow speed, to find and destroy enemy squadron. Consequently have ordered *Defence* to join me after calling at Montevideo for orders. *Canopus* will be employed convoying colliers. From experience of 6 August respectfully submit not to oppose depredations of *Karlsruhe*. May they continue until he meets vessel of superior speed. (*No 14*)

Although Churchill minuted: 'This telegram is very obscure and I do not understand what Cradock intends or wishes', it should have been clear to the Naval Staff that he did not consider it possible to locate and destroy von Spee if his squadron was tied to the *Canopus*: he had therefore ordered the *Defence* to join him. He reasonably assumed that this powerful armoured cruiser was now off the east coast of South America. (See *No 4* on p 63, also p 65.)

Cradock's last two sentences did not, however, help anyone to understand him. By thus recalling the galling way in which the *Karlsruhe* had eluded him in the first days of the war, he meant to imply that it was useless to employ the slower *Defence* to hunt for her. But the Naval Staff was too busy to interpret this oblique reference; they assumed there had been a cipher error. Their consequent appreciation was summed up in a minute to the First Sea Lord on 29 October:

> The situation on west coast seems safe. If *Gneisenau* and *Scharnhorst* have gone north they will meet *Idzumo*, *Newcastle* and *Hizen* [a Japanese battleship which was on her way to the west coast of North America], and will be forced south on *Glasgow* and *Monmouth* who have good speed and can draw them on to *Good Hope* and *Canopus*, who should keep within supporting distance.

And Cradock was told:

> *Defence* is to remain on east coast under orders of Stoddart. This will leave sufficient force on each side. Japanese battleship *Hizen* expected shortly on North American coast, to join *Idzumo* and *Newcastle* and move south towards Galapagos. (*No 15*)

But this message, especially its vital first sentence, did not reach the *Good Hope* until after noon on 1 November, which was too late to affect the outcome. So, too, was this further signal, sent as the result of a telegram from the British Consul at Valparaiso reporting von Spee's appearance off the Chilean coast that morning:

> *Defence* has been ordered to join your flag with all dispatch. *Glasgow* should keep in touch with enemy. You should keep in touch with *Glasgow*, concentrating rest of your squadron including *Canopus*. It is important you should effect your junction with *Defence* at earliest possible moment subject to keeping touch with enemy. (*No 16*)

It was too late, because, in Churchill's words, 'we were already talking to the void'.

5

Von Spee's Triumph

The Battle of Coronel

> Poor old Kit Cradock has gone at Coronel. His death and
> the loss of the ships and the gallant lives in them can be
> laid to the door of the incompetency of the Admiralty.
> They have broken over and over again the first principles
> of strategy.
>
> *Vice-Admiral Sir David Beatty*

A heaving unsettled sea, and over the western horizon an angry
yellow sun is setting below a forbidding bank of wind-charged
clouds. In the centre lies an immense solitary cruiser with a flag
at her masthead blowing out broad and clear in the fast rising
breeze. From half the points of the compass the swift ships of a
cruiser squadron draw in to join their flagship, like wild ducks at
evening flighting home, hurrying back at the behest of their mother-
ship to gather round her for the night.' The quotation comes from
Cradock's *Whispers from the Fleet*, but it might well have been
included in his dispatch reporting the events of 1 November 1914
– if he had survived that Sunday evening's battle off Coronel.

The 'immense solitary cruiser' was HMS *Good Hope*. Completed
in 1902 with a speed of 23 knots, she was armed with two 9·2-inch
and sixteen 6-inch guns, though half of the latter were mounted in
broadside batteries so low down that they could not be fought in
a seaway. And Captain P. Francklin had commissioned her on mobilization with 90 per cent reservists who had steamed her out of
Portsmouth as soon as 2 August, for Halifax where Cradock transferred his flag to her; and in the three months that had since
passed, this scratch crew had carried out only one full-calibre shoot.
The 'ships ... all drawing in to join their flagship' numbered four.
The *Monmouth* shared the *Good Hope*'s deficiencies. Her effective
broadside in a seaway was only six 6-inch guns; and she was near
to being condemned as unfit for further service when she was
hurriedly re-commissioned under Captain Frank Brandt's command

and sent to patrol Britain's trade routes, with no opportunity to weld her company into fighting trim. The only 'swift' ship was the *Glasgow*, of 25 knots, completed as recently as 1911, since when she had been under Captain John Luce's command, so that she was an efficient unit; but only a light cruiser, without armour, with two 6-inch and ten 4-inch guns. The *Otranto*, Captain Edwards, was a 12,000-ton liner, armed with eight 4·7-inch guns, intended for protecting British shipping against attacks by similar vessels, not for fighting enemy warships. Last but not least, the *Canopus*: her predreadnought vintage was of small importance in waters where there was no other battleship with 12-inch guns to match the four she mounted on her armoured hull. But, like the *Good Hope* and *Monmouth*, she, too, had been commissioned on mobilization with a crew of reservists, with no opportunity for carrying out practice firings before she was ordered to the Falklands. She was, nonetheless, a vessel with which von Spee was unlikely to risk an engagement, so that she gave Cradock's force a certain superiority over his opponent's two armoured cruisers and three light cruisers.

Of these the *Gneisenau*, Captain Maerker, and *Scharnhorst*, Captain Schultz, were sister-ships completed five years later than the *Good Hope*, each mounting eight 8·2-inch, all of which could be fought in a seaway by highly trained crews who had won the Kaiser's prize for gunnery efficiency, and 6 5·9-inch weapons. Except for their maximum speed which was now less than 22 knots, both these armoured cruisers were immeasurably superior to the *Good Hope* and *Monmouth*. The *Dresden*, *Leipzig* and *Nürnberg*, the last commanded by Captain Karl von Schönberg, had likewise been commissioned with regular crews before the war clouds gathered; in a duel with the *Glasgow* their one handicap would be an armament of only 4·1-inch guns whose shells weighed less than half those fired by the British vessels' two 6-inch.*

But the *Canopus* was not in company with the British cruisers on 1 November because, as Grant had told Cradock at the Falklands on 22 October, faulty condensers had cut her designed speed of 17 knots to as slow as 12. Moreover, Cradock had no confirmation that von Spee's force was concentrated: he might find one or more of the enemy ships, for whom his three cruisers were a match, and sink them before they could be reinforced. Moreover, if he was to locate the enemy at all in so vast an area, with so many uninhabited bays and islands, he needed both speed and ships, in which respect

* For fuller details of these British and German warships see Appendix C on pp 121–2.

the *Otranto*'s 18 knots were more useful than the *Canopus*'s 12. He did not, however, make this clear in his signal to the Admiralty on 27 October (*No 14* on p 69). By the 29th Cradock had brought his squadron as far north as Vallenar Roads, on no firmer intelligence of the *Scharnhorst* and *Gneisenau* than the Admiralty's signal that they were on the way east between the Marquesas and Easter Island (*No 7* on p 66). For all he knew von Spee intended to take these ships through the Panama Canal, rather than attempt the passage round the Horn, in which case he should meet nothing stronger than the *Dresden*, *Leipzig* and *Nürnberg*. So when the *Glasgow* was ordered into Coronel to send and receive signals, and Luce reported intercepting cipher messages from a German W/T transmitter no more than 150 miles away, Cradock did not hesitate to take the *Good Hope* and *Monmouth* northwards early on the 30th, leaving orders for the *Canopus* to follow.

The battleship reached Vallenar Roads an hour after Cradock's departure, to coal and repair an engine defect, when Grant discovered that his engineer commander was a sick man who had magnified the difficulties of maintaining his ageing machinery and of firing boilers with a scratch crew. The ship could, after all, still do as much as $16\frac{1}{2}$ knots. Grant did not, however, break W/T silence to tell Cradock this, because he did not believe the Admiral would delay his northward progress for the battleship to catch up. Whether Cradock would have kept the *Canopus* with him, if he had not been so misled by the failure of the health of a single man, can only be conjectured.

On the 31st, the *Good Hope* and *Monmouth* were joined by the *Otranto* which had been into Puerto Montt for intelligence; and the *Glasgow* reported having intercepted Telefunken transmissions from the *Leipzig* to a supply ship. Cradock responded by ordering Luce to leave Coronel at once for a rendezvous with the *Good Hope* next day, which dawned fine and clear, with a rising south-easterly wind. Luce brought no fresh news when they met at noon, apart from the Admiralty's signal *No 15* (p 70); but at 1350 further W/T transmissions from the *Leipzig* confirmed Cradock's belief that he would soon meet a single German warship. Ordering his squadron to form a line of search NE by E, 15 miles apart, in the order *Good Hope*, *Monmouth*, *Otranto* and *Glasgow* (nearest the coast), he headed NW by N at a speed of 15 knots. The line was not, however, fully extended by 1620 when Luce sighted smoke on his starboard bow and altered course towards it.

Since von Spee had decided, early in September, to take the Cape

Horn route to the Atlantic, German agents had confirmed the wisdom of his choice. Whilst there were indications of a strong Anglo-Japanese force concentrating off the west coast of North America, he had little to fear off the Chilean seaboard, nor to the immediate east of Cape Horn, if he kept his force together. And 24 hours after leaving Mas a Fuera, he received the encouraging news that Cradock's cruisers were operating independently in the protection of trade, unaware that a German squadron was in the area. He was, therefore, moving down the Chilean coast to the south of Valparaiso, when at 0250 on 1 November he learned from a supply ship, which he had sent into Coronel, that the *Glasgow* had anchored in the Roads at 1900 on the previous day. Since International Law would · require her to leave within 24 hours, the German Admiral ordered the *Scharnhorst* and his light cruisers to guard the northern entrance to this port, and the *Gneisenau* to watch the southern. But in response to Cradock's order, the *Glasgow* slipped away before they could reach these positions: they were still 40 miles to the north of Arauco Bay, with the *Dresden* 12 miles astern, and the *Nürnberg* even more (delayed searching neutral vessels) when, at 1620, the *Leipzig* sighted smoke and hauled out to investigate.

Thus, when the two squadrons first made contact, both Admirals supposed that they were about to overwhelm a single enemy light cruiser. Indeed, by 1640, both the *Otranto* and *Monmouth* had turned to Luce's support. But the *Glasgow*'s Captain had already identified the enemy: swinging his plunging ship round towards the *Good Hope*, and ringing down for full speed, he spanned the 50 miles that separated him from the flagship with a report that the *Scharnhorst* and *Gneisenau* were in company with the *Leipzig*.

Cradock might have escaped to the south: he had plenty of sea room; von Spee did not know that the British armoured cruisers were so near. Moreover, the Germans had steam for only 14 knots; and even when the *Scharnhorst* and *Gneisenau* had worked up to full speed, the British would have the advantage of a couple of knots over their opponents − except for the *Otranto*, and she had every chance with sunset so near. Cradock would also have been acting in accord with Admiralty instructions had he fallen back on the *Canopus*, which was bringing two colliers northwards, some 300 miles to the south. But once he lost touch with von Spee, for whom the Allies had been searching for so long, who could tell when they would find him again? Moreover, it was not essential to sink von Spee's ships; damage would compel them to seek intern-

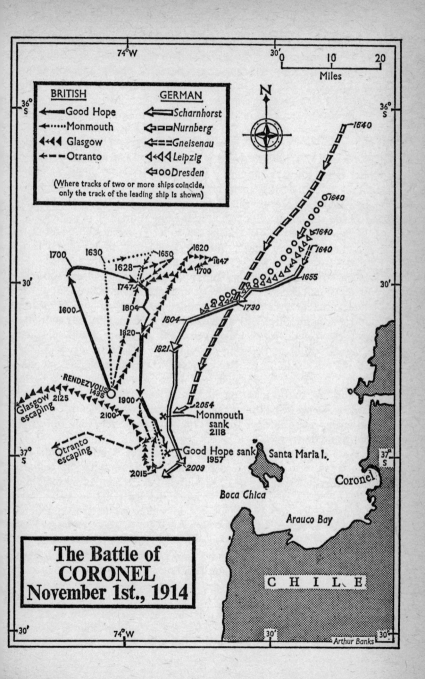

The Battle of
CORONEL
November 1st., 1914

ment in a neutral port. And Cradock's name would not be tarnished by a court-martial charge such as that to which Troubridge had been subjected for conduct that ran counter to the British tradition, epitomized in Nelson's words, that no captain can go far wrong who lays his ship alongside the enemy.

At 1700 Cradock ordered his ships to concentrate on the *Glasgow*: he would force an action in the short period of daylight that remained. Forty-five minutes later the *Good Hope*, *Monmouth*, *Glasgow* and *Otranto* formed a single line ahead on the SE course that would bring them quickly within 6-inch gun range of von Spee, although this headed them into a sea that made it impossible to fight the *Good Hope*'s and *Monmouth*'s main deck guns. Cradock's decision to include the *Otranto* in the line is difficult to understand. 'Perhaps he did not like leaving her to look after herself,' wrote the *Glasgow*'s gunnery officer; but she should have been ordered clear to the west. As it was, Cradock tempered his desire to close the enemy with concern for her safety; at 1850 he signalled: 'I cannot go down and engage the enemy at present leaving *Otranto*.'

Meantime, the *Leipzig* had identified the *Glasgow* and *Monmouth* at 1647, in another eight minutes recognized the *Otranto*, and later still the *Good Hope*, when von Spee no more hesitated than Cradock had done. Ordering the *Nürnberg* and *Dresden* to join him, he steamed at full speed in pursuit. 'The wind was S, force six, with a correspondingly high sea,' he wrote, 'so that I had to be careful not to be manœuvred into a lee position. Moreover, the course chosen helped to cut off the enemy from the neutral coast' — an enemy force inferior to his own, such as he had long hoped to meet and destroy.

At 1804 the British squadron turned four points towards the enemy, only to be thwarted by von Spee conforming: he realized the danger of a fight when his gunlayers were blinded by the glare of the setting sun. At 1818 Cradock radioed the *Canopus*: 'I am now going to attack the enemy,' to which the battleship replied with her position, when the distance between the two forces was still two miles outside the range of their heavy guns. Von Spee, who had been joined by the *Dresden* (the *Nürnberg* was still hull down to the north), was waiting until the sun dipped below the horizon. Not until 1900, when the British ships were silhouetted against the afterglow and the German vessels smudged shapes in the gathering darkness, did von Spee signal his force to open fire at 12,300 yards. 'And with that order [to quote a German source] disaster broke over Cradock's squadron.' The British were within range of

12 of the enemy's 8·2-inch guns to which only the *Good Hope*'s two 9·2-inch could reply. 'Immediately after the *Scharnhorst*, the *Dresden* opened fire on the *Otranto*. The German light cruiser's first salvoes were successful. The English auxiliary turned off and made for the open sea.' Edwards had already signalled Cradock suggesting he should keep out of range, but the only reply he received was never finished: 'There is danger; proceed at your utmost speed ...' Perhaps the Admiral intended him to escape, but because he had not been detached earlier, Edwards supposed he was to stay under the cruisers' protective wing. He did no more than edge the *Otranto* out of the line, just out of range to starboard.

The *Leipzig*'s attempt to engage the *Glasgow* was ineffective for nearly ten minutes; the range was too great. But the *Scharnhorst*'s third salvo put the *Good Hope*'s forward 9·2-inch out of action, whilst the *Gneisenau* destroyed the *Monmouth*'s foremost turret and set her ablaze. The British ships had already opened fire, the *Good Hope* at the *Scharnhorst*, the *Monmouth* at the *Gneisenau*, the *Glasgow* at the *Leipzig*; but 'the impossibility of observing the fall of shot and the indistinctness of the target reduced the chance of hitting to a minimum', and the *Monmouth*'s fire was largely wasted because the *Gneisenau* was beyond the range of her 6-inch guns. Within ten minutes of the Germans' first salvo the result was not in doubt; while Cradock continued to close the range until it was down to 5,500 yards,

the *Good Hope* received serious hits in the fore part of the ship, on the upper bridge, and on the foretop [wrote a German officer]. She was also hit repeatedly amidships, most of these causing fires, whose flames could be seen through the portholes. The after battery was hit several times. Two shells struck the after turret. The *Monmouth* was hit on her fore 6-inch turret, high explosive shell blowing off the roof. A terrific explosion of charges then blew the whole turret off the forecastle. Many shells struck the ship amidships. A column of fire as high as the mast shot up on the starboard side. Between thirty and forty hits were counted. At times three or four fires were burning simultaneously.

An officer in the *Glasgow* noted that

by 1945, when it was quite dark, *Good Hope* and *Monmouth* were obviously in distress. *Monmouth* yawed off to starboard burning furiously and heeling slightly. *Good Hope* was firing only a few of her guns, with the fires onboard increasing their brilliance. At 1950 there was a terrible explosion between her mainmast and her after funnel, the flames reaching a height of over 200 feet, after which she lay between the lines, a black hull lighted only by a dull glow.

No one saw the *Good Hope* go down with all hands around 2000, but Luce could guess her fate. His ship bore a charmed life, in part because the *Dresden* and *Leipzig* had difficulty in fighting their guns in such bad weather: one shell had made a hole on the *Glasgow*'s port waterline aft, which had not impaired her speed. However, now that the German ships were free to concentrate on his ship and the *Monmouth*, Luce realized that to continue the action would be tempting fate: his guns could do nothing against such powerful adversaries. He turned to succour the stricken *Monmouth*: 'Are you all right?' he signalled at 2015. Brandt replied: 'I want to get stern to sea. I am making water badly forward.' 'Can you steer NW?' Luce asked. 'The enemy are following us astern.'

There was no answer. The *Monmouth* could neither fight nor fly. She was badly down by the bows, listing to port with the glow of her ignited interior brightening the portholes. It was essential that there should be a survivor of the action to turn *Canopus* which, if surprised alone, must have shared the fate of the other ships. *Glasgow* increased to full speed and soon left the enemy astern. It was awful having to leave the *Monmouth* but I don't see what else the Skipper could have done [wrote one of the *Glasgow*'s officers].

Luce had also to remember the *Otranto*. Edwards had decided on flight half an hour before: when the *Good Hope* was sorely stricken, he had headed west at maximum speed. At 2125 the *Glasgow* saw 'a searchlight flicker below the horizon. Seventy-five flashes of firing against *Monmouth* were counted, then silence.'

By 2000 von Spee had lost contact with the British force. Manœuvring the *Scharnhorst* and *Gneisenau* to the SW to gain the advantage of the moonlight, he radioed his light cruisers: 'Both British cruisers severely damaged. One light cruiser fairly intact. Chase and attack with torpedoes.' The *Leipzig* steamed towards a dull glare to the NW which Haun supposed to be the *Good Hope* burning, but on reaching this position there was nothing to be seen from the *Leipzig*'s bridge. Not until later did he learn that some of his crew, who were nearer the water, had spotted floating debris from a sunken ship — when it was too late for him to search for survivors. For the same reason it was several days before von Spee knew of the British flagship's fate. Haun had other things to worry him. 'Am between three enemy cruisers; am steering SW', he radioed soon after 2100. But if one of these was the *Monmouth* or the *Glasgow*, the others were the *Nürnberg* and *Dresden*.

The latter had steered SW on receipt of von Spee's order to carry out a torpedo attack. At 2030 Lüdecke sighted the *Glasgow*, but lost contact before he could engage. He then encountered the *Leipzig*, recognizing Haun's ship just in time to avoid putting a torpedo into her. The *Nürnberg* was 25 miles from the *Scharnhorst* at 1700. Closing at high speed, von Schönberg had von Spee's flagship in sight by 1800, but was still too far away to take part in the fight. Receiving his Admiral's order to attack with torpedoes at 2054, he turned his ship towards the bearing on which he had last seen gunfire. But he failed to catch the *Glasgow*: instead, at 2120, he found another ship which, in the words of the German historian,

was recognized to be the *Monmouth*. Her foremost 6-inch turret was missing, but her engines were running and her steering gear was undamaged. As she did not haul down her flag, the *Nürnberg* opened fire at between 1,000 and 600 yards, and fired a torpedo which missed. As this was not replied to, the *Nürnberg* ceased fire and switched off her searchlights; but the *Monmouth* turned towards, either to ram or to bring her starboard guns to bear, so von Schönberg opened fire again, tearing open the unprotected parts of the *Monmouth*'s hull with his shells. She heeled further and further, and at 2128 capsized and went down with her flag still flying. There was no chance of rescue work because columns of smoke were reported from two directions. Moreover, the *Nürnberg*'s boats could not be launched in the heavy sea.

By 2215 von Spee decided that the *Glasgow*, *Otranto* and *Good Hope* had eluded him. With the first two he was not seriously concerned, and the *Good Hope* must have been so heavily damaged that she would make for Valparaiso to effect repairs, where he could persuade the Chilean authorities to intern her. But 'against the *Canopus* we can hardly do anything', and from intercepted W/T signals, von Spee believed her to be nearing the scene. So he altered to NNE until the morning, when he signalled his ships: 'By the Grace of God a fine victory. My thanks and good wishes to the crews.' His satisfaction was justified: he had achieved command of the sea in the south-east Pacific at very small cost, not least because of the poor quality of the British ammunition. The two shells that hit the *Scharnhorst* had failed to explode; the four which struck the *Gneisenau* had done only slight damage that could be easily repaired, and slightly wounded three men. Against this, however, his ships had expended nearly half their ammunition, with no prospect of replenishing it.

The *Canopus* was not so near as von Spee feared. Since receiving Cradock's signal that he was about to engage, Grant had left his colliers and pressed his ship hard to reach the scene; but at 16½ knots he had not come much closer than 200 miles from the action, before the *Glasgow*'s W/T warned him of Cradock's defeat. To go on and find the enemy in that sea meant that the *Canopus* would suffer the same fate as the cruisers without doing them significant damage, because in the prevailing weather the maximum range of the old battleship's guns was well inside that of the German armoured cruisers. She would be better employed covering the retreat of the *Glasgow* and *Otranto*, so she turned and steamed back to her colliers, ordering them to return to Port Stanley round the Horn.

The *Glasgow* had suffered five hits from the *Leipzig*'s and *Dresden*'s shells, but none had done serious damage, and her casualties were negligible. To quote Luce's report:

> The spirit of my officers and men is unimpaired by this serious reverse, and their unanimous wish is that the ship may take part in further operations against the same enemy. I cannot close without expressing my deepest regret at the death of Sir Christopher Cradock and the captains, officers and ships' companies of the *Good Hope* and *Monmouth*, and bearing witness to the determined way in which those ships were fought to the end. Our Admiral's gallantry in immediately attacking a superior force, rather than risk the possibility of losing an opportunity by waiting for reinforcements, though it proved ill-fated, is in accordance with the highest traditions of His Majesty's Navy.

'Poor Kit Cradock,' commented Rear-Admiral Sir Robert Arbuthnot, when he heard the news of the disaster; 'he always hoped he would be killed in battle or break his neck in the hunting field.' Beatty wrote: 'Doubtless it was better to have fought and lost than not to have fought at all.' And this verdict was endorsed by Churchill's successor as First Lord when, in 1916, he unveiled a memorial to Cradock in York Minster.

Why did he attack, deliberately, a force which he could not have hoped either to destroy or put to flight? The German Admiral was far from any port where he could have refitted. If, therefore, he suffered damage, even though he inflicted greater damage than he received, his power might suddenly be destroyed. He would be a great peril as long as his squadron remained efficient, and if Admiral Cradock judged that he himself, and those under him, were well sacrificed if they destroyed the power of this hostile fleet, then there is no man but would say that such a judgement showed the highest courage in the interests of his country. We shall never know his thoughts when it became evident that, out-gunned and outranged, success was an impossibility. He and his gallant comrades lie far from the pleasant homes of England. Yet they have their reward; theirs is an immortal place in the great role of naval heroes.

There were, however, many who, like Beatty in the bitter words quoted at the head of this chapter, condemned the Admiralty for a defeat which, in the words of the German historian, 'dealt the most severe blow that British prestige had suffered for over a century. The myth of its invincibility had been ruthlessly destroyed.' And Churchill chose to answer this accusation in his *World Crisis* shortly after the war:

I cannot accept for the Admiralty any share in the responsibility. The first rule of war is to concentrate superior strength for decisive action and to avoid division of forces or engaging in detail. Cradock showed by his telegrams that he clearly appreciated this. The Admiralty explicitly approved his assertion of these elementary principles.

This could have only one interpretation; that the whole responsibility was Cradock's — and this account would not be complete if it omitted to examine so grave a charge.

From as early as 17 August the Admiralty received warnings that the German armoured cruisers were heading for South America. On 23 August they decreed that 'the destruction of *Scharnhorst* and *Gneisenau* is of the first importance'; but no priority was given to this object. Because von Spee might attack trade in Far Eastern waters, Jerram was ordered to deploy his ships there; and because the British Government encouraged Australia and New Zealand to launch immediate expeditions against Germany's defenceless island colonies, Patey's ships had to protect seaborne expeditions. No ships remained to be moved eastwards across the Pacific. Cradock was, however, moving down the Atlantic coast of South America, and on 6 September the Admiralty told him that the Magellan Straits might be von Spee's destination (*No 3* on p 62). They considered the adequacy of Cradock's squadron to meet this threat, and on 14 September sent him detailed instructions (*No 4* on p 63). In stressing the need to meet the enemy with superior strength, they reiterated an accepted principle of war. Realizing that Cradock did not have this strength, they considered reinforcing him with three armoured cruisers, but whittled these down to one. The *Good Hope*, *Monmouth* and *Defence* might have been adequate; but the *Scharnhorst* and *Gneisenau* could reach South America before the *Defence*; so the Admiralty told Cradock to keep the *Canopus* with him. But nothing in *No 4* indicated that the Admiralty realized that the battleship's slow speed made it impracticable for him to destroy the much faster German cruisers. Nor did they say that, until the *Defence* joined, Cradock was to do no more than search for the *Scharnhorst* and *Gneisenau*, using the *Canopus* as a deterrent against an attack.

The Admiralty had, however, no sooner sent these instructions than von Spee was located off Samoa, when they rejected all the evidence indicating his destination. The Japanese Fleet continued patrolling the western Pacific; the *Australia* was added to the first troop convoy's escort; and Cradock was told that he need no longer keep his cruisers concentrated nor, by implication, have the *Canopus* in support (*No 5* on p 65). Simultaneously, and without informing Cradock, the *Defence* was ordered to remain at Malta. For this the Admiralty had one excuse, von Spee's deceptive NW course on leaving Apia. But they had no justification for repeating it a week later when the German ships appeared 1,350 miles further to the east, off Tahiti, when no fresh action was taken against the possibility of von Spee meeting Cradock, who was now sending some of his ships into the Pacific in pursuit of the *Dresden*, and to stop German trade on the west coast of South America in accordance with *No 5*.

It was not too late to retrieve the situation, even when the Admiralty learned that the *Scharnhorst*, *Gneisenau* and *Nürnberg* were on their way to Easter Island, if decisive action had then been taken to reinforce Cradock. Instead, they instructed him to meet the German force with the *Canopus*, *Glasgow*, *Monmouth* (or *Good Hope*) and *Otranto* (*No 7* on p 66). If he had doubts about the Admiralty's suggestion that his two old armoured cruisers, supported by an even older battleship, were a superior force to the *Scharnhorst* and *Gneisenau,* what must have been his reaction to a suggestion that, now augmented by the *Nürnberg,* they could be countered by only one of his armoured cruisers, again supported by the *Canopus,* together with a light cruiser and an AMC? His reply (*No 8* on p 66), in which he said that von Spee's force was likely to comprise two armoured cruisers and three light cruisers, is remarkable for its restraint; but he confused matters by not making his intentions clear. He had ordered the *Canopus* to the Falkland Islands 'where I intend to concentrate and avoid division of forces', but three of his ships were, apparently, to operate in the Pacific: nor did his amplifying message help the Admiralty to understand him (*No 9* on p 66).

Nonetheless, on the 14th Churchill and Battenberg agreed that Cradock should concentrate at the Falklands, only the *Glasgow* going into the Pacific; and they recognized that, pending reinforcements, his squadron might have to limit its aim to locating and shadowing the enemy. But their reply to Cradock did not say this: he was told only that a force under Stoddart was being sent to the east coast and, 'your concentration of *Good Hope, Canopus, Monmouth, Glasgow* and *Otranto* for combined operations is concurred in', which could be interpreted as authorizing him to provide the Pacific force (*No 10* on p 67). Moreover, he was left with the impression that his aim was still that signalled to him on 14 September, 'to destroy the German cruisers' (*No 4* on p 63). He expressed this clearly when informing the Admiralty that the *Canopus*'s speed limited his squadron to 12 knots, 'but shall trust circumstances will enable me to force an action' (*No 12* on p 68). However, the Admiralty took this message to mean that Cradock was acting in accordance with their latest wishes and concentrating at the Falklands.

They were disillusioned a week later by the Admiral's *No 13* (p 69), but did not intervene for three reasons. Stoddart's force was assembling to the east of South America and could be moved to the Falklands: by the time the signal reached Whitehall Cradock was already in the Pacific: and they believed he was using the *Canopus* to support his cruisers for what they had decided on 14 October should be his task: 'if not strong enough to attack, he will do his utmost to shadow von Spee, pending the arrival of reinforcements'. That this was far from Cradock's interpretation might have been clear from his *No 14* (p 69) in which he referred to destroying the enemy's squadron, and reported that the *Canopus* was so useless for this that he intended she should escort his colliers, the *Defence* taking her place. He did not, however, specify that he intended to dispense with the *Canopus* before the *Defence* joined; and he irritated a busy Admiralty with an obscure reference to his encounter with the *Karlsruhe* on 6 August. These two points explain their reply to the effect that he already had a sufficient force to engage von Spee, his orders to the *Defence* being cancelled (No 15 on p 70), which Luce brought out to him on 1 November, when he was already seeking the *Leipzig*. And this must have confirmed in his mind that he was intended to fight the *Scharnhorst* and *Gneisenau* when he sighted them a couple of hours later, even though he had not been provided with the strength to ensure success.

The measure of the Admiralty's responsibility for Coronel is, then, this. Initially, whilst appreciating the importance of destroying the German armoured cruisers, they employed many of the Allied warships in Far East waters on less vital tasks. In mid-September they made a serious error of judgement in deciding that von Spee was going west instead of east, so that Cradock's squadron was not reinforced. They believed that the *Good Hope* and *Monmouth*, supported by the *Canopus*, were sufficient to deal with von Spee. And their instructions were so badly worded that Cradock supposed he was intended to seek an action even though his force might be inadequate to gain a victory.

Why did the Admiralty make these mistakes? One explanation was expressed by Wemyss: 'The Admiralty needs a large and efficient staff organization. At the commencement of the war this was lamentably inadequate.' In the Napoleonic era the Admiralty could do no more in the way of operating the Fleet than issue orders of a general nature, a task within the personal capacity of Members of the Board, helped by a Secretary and a handful of clerks. In the subsequent century telegraphic communication by landline, cable and wireless gave the Admiralty the power of immediate control over the world-wide dispositions of their ships, and to direct their day-to-day employment, whilst maritime operations were complicated by technical developments such as the introduction of steam and long-range guns, the invention of torpedoes and mines, and the birth of the submarine. These placed the conduct of a naval war beyond the capacity of a few individuals: the Admiralty Board needed trained staff officers to deal with the manifold details, to advise them wisely, and to implement their decisions with clear and comprehensive orders. But successive Boards refused to

recognize this. Although Beresford succeeded in establishing a Naval
Intelligence Department in 1887, this remained no more than an
embryo Naval Staff for another quarter of a century. To Fisher it
was only 'a very excellent organization for cutting out and arrang-
ing foreign newspaper cuttings': he, and Wilson, believed that war
plans should be prepared by the First Sea Lord alone and divulged
to no one.

Fortunately the Agadir crisis of 1911 revealed one dire consequence of this; the Admiralty's and the War Office's plans were so
fundamentally different that Lord Haldane, Secretary of State for
War, told the Prime Minister that he would not remain at the War
Office unless the Admiralty organized a Naval War Staff comparable
with the Army's General Staff. Asquith then appointed the dynamic
Churchill as First Lord to put the Admiralty's house in order. Because he categorically refused to create a Staff, Wilson was replaced
as First Sea Lord, first by Bridgeman, then, in March 1913, by
Battenberg. A Naval War Staff was established in 1912, and a staff
course was grafted on to the Naval War College to train officers for
it. But these changes could not, in the short space of three years,
turn the Admiralty into the efficient machine needed for the effective conduct of a twentieth-century war: such a task requires a
generation. To quote Richmond:

> The War Staff was deficient in all the characteristics needed for
> staff work. The whole of the work passes through the Chief of
> Staff. There is no decentralization, and his mind has to grapple
> with every problem that arises, even in its details. The result
> is that the First Sea Lord and Chief of Staff are so overworked
> that they cannot foresee and provide in advance.

This in large part explains the Admiralty's failings which led to
Coronel. It does not, however, absolve those who were at the
controls. All too often the Director of Operations, Rear-Admiral
Arthur Leveson, rejected his staff's arguments for an adequate force
to be sent to the west coast of South America or, when he accepted
them, failed to press them on his superiors. As Naval Secretary,
Commodore Henry Oliver's duty was limited to feeding the First
Lord with the Naval Staff's views: he is not to be blamed for the
disastrously wrong appreciation which he summed up for Churchill
on 29 October in the minute quoted on p 70. As adviser to the
Board on overseas operations, Admiral Sir Henry Jackson was
chiefly responsible for encouraging the Australian and New Zealand
attacks on New Guinea and Samoa, which required Patey's squadron

to protect these expeditions when it might have been deployed against von Spee's armoured cruisers. Sturdee had assumed control of the newly fledged Naval War Staff less than three months before it was plunged into conducting a world-wide war. He was by nature ill-fitted for his task: his analytical brain lacked the flexibility of mind and incisive ability for quick decisions. And though he had been Chief of Staff to Beresford, he had been brought up to reject the need to delegate. He could not direct the War Staff to prepare an appreciation; he must do it himself. He could not authorize them to draft a signal; he must write it in his own hand. As a result, he was monstrously overwhelmed with work so that urgent action was often delayed. The directing hand should have been Battenberg's, in Fisher's words, 'the very ablest admiral after Wilson that we possess'; and no naval officer doubted that he was the man who should be at the Admiralty's helm in war. But as First Sea Lord he had to deal with a dozen dangers at the same time, of which those in the far seas occupied second place in his mind to those in Home waters. And to be master of the details of ever-changing situations, many of great complexity, without the help of an effective Staff, was too much for any man. But Battenberg also laboured under two other handicaps; he had to expend much of his time and energy contending with a particularly forceful First Lord; and he was distracted by circumstances which led him to write to Churchill on 28 October: 'I have been driven to the painful conclusion that my German birth and parentage have the effect of impairing my usefulness in the Admiralty. I feel it my duty to resign.' But this shameful business does not relieve him of the major responsibility for the Admiralty's part in Coronel, for all that it goes a long way to explain it.

There remains Churchill's part. Until after Trafalgar, the First Lord was both a naval officer and in Parliament: Anson, Hawke, Howe, St Vincent, Barham were as well qualified to conduct the affairs of the Navy as they were to answer for it to the nation. But in the nineteenth century the First Lord became a politician; direct control of the Navy passed to the First Sea Lord. The circumstances in which Churchill was sent to the Admiralty were, however, enough for a man of his calibre to concern himself with naval operations. Much that he did in this sphere is not open to criticism; indeed, he often showed himself to be wiser than his Service colleagues. But his methods of doing business caused friction. He could not confine his zest for war to matters which were within the Admiralty's purview. He was not content with sending a naval

1   The German Surrender   *Painting by Sir John Lavery*

2 German battle-cruisers

3 British battle-cruiser *Inflexible*

4 German battle-cruiser *Goeben*

5 German light cruiser *Breslau*
6 British armoured cruiser *Warrior*
7 British light cruiser *Gloucester*

8 British pre-dreadnought *Irresistible* sinking

9 British monitor *Raglan*

10 German light cruiser *Emden*

11 End of the *Emden*

12 Australian light cruiser *Sydney*

13 Rear-Admiral Troubridge

14 Rear-Admiral Cradock

15 Captain von Müller

16 Vice-Admiral Sturdee *Drawing by Francis Dodds*

17 Howard Kelly as a rear-admiral

18 British armoured cruiser *Good Hope*

19 German armoured cruiser *Scharnhorst*

brigade to defend Antwerp in October: he must suggest that he assume personal command. The Cabinet rejected this, but only after he had been away from London for a week at a critical time for Coronel. Although the attention which he gave to von Spee's approach to South America was, therefore, spasmodic, it is clear that, by arrogating to himself a part of the First Sea Lord's task, he should have accepted a share of the responsibility for the disaster.

The action of the Admiralty on 3 November, two days after Coronel, supports these criticisms. Forced to find a new First Sea Lord, Churchill brought Fisher back: he might be 74, but much of his dynamic genius remained. On 30 October Churchill accompanied him to the War Room and 'went over the positions and tasks of every vessel. The critical point was clearly in South American waters. Speaking of Cradock's position, I said: "You don't suppose he would try to fight them without the *Canopus*?" He did not give any decided reply.' But as soon as von Spee was reported off the coast of Chile, Fisher realized the inadequacy of Cradock's force and the danger inherent in his intentions. Unhappily, it was already too late by the time *No 16* (p 70), in whose wording the new directing hand is clear, went out. In short, and in the words of a *Morning Post* leader, 'by attacking the memory of a heroic martyr to his duty and his orders, the First Lord cast the blame upon the principal victim of his own error of judgement. He would have been wiser to have left the reputation of the dead sailor alone.'

Two days after Coronel the *Scharnhorst*, *Gneisenau* and *Nürnberg* anchored in Valparaiso Roads, whilst the *Dresden* and *Leipzig* went to Mas a Fuera. But von Spee's heartwarming reception by the people of the Chilean capital was offset by news that Japanese reinforcements were heading for North America to bar his way to Panama, and by this signal from Berlin: 'You are advised to try and break through with all your ships and return home.' To break through a ring that was held by the whole might of the British Grand Fleet? But what other course was there? By the time the German squadron was reunited at Mas a Fuera, the Admiral had almost made up his mind that he would next attack the South Atlantic trade routes – almost, but not quite, because the strain of his exceptionally difficult command had impaired his capacity for incisive thought. Since the British would clearly react to the news of his recent victory by dispatching strong forces to hunt him down, the sooner his squadron rounded the Horn the better; but he hesitated to make this crucial move. In contrast to his voyage across the Pacific, when he spent very little time in harbour, von Spee remained at Mas a Fuera whilst he sent the *Dresden* and *Leipzig* to visit Valparaiso. Not until 15 November did he sail his force south, leaving the *Prinz Eitel Friedrich* behind to make W/T transmissions which might mislead the Allies into supposing his ships still to be in the Pacific.

On the 21st the five cruisers anchored in St Quentin Bay, to fill more than their bunkers from colliers that had slipped out of Chilean ports. When they sailed again five days later, their decks were piled with coal so that they could make the long voyage round the Horn and up to Port Santa Elena, where colliers out of Montevideo would meet them on 5 December. The *Dresden* brought from Valparaiso a letter in which Berlin amplified their above-quoted signal:

> Cruiser warfare in the Pacific offers few prospects of success. In the Atlantic it is possible only for ships operating in groups strong enough to meet the enemy squadrons now patrolling the trade routes. On the other hand it is becoming more and more difficult to coal groups of ships. It is therefore left to your discretion to break off cruiser warfare and make your way home. You may succeed if your plans are accompanied by good luck. You should notify your intentions in good time to obtain the cooperation of the High Seas Fleet in breaking through the enemy's patrols in the North Sea.

Von Spee's response was a signal telling an anxious *Admiralstab*: 'The Cruiser Squadron intends to break for home', to which he added the warning that his heavy ships had expended half their ammunition and his light cruisers rather more. At St Quentin von Spee also learned that the German naval agent in San Francisco had asked Berlin to help his return by sending a battlecruiser into the North Atlantic; but he does not appear to have received the discouraging answer that this was 'impossible'.   The same German agent seems also to have been the only man to urge the need for haste, signalling von Spee on 11 November: 'If the squadron decides to return home it appears advisable for it to leave immediately. In my opinion it is dangerously situated.' But the Admiral connected this with a report dated 7 November, that the *Defence*, *Cornwall*, *Carnarvon*, *Bristol*, *Glasgow* and *Canopus* were all at the Falkland Islands; whereas he had more recent news from Montevideo that Stoddart's force had left to deal with a Boer rising in South Africa.

This intelligence was anything but true. In the 48 hours after Coronel, the *Canopus* had a very anxious time.

We could only manage 15 knots and the *Scharnhorst* and *Gneisenau* can do 22, so we might easily have been caught. We expected to meet the enemy when we reached the Magellan Straits, but no, they were not there. Soon after this we heard from the *Glasgow*.

And on 6 November the two ships met in Lomas Bay, to learn that the *Otranto* was also safe, and to allow Luce to signal a brief report on Cradock's defeat to the Admiralty. A substantial account of this had, however, already reached London on the 4th, gleaned from von Spee's visit to Valparaiso; and on this the First Lord and First Sea Lord took drastic steps. Stoddart was told:

> *Carnarvon* and *Cornwall* should join *Defence* off Montevideo. *Canopus*, *Glasgow* and *Otranto* have been ordered there. *Kent* from Sierra Leone has also been ordered to join your flag. Enemy is likely to come on to Rio trade route. Reinforcements will meet you shortly from England.

Another signal went to the Governor of the Falkland Islands:

> German cruiser raid may take place. All colliers should be concealed in unfrequented harbours. Be ready to destroy supplies useful to enemy on ships being sighted.

A third signal was much more important. Churchill proposed sending a battlecruiser to reinforce Stoddart; 'but I found Lord Fisher in bolder mood. He would take two of these powerful ships.' The C-in-C Grand Fleet was instructed to

> order *Invincible* and *Inflexible* to fill up with coal at once and proceed to Plymouth with all dispatch. They are urgently needed for foreign service.

'Sir John Jellicoe rose to the occasion and parted with his two battlecruisers without a word,' when a personal message from the First Lord explained the service for which they were needed, although he had just lost the dreadnought *Audacious* in a field laid off Malin Head by the minelayer *Berlin*, in the course of a foray for which her victim's name is the aptest of adjectives. But he made a vigorous protest a week later when the Admiralty ordered him to send the *Princess Royal* into the Atlantic to guard against von Spee coming through the Panama Canal – albeit in vain. Churchill and Fisher insisted on taking the calculated risk of reducing the Grand Fleet's marginal superiority over the High Seas Fleet, because the new battlecruiser *Tiger* was now in commission, and three new battleships were nearly ready for sea. But the determined courage of these two giants was not matched by Devonport Dockyard: when the *Invincible* and *Inflexible* arrived in the Hamoaze, the Admiral Superintendent signalled that 13 November was the earliest date by which they could be ready to leave. Fortunately, Churchill again rose to the occasion: with Fisher's agreement he signed this order – and sealed von Spee's fate:

> Ships are to sail on Wednesday 11th. They are needed for war service and dockyard arrangements must be made to conform. You are held responsible for the speedy dispatch of these ships in a thoroughly efficient condition.

They sailed accordingly, with the *Invincible* flying the flag of Vice-Admiral Sir Doveton Sturdee.

On returning to the Admiralty ten days before, Fisher had declared a fierce allergy for this man who had been an ally of Beresford's. But Churchill was always loyal to a trusted colleague: Fisher had to be appeased, but not to the extent of making the Chief of the War Staff a scapegoat for Coronel: he could relieve Jerram at Singapore, with the importance of the China Station enhanced by adding Patey's and Pierse's areas to it. Sturdee declined, because his headquarters would be ashore; he was quite willing to serve under Fisher until a sea command became available. But when the news of Coronel reached Whitehall, and the First Sea Lord decided to send two battlecruisers to the South Atlantic, Sturdee chanced to mention that he had suggested such a move before the disaster, only to have it turned down – which provoked Fisher to declare that he would not tolerate that 'd—d fool' at the Admiralty for one day longer. Churchill's inspired solution to this impasse was conveyed to Sturdee in these words: 'The destruction of the German squadron concentrated on the west coast of South America is an object of high and immediate importance, and I propose to entrust this duty to you.'

Born in 1859, Sturdee had made his first mark as an exceptionally clever torpedo specialist. His skilful handling of a tricky international situation in Samoa, where there was a dispute between Germany and the United States in 1899, gained him early promotion to captain. A period as Assistant Director of Naval Intelligence preceded command of several cruisers in Home waters before he became Beresford's Chief of Staff, first in the Mediterranean, subsequently in the Channel Fleet. Promoted to flag rank in 1910, he was appointed to command a squadron of dreadnoughts, then to be senior cruiser admiral in the Home Fleet, by which time Jellicoe knew him as 'an officer who had made a special study of tactics'. When war came he had the reputation of being 'a sea officer of keen intelligence and great practical ability – a man who could handle and fight his squadron with the utmost skill and resolution'. Physically on the small side, with features marked by an impressive Roman nose, his personality was well described by an American correspondent: 'Along with the peculiar charm and alertness which we associate with sailors, he has the quality of the scholar, with a suspicion of merriness in his eye. He is so gentle-mannered.'

The *Invincible* and *Inflexible* left England under orders to 'proceed to South American waters. Your most important duty is to search for the *Scharnhorst* and *Gneisenau* and bring them to action. All other considerations are to be subordinated to this end.' Enough has been said of ships such as these in Chapter Two to show their superiority over von Spee's armoured cruisers. But Stoddart's force was also to come under Sturdee's orders, and he was authorized to withdraw the *Bristol* and the AMC *Macedonia* from their search for the elusive *Karlsruhe*. In two other respects, however, the Admiralty's orders reflected the inadequacies of the Naval Staff: there was no mention of the need for the battlecruisers to reach their destination with dispatch, nor that their movements should be kept secret.

Many other steps were taken to deal with the German squadron. Japanese forces were sent to Suva and the Carolines to cover Australia and New Zealand, so that the battlecruiser *Australia* could join the Allied ships off the west coast of North America. The *Defence* was ordered to reinforce the cruisers *Minotaur*, *Dartmouth* and *Weymouth* and the old battleship *Albion* at the Cape, in case the British expedition against German South-West Africa should draw von Spee's ships there. West African waters were to be guarded by five cruisers and the pre-dreadnought *Vengeance*. Her sister-ship, the *Glory*, plus the cruisers *Berwick*, *Lancaster* and *Condé* were to watch the Caribbean, as well as the *Princess Royal*. In short, and to quote Churchill: 'To compass the destruction of five warships, it was necessary to employ nearly thirty, and this took no account of the powerful Japanese squadrons, of French ships, or of AMCs.' In the event, however, none of these world-wide movements was of comparable importance to those off the east coast of South America. The concentration ordered off Montevideo did not prove wholly practicable. When the *Canopus* signalled that she must spend five days at the Falklands repairing her engines, the Admiralty ordered Grant to remain in Stanley Harbour. Moor ship so that your guns command entrance. Be prepared for bombardment from outside the harbour. Stimulate Governor to organize local forces and make determined defence. Arrange observation stations on shore to enable you to direct fire on ships outside. No objection to your grounding ship to obtain a good berth—

instructions with which Grant complied before von Spee ended his stay at Mas a Fuera. And the *Glasgow*, which went north to meet the *Defence* (now Stoddart's flagship), *Cornwall*, Captain W. M. Ellerton, *Carnarvon*, Captain H. L. Skipwith and *Orama* at English Bank on the 11th, had to be detached to Rio for docking. But the rest of Stoddart's ships joined the armoured cruiser *Kent*, Captain J. D. Allen, and the AMC *Edinburgh Castle* off the Abrolhos Rocks on the 17th.

This was the day the *Invincible* and *Inflexible* reached St Vincent, to sail again as soon as both ships had coaled. The Western Telegraph Company's cable operators passed news of this call at the Portuguese Cape Verde Islands to their opposite numbers in South America. Moreover, as he crossed the Atlantic, Sturdee stopped to examine merchant ships, any one of which might have reported his battlecruisers. It is not therefore surprising that, by 24 November, German agents in Montevideo believed that Sturdee had arrived at the Abrolhos Rocks. Fortunately, they failed to appreciate the immediate importance of this intelligence: they passed it to von Spee in a letter conveyed by one of the colliers ordered to Port Santa Elena, a rendezvous the German Admiral was not destined to keep. (This intelligence *may* have been telegraphed to von Spee via Punta Arenas, but if it was, he must have dismissed it as a British deception, believing that the Grand Fleet could not spare two such powerful ships to go so far afield.) Montevideo's news was, nonetheless, premature: the two battlecruisers did not meet Stoddart's squadron until 26 November, when they coaled and transferred stores, whilst Stoddart shifted his flag to the *Carnarvon* so that the *Defence* could leave for the Cape. However, Luce, on rejoining from Rio, urged Sturdee to go on to the Falklands with all possible speed, with the result that the whole force sailed after 48 hours at the Abrolhos Rocks instead of the 72 that had been planned, notwithstanding these fresh instructions from the Admiralty:

Scharnhorst's squadron was at Mas a Fuera on 15th; later evidence points to their presence in St Quentin on 21st. Proceed south with whole squadron. Use Falkland Islands as main base for colliers. After coaling proceed to Chilean coast, avoiding letting your large ships be seen in Magellan Straits. Search the Straits' inlets and channels.

Here was belated mention of the need for secrecy, but still nothing about proceeding with dispatch, when von Spee could be in the South Atlantic by the end of the month, because Whitehall did not believe this to be his intention. Moreover, the battlecruisers were confidently expected to reach the Falklands as soon as 3 December. The Naval Staff did not appreciate that, although Sturdee's force could make a good 16–18 knots, the Admiral preferred to husband his fuel, and to search for enemy shipping as he steamed south. And notwithstanding Luce's premonition, when Sturdee ordered battle practice firings, and the target-towing wire fouled one of the *Invincible*'s propellers, he stopped the whole squadron for 12 hours while divers cleared it, instead of sending all but his flagship on ahead, subsequently catching them up.

Sturdee did not, therefore, reach the Falklands until four days after the Admiralty's expectation. Fortunately, the German squadron had run into heavy weather after leaving St Quentin on 26 November, which delayed it rounding Cape Horn until the night of 1 December. Furthermore, the *Dresden* reported that she now had insufficient fuel to reach Port Santa Elena. To remedy this, von Spee captured the British barque *Drummuir* with 3,000 tons of coal, and took her to an anchorage off Picton Island, where his force stayed coaling until the 6th. Even so, this further delay would not have influenced events but for a fresh decision taken by von Spee whilst his ships lay in this desolate outpost of southern Patagonia. Since German agents had confirmed the absence of British warships from the Falklands, he would destroy the islands' W/T station and coal stocks. Fielitz, his Chief of Staff, and von Schönberg favoured this: Maerker, Lüdecke and Haun thought it a mistake. They doubted that Stoddart's ships had sailed for South Africa; they recommended steering well to the east of the Falklands and appearing without warning off the Plate. They were right: if von Spee was to take any action against the Allies before running for home, he should have lost no time in making a descent on the Plate trade, which would have paid him the richest of dividends. But to the German Admiral such attacks were the least important aspect of cruiser warfare; as he had raided enemy islands in the Pacific, so he would pursue the same strategy in the Atlantic. On the 7th he issued these orders:

When *Gneisenau* and *Nürnberg* are detached, they will proceed at 14 knots to a point to the east of Cape Pembroke from which Stanley Harbour* can be overlooked. If clear, *Nürnberg* will reconnoitre as far north as Berkeley Sound, while *Gneisenau* lowers boats off Port William to sweep entrance clear of mines. *Nürnberg* will then proceed into Port Stanley and embark stores and do destruction. *Gneisenau* will follow as far as channel connecting Port William with Port Stanley, anchoring and sending armed cutters to the town with an ultimatum to the Governor. The cutters will be covered by *Nürnberg*. The two ships will rejoin the squadron not later than 1930.

Thus the die was cast for an operation which, apart from being a strategical blunder, could have been carried out a fortnight before if von Spee had displayed the urgency which the situation demanded after Coronel. It is, however, also true that events would have taken a different course if Sturdee had responded to the speed with which Churchill and Fisher dispatched the *Invincible* and *Inflexible*, and had arrived several days earlier at the Falklands, and gone on into the Pacific before 7 December. When neither Admiral appreciated the importance of time in war, months could have elapsed before the British C-in-C located his opponent. But Fortune chose to give Sturdee his golden moment less than four weeks after his departure from England.

* Stanley Harbour is a bay divided into two anchorages by a narrow channel. Port William is the outer, deeper anchorage; Port Stanley the inner anchorage off the tiny, timber-built town of Stanley (pop 1,000). Cape Pembroke, with its lighthouse, is the southern of the two points forming the entrance to Port William.

Appendix B
A Note on Naval W/T Communications in 1914

Because the ship-shore range, and vice versa, of W/T in 1914 was measured in hundreds of miles, not the thousands of today, the Admiralty and the *Admiralstab* could not maintain direct communication with their ships outside Home waters. Signals to and from vessels in the 'far seas' were normally routed through one of the W/T stations which both Navies had established in their colonies, which were connected by cable with Europe – 'normally', because some areas of the Atlantic, Pacific and Indian Oceans were outside the range even of these stations. Thus, signals from Whitehall to HM ships off the south-*east* coast of South America were sent by cable to Montevideo, whence the Uruguayan Government allowed them to be passed by Cerrito W/T station to the Falkland Islands, from where they were re-transmitted to ships at sea, which, for their own signals, used the reverse route. Either way, signals were subject to delay, which could be as much as two or three days when atmospheric conditions were poor.

On the other hand, HM ships off the south-*west* coast of South America were seldom in W/T touch with the Falklands owing to the intervening mountain barrier. Moreover, the use of W/T stations in Chile was impracticable because that Government, unlike the Uruguayan, prohibited the transmission and reception of messages in cipher. Signals from the Admiralty had, therefore, to be sent by cable to a British consul, to await collection, which is the reason, for example, why Cradock sent the *Glasgow* into Coronel on 1 November 1914. In these circumstances signals were sometimes delayed in transit by as much as a week or more. Communication between Berlin and ships in the Pacific suffered similar restrictions, with the further disadvantage that Germany had no shore W/T station there after Jerram's destruction of Yap on 12 August 1914. Hence, for example, the visit of the *Nürnberg* to Honolulu at the end of that month. On the other hand, when von Spee reached South American waters, both the *Admiralstab* and the agents on whom he depended for intelligence and supplies could communicate with him by cabling messages to one of their consuls, for re-transmission by a German merchant ship immobilized by the British blockade, in flagrant breach of regulations which prohibited the use of W/T by belligerent vessels lying in neutral harbours. And von Spee used the same route to send signals to Berlin and German agents in America.

The introduction of W/T at the beginning of the twentieth century greatly facilitated control of naval operations: it was, nonetheless, a two-edged weapon. Chapter Four exemplifies the consequences of the Admiralty succumbing to the temptation to use it to interfere with the man on the spot. As important, the spark transmitters used in 1914 could be intercepted relatively easily by any ship within range. A ship which used its transmitter either to send a message, or to answer a call by another ship or shore station, was therefore likely to reveal her presence to any enemy vessel in the same area. Moreover, although ships could not then measure the bearing of a W/T transmission, they could estimate its range, distinguish whether it was British or German by its note, and sometimes identify the call-sign. As C-in-C of a station so vast as that covered by the China Squadron, Jerram found the need for his flapship to maintain W/T silence, when he was at sea in her in September 1914, such a handicap that he moved into headquarters ashore in Singapore. But in the days immediately preceding Coronel, when the *Good Hope*, *Canopus* and *Glasgow* were separated, Cradock had to accept the risk that, by using W/T, his ships would reveal their presence in that area. Von Spee, on the other hand, with the advantage of having his ships concentrated, used only the W/T transmitter of one light cruiser for all his messages, thereby deceiving his adversary into the fatal supposition that there was no more than the *Leipzig* off Coronel. The Germans were as cautious over using W/T when they rounded the Horn so as to give no warning of their approach to the Falklands. But neither did von Spee learn through W/T intelligence of the arrival of a powerful British force because, when the battlecruisers (which had kept strict W/T silence whilst crossing the Atlantic) joined Stoddart's force at the Abrolhos Rocks, Sturdee arranged that any signals which he might have to send should be transmitted by the *Bristol* or *Glasgow*, whose presence off the east coast of South America was already known to the enemy.

6

Sturdee's Revenge

The battle of the Falkland Islands — The hunt for SMS Dresden *—
The end of SMS* Königsberg

> It was an interesting fight off the Falkland Islands, a good
> stand-up fight, and I always like to say I have a great re-
> gard for my opponent, Admiral von Spee. At all events he
> gave our squadron a chance by calling on me the day
> after I arrived.
>
> *Vice-Admiral Sir Doveton Sturdee*

Sturdee's fleet reached the Falklands at 1030 on 7 December, to
the immense relief of the Governor and Grant who had been
expecting the Germans hourly since 25 November. The former had
enrolled every able-bodied man into a local defence force, and sent
the women and children into the hinterland. The latter had beached
the *Canopus* in Port Stanley, transforming her into a fort, with
observation posts ashore. He had also laid a minefield across the
entrance to Port William, and landed 12-pounders manned by a
detachment of Royal Marines. The Falklands were not, however,
Sturdee's first concern; believing von Spee to be still off Valparaiso,
he decided that, 'to reach the Chilean coast at the earliest possible
date, all ships should remain for only 48 hours'. So that all could
replenish with the least possible delay from the only two colliers
available, the light-draught *Bristol* and *Glasgow* were sent into Port
Stanley, whilst the battlecruisers, together with the *Carnarvon*,
Cornwall and *Kent*, anchored in Port William. Only the AMC *Macedonia* remained on patrol outside — when the enemy was less than
a day's steaming away.

The German squadron had first sight of the Falklands as early as
0230 next morning. Three hours later von Spee signalled the
Gneisenau and *Nürnberg* to proceed in execution of previous orders.
Around 0830 Maerker distinguished the masts of the W/T station,
and a column of smoke to the east from a vessel entering harbour,

the *Macedonia*. But over the neck of land between Cape Pembroke and Port Stanley he could see nothing except a cloud of black smoke from which he deduced that, as when von Spee's force approached Papeeté, the coal stocks were being fired. Not until 0900 did the *Gneisenau*'s gunnery officer make out the funnels and masts of warships in the harbour. Maerker then knew that he had been right in refusing to believe that Stoddart's squadron had sailed for South Africa; but he would not accept his control top's next report – of four *tripod* masts in Port William: there could be no dreadnoughts in the South Atlantic. He continued to take the *Gneisenau* and *Nürnberg* towards their appointed position five miles from Cape Pembroke, as he signalled von Spee that, in addition to three British 'County' class cruisers and one light cruiser in Stanley Harbour, there *might* also be two larger ships – but of no greater significance than '*Canopus*' class pre-dreadnoughts.

Grant's look-outs on Sapper Hill spotted the approaching German ships shortly before 0800. At 0756 the signal, 'Enemy in sight', flew to the *Canopus*'s masthead, and the *Glasgow* fired a gun to draw attention to it. Two amplifying reports followed; the first that the enemy comprised 'a four-funnelled and a two-funnelled man-of-war in sight SE steering northwards'; the second increasing the approaching force to seven vessels, five of them warships. Sturdee could have no doubt that this was von Spee's squadron about to attack the Falklands, when his ships were anything but ready to take advantage of such an unexpected opportunity for annihilating the only substantial German force outside the North Sea. The *Invincible* and *Inflexible* had the two colliers alongside: the *Kent*, *Cornwall* and *Bristol* had not yet begun to replenish their bunkers: only the *Carnarvon* and *Glasgow* had completed with fuel. Moreover, the *Kent* was the only ship with steam at less than two hours' notice, whilst both the *Bristol* and *Cornwall* had an engine opened up for repairs. Against these handicaps Sturdee had an advantage all his own: 'no man ever saw him rattled'. As quietly and calmly as in a peacetime exercise, he gave orders for the *Kent* to weigh and proceed out of harbour, for the battlecruisers to cast off their colliers, and for all ships to raise steam for full speed and report when ready to proceed: then he went below for breakfast.

He was on deck again by 0845 to see the *Kent* leaving harbour; but it would be another hour before the battlecruisers and the *Carnarvon* and *Glasgow* could weigh, and longer still before the *Bristol* and *Cornwall* were ready. In that time much could happen; as Churchill wrote:

I was working in my room when Oliver [who had relieved Sturdee as Chief of War Staff] entered with this telegram from the Governor of the Falkland Islands. 'Admiral von Spee arrived at daylight this morning with all his ships and is now in action with Admiral Sturdee's whole fleet, *which was coaling.*' These words sent a shiver up my spine. Had we been taken by surprise and, in spite of our superiority, mauled, unready at anchor?

Von Spee could, indeed, have closed Stanley Harbour, overwhelmed the *Kent*, and raked the rest of the British force with gunfire when it could bring no more than a small part of its superior armament to bear. But, for the moment, Sturdee could do no more than order the *Canopus* to open fire as soon as the *Gneisenau* and *Nürnberg* were within range, his battlecruisers to be 'ready to open fire at any moment', and the *Carnarvon* to clear for action and 'engage enemy as they come round the corner'. Twenty tense minutes passed before Sapper Hill reported that the *Gneisenau* and *Nürnberg* had trained their guns on the W/T station. Grant responded by firing a salvo from his ship's four 12-inch guns at their maximum range of 13,500 yards.

On the previous evening word was passed that we would carry out a practice shoot the following morning. To get one up on their deadly rivals in the fore turret, the after turret's crew crept out privily by night and loaded with practice shell. Next morning there was no time to unload for a real battle. The results of this naughtiness was very interesting; the *Gneisenau* was well outside our extreme range, and live shell from the fore turret burst on impact with the water, but those from the after turret ricocheted, and one of them scored a hit!

Maerker had increased speed as soon as he saw the *Kent* leave harbour, hoping to cut her off, but when this freak shot from the *Canopus* struck the base of the *Gneisenau*'s after funnel, he turned sharply away. Von Spee was of the same mind: 'Do not accept action,' he signalled. 'Concentrate on course E by N and proceed at full speed.' So the *Canopus* did not fire again; but she had served her purpose; by 0930 the German Admiral had turned to the east, and detached his supply ships to return to Picton Island. He had chosen flight instead of taking his one chance of avoiding nemesis by engaging the British ships whilst they were still in harbour; because he did not know how unprepared they were; because he would not risk an action with the two pre-dreadnoughts that Maerker had reported, whose presence the *Canopus*'s salvo seemed to have confirmed; and because he believed his squadron to be the faster. Not until 1100, when all five German cruisers were steering a south-easterly course at 22 knots, in the order *Gneisenau*, *Nürnberg*, *Scharnhorst*, *Dresden* and *Leipzig*, did he learn that the British force included two battlecruisers which would be able to overhaul him before the sun went down.

In the engine and boiler rooms of the British ships officers and men rose splendidly to the occasion, as they were to do throughout the day. The *Glasgow* had steam by 0945. A quarter of an hour later, Stoddart in the *Carnarvon* followed Luce's ship out of harbour. It was not much longer before the *Invincible* and *Inflexible*, and then the *Cornwall*, joined the watching *Kent*, and Sturdee was able to hoist that most exhilarating of signals: 'Chase!' The *Bristol* was the last to leave, at 1100; but well before that Sturdee knew that he had von Spee at his mercy, and decided against an immediate engagement. The smoke from his battlecruisers, made by burning both coal and oil to achieve their full speed, made it difficult to see the enemy. He reduced to 24 knots, ordered the *Inflexible* to haul out on his flagship's starboard quarter, stationed the *Glasgow* three miles on his port bow where she could keep the enemy in sight without coming in range, and instructed the *Kent* to drop back to his port beam. Shortly after this he reduced again, to 19 knots, so that the slower *Cornwall* and *Carnarvon* might catch up – and signalled that before action was joined ships' companies would have time for their midday meal.

Around 1130 the *Bristol* wirelessed a report of 'colliers or transports' approaching the Falklands. Suspecting a German attempt to make an armed landing, Sturdee instructed Fanshawe to take the *Macedonia* under his orders 'and destroy transports'. By 1500 the colliers *Baden* and *Santa Isabel* had been found and overtaken. Forgetting a sentence in Sturdee's *Fighting Instructions* – 'The opportunity might occur to capture the enemy's colliers' – he sank both these ships with their valuable cargoes, after taking off their crews. This occupied the *Bristol* and *Macedonia* until 1900, by which time a third German supply ship, the faster *Seydlitz*, had made good her escape under cover of darkness – but only to seek internment in the Argentine port of San Antonio.

'At about 1220,' onboard the *Inflexible*, 'the Skipper came aft and said that the Admiral had decided to get on with the work. The men on deck cheered.' Seeing that the *Carnarvon* was still six miles

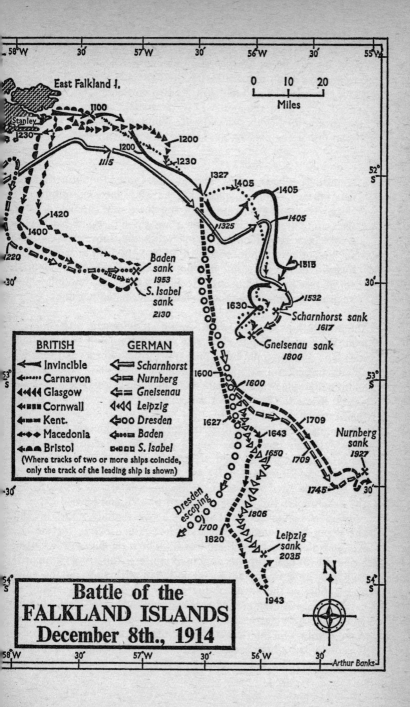

Battle of the
FALKLAND ISLANDS
December 8th., 1914

astern, and that it would take him too long to come within range of
his opponent if he remained with the *Kent* and *Cornwall*, Sturdee
decided to begin the attack with his two battlecruisers. Speed was
worked up to 26 knots, and at 1247 the signal, 'Engage the enemy',
flew to the *Invincible*'s masthead. Minutes later, the *Inflexible*
opened fire at the *Leipzig*, at the rear of the enemy line, at 16,500
yards.

> It must have been a very pretty picture [noted the former's gun-
> nery officer]. A blue cloudless sky, the atmosphere extraordinarily
> clear, the two battlecruisers forcing their way through a calm
> sea, white water boiling in their wakes, masses of black oily
> smoke from their funnels, against which the many white ensigns
> showed up in striking contrast. Ever and anon the roar from the
> forward turret guns and heaving masses of chocolate-coloured
> cordite smoke tumbling over the bows, a long wait, and tall white
> splashes growing out of the sea behind the distant enemy.

The British ships were still on a south-easterly course, with the Germans running parallel to them fine on the starboard bow, so that
each battlecruiser could bring only two turrets to bear; and with no
aids to fire control except for a couple of short-base rangefinders,
and the most elementary of rate and deflection calculators and range
clocks, it was the best part of half an hour before their shells found
their targets.

Von Spee then realized that it could only be minutes before the
lagging *Leipzig* received a damaging hit; he recognized, too, that
his armoured cruisers could no longer avoid action. At 1320, he
signalled the *Dresden*, *Leipzig* and *Nürnberg* 'to leave the line and
try to escape'; and as soon as they swung away to the south, he led
the *Scharnhorst* and *Gneisenau* round to ENE and opened fire. But
Sturdee 'was an officer who had made a special study of tactics', and
the *Fighting Instructions* which he had issued before leaving the
Abrolhos Rocks included these words: 'The main duty of the battlecruisers is to deal with the armoured cruisers. The British armoured
and light cruisers should not seek action with them in the early
stages but, in the event of the enemy's light cruisers trying to
escape, deal with them.' And no more was needed for Luce, Ellerton
and Allen to swing the *Glasgow*, *Cornwall* and *Kent* in pursuit as
soon as they saw the German light cruisers turn away. Because the
Carnarvon lacked the speed to catch them, and because two British
armoured and one light cruiser should be ample to deal with three

German light cruisers, Stoddart continued to follow the battle-cruisers.

The battle was thus divided into a number of separate actions. The critical one began with a chase on parallel easterly courses, the *Invincible* engaging the *Scharnhorst*, the *Inflexible* the *Gneisenau*, at a range which Sturdee brought down to 13,500 yards. Despite the great disparity in strength between the two sides, it was far from a one-sided contest. 'The German shooting was excellent; they straddled us time after time'; and at 1344 the *Invincible* was hit. Sturdee's intention to fight at a range within that of his own guns, but outside that of the enemy's, had been frustrated by the Germans having the lee position. The smoke from the battlecruisers was blowing towards the enemy, obscuring the British gunlayers' view of their targets, and making spotting almost impossible. It prevented them from seeing that they had scored two hits on the *Gneisenau* already, one below the waterline, and that the *Scharnhorst* had also suffered. To ensure that the enemy did not cripple one of his battle-cruisers with a lucky shot, Sturdee altered two points to port and opened the range, which brought a lull in the action. But von Spee forestalled his attempt to get to leeward by a large alteration of course to the south: Sturdee could only haul round after him and, at 1445, close the range again and reopen fire. Von Spee's response, this time, was a sharp alteration of course towards the British battlecruisers to enable the *Scharnhorst* and *Gneisenau* to use their 5·9-inch guns at a range of 10,000 yards, as well as their heavier weapons. And, by 1515, this was so effective that Sturdee swung his ships through 32 points in an attempt to clear the smoke that fouled the range, which opened it to 14,000 yards.

The British ships were not the only ones thus handicapped. When a splinter cut the halyards of von Spee's flag, Maerker signalled the *Scharnhorst*: 'Why is the Admiral's flag at half-mast? Is he dead?' He received the reply: 'I am all right so far. Have you hit anything?', to which Maerker had to answer: 'The smoke prevents all observation.' Von Spee replied with a generous acknowledgement of Maerker's misgivings over the attack on the Falklands: 'You were right after all.' The weight of British metal was taking its toll of the German ships. (Each battlecruiser's broadside weighed nearly 3,500 lb; each German armoured cruiser's little more than 1,500 lb.) According to their historian,

the heavier British shells easily penetrated the casemate decks and played havoc in the compartments below. The damage increased continually, especially in the *Gneisenau*. The 5·9-inch casemates suffered severely; the wireless room was demolished; No 1 boiler room was flooded and had to be abandoned; No 3 boiler room also began to fill.

But the *Scharnhorst* was also holed fore and aft below the waterline so that she was drawing three feet more than normal; she was on fire in several places; and by 1530 her third funnel had been shot away, when her gunfire slackened perceptibly.

Such hits as the two German ships scored on the British battle-cruisers did nothing to reduce their fighting value. In sharp contrast, the Germans had so many guns put out of action on their engaged side that von Spee swung ten points to starboard to bring their other broadsides to bear. This enabled Sturdee to cross his opponent's wake and, at last, to gain the lee position, when he noted, 'the effect of the British fire on the *Scharnhorst* became more and more apparent; a shell would cause a large hole in her side through which could be seen a red glow of flame'. But 'although our shots were falling all over the *Scharnhorst*', the *Inflexible*'s gunnery officer 'could not stop her firing. I remember asking my rate operator, "What the devil can we do?" when she suddenly shut up as when a light is blown out.' To quote Sturdee: 'At 1604 the *Scharnhorst*, whose flag remained flying to the last, suddenly listed heavily to port, and it became clear that she was doomed. The list increased very rapidly until she lay on her beam ends; at 1617 she disappeared' – five minutes after the *Carnarvon* managed to catch up, and add the fire of her 7·5-inch guns to the larger weapons of the battlecruisers. The German flagship went down with her entire crew, including the brave von Spee.

Maerker had already received one last signal from his Admiral: 'Endeavour to escape if your engines are still intact', but 'the poor devils onboard must have known that they were doomed. The *Gneisenau*'s fore funnel was leaning against her second, and she had a large hole through her fourth. Her foremast was all skewy, too;' and the damage to her boiler rooms had reduced her speed to 16 knots. But though battered and blazing, and under a hail of fire from three ships on different bearings, she continued to fight with such of her guns as remained. As late as 1715 she secured a hit on the *Invincible*.

At 1730 she turned towards Sturdee's flagship with a heavy list to starboard and appeared stopped, with steam pouring from her exhaust pipes, and smoke from fires rising everywhere. But she continued to fire with a single gun. At 1740 our three ships closed in, and the flag flying at her fore-truck was hauled down, but the flag at the peak continued flying. At 1750, 'Cease fire' was made. The *Gneisenau* was then sinking. She went over slowly and gave ample time for injured men to get on deck before she quietly disappeared. Within a few minutes we were up to the survivors, some 200 men supporting themselves with hammocks, belts, spars, etc.

Having expended all his ammunition, lost steam from all boilers and suffered some 600 of his crew killed and wounded, Maerker gave orders to scuttle his ship.

He called for three cheers for His Majesty and the *Gneisenau* was then abandoned. I [one of her officers] fell into the water on the starboard side as she capsized. Men clinging to objects around me were singing patriotic songs. There were 270 to 300 in the water, but the temperature was only 39°F, and during half an hour's immersion many perished.

When the *Carnarvon* was slow to join the *Invincible* and *Inflexible* in the work of rescue, Sturdee dropped his mask of imperturbability for the only time on that eventful day: 'Lower all your boats at once', he signalled her twice.

We got about fifty onboard* [wrote one of the *Inflexible*'s officers]. We were busy getting out clothes, etc for them, and by dinner-time we had several in the mess. Most of them could not sleep that first night, the scenes in their ships were so terrible. To see one's best friend rush on deck, one huge wound covered with blood, and just have time to send his love home, is terrible. But we were all good friends after the fight, and agreed that we did not want to fight at all, but had to. Over 2,000 of them must have been killed or drowned, but they fought magnificently, and their discipline must have been superb.

That evening Sturdee signalled the senior German survivor:

The Commander-in-Chief is very gratified that your life has been spared. The *Gneisenau* fought in a most plucky manner to the end. We so much admire the good gunnery of both ships. We sympathize with you in the loss of your Admiral and so many

---

* The actual numbers rescued were: by the *Invincible*, 108; by the *Inflexible*, 62; by the *Carnarvon*, 20. They did not include Spee's younger son, Heinrich.

officers and men. Unfortunately the two countries are at war; the officers of both navies, who can count friends in the other, have to carry out their countries' duties which your Admiral, Captains and officers worthily maintained to the end.

Commander Pochhammer replied:

I thank Your Excellency very much for your kind words. We regret, as you, the course of the fight, as we have learned to know during peacetime the English Navy and her officers. We are all most thankful for our good reception.

Officers and men of the *Scharnhorst* and *Gneisenau* had fought to the end against overwhelming odds, in an action in which von Spee went to an honourable death, for all that the battle was as much due to his own mistakes as to the swift dispatch of strong British reinforcements. The destruction of the German armoured cruisers could not, however, have been achieved without the skill and steadiness in action for which the Royal Navy had long been famous. It was as much a triumph for the British ships' engine- and boiler-room crews as for those who manned their turrets. But, above all, it was due to Sturdee's calm, incisive reaction to the unexpected arrival of von Spee's force at the Falklands, and to his subsequent skilful handling of his squadron. With justice did he say to his Flag Captain that eventful evening: 'Well, Beamish, we were sacked from the Admiralty, but we've done pretty well today.'

The *Invincible*, which had borne the brunt of the enemy fire, had no man killed or wounded; though struck by 22 shells, the majority of 8·2-inch calibre, her efficiency was affected only to the extent of one 4-inch gun out of action and one bunker flooded. On the other hand, the *Inflexible* received only three hits that caused no significant damage, but which killed one seaman and slightly wounded two others. This was the reward of Sturdee's decision to engage his opponent at long range; but in another respect it was more costly than he had expected. The two battlecruisers had each fired 600 rounds, the greater part of their 12-inch ammunition, when there was no stock nearer than Gibraltar. The Navy had only recently passed out of the era of close-range fire, when more than 50 per cent of hits could be expected: not until later in the war would it be realized that, at ranges over 10,000 yards, the rate of hitting was as low as five per cent. Fortunately, in the days that followed 8 December 1914, Sturdee had no reason to expect a further encounter with anything larger than a light cruiser.

How, meantime, had the *Kent*, *Cornwall* and *Glasgow* fared in their pursuit of the *Dresden*, *Leipzig* and *Nürnberg*? When, soon after 1300, von Spee ordered his light cruisers to 'try to escape', all three swung on to southerly courses in the hope of reaching the comparative safety of Tierra del Fuego. Lüdecke's *Dresden* soon drew ahead, Haun's *Leipzig* lagged behind. The *Kent* being to port of the *Cornwall* and the *Glasgow* to starboard, Ellerton signalled Allen and Luce: 'I will take *Leipzig* if *Kent* takes *Nürnberg* and *Glasgow* takes *Dresden*.' But though the *Glasgow* could steam faster than the two armoured cruisers, Luce (who was senior officer) replied: 'I fear I am gaining very slowly on *Dresden*. Having already engaged *Leipzig* I feel I must stand by you.' Since he doubted whether the *Glasgow* could overhaul the *Dresden* before dark, and feared that the *Cornwall* would be unable to catch the *Leipzig*, he must fight a delaying action with the latter until the *Cornwall* had her measure.

At 1450 the *Glasgow* opened fire with her two 6-inch guns. Deciding that the *Leipzig* had small chance of eluding her, Haun responded with an alteration of course that brought his 4·1-inch guns within range.

Twenty minutes after fire had been opened the *Leipzig* received her first hit [wrote her navigating officer]. A shell struck the superstructure before the third funnel and passed through the upper deck into a bunker which happened to be the one in use, which caused a temporary diminution of the forced draught in Nos 3 and 4 boiler rooms. Our fire was severely hampered by the fact that only three guns on the starboard side, and occasionally the aftermost gun on the port side, were in action.

The *Leipzig*'s fire was, nonetheless, accurate enough to score two hits in a running fight lasting an hour, which deterred Luce from closing to within range of the *Glasgow*'s 4-inch armament, until Ellerton was able to bring the *Cornwall* into action at 1617. This was in time for the larger ship's heavier guns to dispose of the *Leipzig* before dark. Unfortunately Luce was not now in a position to go after the fleeing *Dresden*: the *Leipzig* had damaged one of the *Glasgow*'s boilers, reducing her speed; moreover Lüdecke's ship was obscured by mist and rain.

Haun turned the *Leipzig*'s guns on to his new, more powerful opponent, but with little effect.

At 1642 the *Cornwall* [wrote Ellerton] hit the *Leipzig*'s foretopmast and carried it away. At 1703 I turned to starboard and poured in my whole broadside, range 8,275 yards. By 1806 she was on fire.

Luce supported Ellerton, first by engaging the *Leipzig* from the same side, then from the opposite quarter. Slowly closing the range, the fire of the two British ships became more and more effective until, at 1930, the *Leipzig*'s gunnery officer,

> after making a tour of the guns and finding no more ammunition, reported that her means of defence were exhausted. Haun turned to his torpedo officer, and said: 'Go ahead, it's your turn now.' Between 1950 and 1955 three torpedoes were loaded and fired, but we obtained no hits, for the enemy kept out of range.

The *Glasgow* and *Cornwall* then approached to see if the *Leipzig* had struck her colours, but since her ensign was still flying, Luce again opened fire. There was no response.

> Many men sought shelter behind the gun shields but were mown down in heaps by shell splinters that ricocheted from the conning tower. Others decided to jump overboard and swim towards the enemy, but the cold water numbed them. The survivors stood with the Captain on the forecastle as darkness fell,

and Luce signalled: 'I am sending boats to save life.' It was 2030 when Haun gave his final order, to abandon ship, as the *Leipzig* heeled over to sink rapidly by her bows, her flag still flying.

Luce and Ellerton had achieved this at very small cost: the *Glasgow* had received two hits which caused the death of one man and wounded four; the *Cornwall* had been struck 18 times, but had suffered no casualties and no worse damage than two flooded bunkers. In sharp contrast, the British ships could rescue only seven officers and 11 men from the *Leipzig*, Ellerton regretting 'that an officer as gallant as Captain Haun was not saved'. Of his own ship's company, Luce wrote: 'After our experiences on 1 November their one idea has been to wipe out that reverse to His Majesty's arms, and it is a source of much gratification that we have been able to take part in the destruction of the enemy's squadron which inflicted this upon us.' Unfortunately, for Sturdee rather than himself, he had allowed the *Dresden* to escape.

The Admiral called for reports from his detached ships soon after 1800, when he broadcast the news of the sinking of the *Scharnhorst* and *Gneisenau*. Fanshawe answered that the *Macedonia* was proceeding to Port Stanley with the crews of the two German colliers, asked for orders for the *Bristol*, and was instructed to join the flagship. When there were no other replies, Sturdee decided to search towards Cape Horn, while Stoddart took the *Carnarvon* to reinforce the *Orama*, against the possibility that the British colliers, that were due at the Falklands on the 10th, might be attacked by one of the German light cruisers. When he received Luce's report nearly four hours later, he ordered him to take the *Glasgow* and *Cornwall* to the Magellan Straits, so that the *Dresden* should not escape by that route. Early next morning, however, Sturdee learned that both cruisers had expended nearly all their ammunition, and that the *Cornwall* was seriously short of coal, so all three were diverted to Port Stanley. He also detached the *Bristol* to the sparsely populated West Falkland Island to cover the possibility that the *Dresden* might go there. At the same time, he became so concerned at the continued absence of news from the *Kent*, that he ordered Luce to take the *Glasgow* and *Macedonia* out to search for her. But before they could sail, Allen's ship was sighted from Sapper Hill, whence Sturdee received a signal explaining why he had had to wait so long for news of her.

I steered [wrote Allen] after the *Nürnberg* at the utmost possible speed. The stokers responded magnificently: the maximum horsepower of the ship was exceeded by 5,000. The range appeared to be decreasing; and at 1700 the *Nürnberg* opened fire with her two stern guns, quickly found the range, about 12,000 yards, and from then onwards her shooting was remarkably accurate. The *Kent* fired two guns every few minutes at extreme elevation to try and reach her. When she came within range at 1709 I fired salvoes continuously. We gradually closed until it dropped to 7,000 yards, when the *Nürnberg* altered course to port, bringing her whole broadside to bear. I altered course to port, too, and opened fire with all the *Kent*'s starboard guns. We steered on converging courses until the range decreased to 3,000 yards, when the *Kent*'s shells were bursting all over the *Nürnberg*. By 1802 she was on fire forward, and her speed had decreased. By 1835 she was practically stopped and had ceased firing. I steamed towards her until I could see that she was still flying her colours, when I again opened fire. Five minutes later she lowered her colours. I immediately ceased firing. As she was now well down by the stern and had a list to starboard, I ordered all available boats to be got ready for saving survivors. At 1926 she heeled right over to starboard and slowly sank. Twelve officers and men were picked up [von Spee's elder son, Otto, was not among them] but only seven survived, the remainder being dead when brought onboard or dying shortly afterwards. I remained in the vicinity till 2100, then hoisted boats and proceeded towards the Falkland Islands. I was unable to make any W/T signals as a shell had passed through the office and damaged the instruments. I regret to report that during the action four of my men were killed and twelve wounded. The *Kent* was struck 38 times but there is no serious damage. I wish to express my admiration of the very gallant and determined manner in which the Captain, officers and men of the *Nürnberg* fought their ship.

Allen had, in fact, been very near to losing his own ship: his report records:

Only one fire occurred during the action, in A3 casemate. A shell struck the gunport and burst; the flash must have ignited one or more charges inside the casemate, as a flame went down the hoist into the ammunition passage. There was a charge at the bottom of the hoist at the time, but fortunately the man standing there, Sergeant Charles Mayes, RMLI, had the courage and presence of mind to throw it away and flood the compartment, which prevented the fire spreading. There can be no doubt that the ship narrowly escaped being blown up as, had a charge caught fire in the ammunition passage, the flash would have set other charges on fire and reached the magazine before the watertight doors could have been closed.

The Admiralty recognized Mayes's heroism with the Conspicuous Gallantry Medal. Unfortunately they did not appreciate the wider implications of this near-disaster – with fateful consequences to be related in later chapters.

Sturdee now knew that in as little as six weeks of leaving the Admiralty he had fulfilled the task entrusted to him. Though surprised by the enemy in circumstances that would have rattled many men, he had scored a victory as decisive as any in British history, the last to be fought between ships in the old style by gunfire alone, unaided by aircraft and in waters free from minefields and submarines. To Fisher, Churchill wrote: 'This is your show and your luck. I should have only sent one greyhound [i.e. battlecruiser] and *Defence*. Your flair is quite true' – a gesture which the First Sea Lord acknowledged with the words: 'Your letter pleasant ...'. The consequences 'affected our position in every part of the globe', commented the First Lord. 'The strain was everywhere relaxed. All our enterprises, whether of war or commerce, proceeded without hindrance. Within 24 hours orders were sent to a score of British ships to return to Home waters.' King George V signalled Sturdee: 'I heartily congratulate you and your officers and men on your most opportune victory,' to which the Admiralty added: 'Our thanks are due to yourself and to your officers and men for the brilliant victory you have reported.' But when he brought the *Invincible* and *Inflexible* back to the Falklands on 11 December, after a search for the *Dresden* that had been hindered by fog, Sturdee had to write:

> The Commander-in-Chief wishes to congratulate all the ships of the squadron on the success of their main encounter with the enemy's squadron, and to thank the Rear-Admiral, Captains, officers and men for their individual assistance in attaining this great result.* The zeal and steadiness under fire of all hands was most noticeable. But the victory will not be complete until the remaining cruiser is accounted for, and directly the squadron is coaled, a further organized search will be made.

The *Dresden* lost sight of her pursuers by 1700 on 8 December. A couple of hours later Lüdecke knew from intercepted W/T traffic that the rest of von Spee's squadron had been destroyed. Since the *Baden* and *Santa Isabel* had reported being chased by British warships, he concluded that they would be unable to return to Picton Island. Because he also thought the entrance to the Magellan Straits would be guarded by the enemy, he steered well to the south of Cape Horn. Next morning the *Dresden* was off the entrance to Cockburn Channel, on the western side of Tierra del Fuego, and that afternoon Lüdecke anchored her in Sholl Bay, where he thought himself sufficiently safe to land men to fell timber to augment his remaining coal. But the arrival of a Chilean destroyer, to draw his attention to the convention limiting a belligerent's stay in neutral waters to 24 hours, left Lüdecke with no alternative but to proceed to Punta Arenas, where the *Dresden* anchored on the 12th. Sturdee learned of this from the British Consul early next morning, and immediately ordered the *Inflexible*, *Glasgow* and *Bristol* to head there, whilst the *Carnarvon* and *Cornwall* sailed to work down the coast from Port

---

* Sturdee gave no special credit to Luce for the British squadron's timely arrival at the Falklands (see p 93). Indeed, when Luce mentioned it he was coldly received. Sturdee had no wish to be reminded of how near he had been to missing his opponent because of his leisurely progress south.

Madryn in case the *Dresden* should double back into the South Atlantic.

Meantime, at the Admiralty, Churchill and Fisher had reached agreement that, although the *Karlsruhe*, *Kronprinz Wilhelm* and *Prinz Eitel Friedrich* remained to be located as well as the *Dresden*, the *Invincible* and *Inflexible* must return to Home waters. They were less in harmony over Sturdee's future. Fisher wanted him to transfer his flag to a cruiser and remain in charge of the hunt, although this task did not warrant such a senior flag officer. Churchill realized the First Sea Lord's motive: inwardly seething at the praise being lavished on his *bête noire*, Fisher wanted to prevent, for as long as possible, Sturdee enjoying the public acclaim he would receive when he returned to England. So the First Lord overruled him: Sturdee was ordered to return with the *Invincible* and *Inflexible*, leaving the *Canopus* as guardship at the Abrolhos Rocks, and the other ships to hunt for the *Dresden* under Stoddart's command. But when the Admiralty heard that Lüdecke had been allowed to coal at Punta Arenas, Sturdee was told to use his discretion over the return of the battlecruisers; 'object is destruction of the *Dresden*, not internment. Press your chase.' He answered that he intended to sail for England in the *Invincible* on the 16th, whilst the *Inflexible* continued the search until the 29th, when she would have to return to the Falklands for coal, and would then leave for home.

Lüdecke had, however, done more than slip out of Punta Arenas with full bunkers before the *Inflexible*, *Bristol* and *Glasgow* could arrive: on 14 December the *Dresden* found refuge in lonely Hewett Bay. And when the 18th brought no news of her, Fisher's smouldering wrath took fire. He ordered Sturdee to return home at once, adding: 'Report fully reason for the course which you have followed since the action,' because, as he wrote to Jellicoe on the 20th, Sturdee's 'criminal ineptitude in not sending a vessel to Punta Arenas at the close of the action has disastrously kept from you light cruisers now hunting *Dresden*'. But if Sturdee suspected a sting in the Admiralty's signal, he did not show it in his reasoned reply, in which he confirmed that the *Inflexible* was following the *Invincible* to St Vincent, where both would replenish with ammunition.

For the next fortnight it seemed that Fisher was satisfied – until on 3 January the Admiralty abruptly signalled:

Explain why neither *Inflexible*, *Invincible*, nor any other vessel proceeded immediately on completion of action to Punta Arenas to cable Admiralty, and also to obtain information from British Consul.

Sturdee answered: 'Reasons for actions taken were given in my reply to your signal of 18 December.' Fisher repeated his inquiry, because 'your previous reply does not answer the question'. To this, Sturdee gave more than a clear and adequate explanation: he concluded: —

> Their Lordships selected me as C-in-C to destroy the two armoured cruisers and I endeavoured to the best of my ability to carry out these orders. I submit that my being called upon in three separate telegrams to give reasons for my subsequent action was unexpected.

Many admirals would have phrased this protest in less moderate terms. Sturdee's received this sharp rebuke: 'Last paragraph of your signal is improper and such observations must not be repeated.' But for the moment Fisher could not pursue his vendetta beyond adding: 'Their Lordships await your written report and dispatches before coming to any conclusion.'

The *Invincible* berthed at Gibraltar on 11 January. Sturdee's report reached the Admiralty five days later. Churchill did not doubt that the victor of the Falklands had done all that was reasonably possible to locate the *Dresden* in the days after the battle, and that he well deserved another major appointment at sea: on the 21st Sturdee was offered command of the 4th BS, of eight dreadnoughts in the Grand Fleet. But Fisher's vindictive spirit was not quenched: when Sturdee reported to the Admiralty, he was kept waiting for several hours before the First Sea Lord consented to receive him for an interview restricted to a cold five minutes, during which nothing was said of his victory over von Spee, only of his failure to catch the *Dresden*. And when Fisher heard that Sturdee had been summoned to Buckingham Palace to give the King an account of the battle, he tried to prevent him having this satisfaction by ordering him to leave immediately for Scapa Flow; but Sturdee insisted on deferring his departure for 48 hours. Subsequently, the First Sea Lord emasculated Sturdee's dispatch before allowing it to be published in the *London Gazette*. But neither by such insults, nor by other means, did he dim the Admiral's glory. Many were the letters that Sturdee received, such as this:

> I don't know how to express all I feel about your most glorious victory. It's too splendid — and oh, if you knew what the whole

Navy and the Nation are saying about it – it's just grand. It was all so complete and perfect.

And in the list of honours and awards for the battle he became the first officer to receive the traditional baronetcy for a successful action at sea for more than a century.

The search for the *Dresden* continued for nearly three months after the *Inflexible*'s withdrawal, occupying a number of British and Allied warships that were needed elsewhere. Otherwise Lüdecke did little damage to the Allied cause: he did not come from the same corsair stable as von Müller. For both the crux was coal, but, whereas the *Emden*'s Captain was determined to find it in the holds of the Allies' colliers, the *Dresden*'s waited for German agents to send it in neutral bottoms – and waited in vain. He remained in lonely Hewett Bay until 26th December, then moved to the more secluded Weihnachts Bay where the supply ship *Sierra Cordoba* joined him on 19 January. But she carried insufficient coal for the *Dresden* to wage cruiser warfare. On 21 January Berlin signalled the *Dresden* to return to Germany. Lüdecke replied that he intended 'to break through to west coast of South America and carry on commerce warfare in East Indies if sufficient coal is procurable'. On 10 February Berlin told him: 'Further coal supplies for Pacific and Indian Oceans impossible,' and again advised returning home. Lüdecke's response was to leave Weihnachts Bay on the 14th and head for an area to the south of Juan Fernandez, where in the course of three weeks he sighted and sank one small British sailing vessel.

Such caution explains the failure of all Stoddart's efforts to locate the *Dresden* for so long as three months. Indeed, his squadron of cruisers and AMCs might have been required to search for another three, if the Admiralty had not procured a vital telegram from a German agent in Chile. Deciphered, this revealed that a collier was to rendezvous with the *Dresden* 300 miles west of Coronel on 5 March. The *Kent* was ordered to investigate, but Allen could not reach this position until the 7th, when he discovered nothing. The fog that veiled the scene next day cleared in the afternoon, to reveal not the collier, but the *Dresden* herself. She was, however, 12 miles to the west, too far for the *Kent* to catch her before dark.

But she was not to escape. Since the collier had not arrived, the *Dresden* had insufficient coal to go farther than Mas a Fuera, where Lüdecke anchored early on the 9th and informed the Governor that he would allow his ship to be interned as soon as a Chilean warship could arrive for this purpose. He hoped a collier would join him first. But Luce was already bringing the *Glasgow* and *Orama* north to join the *Kent*; and when the three ships approached Cumberland Bay at daylight on the 14th, the senior British Captain did not hesitate over the niceties of International Law. Since the *Dresden* had remained at this neutral island for well over the authorized 24 hours, the *Glasgow* closed to 8,400 yards, and at 0850 opened fire, her first two salvoes scoring hits. The *Kent* joined the action. The *Dresden* returned her opponents' fire. But in three minutes she had suffered enough damage for Lüdecke to hoist a white flag, when the British vessels broke off the engagement and awaited a boat flying a flag of truce. However, Lüdecke had no intention of allowing his ship or her company to fall into enemy hands: whilst Luce was parleying with Lieutenant Canaris* and parrying the protests of an incensed Chilean Governor, the German Captain detonated her forward magazine after he and his crew had reached the safety of a neutral shore.

A month before this Allied success, the Admiralty had the satisfaction of solving the mystery of why they had received no reports of the *Karlsruhe* for so long: of why Köhler, who had managed to elude Cradock in the Bahamas in August 1914, and then moved down to the Pernambuco area to capture or sink 76,500 tons of Allied shipping by the end of October, had done nothing since then, except be a potential threat to the Atlantic trade routes. As von Spee was closing Coronel for his encounter with Cradock, the *Karlsruhe* was nearing Barbados to raid this island's defenceless capital. But fate, in the guise of unstable ammunition, such as destroyed the British cruiser *Natal* in Cromarty Firth on New Year's Day 1915, intervened: the *Karlsruhe* was rent by the spontaneous explosion of her magazines. The forepart, with Köhler and the majority of his crew, sank at once: the after part remained afloat long enough for the cruiser's two tenders to rescue 140 of her officers and men. The senior of these, Commander Studt, who showed much the same determination to return to Germany as von Mücke of the *Emden*, scuttled one tender, then headed the larger, the liner *Rio Negro*, for Iceland. With the advantage of the long winter nights in northern latitudes and a fierce gale, she

---

* Canaris not only eluded internment in Chile but later rose to the rank of admiral, to command the *Abwehr* in the Second World War, and to be executed for his part in the 1944 plot against Hitler.

slipped through the British blockade to reach Ålesund in Norway. And from there Studt, and the rest of the *Karlsruhe*'s survivors, reached Germany early in December, to the consternation of the *Admiralstab,* which had just signalled Köhler to 'return home; your work is done'.

If Berlin could remain in ignorance of the *Karlsruhe*'s unhappy end for more than a month, it is not surprising that Whitehall heard nothing for another two. Be this as it may, the rounding-up of the *Dresden* left only one of the German warships, which had been at large at the outbreak of the war, to be accounted for. At the end of July 1914, Captain A. D. Looff had taken the *Königsberg,* a similar ship to the *Leipzig,* out of Dar-es-Salaam in German East Africa, to elude both Pierse's East Indies Squadron and Rear-Admiral Herbert King-Hall's Cape Squadron. Fortunately, the former soon had other commitments; the only Allied ships that could be spared to search for the *Königsberg* in the western part of the Indian Ocean were King-Hall's old and slow cruisers *Astraea*, *Hyacinth* and *Pegasus*. And, of these, the first dealt Looff a shrewd blow almost at the outset: appearing off Dar-es-Salaam early on 8 August, Captain A. C. Sykes not only destroyed the W/T station by gunfire, but frightened the harbour-master into scuttling the floating-dock across the entrance. The *Königsberg* was thus denied both her communication link and access to the only German port in the area.

For this, however, Looff was to have his revenge. After spending a week on the trade routes off Aden, where he sank the 6,000-ton SS *City of Winchester*, he turned his ship south for a safe anchorage in the delta of the Rufigi; and there, in mid-September, he learned that the *Pegasus* had arrived at Zanzibar to clean her boilers. At first light on the 20th, the armed tug, which Commander John Ingles placed on guard off this island, was surprised before she could give the alarm, so that one of the *Pegasus*'s officers, who was sleeping on deck, was suddenly awakened at 0515 by

two shells screaming over my head. I flew forward to my station in the top, to see the *Königsberg* about four miles away firing like mad. Our men dashed to their stations, but shells were falling fast and did fearful execution. Our guns [eight 4-inch] were soon at it, but could not reach her by 1,000 yards. Suddenly a shot pitched 20 yards in front of me, throwing spray right over the topmast. Then the fore control told me they could get nothing through to the guns, so I shouted to the after control to take over. But by now all our guns had ceased firing, and I heard someone say, 'Surrender!' I shouted, 'No surrender'; but a few seconds later several voices said, 'Captain's order, sir': and I saw the white flag was up. Before the Germans could see this, they fired nine more rounds. Although water was gushing in, we contrived to stop it partially with a mat; but the ship went on listing. So I lowered all boats and put all hands on to getting the wounded ashore.

It was then a question whether we were prisoners of war, but as the *Königsberg* had steamed away I considered we were not. As the ship appeared to be sinking, the Captain gave the order to abandon her, but when we were about 50 yards away the steamer *Kilwa* came along, and I begged to be allowed to go back, so that the ship could be towed down harbour to a sandspit where we grounded her. But as the shore was very steep she slipped off. Although the engagement had lasted barely 15 minutes, the time was about 1300 when, soon after this, the *Pegasus* capsized. We had 102 casualties; 42 killed and the rest wounded. The Captain was undoubtedly right to haul down the flag. What else could we do? We could not reach the *Königsberg* with our old guns, and we had no steam: it was useless going on against such hopeless odds.

From this success the *Königsberg* returned to the Rufigi delta. Her engines needed a major overhaul, for which the parts had to be sent overland to the workshops of Dar-es-Salaam. By the time they were returned, Looff's ship had been located by the light cruisers *Chatham*, Captain S. R. Drury-Lowe, *Dartmouth* and *Weymouth*, which the Admiralty had detached from troop convoy escort duty to ensure that the *Königsberg* did not again strike such a blow to Britannia's pride. But although the task of finding her occupied these ships for only ten days, her destruction was to take many months. The humid mangrove swamps concealed the *Königsberg* so well that these three light cruisers' gunfire was ineffective from seaward, whilst a bar that could only be crossed at high water springs, and an improvised minefield, deterred them from making a closer approach. For the moment they could do little more than maintain a blockade to ensure that their cornered prey did not escape. Realizing, however, that the Admiralty could ill afford to employ three modern ships on this wearisome task, Drury-Lowe converted the collier *Newbridge* into a blockship. And on 10 November he sent her, with an escort of armed steamboats, into the branch of the delta which led to the *Königsberg*'s lair. Despite heavy artillery fire from both banks, Commander R. Fitzmaurice of the *Chatham* succeeded in sinking his charge in her planned position. Unfortunately this success only made it more difficult for the *Königsberg* to put to sea; Looff could still work his ship out through another channel. But the German Captain was well aware that any such move would mean swift nemesis for his ship; whereas for as long as he kept the Imperial naval ensign flying, for so long would he keep several British cruisers from operating against Germany elsewhere. Instead of attempting to escape, he moved the *Königsberg* farther up the Rufigi, where she could be made impregnable against all orthodox forms of attack.

In December Drury-Lowe tried to get at her with aircraft, but the only two RNAS machines that were available to him were soon damaged beyond repair. Early in the New Year, more for *amour propre* than strategic sense, the *Admiralstab* decided that the *Königsberg* should attempt to return home. But first she needed fuel. In the long nights of February, the collier *Rubens* broke out of the North Sea – only to be intercepted by the *Hyacinth*, in which King-Hall was coming north to take charge of the Rufigi operations. The *Königsberg*'s ultimate fate was then settled by the redoubtable von Lettow-Vorbeck, German Army Commander in East Africa; Looff was required to land as many of his crew as he could spare to help with the defence of this German colony. He kept only 220 officers and men, enough to ensure that his ship did not fall into enemy hands, but not enough to take her to sea.

In April King-Hall tried further attacks with aircraft of No 7 Squadron RNAS, but to no avail. The Admiralty then, at last, agreed to a proposal which Drury-Lowe had put forward in November: two shallow-draught monitors, the *Severn* and *Mersey*, each armed with two 6-inch guns, left Britain for East Africa. On 6 July 1915 these vessels, under the command of Commander Eric Fullerton, crossed the bar and steamed up the tortuous channels of the Rufigi. Despite fierce fire from both banks, they reached a point which was supposed to be 10,000 yards from the *Königsberg*, where they should have been within effective range of their own guns, but beyond that of the enemy's smaller-calibre weapons. But the charts proved misleading; when the monitors opened fire at 0630, with aircraft to spot their fall of shot across the dense mangrove jungle, the German light cruiser replied with broadsides. And these were so effective that, in little more than an hour, a damaged *Mersey* was obliged to withdraw; and in another two hours Fullerton had to concede that the *Severn* had also failed.

But this was Looff's final fling. A week later, having completed repairs, the two monitors tried again. This time, Fullerton's flotilla carried out a five-hour bombardment, eventually closing to 7,000 yards. When they ceased fire at 1420, the *Königsberg* had been reduced to a battered wreck, which was then abandoned by the wounded Looff and the surviving members of his crew.

The destruction of the *Königsberg* brought down the curtain on the war in the far seas. No German warship was ordered out from Kiel or the Jade to raid the trade routes. Von Tirpitz's battleships and battlecruisers lacked the endurance for operations outside the North Sea, and the High Seas Fleet was too short of light cruisers to spare any of these. A number of merchant ships were, however, converted into AMCs, with their guns, torpedoes and mines concealed beneath the trappings of their peacetime status. For the best part of two years, Allied cruisers had to be employed searching for these marauders, and in providing escorts against their attacking troop convoys. They were, however, never more than a nuisance, sinking little shipping, Britain having an abundance of cruisers with which to counter them.

Germany's conspicuous failure to continue the war in the wide oceans is well illustrated by the careers of five of these vessels. The *Moewe*, of 4,798 tons, armed with four 5·9-inch guns and four 19·7-inch torpedo tubes, and carrying 300 mines, left Hamburg in December 1915. A four months' cruise in the South Atlantic was followed by another beginning in November 1916, from which Commander Count zu Dohna returned with a total bag of 34 Allied merchant ships, and the pre-dreadnought *King Edward VII* which was sunk on a mine he laid off Cape Wrath. The *Moewe*'s record was, however, exceptional. The *Greif*, of similar size and armament, was sunk in February 1916 by the light cruiser *Comus* and the AMCs *Andes* and *Alcantara*, two days after leaving Germany for her first cruise – though not before Commander Tietze had dispatched the *Alcantara*. The *Wolf* sailed in December 1916, to lay mines off the Cape, and land ammunition that would enable von Lettow-Vorbeck's beleaguered garrison to hold out until the end of the war. But Commander Nerger's subsequent cruise in the Indian Ocean brought him a total bag of only 12 Allied ships. One of the *Moewe*'s prizes, the British SS *Yarrowdale*, was given a concealed armament of five 5·9-inch and four 3·4-inch guns plus two torpedo tubes, and renamed *Leopard*. But Commander von Laffert's attempt to elude the British blockade was no more successful than Tietze's; as his ship tried to break out of the North Sea in March 1917, she was intercepted by the armed boarding vessel *Dundee* and sunk by the cruiser *Achilles*.

The luckiest of these raiders was the 25-year-old, ertswhile American *Pass of Balmaha*, a 1,571-ton sailing vessel captured by *U36* and renamed *Seeadler*. Disguised as the Norwegian SS *Rena*, she was intercepted by British patrols to the north of the Shetlands; but the boarding party discovered neither her two 4·1-inch guns nor her two torpedo tubes; nor did they realize that Lieutenant-Commander Count Felix von Luckner's unusually large Norwegian-speaking crew were Germans to a man. She was allowed to pass the Allied blockade, to operate first in the South Atlantic, then in the Pacific. But though the *Seeadler* proved an armed sailing vessel's ability to avoid detection, she also showed how small were her chances of achieving much. Von Luckner had the advantage of being an officer of the German naval reserve with many years' experience of the ways of merchant ships, especially in Far East waters. He had, too, the luck to be away from the *Emden*, which he joined in August 1914, in charge of one of von Müller's prizes at the time that this light cruiser fell a victim to HMAS *Sydney*. Nonetheless, he was never the 'sea devil' that he afterwards flamboyantly claimed: on the contrary, he provided the tamest of curtains to Act One of the war at sea when, after sinking only ten Allied ships, he wrecked his ship on the Fiji Islands in August 1917.

Appendix C

Particulars of the ships involved at Coronel and the Falklands

Ship	Type	Year of completion	Displacement (tons)	Guns (with max. range in yds)	Designed speed (knots)	Principal armour	Commanded by	Complement
BRITISH Canopus	Battleship	1900	12,950	4 12" (13,500) / 12 6" (10,000)	18·5	6" belt / 12" barbettes / 8" turrets	Captain H. S. Grant	750
Inflexible	Battle-cruisers	1908	17,250	8 12" (16,400) / 16 4"	25·5	6" belt / 7" barbettes / 7" turrets	Captain R. F. Phillimore	
Invincible		1909					Captain T. P. H. Beamish / Flagship of Vice-Admiral / Sir Doveton Sturdee	780
Carnarvon	Armoured cruiser	1904	10,850	4 7·5" (12,000) / 6 6" (11,200)	22	6" belt / 6" barbettes / 5" turrets	Captain H. L. d'E. Skipwith / Flagship of Rear-Admiral / A. P. Stoddart	650
Cornwall	Armoured cruisers	1904		14 6" (11,200)	23	4" belt / 5" barbettes / 5" turrets	Captain W. M. Ellerton	675
Kent		1903	9,800				Captain J. D. Allen	
Monmouth		1903					Captain F. Brandt	

Ship	Type	Year of completion	Displacement (tons)	Guns with max. range in yds)	Designed speed (knots)	Principal armour	Commanded by	Complement
Defence	Armoured cruiser	1908	14,600	4 9·2" (12,500) 10 7·5" (12,500)	23	6" belt 7" barbettes 6–8" turrets		755
Good Hope	Armoured cruiser	1902	14,100	2 9·2" (12,500) 16 6" (11,200)	24	6" belt 6" barbettes 5" turrets	Captain P. Francklin *Flagship of Rear-Admiral* Sir Christopher Cradock	900
Bristol	Light cruisers	1911	4,800	2 6" (11,200) 10 4" (9,800)	26	None	Captain B. H. Fanshawe	450
Glasgow							Captain J. Luce	
GERMAN *Gneisenau*	Armoured cruisers	1907	11,600	8 8·2" (13,500) 6 5·9" (11,200)	22·5	8" belt 6" barbettes 6½" turrets	Captain Maerker	765
Scharnhorst							Captain F. Schultz *Flagship of Vice-Admiral* von Spee	
Dresden	Light cruiser	1909	3,650	10 4·1" (10,500)	24·5	None	Captain Lüdecke	360
Leipzig	Light cruiser	1906	3,250	10 4·1" (10,500)	22	None	Captain Haun	290
Nürnberg	Light cruiser	1908	3,550	10 4·1" (10,500)	24·5	None	Captain K. von Schönberg	320

ACT TWO

Home Waters

7

First Blood

> The British battle fleet is like the queen on the chess board; it may remain at the base but it still dominates the game. It is the final arbiter at sea; to lose it is to lose the game.
>
> *Admiral of the Fleet Lord Chatfield*

The scene changes; from the far seas to Home waters, from cruiser warfare to the opposing battle fleets. When the British Home Fleet reached its war station on 1 August 1914, it had been under the command of the 62-year-old Admiral Sir George Callaghan for nearly three years. Next day, Vice-Admiral Sir John Jellicoe, who was seven years his junior, arrived at Scapa Flow, knowing that 'in certain circumstances' he might be appointed C-in-C. He had already protested to Churchill and Battenberg against the command being changed on the eve of war: now he signalled: 'You court disaster if you carry out your intention. Fleet is imbued with loyalty for C-in-C.' But both First Lord and First Sea Lord were 'doubtful as to Callaghan's health and physical strength being equal to the immense strain that would be cast upon him': early on the 4th Jellicoe was ordered to open a sealed envelope containing his appointment to the supreme command of an armada to which was given the historic title of Grand Fleet. This left him no alternative but to proceed onboard the *Iron Duke* where, 'a signal having been received ordering the fleet to sea, Sir George arranged to leave before its departure at 0830'.

Son of a master mariner, Jellicoe had first achieved distinction as a specialist in gunnery. He had narrowly escaped death on three occasions: from a horde of hostile *fellaheen* after the bombardment of Alexandria (1882); from the *Victoria* when she was sunk in collision with the *Camperdown* (1893); and when the international naval brigade failed to relieve the Peking legations (1900). He had been one of Fisher's 'brains' who helped to design the *Dreadnought*. His skilful administration when Third Sea Lord had done much to ensure that Britain maintained her battleship strength over Germany. As a flag officer afloat he had shown exceptional ability in handling a fleet before returning to the Admiralty to be Second Sea Lord in 1912, by which time there were very few in the Navy who questioned Fisher's wisdom in grooming him to be 'Nelson at Cape St Vincent until he becomes boss at Trafalgar when Armageddon comes'. No one realized that he 'had all the Nelsonic virtues save one'; that he was 'totally lacking in the great gift of insubordination.' No one could foresee that he was one of those great men of war whose avenging sword would be blunted too soon by advancing years and the burden of great responsibilities.

To the 20 dreadnoughts that formed the core of the Grand Fleet when Jellicoe hoisted his flag in the *Iron Duke*, two more were soon added, giving a margin of eight over the enemy's 14. Germany had, however, some 20 older battleships available, so the Admiralty augmented the Grand Fleet with a squadron of eight 'King Edwards' from Britain's 32 pre-dreadnoughts. Jellicoe also had a larger number of cruisers and destroyers, whilst against Germany's four battle-cruisers (including the hybrid *Blücher* which mounted nothing larger than twelve 8·2-inch guns), he had five under Vice-Admiral Sir David Beatty in the *Lion*. Twelve years younger than his C-in-C, this sprig of the Anglo-Irish gentry had won the DSO on the Nile (1896). He, too, was wounded in the Boxer rebellion, when his outstanding services gained him captain's rank at the exceptional age of 29. But he then spent so much time ashore that he reached the top of the list without the necessary qualifications for flag rank. Fisher swept this obstacle aside; in 1910, by special Order in Council, Beatty became the youngest admiral since Nelson. Even so, his subsequent refusal to serve as second-in-command of the Atlantic Fleet would have terminated his career, but for a chance meeting with Churchill who persuaded him to become his Naval Secretary. And in the next fifteen months the First Lord realized that Beatty 'viewed naval strategy and tactics in a different light from the average naval officer. His mind had been rendered quick and supple by polo and the hunting field. I had no doubt, when command of the Battlecruiser Squadron fell vacant in 1913, in appointing him over the heads of all.' Inevitably this roused jealousy, but Beatty soon proved that he could lead these great ships with all the dash that characterized him in the saddle. He had, too, the extrovert *panache* that Jellicoe lacked; the rakish angle of his cap and his unorthodox six-button jacket became as well known as 'Monty's' battledress and beret. In many other ways he was the antithesis of his C-in-C, but there was no discord between them – at least not until after 31 May 1916. Though Jellicoe paralleled his own lack of 'the great gift of insubordination' with the firmest of control over his Battle Fleet, he had the wisdom to ride the commander of his cavalry on the lightest of reins, to which Beatty responded with the loyalty of a trusted surbordinate.

If, then, the Grand Fleet was both stronger than the High Seas Fleet, and commanded by two such redoubtable men as these, why did nearly two years elapse before they clashed in battle? The strategy of close blockade with which Cornwallis and Nelson confined Ganteaume, Latouche-Tréville and Villeneuve in Brest and Toulon was no longer possible. Coal-fired ironclads could not remain at sea for more than a week before they must refuel: minefields kept them away from enemy harbours; submarines, against whose unseen presence there was no adequate defence, could sink a battleship with a single torpedo. Bridgeman and Battenberg had, therefore, evolved a new strategy of distant blockade. The High Seas Fleet was to be confined to the North Sea by a fleet based on Scapa Flow, which the Admiralty believed to be beyond the range of Germany's U-boats. Light cruisers and destroyers at Harwich, under Commodore Reginald Tyrwhitt, whose conspicuous ability was to gain him the unique distinction of retaining the same command throughout the war, would clear the southern North Sea of enemy light craft and minelayers. And a Channel Fleet of 17 pre-dreadnoughts would close the Straits of Dover. But, though blockade was the proper strategy for the stronger Navy, the ultimate aim remained – to bring the enemy fleet to battle and destroy it, as Hawke had done when Conflans slipped out of Brest and was driven into Quiberon Bay. And the Admiralty expected to achieve this as early as August 1914, because von Tirpitz had so often boasted that he had built the High Seas Fleet to break Britain's paramount power. Before Whitehall's ultimatum expired, Jellicoe was ordered out of Scapa for the first of a series of sweeps across the North Sea, in the confident hope that the German battle fleet would also sortie to prevent the British Expeditionary Force crossing the Channel.

But September came without the German heavy ships leaving the Heligoland Bight. For all his bellicosity von Tirpitz's authority was circumscribed. Admiral von Pohl's *Admiralstab* was responsible for naval operations, not the Secretary of the Navy's *Reichsmarineamt*; and von Pohl was chiefly concerned to avoid displeasing a Kaiser

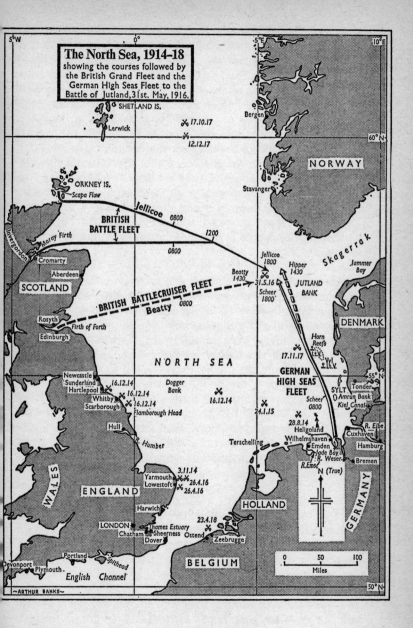

The North Sea, 1914–18

showing the courses followed by
the British Grand Fleet and the
German High Seas Fleet to the
Battle of Jutland, 31st. May, 1916.

SHETLAND IS.

✠ 17.10.17

✠ 12.12.17

60° N

NORWAY

Bergen

Lerwick

ORKNEY IS.

Scapa Flow

Stavanger

Jellicoe 0800

BRITISH
BATTLE FLEET

1200

Invergordon

Moray Firth

0800

Cromarty

Jellicoe
1800

Hipper
1430

Jammer
Bay

Skagerrak

Aberdeen

SCOTLAND

Beatty
1430

31.5.16

Scheer
1800

JUTLAND
BANK

BRITISH BATTLECRUISER FLEET

Beatty 0800

DENMARK

Rosyth

Firth of Forth

Edinburgh

NORTH SEA

Horn
Reefs

L.V.

17.11.17

55° N

GERMAN
HIGH SEAS
FLEET

SYLT

Tonder

Newcastle

Sunderland

Hartlepool 16.12.14

Dogger
Bank

16.12.14

Amrun Bank

Whitby ✠ 16.12.14

Kiel Canal

Scarborough ✠ 16.12.14

16.12.14

✠ 24.1.15

Scheer
0800

Flamborough Head

R. Elbe

Hull

28.8.14

Heligoland

Cuxhaven

Wilhelmshaven

Hamburg

R. Humber

Terschelling

Emden

Jade Bay

Bremen

R. Weser

R.Ems

N (True)

3.11.14

Yarmouth

26.4.16

Lowestoft 26.4.16

WALES

ENGLAND

Harwich

HOLLAND

GERMANY

LONDON

Chatham

Thames Estuary

Sheerness

Dover

23.4.18

Ostend

Zeebrugge

BELGIUM

0   50   100

Miles

Devonport

Portland

Spithead

Plymouth

English Channel

50° N

~ARTHUR BANKS~

who had as little understanding of sea power as Napoleon. Confident that Paris would quickly fall to his Army, the Emperor would not hazard his Navy against a Fleet that 'had the advantage of looking back over a hundred years of proud tradition which must have given every man a sense of superiority based on the great deeds of the past'. The High Seas Fleet was only to go beyond the Horn Reefs–Terschelling line 'if a favourable opportunity to strike offers itself': otherwise it was to wage 'guerilla warfare until we achieve such a weakening of the English Fleet that we can safely send out our own'. An inferiority complex was not, however, the only reason for the Kaiser's insistence on a 'fleet in being'. Von Tirpitz and von Pohl supposed that the British would attempt a close blockade, which would enable them to reduce the Grand Fleet's superiority by mines and torpedoes; they also believed that the High Seas Fleet should be conserved to prevent a British landing on Germany's North Sea coast.

Small groups of German lightcraft did, however, make two sorties across the southern North Sea, on 21 and 23 August, which decided the Admiralty to approve an *ad hoc* plan of retaliation devised by the commander of the 8th Submarine Flotilla, the spirited Commodore Roger Keyes. Tyrwhitt's Harwich Force would raid the enemy's patrols in the Heligoland Bight at dawn on 28 August. This should do more than inflict damage on a flotilla of torpedo-boats, supported by a couple of light cruisers; it ought to draw German heavy ships out of the Jade to where seven 'D' and 'E' class submarines, of 600–800 tons, armed with 18-inch torpedo tubes, would be lying in wait to the north and west of Heligoland, under Keyes's control in the destroyer *Lurcher*, with the *Firedrake* in company. But, as so often happens in war, things didn't quite work out that way. Jellicoe wanted the whole Grand Fleet to join in, but the Admiralty would not risk more than the BCS and Commodore W. E. Goodenough's 1st LCS – and failed to inform Tyrwhitt and Keyes that these would be taking part, as they also omitted to tell Beatty and Goodenough that British submarines would be on the scene. Fortunately, Tyrwhitt's ignorance was remedied, just in time, by a chance encounter between his force and Goodenough's squadron at first light on the 28th.

From this meeting 70 miles to the north of Heligoland, Tyrwhitt in the *Aresthusa*, a new light cruiser with a mixed armament of two 6-inch and six 4-inch guns, led 16 destroyers of the 3rd DF towards Germany's island fortress, followed by Captain W. F. Blunt in the light cruiser *Fearless*, armed with ten 4-inch guns,* with 15 boats of the 1st DF. Goodenough in the *Southampton*, with five more 'Town' class light cruisers, all but one armed with eight or nine 6-inch guns, was in close support eight miles astern. Beatty's five battlecruisers, the *Lion, Queen Mary* and *Princess Royal*, each with eight 13·5-inch guns, and the *Invincible* and *New Zealand*, with eight 12-inch guns apiece, awaited developments 40 miles to the NW.

Shortly before 0700 Tyrwhitt sighted torpedoboats *G194* and *V187*, two of the patrolling German flotilla that were hunting one of Keyes's submarines. He at once opened fire and gave chase, as the enemy sought safety in a mist that limited visibility to under five miles. This brought the British force within range of the expected German light cruisers, the 4·1-inch-gunned *Stettin* and the older *Frauenlob*, with whom the *Arethusa* and *Fearless* had a sharp engagement, around 0800, close to the west of Heligoland. When the *Frauenlob*'s bridge was destroyed by a 6-inch shell, the Germans withdrew behind this fortress – but not before one of them had inflicted damage to the *Arethusa*'s engine room. Tyrwhitt's force then began its planned sweep to the west, which brought it into further contact with patrolling units of the 1st TBF. And again these fled into the mist, except for their leader, *V187*, which was cut off from her base. According to one of her officers,

> the enemy fire was very heavy. At 0905 both turbines were hit. When Captain Lechler was severely wounded beside me, I gave the order to prepare explosive charges, then took the helm myself, hoping to ram the last destroyer in the enemy line; but the rudder could not be put hard over, and the boat was moving too slowly. All ammunition being expended, I ordered the explosive charges to be fired and the crew to abandon ship. *V187* sank with her flag flying. The English destroyers lowered boats to rescue her crew. I was picked up by the *Lizard* and well cared for.

A German cruiser appeared before the *Defender* could rehoist one of her boats, but Lieutenant-Commander E. W. Leir surfaced submarine *E4* and rescued the castaways.

There followed the first consequences of the Naval War Staff's inadequate orders. Keyes sighted Goodenough's squadron and reported them as enemy cruisers, with the result that Tyrwhitt turned back to help the *Lurcher* and *Firedrake*, and ordered the 1st LCS

---

* For further details of these two cruisers and of other ships involved in this action, see Appendix D on pp 139–40.

to chase the newcomers – in effect to chase themselves. Fortunately, Keyes soon identified the *Southampton* – though not before one of his submarines had made an unsuccessful torpedo attack on her. Moreover, when Goodenough signalled that he was withdrawing from an area in which he now knew Keyes to be operating, in order to avoid the danger of a further similar incident, Beatty accepted the risk of ordering him back to Tyrwhitt's support, as the latter's force resumed its delayed sweep to the west.

Beatty's courage was rewarded. At 1100 the partially crippled *Arethusa* was engaged by the twelve 4·1-inch guns of the *Strassburg*, the first of several light cruisers to leave harbour in response to reports of Tyrwhitt's raid. The 1st DF drove her off into the mist. The *Mainz* then appeared out of the Ems and was chased to the north until, at 1145, according to one of her officers,

> masses of smoke were suddenly seen from three 'Birmingham' class cruisers. The *Mainz* turned hard a-starboard as their salvoes fell close aboard, but she soon received her first hit. Our fire was directed on these new opponents as we headed SSW at 25 knots, making heavy smoke. Then another 'Birmingham' class cruiser appeared to port and, further forward, six destroyers. In our action with these the rudder was jammed by an underwater hit and, although the port engine was stopped, the *Mainz* slowly turned to starboard until she was again within range of the first three cruisers. By 1220 most of our guns and their crews were out of action.

'The *Mainz* was immensely gallant,' wrote one of Tyrwhitt's officers. 'The last I saw of her she was absolutely wrecked, her whole amidships a fuming inferno. She had one gun forward and one aft still spitting fury and defiance, like a wild cat mad with wounds.' But when she 'received a torpedo hit on the port side amidships, the Captain ordered "abandon ship" and left the conning tower, to be killed outside. Then the English ships ceased firing and, with great energy, began fishing survivors out of the water. One destroyer [Keyes's *Lurcher*] was able to come alongside and take our wounded aboard before the *Mainz* turned over to port and sank at 1310.'

An hour before this, Tyrwhitt was faced with a fresh threat: his force was engaged by the *Cöln*, flagship of Rear-Admiral Maass, commander of all the High Seas Fleet's torpedoboats, who had hurried out of Wilhelmshaven towards 'the sound of the guns'; also, for the second time, by the *Strassburg*. Both German light cruisers were driven off, but only after they had inflicted serious damage on the *Laertes*, *Laurel* and *Liberty*, of the 3rd DF. And there was worse to come: at 1230 three more German light cruisers, the *Stralsund*, the *Danzig* and the old *Ariadne* which had been completed back in 1901, appeared together with the *Stettin*, all armed with ten or twelve 4·1-inch guns. Tyrwhitt and Blunt did not hesitate to engage them, but with the *Arethusa* and three destroyers already crippled, it seemed that the Harwich Force would be overwhelmed.

An hour earlier, however, to quote Beatty,

signals received at 1125, 1128 and 1130 [from Tyrwhitt and Blunt] were the first news we [in the *Lion*] had since 0955 as to the movements of the flotillas, or the result of an action which had been in progress for three and a half hours. The situation appeared extremely critical; the flotillas had advanced on their sweep only ten miles since 0800, and were only 26 miles from an enemy base in their rear. With another base 25 miles on their flank, there was a possibility of a grave disaster. At 1130 I decided that the only course possible was to take the BCS at full speed to the eastwards. To be of any value the support must be overwhelming, and I did not deem the 1st LCS to be strong enough. I had not lost sight of the danger to my squadron from U-boats, mines, our own submarines, and the possible sortie of a large enemy force.

'Am I justified in going into that hornets' nest with these great ships?' Beatty asked his Flag Captain. 'If I lose one it will be a great blow to the country.' A. E. Chatfield's advice was very different to that which Wray had given Troubridge less than a month before. 'Surely we must go,' he said, which decided Beatty to take a calculated risk, whereby he enjoyed the success that attends the bold. By 1135 the BCS was heading ESE at full speed to Tyrwhitt's rescue: 'by steaming hard the *Lion* fairly flew at 28 knots', and soon after 1230

there straight ahead of us [wrote an officer of one of Tyrwhitt's hard-pressed destroyers] in lovely procession, like elephants walking through a pack of 'pi-dogs', came our battlecruisers. How solid they looked, how utterly earth-quaking! We pointed out our latest aggressors to them and they passed down the field of battle. And we went west while they went east, and a little later we heard the thunder of their guns.

Two salvoes sent the *Cöln* to the bottom, with Admiral Maass, his Flag Captain and all but one of her crew. The *Ariadne* was only a shade more fortunate: according to one of her officers,

> the *Lion* and another English battlecruiser fired at us for about half an hour at ranges from 6,000 down to 3,000 yards, scoring many hits that started numerous fires which could not be extinguished because the fire mains were destroyed. Towards 1330 the enemy turned away to the west. I assume that he could no longer make out the *Ariadne* through the smoke from the fires. It was impossible to remain onboard because of the smoke and heat, and because the ready-use ammunition began to explode. So the crew assembled on the forecastle, and three cheers were given for the Kaiser, after which *Deutschland über Alles* was sung. Then, shortly before 1400, the *Danzig* approached and sent boats for the wounded. The rest of the crew jumped overboard and swam to the *Danzig* and the *Stralsund*. When the fires died down, and the explosions became less frequent, I requested the Captain of the *Stralsund* to take the *Ariadne* in tow. But at 1510 she heeled over to port and capsized. Our losses were 59 dead and 43 wounded.

The mist that veiled the *Ariadne*'s last hour saved the *Danzig*, *Stralsund*, *Stettin* and *Strassburg* from a like fate, the last of these being especially fortunate. When Beatty lost contact with the enemy soon after 1300, he signalled the whole British force to retire, so that Tyrwhitt's damaged vessels could make good their withdrawal before German heavy ships appeared on the scene. Soon after the BCS then turned for home, they sighted a lone warship at a range as short as 8,000 yards. She was the *Strassburg*; but because most German light cruisers had only three funnels, her four misled Beatty's ships to suppose that she might be one of Goodenough's 'Town' class. By the time they decided to challenge her identity, she had disappeared into the haze that played so large a part throughout the battle.

The whole Harwich Force, including Tyrwhitt's severely damaged flagship and the destroyer *Laurel*, both of which had to be taken in tow, limped safely home. So, too, did Keyes's flotilla withdraw from a hornet's nest without further incident. But an eventful day might have finished otherwise had the celerity with which as many as six German light cruisers hurried to sea to reinforce the patrolling *Frauenlob* and *Stettin* been paralleled by Rear-Admiral Franz Hipper's 1st SG. The battlecruisers *Blücher*, *Moltke*, *Seydlitz* and

Von der Tann, all lying in Wilhelmshaven Roads, were ordered to raise steam as early as 0820, the last named being ready to weigh by 1015. She was, however, told to await the *Moltke* which was not ready until 1210. And if these ships were then too late to prevent Beatty sinking the *Ariadne*, how vain was Hipper's subsequent attempt to pursue the BCS, because it was after 1500 by the time his flagship, the *Seydlitz*, which had to await the tide before she could cross the bar, and the *Blücher* joined their consorts.

The action was a clear British victory; three German light cruisers and one torpedoboat sunk, with the loss of more than 1,000 officers and men, at the cost of one light cruiser and three destroyers damaged, but soon repaired, and less than 50 casualties. And the hero of the day was Beatty; in him the spirit of Nelson lived again. The raid had, however, been too near a disaster to be repeated. Keyes's plan was exposed as rash; his attempt to control a flotilla of submarines by hazarding a couple of destroyers in such dangerous waters was ineffective. And the Admiralty learned the need to issue clearer orders for future operations in the North Sea, both to ensure the cooperation of all forces taking part and to avoid losing a British ship to a torpedo from one of their own submarines. But there was another lesson, of fateful consequence to the future, which the Germans marked but were careful to conceal; that British shells were of such poor quality that many broke up on impact, so that instead of penetrating and dealing death blows, they often inflicted no more than superficial wounds.

The Germans learned much else from the Imperial Navy's first sea battle. An outer patrol line of U-boats, 60 miles from Heligoland, was needed to give advance warning of any further British incursion, and more defensive minefields were laid to ensure that these were an effective obstacle. The torpedoboat patrol and its supporting light cruisers would not risk another engagement with possibly superior enemy forces; it would retire immediately under the guns of Heligoland, the enemy being dealt with by whole squadrons of adequate strength, not by light cruisers and heavier ships hurrying to sea in 'penny numbers' as each raised steam. More important than these professional lessons, however, was the moral effect of such a defeat, which was, in von Tirpitz's words, 'fateful in its after-effects on the work of our Navy'. As the 'miracle on the Marne' put paid to the Kaiser's expectations of an early victory on land, he accepted the Heligoland Bight action as confirmation that the British Fleet was still imbued with the offensive spirit that had triumphed in the Napoleonic wars; and he amplified his restrictive instructions to make clear that his own Fleet was 'to hold itself back and avoid actions which can lead to greater losses'.

There was, also, another very different reason why the Grand Fleet did not again venture a similar battle. The ramming of *U15* by the light cruiser *Birmingham* gave Jellicoe evidence as early as 9 August that German submarines might be able to operate in the northern part of the North Sea. More ominously, on 1 September one was reported inside Scapa Flow. Though subsequently dismissed as false, this was soon shown to be possible. On 23 November, *U18* penetrated the Pentland Firth and Hoxa Sound. Her periscope was sighted, and she was rammed by patrolling destroyers, forcing Lieutenant-Commander von Hennig to surface his boat, to save the lives of his crew by surrendering east of the Pentland Skerries. He had found no targets for his torpedoes because the 1 September alarm convinced Jellicoe that the Admiralty was wrong in believing the Orkneys beyond U-boat range. Until Scapa's defences were strengthened, he must move his base to Loch Ewe; and, when a U-boat was reported there on 7 October, to the more remote Loch Swilly. This Irish harbour was, however, so far from the North Sea that the Grand Fleet could only use it to coal; otherwise it had to remain at sea, with the consequence that its ships were increasingly subject to defects. Indeed, by the end of October, when Jellicoe had 23 dreadnoughts and seven battlecruisers under his command, four were refitting, two were under repair after being in collision, and the *Audacious* had been sunk by a single mine. Moreover, for so long as there were enemy cruisers abroad, the Admiralty might detach battlecruisers to counter them, as with the *Invincible, Inflexible* and *Princess Royal* after Coronel. Since the competent but uninspired Admiral von Ingenohl could always plan a sortie for a day when all his 16 dreadnoughts and five battlecruisers were available, the effective strength of the Grand Fleet was no more than that of the High Seas Fleet. Nor was this all: to his conviction, derived from his years at the Admiralty, that the German dreadnoughts were, ship for ship, better built than the British (to be confirmed by *Goeben*'s survival after striking three mines, as related in Chapter Two, whereas the *Audacious* succumbed to one), Jellicoe added a healthy respect for the fighting qualities of the Imperial German Navy, on the evidence of the *Mainz*'s gallantry in the Heligoland Bight.

All this led the British C-in-C to inform the Admiralty on 30 October 1914 that

20 British pre-dreadnought *Canopus*

21 British light cruiser *Glasgow*

22 German light cruiser *Dresden*

23 British 'Lion' class battle-cruisers

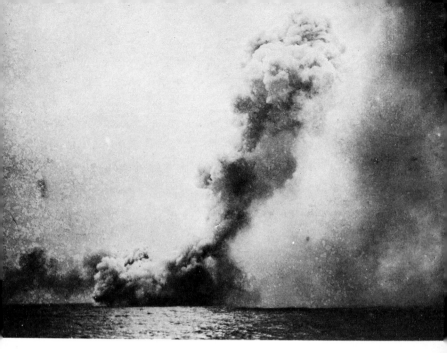

24 Destruction of the *Queen Mary*

25 British 'Orion' class dreadnoughts

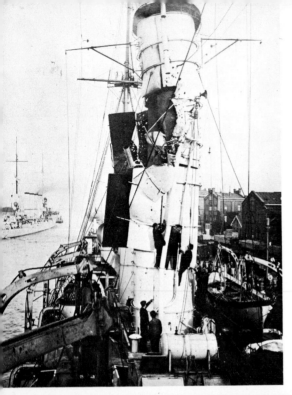

26 *Frauenlob* after Heligoland Bight action

27 German heavy cruiser
Blücher sinking at the
Dogger Bank battle

experience of German methods makes it possible to consider the manner in which they are likely to be used tactically in a fleet action. They rely to a great extent on submarines, mines and torpedoes, and they will endeavour to make the fullest use of these. However, they cannot rely on having their full complement of submarines and minelayers in a fleet action unless the battle is fought in the southern North Sea. My object will therefore be to fight the fleet action in the northern portion of the North Sea.

There would be no battle unless the High Seas Fleet ventured further out than, unknown to the Admiralty or Jellicoe, the Kaiser would allow. Jellicoe's strategical conclusion was paralleled by his tactical ones; submarines with the German battle fleet

can be countered by judicious handling of ours, but will probably involve a refusal to move in the invited direction. If the enemy turned away from us, I should assume the intention was to lead us over mines and submarines, and decline to be drawn. This might result in failure to bring an enemy to action as soon as is expected and hoped, but with new and untried methods of warfare, new tactics must be devised. These, if not understood, may bring odium upon me, but it is quite possible that half our battle fleet might be disabled by underwater attack before the guns opened fire at all. The safeguard will consist in moving to a flank before the action commences. This will take us off the ground on which the enemy desires to fight, and may result in a refusal to follow me; but if the battle fleets remain in sight of one another, I should feel that, after an interval of high-speed manœuvring, I could safely close.

To submit such cautious ideas to an Admiralty that was not only about to arraign Troubridge before a court martial but was headed by men so offensively minded as Churchill and Fisher, showed moral courage. For had Jellicoe been a student of history, he would have remembered that Britain has seldom achieved victory at sea by material might. At St Vincent Jervis had only 15 sail-of-the-line against Spain's 27. In the words of the German Vice-Admiral Livonius: 'It was the genius of her captains and admirals which produced Britain's glorious victories.' Nor could Jellicoe claim that steam and steel had reduced the importance of the human factor, because Togo had annihilated a stronger force at Tsushima. However, although Admiral Sir A. K. Wilson argued the difficulties of submarines operating tactically with a surface fleet, the Admiralty assured Jellicoe 'of their full confidence in your contemplated conduct of the fleet in action'. Fisher was, in truth, more interested in a scheme for ending the deadlock in Flanders which had captured Churchill's imagination: they were planning an armada of 600 vessels to land an army on the Baltic coast only 90 miles from Berlin, with no effective Naval Staff to advise them against anything so foolhardy. And although this was superseded, in the year and a half that elapsed before Jutland, by the Gallipoli campaign, which led to the First Lord and the First Sea Lord being relieved by Balfour and Admiral Sir Henry Jackson in May 1915, neither the Admiralty nor Jellicoe altered their ideas of how the Grand Fleet should be employed. 'I take the fullest responsibility for approving the answer proposed by the First Sea Lord,' wrote Churchill. 'There was no reason in the first phase of the naval war for seeking a battle except in the best conditions, but I do not accept any responsibility for the actual conduct of Jutland which took place in conditions of relative strength different from those which existed in October 1914.'

Comment on Jellicoe's tactics is best reserved until later; but there was wisdom in his decision not to be drawn into the southern North Sea. Such caution might not accord with tradition, but no previous British admiral had had to contend with mines and submarines. Destruction of the enemy is not to be sought without regard for the consequences of failure, inability to maintain command of the sea by blockade. Churchill's oft-quoted words, that Jellicoe was 'the only man on either side who could lose the war in an afternoon', may have been an exaggeration: but the reverse of this comment was anything but true. A decisive British victory over the High Seas Fleet would have done little towards weakening the German Army's stranglehold on the Continent of Europe – though it would have released destroyers to combat the U-boats and, perhaps, allowed British squadrons to penetrate the Baltic.

Be this as it may, although Jellicoe's caution, combined with the Kaiser's restrictions, delayed a major clash for nearly two years, there were several lesser engagements. On 17 October four German torpedoboats were wiped out whilst attempting to lay mines off the Thames. And when von Ingenohl pressed to be allowed to retaliate, the *Admiralstab* replied that, whilst 'the battle fleet must avoid heavy losses, there is nothing to be said against the battle-cruisers trying to damage the enemy'. So, on 3 November the German C-in-C sent Hipper's 1st SG to bombard Yarmouth. This fishing port was too far south for the Grand Fleet to reach the scene in time, and Tyrwhitt also failed to intercept the German force as it retired from a venture which cost them the large armoured cruiser *Yorck* on one of their own defensive mines at the mouth of the Jade. But as a consequence of this, Beatty's battle-cruisers were moved south to Cromarty, and Vice-Admiral Brad-ford's 'King Edward VIIs' to Rosyth. Moreover, since submarines patrolling off Heligoland had proved an unreliable substitute for the frigates that Nelson stationed off Cadiz to report enemy ships leaving port, a chain of direction-finding stations was erected to locate their W/T transmissions. And this source of intelligence was soon supplemented by a more fruitful one: from the cruiser *Magdeburg*, wrecked in the Gulf of Finland on 26 August, salvaged copies of the German Navy's codes were sent to London, and by December Room 40 OB (Old Admiralty Building) was able to de-cipher enough German signals to give warning of future sorties by the High Seas Fleet.

From the Falklands battle von Ingenohl learned that at least two of Beatty's battlecruisers were away in the Atlantic. Such an opportunity to inflict damage on a weakened Grand Fleet was not to be missed. Room 40 learned that he intended his battlecruisers to raid the Yorkshire coast at dawn on 16 December – but not that the German Battle Fleet would be out in support. Jellicoe was in-structed to send no more than Vice-Admiral Warrender's 2nd BS and Rear-Admiral Pakenham's 3rd CS south to join Beatty's four battlecruisers, Goodenough's 1st LCS and Tyrwhitt's Harwich Force, when these were ordered to sea. The Admiralty's under-estimation of the enemy's strength was, however, more than com-pensated by the German C-in-C's reaction to a dawn contact, in squally weather south of the Dogger Bank, between his torpedo-boats and Beatty's destroyers. Whilst Beatty was deterred from pursuing what he supposed to be no more than a detached flotilla, by reports that German heavy ships had appeared off the Yorkshire coast, von Ingenohl believed that he was about to run into the whole Grand Fleet. Fearful of the All Highest's wrath, he reversed course at 0545 and hurried back to the Jade, although this turned the snare he had planned for his opponent into a trap for his own battle-cruisers.

By the time that the light cruiser *Kolberg* had laid her mines off Filey, the *Derfflinger* and *Von der Tann* had fired on the undefended seaside resorts of Scarborough and Whitby, and the *Seydlitz*, *Moltke* and *Blücher* had inflicted greater damage on the port of Hartlepool, their three possible escape routes through the east coast minefields were barred by Warrender's 2nd BS and Tyrwhitt's force to the south, Beatty's battlecruisers in the centre, and Bradford's 3rd BS to the north. Hipper chose the centre gap for his retirement, and there his ships were duly sighted by Goodenough in the *Southampton* shortly before noon. Since she was wing ship of a light cruiser screen ahead of the British battlecruisers, the *Birmingham*, *Nottingham* and *Falmouth* swung round to their Commodore's support – until Beatty signalled, 'Resume station'. He intended this to apply only to the *Nottingham* and *Falmouth*; but his order was passed to all four light cruisers, with the lamentable consequence that the *Southampton* and *Birmingham* quickly lost touch with the enemy. However, all was not yet lost: soon after this the *Orion*, flying the flag of Rear-Admiral Sir Robert Arbuthnot, second-in-command of Warrender's squadron, sighted Hipper's light cruisers and destroyers through a gap in the rain squalls. His Flag Captain, F. C. Dreyer, 'put our guns on the leading light cruiser, and asked Sir Robert's permission to open fire, but he said, "No, not until the Vice-Admiral signals 'open fire'." But the German force had hauled away to the northward before Warrender saw them and our golden moment had been missed.'

Hipper's 1st SG was thus able to slip through the British net, with the help of typical North Sea winter weather, a signal error by Beatty's flagship (Beatty's Flag Lieutenant was not a signal specialist), and Goodenough's and Arbuthnot's belief in rigid obedience to superior orders, which had been misguidedly bred by the Victorian Navy in the last decades of a century of peace. On Beatty such missed opportunities 'left a mark which nothing can eradicate except total destruction of the enemy. We were within an ace of accomplishing this. Our advanced ships had sighted them! I can't bear to write about it.'

Appendix D

Particulars of principal ships involved in the Heligoland Bight action

Type	Name	Year of completion	Displacement (tons)	Main armament	Designed speed (knots)	Notes
BRITISH Light cruisers	*Arethusa*	1914	3,510	{ 2 6" 6 4" }	29	Broad pendant of Commodore R. Tyrwhitt
	Fearless	1913	3,350	10 4"	26	Captain W. F. Blunt
	Southampton	1912	5,400	8 6"	25·5	Broad pendant of Commodore W. E. Goodenough
	Birmingham	1914	5,440	9 6"	25·5	
	Nottingham	1914	5,440	9 6"	25·5	
	Lowestoft	1914	5,440	9 6"	25·5	
	Falmouth	1911	5,250	8 6"	25·5	
	Liverpool	1910	4,800	{ 2 6" 10 4" }	26	
Battlecruisers	*Lion*	1912	26,350	8 13·5"	27	Flag of Vice-Admiral Beatty
	Queen Mary	1913	27,000	8 13·5"	28	
	Princess Royal	1912	26,350	8 13·5"	27	
	Invincible	1909	17,250	8 12"	25·5	Flag of Rear Admiral Moore
	New Zealand	1912	18,800	8 12"	26	

APPENDIX D – continued

Type	Name	Year of Completion	Displacement (tons)	Main armament	Designed speed (knots)	Notes
GERMAN Light cruisers	Stettin	1907	3,550	10 4·1"	24	
	Frauenlob	1903	2,700	10 4·1"	21·5	
	Strassburg	1912	4,550	12 4·1"	28·5	
	Mainz	1909	4,360	12 4·1"	26·5	SUNK
	Cöln	1911	4,360	12 4·1"	26·5	Flagship of Rear-Admiral Maass. SUNK
	Stralsund	1912	4,550	12 4·1"	28·5	
	Danzig	1907	3,280	10 4·1"	22	
	Ariadne	1901	2,660	10 4·1"	21·5	SUNK

8

The Long Wait

The battle of Dogger Bank – The bombardment of Lowestoft

We were haunted by the fear that possibly 'the day' might never come.

Vice-Admiral Sir David Beatty

British public opinion condemned the bombardment of Hartlepool, Scarborough and Whitby, which killed 122 innocent civilians and wounded 433, as characteristic Hun brutality. The Admiralty was also criticized for the Navy's failure to prevent such a dastardly attack on Britain's east coast. So Beatty's battlecruisers were moved yet further south, from Cromarty to Rosyth, shortly before Christmas 1914, where they should be even better placed to intercept a further raid.

Jellicoe's margin of strength was now at its nadir: though Beatty had five battlecruisers to match Hipper's four, plus the *Blücher*, the British C-in-C had no more than 18 dreadnoughts plus eight pre-dreadnoughts to pit against a possible 17 dreadnoughts and a score of older battleships. That the Germans should make another sortie early in the new year, after a British raid on Cuxhaven by planes from the seaplane-carriers *Engadine*, *Riviera* and *Empress* had been thwarted by one of the worst gales in living memory, was therefore no surprise. On 23 January 1915, Hipper's 1st SG (less the *Von der Tann*, in dockyard hands) left the Jade, accompanied by the 2nd SG of four light cruisers, and two flotillas of torpedoboats, with orders to raid the British Dogger Bank patrols and fishing fleet at dawn next day. Room 40 gave enough warning of this for the Admiralty to take well-judged and properly coordinated counteraction. Beatty's battlecruisers, now organized in two squadrons, the 2nd being under the command of Rear-Admiral Sir Archibald Moore with his flag in the *New Zealand*, accompanied by Goodenough's 1st LCS, were ordered to rendezvous with Tyrwhitt's Harwich Force of three light cruisers and two-and-a-half destroyer flotillas, at 0700 on the 24th in a position which should be between

Hipper's force and its base. Bradford's 3rd BS and Pakenham's 3rd
CS would be 40 miles to the NW, to intercept Hipper if he turned
north; and Jellicoe was allowed to bring his Battle Fleet south in
support, although it could not reach the area before the afternoon.

Events proved the accuracy of the Admiralty's intelligence. As
the *Lion*, leading the *Tiger* and *Princess Royal*, followed by the *New
Zealand* and *Indomitable*, made their appointed rendezvous with
the *Arethusa* to the NE of the Dogger Bank, the *Aurora*, another
of Tyrwhitt's light cruisers which was spread 12 miles to the south,
reported sighting the *Kolberg*. Hipper began to close this wing ship
of his light cruiser screen, until he received reports of smoke from
further British ships to the NW. Rather than risk an engagement
with what he believed to be a squadron of British battleships, he
then turned SE for home, albeit without increasing to the *Blücher*'s
maximum speed of 23 knots. Beatty had, meantime, reacted to the
Aurora's brief engagement with the order to chase, so that by 0730
Goodenough, five miles ahead of the *Lion*, had the German battlecruisers in sight. Half an hour more and Beatty, whose 1st BCS had
worked up to 27 knots, leaving the 2nd BCS trailing astern at 25,
saw his quarry on the horizon. Although the visibility was extreme,
the Germans suffered the disadvantage of the weather gauge – there
was a fair breeze from the NE: smoke pouring from the funnels of
the *Seydlitz* (flag), *Moltke*, *Derfflinger* and *Blücher* prevented Hipper
identifying his pursuers until 0840, by which time the range was
down to 25,000 yards, and it was too late to avoid battle.

At 0900 the *Lion* opened fire on the *Blücher*, and was soon joined
by her consorts, to which the 1st SG replied by concentrating on the
British flagship. As Beatty continued to overhaul the enemy, he
ordered his heavy ships to engage their opposite numbers, intending
the *Seydlitz*, *Moltke* and *Derfflinger* to be the targets of the 13·5-
inch-gunned *Lion*, *Tiger* and *Princess Royal*, leaving the *Blücher* to
be dealt with by the 12-inch-gunned *New Zealand* and *Indomitable*.*
But the *Tiger*'s Captain H. B. Pelly supposed that, with five ships
against four, two should concentrate on the leading enemy vessel.
For some fifteen minutes the 11-inch-gunned *Moltke* was left with
no ship engaging her, and the *Tiger*'s fire on the *Seydlitz* was ineffective because she spotted the *Lion*'s shell splashes as her own.
However, to a young officer in the *Aurora*,

it was wonderful to see our battlecruisers steaming at top speed
with spurts of flame and brown smoke issuing every minute or so

* For further details of the battlecruisers of both sides involved in this battle
see Appendix E on p 154.

from their bows and sides – and in the far distance the enemy's guns flashing in reply. From shots falling in the water there were tall columns of white spray. From others there was, more ominously, no splash as they scored a hit which caused black smoke and bright flashes from the injured craft. It was all very exciting: to make a long story short – they got HELL!

At 0930, with the range still as much as 17,500 yards, the *Lion* scored a success that was as fateful in its consequences for this action as it was to be at Jutland a year and a half later. To quote von Ingenohl:

> A 13·5-inch shell pierced the barbette armour of the aftermost turret of SMS *Seydlitz* at the level of the working chamber. The charges being brought up were ignited by the explosion, the flash shooting upwards into the gunhouse and downwards into the magazine, in both places setting fire to charges being delivered to the guns. The magazine crew tried to flee forward by opening the doors into the handing room of the adjacent turret, so that the flash set fire to the charges there and spread to the adjacent magazines and upwards as far as the gunhouse. Thus the crews of both turrets were killed by one hit.

And, but for the prompt action of the *Seydlitz*'s executive officer in flooding both magazines, it is unlikely that the ship would have survived.

Hipper's reaction to this near-disaster was an urgent appeal to von Ingenohl to bring his Battle Fleet to the rescue; but with the Jade some 150 miles away, it must be several hours before it could intervene – hours in which much could happen. By 0950 the *Seydlitz* was not the only severely damaged German ship: the *Blücher* was also badly battered. The British went largely unscathed until shortly after 1000 when the *Lion* was hit by three 12-inch shells from the *Derfflinger*, of which one pierced her port feed tank, slowing her engines, with the result that, as Beatty ordered his battlecruisers to 'proceed at your utmost speed', the *Lion* began to lag behind. A quarter of an hour later the *Blücher*'s speed was down to 17 knots, and Hipper turned south 'to commence a circling action which would have supported her. But since two of the *Seydlitz*'s turrets were out of action, since there was a lot of water in the ship aft, and since only 200 rounds of main armament ammunition remained, I decided that this was likely to lead to heavy losses. So I turned again to SE' – and left the *Blücher* to her fate.

With Beatty ordering the *Indomitable* to intercept her, and his other ships to 'close the enemy as rapidly as possible', it seemed that the British would score an annihilating victory. The *Lion* might be unable to keep up, but the *Tiger*, *Princess Royal* and *New Zealand* had the advantage of several knots speed over the damaged *Seydlitz*, the *Moltke* and the *Derfflinger*; so that these three German battlecruisers should not be able to escape from the devastating fire of the heavier British guns. But this was not to be; at 1050 the *Lion* received a further hit which put her remaining dynamo out of action, and deprived her of all means of signalling except by flags. Ten minutes later Beatty saw what he believed to be a submarine's periscope on his flagship's starboard bow. Suspecting a U-boat trap, he ordered his squadron to turn away, 90 degrees to port. Then he realized that so large a turn would open the range too much, and told Ralph Seymour to hoist 'Course NE', to limit the turn to 45 degrees. So far so good — but only so far. When the *Lion* had dropped so much astern of her consorts that Beatty was near to losing all control of the battle, he gave a further order: 'Attack the enemy's rear.' Seymour hoisted this when the flags for 'Course NE' were still flying, so that both were read together as meaning: 'Attack enemy bearing NE'. And because this was the *Blücher*'s bearing, Moore supposed that he was to deal with her: the *Tiger*, *Princess Royal* and *New Zealand* swung round to join the *Indomitable* in completing the destruction of the Germans' lame duck. At a loss to understand why his hounds were pursuing a false scent, Beatty made one last attempt to give them a fresh lead. He ordered Seymour to hoist, 'Engage the enemy more closely', only to learn that, since Trafalgar, this had been expunged from the signal book and replaced by the uninspired euphemism, 'Keep nearer the enemy'. This was, however, of no consequence: the *Lion*'s flags could not now be read by any of Beatty's ships except the destroyer *Attack*. Ordering her alongside, the Admiral jumped aboard and went after the rest of his force, but it was noon by the time he could rehoist his flag in the *Princess Royal*.

From *L5*, the only zeppelin on reconnaissance over the North Sea that day — of which Hipper made no use to check his belief that Beatty's battlecruisers had a squadron of dreadnoughts at their back — Lieutenant-Commander Heinrich Mathy saw

a tremendous picture, although we could hear almost nothing of the thunder of the guns, because of the noise of our engines. The *Blücher* was left behind as our forces steamed off and she was unable to follow. The four English battlecruisers fired at her together. She replied for as long as she could, until she was completely shrouded in smoke and apparently on fire. At 1207 she heeled over and capsized. We then observed the enemy's withdrawal, and followed our forces as rearguard. You can imagine how distressing it was for me to watch the *Blücher* capsize, and be helpless to do anything but observe and report. We didn't drop bombs on the English ships. We had no chance because the clouds were at 1,300 feet. If we had dared to fly over them at this altitude, we would have been shot down.

The *Blücher* sustained hits by seven torpedoes in addition to more than 70 shells before she sank, by which time the rest of Hipper's fleeing force was over the horizon, leaving Beatty in a position, to quote Seymour's words, 'like trying to win the Derby after a bad fall at Tattenham Corner'. There was nothing more that he could do except ensure that the *Lion* was taken in tow by the *Indomitable*, and escorted safely home to lick her wounds in Rosyth Dockyard.

'The sinking of the *Blücher* and the flight, after heavy injuries, of the other German ships was a solid and indisputable result', wrote Churchill. The British casualties were limited to 15 killed and 80 wounded, whereas the Germans lost 954 killed, with 80 wounded, and 189 prisoners saved by British destroyers despite machine-gun fire from the heartless pilot of an interloping seaplane from Borkum. But it would have been a more decisive victory if Beatty had not been deprived of control at the critical juncture, and if Moore had not chosen to destroy one already crippled cruiser, instead of continuing in pursuit of the main enemy force. He 'ought to have gone on, had he the slightest Nelsonic temperament in him, regardless of signals. In war the first principle is to disobey orders. Any fool can obey,' wrote Fisher. But, like all his contemporaries, Beatty's second-in-command had been schooled to implicit obedience. Moreover, Beatty had contributed to Moore's conduct: his signal, 'Attack the enemy's rear', was as unnecessary as it was open to misinterpretation. For this reason he refrained from condemning Moore, leaving the Admiralty to remove him quietly from the Grand Fleet. But a court martial would have done more to drive home the lesson that, for the second time in two months, the Grand Fleet had lost the chance of inflicting a decisive defeat through a flag officer complying too rigidly with superior orders instead of using his own judgement and initiative. Again, too, there were serious signal mistakes from which Beatty failed to realize the need to acquire a flag lieutenant on whom he could depend for the accurate transmission of his orders.

In sharp contrast the Germans were quick to profit from the near-loss of the *Seydlitz*. Around the turn of the century there was a significant change in warship gun-turret design. In the *Canopus* and earlier pre-dreadnoughts (including their foreign contemporaries because most of these were the product of British brains), the powder charges were lifted up each turret trunk in a single hoist from magazine to gunhouse (see diagram, p 148). To safeguard the ammunition stowed in the magazines from the flame from an explosion passing down the trunk, the magazines were fitted with self-sealing revolving scuttles through which the charges were passed to the hoist. But in the 'Formidable' and later classes, these scuttles were omitted: instead, the charges were lifted up the trunk to a working chamber, which was intended to prevent the flame from an explosion passing down the trunk, and there transferred to a second hoist which raised them to the gunhouse (see diagram, p 148). Unfortunately, those who conceived this change had little understanding of the flash-like qualities of the flame from an explosive fire, as von Ingenohl's advisers discovered from the burnt-out after turrets in the *Seydlitz*: to quote from his report:

> The working chamber is a danger to the entire turret. In all new construction it must be eliminated. Shell and propellant hoists must be equipped with doors which close automatically after the cages have passed. The charges must be delivered to the guns in a flame-proof covering. The doors connecting the magazines of adjacent turrets must be secured with padlocks to prevent premature opening, the key must be in the custody of the turret officer and the order to open only given when all the turret's ammunition has been fired [and it is necessary to obtain ammunition from the adjacent turret].

So, whilst the Royal Navy remained in ignorance of this serious defect in the turrets of all its dreadnought battleships and battlecruisers, Germany had time enough to correct it in hers before the High Seas Fleet's next encounter with the Grand Fleet. But against this advantage must be set Germany's failure to learn another lesson of potentially greater importance. Von Ingenohl might write: 'It must be considered a remarkable coincidence that our cruisers should encounter the enemy precisely at dawn. It appears as if the enemy had intelligence concerning the operation.' But the *Admiralstab* replied: 'Not apparent by what means,' and recommended additional precautions against the possibility of there being a British agent 'who is supposed to be a German in Kiel who usually passes on his messages through inconspicuous newspaper advertisements'. Room 40 remained the best-kept secret of the war.

The loss of the *Blücher* was, in one sense, Fisher's victory. By keeping secret the design of his first battlecruisers, he misled von Tirpitz into believing that they were no more than large armoured cruisers against which a vessel with twelve 8·2-inch guns would suffice. The 11-inch-gunned *Von der Tann* was not completed until two-and-a-half years after the *Invincible*, with the consequence that von Ingenohl could only organize an adequate 1st SG by including a ship that was no more a match for the British 12-inch and 13·5-inch weapons than the *Scharnhorst* and *Gneisenau* had been. For this reason, and in the light of the Kaiser's insistence that the High Seas Fleet should avoid battle with a superior force, Hipper was not made a scapegoat for the disaster. To quote Captain von Egidy of the *Seydlitz*:

> The plans for the operation did not take into account the likelihood of English warships being in the North Sea. The 24th has demonstrated how precarious a situation battlecruisers can find themselves in when sent into battle without the Battle Fleet's support. If we had known that our main body was behind us, Hipper would not have been forced to abandon the *Blücher*: we could have saved this ship, just as the English saved the *Lion*.

Captain Zenker, who, like many other German officers, could not forgive von Ingenohl for failing to press on and destroy Warrender's 2nd BS on 16 December 1914, was much more severe in a memorandum to von Pohl:

> The blame for such an unfavourable result lies with the C-in-C. His belief that the English fleet was coaling in Scapa Flow is not a valid justification for making no provision for an encounter with stronger enemy forces. Our previous advances to the English east coast have had such an effect on English public opinion that it should have been expected that strong forces would be in the North Sea. Also from previous experience, it should have been no surprise to find that the enemy had warning of our sortie. Such lack of foresight and prudence is all the more astonishing and regrettable because the C-in-C has already been excused for the defeat on 28 August [the Heligoland Bight action]; and in the

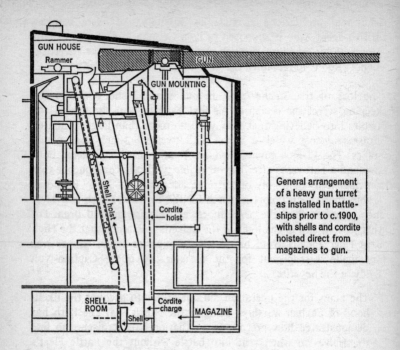

GUN HOUSE
Rammer
GUN
GUN MOUNTING
Shell hoist
Cordite hoist
SHELL ROOM
Shell
Cordite charge
MAGAZINE

General arrangement of a heavy gun turret as installed in battleships prior to c.1900, with shells and cordite hoisted direct from magazines to gun.

BATTLESHIP TURRETS

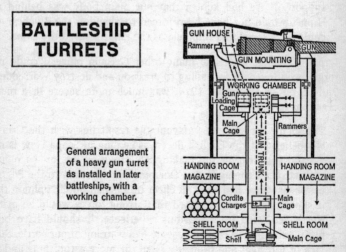

GUN HOUSE
Rammer
GUN
GUN MOUNTING
WORKING CHAMBER
Gun Loading Cage
Main Cage
Rammers
MAIN TRUNK
HANDING ROOM MAGAZINE
HANDING ROOM MAGAZINE
Cordite Charges
Main Cage
SHELL ROOM
Shell
SHELL ROOM
Main Cage

General arrangement of a heavy gun turret as installed in later battleships, with a working chamber.

two operations against the English east coast only luck enabled him to avoid painful consequences. The only way to avoid further disasters from such obstinate inflexibility is to change the C-in-C.

The Kaiser agreed: to no avail was von Ingenohl's plea that the 1st SG must have sunk one British battlecruiser: he was ordered to strike his flag, and von Pohl was appointed in his place, the Emperor being well assured that he was a man who would not urge further sorties that would hazard the larger ships of the High Seas Fleet.

The Dogger Bank battle also had repercussions on the British side. Jellicoe moved one of his battle squadrons south to Cromarty; and Beatty's Rosyth force was strengthened to seven battlecruisers and three light cruiser squadrons (including Goodenough's which was renumbered the 2nd), that were now known as the Battlecruiser Fleet. Moreover, on 23 March Jellicoe addressed these prophetic lines to Beatty:

> I imagine the Germans will try to entrap you by risking their battlecruisers as a decoy. They know that the odds are that you will be 100 miles away from me, and can draw you down to the Heligoland Bight without my being in effective support. This is all right if you keep your speed, but if some of your ships have their speed badly reduced in a fight with their battlecruisers, or by submarines, their loss seems inevitable if you are drawn into the High Seas Fleet with me too far off to extricate them before dark. The Germans know you very well and will try to take advantage of that quality of 'not letting go when you have once got hold', which you possess, thank God. But one must concern oneself with the result to the country of a serious decrease in relative strength. If the game looks worth the candle the risks can be taken. If not, one's duty is to be cautious. I believe you will see which is the proper course, and pursue it victoriously.

A year was, however, to elapse before the Germans sprang the trap of which Jellicoe so percipiently warned his subordinate. The British battle fleet was increased to 27 dreadnoughts, the German strength remaining at 17, and the Battlecruiser Fleet grew into three squadrons of nine battlecruisers, the 1st SG being augmented only by the *Lützow*. So von Pohl refrained from sending his battle fleet farther than the Horn Reefs, even when Jellicoe added raids on the Skagerrak to his periodical sweeps across the North Sea.

The first month of 1916 brought a significant change in Germany's fortunes: von Pohl was found to be mortally ill and, under strong pressure from many senior naval officers, the Kaiser appointed in his place the more aggressive, offensive-minded Vice-Admiral Reinhard Scheer. Four years younger than Jellicoe, his advancement had been slow: he did not outshine his contemporaries until appointed to command a torpedoboat flotilla at the turn of the century. But thereafter he had risen to be Chief of Staff in the High Seas Fleet before the war; to command the pre-dreadnoughts of the 2nd BS in 1914; and subsequently the dreadnoughts of the 3rd BS. In him the High Seas Fleet gained a vigorous leader of undoubted talent, ability and experience; and Jellicoe was faced with an opponent as doughty as Hipper had already proved himself to be of Beatty.

Nor was Scheer slow to unsheath his sword. As early as February 1916, a British minesweeping flotilla, operating near the Dogger Bank, was overwhelmed by German light forces which made good their escape before Beatty and Tyrwhitt could reach the area. In the same month the zeppelins of the High Seas Fleet intensified their night raids on Britain. But neither of these operations satisfied von Falkenhayn's demands for the Imperial Navy to mount an offensive that would compel the Allied armies to relax their grip on Verdun. On 23 February 1916, the Kaiser agreed that the High Seas Fleet should undertake operations designed to trap and overwhelm weaker elements of the Grand Fleet. And as soon as March Scheer sent his cruisers out, with two battle squadrons in support – but the Admiralty learned of their sailing too late to order the Grand Fleet to sea to intercept. Ten days later the Harwich Force escorted the seaplane-carrier *Vindex* to the entrance to the Skagerrak for an attack on the zeppelin sheds at Tondern, from which Tyrwhitt's retirement was delayed by two collisions between his ships. As Scheer left the Jade intent on their destruction, Beatty sped south to their rescue. Early on the 26th it seemed that the Battlecruiser Fleet would meet the German Battle Fleet without Jellicoe's support; but a rising gale decided Scheer to return to harbour rather than risk battle in a storm.

The High Seas Fleet next put to sea on 21 April in the erroneous belief that Tyrwhitt was about to make a second attack on Tondern. Room 40 gave enough warning for Jackson to order the Grand Fleet out; but before Jellicoe could reach the Skagerrak, Scheer concluded that Tyrwhitt's attack had been postponed and returned to the Jade. Jellicoe held on until his Battlecruiser Fleet ran into a dense fog, in which the battlecruisers *Australia* and *New Zealand* were in collision, obliging Beatty to return to Rosyth; and in which the dread-nought *Neptune* collided with a neutral merchant vessel, and three destroyers were likewise crippled, so that Jellicoe was back at Scapa early on the 24th.

His ships were still refuelling when he received news of the Easter Rebellion in Dublin, and a warning that a sympathetic move by the High Seas Fleet was expected. Scheer planned a bombardment of Lowestoft designed to draw British units into the maw of the whole High Seas Fleet. He suffered an early setback when the *Seydlitz* was mined soon after putting to sea on the 24th; but he did not allow the need for Rear-Admiral Boedicker to transfer his flag to the *Lützow* (Hipper was away ill) to delay his advance towards the English east coast. However, this incident involved the exchange of a number of urgent W/T messages from which an alert Room 40 learned what was afoot. At 1950 the whole Grand Fleet was ordered to sea. So, too, was the Harwich Force, Tyrwhitt being given a specific position in which to intercept the enemy. Fortunately, the Commodore judged this to be misconceived and, with the Nelsonic gift of insubordination that so many others lacked, ignored the Admiralty's orders and headed towards Lowestoft. He was re-warded at first light (0350) on the 25th by sighting the four German battlecruisers, which he tried to entice to the south in pursuit. But Boedicker was not to be deflected from his objective: at 0410 he began a ten-minute bombardment which destroyed 200 of Lowestoft's houses. He then swung north to make a similar attack on Yarmouth. This time Tyrwhitt's tactics succeeded: the German battlecruisers had no sooner opened fire than Boedicker had to respond to an urgent call for support from his light cruisers. He might have destroyed his spirited but puny opponent; he chose to retire his whole force eastwards towards Scheer's Battle Fleet which had already (0520) reversed course for home. Tyrwhitt went after him until 0845 when the Admiralty, fearful of the outcome of a contest recalling that between David and Goliath, called off the chase – with the unfortunate consequence that Beatty, who was coming south at full speed, also turned for home, just when Boedicker's Scouting Groups were within 45 miles of the Battle-cruiser Fleet.

Jellicoe retaliated on 3 May by sailing two forces, the one to lay mines off the German swept channels, the other to make a second attack on Tondern, with his Battle Fleet and the Battlecruiser Fleet in support, in the hope that these operations would draw the High Seas Fleet. But the minelaying went undetected, and all but one of the carrier-borne seaplanes of the infant Royal Naval Air Service were unable to take off in the prevailing swell. Moreover, Scheer's attentions were diverted by the need to succour eight of his zeppelins which chanced to be returning from a raid on Britain; not until late on 4 May did he realize that the Grand Fleet was out, by which time Jellicoe had ordered his ships to return to port.

The German Chancellor cited the Lowestoft raid as evidence that Britain no longer held command of the sea. In Britain 'the impunity with which the enemy had insulted our east coast' so shocked public opinion that the First Lord, now Arthur Balfour, promised a further redeployment of the Fleet. To protect the Thames approaches against such a raid, Bradford's 3rd BS, of pre-dreadnoughts plus the *Dreadnought* herself, was moved south to an anchorage in the estuary. And Jellicoe's Battle Fleet was to be moved down to Rosyth, from Scapa and Cromarty, as soon as the anti-submarine defences of the Firth of Forth could be extended to cover so large a number of ships. Pending this, the Battlecruiser Fleet was to be strengthened by the 4th or 5th BS. At the same time, Beatty, who shared Jellicoe's concern at the lack of facilities for practice firings at Rosyth, was to send his battlecruisers in turn to Scapa. This last decision was, however, taken too late to do more than improve the gunnery of one of his squadrons before the High Seas Fleet's next sortie.

This chapter and the last one have marked the different strategies of the two Navies, sketched the characters and qualities of their principal leaders, and said something of the merits and shortcomings of their ships and methods. Another important difference remains to be mentioned. To the British the gun was the decisive weapon. To Jellicoe, a gunnery specialist, the overriding purpose of his battlecruisers and cruisers was to enable his battle fleet to gain contact with the enemy's battle fleet with which he intended to fight a gun duel on parallel courses, initially at 15,000 yards so as to be outside torpedo range but decreasing to 10,000, all under his flagship's close control. His destroyers' chief purpose was, likewise, to use their guns to beat off enemy torpedoboat attacks. Except that the 5th BS would be stationed where its higher speed might enable it to turn the enemy line, preferably in the van, there was little left in his *Grand Fleet Battle Orders* of the flexible concept of a battle that he had embodied in the war orders that he had produced in 1912 whilst second-in-command of the Home Fleet, in which he fully recognized 'the whole art of tactics, amassing superior forces against part of the opposing fleet'. The German Navy, on the other hand, being of such recent creation as to be unhampered by the traditional dominance of the gun, believed that the torpedo should be decisive. For Scheer, a torpedo specialist, his battlecruisers and cruisers had the task of enabling his Battle Fleet to gain contact with a part of the Grand Fleet whilst avoiding the whole of it. His battleships would only fight a gun duel if they encountered a weaker enemy force; if they met a stronger one they would retire under cover of smoke. And his torpedoboats' prime duty was to attack the enemy battle fleet with torpedoes. Moreover, Scheer did not intend his U-boats or minelayers to operate with his Battle Fleet, in contradistinction to Jellicoe's expectations.

In short, the British and German concepts of a fleet action were as incompatible as their differing strategies. As the latter had prevented a clash between the Grand Fleet and the High Seas Fleet for the best part of two years, so was the former likely to deprive Jellicoe of a decisive victory when they did meet, unless he managed to manœuvre his opponent into a position from which he could not evade the British dreadnoughts' heavier broadsides. Moreover, Jellicoe depended on clear weather and contact sufficiently early in the day to allow a prolonged action. Poor visibility would favour Scheer's design of inflicting damage on an inferior British force, just as contact late in the day would facilitate his escape from a more powerful one under cover of darkness.

All this should be remembered in judging the achievements of Jellicoe and Scheer when, on 31 May 1916, the fortunes of war allowed four months of lunge and counter-lunge to culminate in a clash between the two fleets.

Appendix E

Particulars of Battlecruisers at the Dogger Bank Battle

Name	Year of completion	Displacement (tons)	Main armament		Armour	Designed speed (knots)	Notes
BRITISH							
Lion	1912	26,350	8	13·5"	9" belt	27	Flag of Vice-Admiral Beatty
Tiger	1914	28,500	8	13·5"	9" turrets	28	
Princess Royal	1912	26,350	8	13·5"		27	Flag of Rear-Admiral Moore
New Zealand	1912	18,800	8	12"	6" belt	26	
Indomitable	1908	17,250	8	12"	7" turrets	25·5	
GERMAN							
Seydlitz	1913	25,000	10	11"	12" belt 10" turrets	27	Flag of Rear-Admiral Hipper
Moltke	1911	23,000	10	11"	10·5" belt 9" turrets	25·5	
Derfflinger	1914	26,600	8	12"	12" belt 10·5" turrets	26	
Blücher	1909	15,840	12	8·2"	7" belt 7" turrets	25	SUNK

9

Beatty versus Hipper

Jutland: the battlecruiser action

On the afternoon of Wednesday 31 May a naval engagement took place off the coast of Jutland. The British ships on which the brunt of the fighting fell were the Battlecruiser Fleet supported by four fast battleships.

Admiralty communiqué, 2 June 1916

From the bombardment of Lowestoft Scheer learned an important lesson: that although this operation had 'forced the enemy to send out his forces', the High Seas Fleet had crossed the North Sea too far south to trap any part of Jellicoe's fleet. He designated Sunderland, much farther to the north, as the next target for Hipper's battlecruisers, on 17 May 1916. But this plan would only be executed if Scheer's zeppelins reported that the Grand Fleet was not already at sea for some sweep of its own; and if as many as 17 U-boats were able to decimate Jellicoe's and Beatty's strength by laying mines off the British bases, and by torpedoing any units seen to leave them.

Too late to recall these submarines, Scheer learned that the *Seydlitz* would be undergoing repairs for longer than he had expected; moreover, seven ships of his 3rd BS developed condenser defects. The operation was, therefore, postponed to the 23rd, when *U47* reported Sunderland clear for the attack. Unfortunately, the *Seydlitz* was still not ready, which required Scheer to order a further postponement, this time to 29 May, which was very near to the last day his U-boats could remain on patrol. By this time, too, British patrols had destroyed *U74*; another boat had developed leaks in her tanks, compelling her to return with her mines unlaid; *U75* had laid hers to the west of the Orkneys (where, on 5 June, they were destined to sink the cruiser *Hampshire* when she was carrying Kitchener on a mission to Russia); and although *UB27* managed to penetrate the Firth of Forth, her Captain's plan to torpedo the Battlecruiser Fleet at anchor was foiled by the anti-submarine nets off Inchkeith. As a consequence of these and other vicissitudes, only four U-boats remained in positions where they could sight the Grand Fleet leaving harbour. So, when adverse winds prevented zeppelins taking the air on 30 May, Scheer decided to execute a less risky, alternative plan. His fleet would draw the British by attacking merchant shipping to the west of the Skagerrak, and by showing itself off the SW coast of Norway, for which purpose all units were to assemble in the outer Jade by 2000.

The 1st SG, of five battlecruisers with Hipper's flag in the *Lützow*, sailed at 0200 next morning, accompanied by the 2nd SG, of four light cruisers under Boedicker in the *Frankfurt*, and 30 torpedoboats of the 2nd, 6th and 9th flotillas, led by Commodore Heinrich in the light cruiser *Regensburg*. These were followed by Rear-Admiral Behncke in the *König* heading the seven dreadnoughts of the 3rd BS; by Scheer himself in the *Friedrich der Grosse*, leading Vice-Admiral Schmidt's eight dreadnoughts of the 1st BS; and by Rear-Admiral Mauve in the *Deutschland* with five more pre-dreadnoughts of the 2nd BS – the inclusion of these last ships which, with their slow speed and limited gunpower, would be a serious handicap if Scheer ran into Jellicoe's Battle Fleet, being a last-minute decision compounded of Mauve's protests against being left behind to guard the Heligoland Bight and of his C-in-C's sentimental regard for his old command. The three battle squadrons were accompanied by the 4th SG of five light cruisers under Commodore von Reuter in the *Stettin*, and by Commodore Michelsen in the light cruiser *Rostock*, leading 32 torpedoboats of the 1st, 3rd, 5th and 7th flotillas. By 0800 on 31 May Scheer's Battle Fleet was following 50 miles astern of Hipper's force, up the swept channel towards the Horn Reefs in fine weather that was marred only by a NW breeze (which was to back to SW later in the day) of sufficient force to prevent his fragile zeppelins leaving their sheds.*

Meantime, in the third week of May, Rear-Admiral the Hon Horace Hood's 3rd BCS had gone north to Scapa for gunnery practices, Rear-Admiral Hugh Evan-Thomas's 5th BS taking its place at Rosyth. Neither Jellicoe nor Beatty issued instructions for using these temporarily attached squadrons with their own forces: the latter intended Evan-Thomas to rejoin C-in-C, who would send Hood on ahead to the Battlecruiser Fleet if the Grand Fleet should be ordered to sea – as, for example, on 2 June when Jellicoe planned to sweep into the Kattegat in the hope of drawing the

* For further details of the High Seas Fleet at Jutland see Appendix G on p 200.

High Seas Fleet. But before this operation could be executed, the Admiralty noted the unusual concentration of U-boats in the North Sea; then, on 30 May, learned from Room 40 that Scheer had ordered the High Seas Fleet to assemble in the outer Jade. The Harwich Force and the 3rd BS in the Thames Estuary were promptly brought to one hour's notice for steam. By 1740 enough further intelligence was available for Jellicoe and Beatty to be told: 'Germans intend operations commencing tomorrow. You should concentrate to eastwards of Long Forties' – 60 miles east of the Scottish coast. So the whole Grand Fleet sailed from Scapa, Cromarty and Rosyth, Beatty being instructed to take the Battlecruiser Fleet to a position 100 miles NW of the Horn Reefs at 1400 on the 31st, at which time Jellicoe's Battle Fleet would be 65 miles to the north, coming south. If there was no news of the enemy by that hour, Beatty was to turn north and join Jellicoe.

The *Lion* led the Battlecruiser Fleet to sea at 2130, the 1st BCS under Rear-Admiral O. de B. Brock in the *Princess Royal* being followed by the 2nd under Rear-Admiral W. C. Pakenham* in the *New Zealand*. These five ships were accompanied by four of the 5th BS with Evan-Thomas's flag in the *Barham*; by the 1st, 2nd and 3rd LCS, each of four ships, commanded respectively by Commodore E. S. Alexander-Sinclair in the *Galatea*, by Goodenough in the *Southampton* and by Rear-Admiral T. D. W. Napier in the *Falmouth*; by the two light cruisers and 27 destroyers of the 1st, 9th, 10th and 13th flotillas; and by the small seaplane-carrier *Engadine*. At the same hour the Battle Fleet left Scapa and Cromarty; 24 dreadnoughts, including Jellicoe's flagship, the *Iron Duke*, divided into the 1st BS commanded by Vice-Admiral Sir Cecil Burney in the *Marlborough*, the 2nd BS by Jerram in the *King George V*, and the 4th BS by Sturdee in the *Benbow*. With them went the 3rd BCS led by Hood in the *Invincible*; the 1st and 2nd CS, each of four armoured cruisers, the one commanded by Arbuthnot in the *Defence*, the other by Rear-Admiral H. L. Heath in the *Minotaur*; Commodore C. E. Le Mesurier's 4th LCS of five ships led by the *Calliope*; seven other light cruisers; 50 destroyers of the 4th, 11th and 12th flotillas; and the fast minelayer *Abdiel*. Thanks to Room 40, the Grand Fleet was at sea four-and-a-half hours before the first units of the High Seas Fleet left the Jade.†

The Battlecruiser Fleet was sighted around 0500 on 31 May by

---

* Who, as British Naval Attaché in Tokyo, was onboard Togo's flagship at Tsushima (1905).

† For further details of the Grand Fleet at Jutland see Appendix F on p 194.

U32 which, after missing the *Galatea* with her torpedoes, and being nearly rammed by the *Phaeton*, reported two dreadnoughts, two cruisers and several destroyers steering SE. An hour later *U66* signalled an unsuccessful attack on eight dreadnoughts (Jerram's squadron), accompanied by light cruisers and destroyers, heading NE from Cromarty. These messages being contradictory, the German C-in-C held his northerly course. His U-boats had, in fact, and despite their initial numbers, neither provided him with useful intelligence nor reduced the strength of the Grand Fleet which was now heading towards the High Seas Fleet in overwhelming force.

	Grand Fleet	High Seas Fleet
Battleships: dreadnoughts	28	16 ⎫ 22
pre-dreadnoughts	—	6 ⎭
Battlecruisers	9	5
Armoured cruisers	8	—
Light cruisers	26	11
Destroyers/Torpedoboats	77	61
Seaplane-carrier	1	—
Minelayer	1	—

Moreover, the British battle fleet opposed 264 guns of 12- to 15-inch calibre, the latter firing projectiles of 1,920 lb, against the Germans' 200 whose 11- and 12-inch projectiles were of less than half this weight. Similarly, the Battlecruiser Fleet had the benefit of 80 guns of 12- to 13·5-inch calibre against the German battlecruisers' 44 of only 11- and 12-inch. Nor were these the Grand Fleet's only advantages. Four of Beatty's battlecruisers steamed faster than any of Hipper's. Jellicoe's battle fleet was a knot faster than Scheer's — four knots faster if the German C-in-C kept Mauve's 2nd BS in company. The British 5th BS was as fast as the *Moltke* and *Von der Tann*, and more heavily armed and armoured than any German vessel. And Scheer and Hipper were so short of cruisers that they had to use torpedoboats to augment their look-out screens. Indeed, the German force matched the British in only one respect; it was armed with as many torpedoes, 362 19·7-inch and 107 17·7-inch, against 382 21-inch and 75 18-inch. In sum, Jellicoe had a fleet double the size of Scheer's, and able to fire more than twice the weight of shell. Moreover, in addition to the six British dreadnought battleships and battlecruisers which were elsewhere on this date, seven more were building, whereas Scheer's only reserves were two recently completed and two on the stocks. Surely, then, in sharp contrast to the first year of the war (and despite reports suggesting that the High Seas Fleet included two more dreadnoughts, and that most of its battleships had been rearmed with bigger guns), the British C-in-C could risk the loss of some of his dreadnoughts in a determined attempt to maul, if not destroy, his opponent – some, but not many, if he had regard for the possibility that the USA might be sufficiently provoked by the stringent British blockade to declare war against the Allies, in which even the Grand Fleet would have to counter a second enemy Battle Fleet in the Atlantic. As surely, if Scheer failed to avoid so great a force, he must suffer a decisive defeat.

At 0500 on 31 May Jellicoe's Battle Fleet altered course to S50E, at 16 knots, for the rendezvous towards which Beatty's battlecruisers were heading east at 19 knots (see map, p 127). But Tyrwhitt, after reminding the Admiralty that the Harwich Force was still in harbour, was told to remain there, because as late as 1235 the Admiralty had 'no definite news of enemy. It was thought fleet had sailed but directionals place flagship in Jade' – for reasons explained by Admiral Sir William James:

> The Room 40 staff were, in the eyes of the Operations staff, very clever fellows who could decipher signals, but any suggestion that they should interpret them would have been resented. On the morning of 31 May, the Director of Operations [Rear-Admiral Thomas Jackson] asked them where directionals placed call-sign DK. On being told 'in the Jade', he went out without asking questions. If he had discussed the situation he would have learned that DK was the German C-in-C's harbour call-sign, and that when he went to sea he transferred it to a harbour station.

This lack of cooperation led the Admiralty to signal Jellicoe and Beatty that, if any part of the High Seas Fleet was out, it did *not* include Scheer's Battle Fleet. Jellicoe did not therefore alter his orders to Beatty to turn north at 1400, when 65 miles should have separated their forces. The C-in-C had adopted this distance, instead of a tactically more desirable 40 miles, so that his Battle Fleet could cover the 10th CS, which was enforcing the blockade between the Shetlands and Norway, whilst the Battlecruiser Fleet went far enough south to counter a further German raid on the east coast.

  To be ready for his turn to the north, Beatty stationed the 2nd BCS three miles ENE of the 1st, and the 5th BS five miles NNW from the *Lion*. But, having been delayed half an hour examining suspicious trawlers, he held his SE course until 1415 before hauling down the signal for his force to swing round to N by E. Alexander-Sinclair's, Napier's and Goodenough's light cruisers were then spread on a lookout line running ENE–WSW, eight miles SSE from the *Lion*. The *Galatea*, wrote one of her officers,

> was just about to turn when a merchant ship was sighted to the east blowing off steam, so the Commodore held on and a Hun destroyer was observed to leave her side. Action stations were at once sounded, and as I went up on to the forecastle I was deafened by the 6-inch gun firing. I nipped into my little coding office and the first enemy report rattled down the tube from the bridge.

Since Scheer had heard nothing to suggest that he might encounter British ships, his Battle Fleet was still on its course for Norway, with Hipper's Scouting Groups 60 miles to the north. Thus, at 1415, all unknown to Hipper and Beatty, as little as 50 miles separated their battlecruisers. Moreover, Beatty's turn towards Jellicoe had brought him on to a similar course to Hipper's, with the wings of their respective screens separated by little more than 20 miles. They might, nonetheless, have missed seeing each other but for the chance that a Danish steamer passed midway between them. Captain Madlung of the light cruiser *Elbing*, on the western wing of Hipper's screen, sent two torpedoboats to board this innocent vessel, which brought them in sight of the *Galatea* on the eastern wing of Beatty's screen – a contact that was reported by both Madlung and Alexander-Sinclair at 1428, as the *Elbing*'s guns answered the *Galatea*'s, and drew first blood at 15,000 yards. By this chance began what was to be known as the Battle of Jutland to the British, of the Skagerrak to the Germans; with neither C-in-C knowing that the other's fleet was at sea, Scheer because his zeppelins had been unable to take the air, Jellicoe because the Admiralty had misinterpreted the intelligence in their possession.

Here a note of caution must be sounded before unfolding how the action developed. The difference between the *Victory* and a twentieth-century battleship is too great for a student of Trafalgar to be tempted into a facile misjudgement of Nelson's tactics; but the 'Queen Elizabeth' class is well remembered for the notable part these ships played in the Second World War. In the years that elapsed between 1916 and 1939 there were, however, several crucial technical innovations. Neither Jellicoe nor Scheer had aircraft, apart from Germany's unreliable zeppelins and the few 'sticks and string' seaplanes in the *Engadine*. (The larger seaplane-carrier *Campania* should have accompanied the British Battle Fleet, but was delayed sailing until 0200 on 31 May by a signal error and by an engine defect; and at 0500 Jellicoe ordered her to return to harbour rather than risk her loss to a U-boat as she was trying to overtake the *Iron Duke*.) For news of the enemy both Cs-in-C had to spread their cruisers well over the horizon ahead of their battle fleets. Moreover, the great size of the two fleets, coupled with the increase in gun range since Tsushima, made it impossible for their Cs-in-C to control the battle (as every fleet commander before them had done, down to and including Togo and Rozhestvensky) from what they could see for themselves from their flagships' bridges: both depended on reports signalled by their captains. But, although warships were now equipped with W/T, its message capacity was, by later standards, limited: most signals had to be passed by flags or searchlight, methods that were relatively slow. As important, the only means available for plotting these reports were inadequate for providing a comprehensive picture of the battle, more especially when it was confused by discrepancies between ships' positions consequent on many being fitted with nothing better than a magnetic compass. A natural hazard increased these handicaps when radar had yet to be conceived: although the weather was fine, a mist limited visibility to eight miles at the outset, and thickened as the day wore on until, with the addition of funnel smoke from more than two hundred vessels steaming at full speed, plus the brown cordite fumes from their guns, no admiral or captain could see more than a few of his own ships, and had, moreover, only fleeting glimpses of an enemy who disappeared as soon as he had been the target for half a dozen salvoes. In effect, the British and German fleets were compelled to fight much of Jutland as if blindfolded, a disadvantage suffered by neither Nelson nor Togo when they annihilated their enemies.

The inherent inaccuracy of long-range gunfire before the days of radar must also be remembered. Dreadnoughts had achieved results comparable with ships-of-the-line in peacetime practices: 70 per cent of hits at a target towed at eight knots on a predetermined parallel course at 8,000 yards. But war had shown that at ranges of 12,000 yards and over, with ships steaming at 20 knots or more, and with the enemy's course unknown, five per cent of hits was the best that could be expected. A prolonged gunnery duel was therefore necessary to achieve a decisive result, as at the Falklands, unless lucky hits should be scored early in the action, as on the *Lion* and *Blücher* at the Dogger Bank. But whilst British dreadnoughts had the better fire-control equipment, in particular Admiral Sir Percy Scott's director and Captain F. C. Dreyer's 'table', the Germans had stereoscopic rangefinders that were more accurate than the British coincidence type. The German ships were, therefore, more likely to score hits with their initial salvoes, but the British were better fitted to 'hold' their targets once they had found the range, which gave the advantage to the former in fleeting engagements, to the latter if an action was prolonged.

To return to the opening of the battle; as the other four ships of the 1st LCS hurried to the *Galatea*'s support, Beatty reacted to Alexander-Sinclair's initial report with a signal ordering his force to swing back to SSE. The 1st BCS followed the *Lion*, and the 2nd also turned, but the *Barham* was too far away to read the *Lion*'s flags. Though Evan-Thomas saw the battlecruisers turning, and his Flag Captain, A. W. Craig, urged him to conform, the Rear-Admiral insisted on waiting until the *Lion* passed the new course by searchlight seven minutes later. By this time the *Barham* had altered to the port leg of a zigzag, turning her squadron even farther from SSE, and Beatty had increased speed to 22 knots. So when the 5th BS turned, the *Barham* was as much as ten miles astern of the *Lion*, with no margin of speed to catch up. A signal error, coupled with Evan-Thomas's refusal to act without orders, thus deprived the battlecruisers of the immediate support of the four most powerful ships in the Grand Fleet. This 'failure' (Jellicoe's word) by Beatty to concentrate his force was to have more serious repercussions than a comparable mistake made by the German battlecruisers. Whilst Boedicker's light cruisers were speeding to the *Elbing*'s support, the *Lützow* misread her sighting report as of 24–26 battleships, which impelled Hipper to turn sharply away to SSW. It was not, however, long before he accepted the evident inaccuracy of this signal, and at 1452 swung back to WNW and increased to 23 knots, in the confident belief that he was about to destroy a squadron of British light cruisers. Meanwhile, Alexander-Sinclair, in pursuit of the *Elbing*, had been able to signal at 1440: 'Have sighted large amount of smoke bearing ENE,' to which he added that this came from 'seven vessels besides destroyers and cruisers, which have turned north'. This made clear to Beatty 'that the enemy was to the north and east and that it would be impossible for him to round the Horn Reefs without being brought to action'. Nonetheless, he continued to lead his battlecruisers at 25 knots towards the 'sound of the guns', despite the distance which separated them from the 5th BS whose best speed was only 24 knots.

At 1447 Beatty ordered the *Engadine* to send up one of her Short seaplanes. Though Lieutenant-Commander Robinson's crew beat their best time for this evolution, it was 21 minutes before Flight-Lieutenant F. J. Rutland and his observer, Assistant-Paymaster G. S. Trewin, were airborne, and half an hour before they sighted the enemy and

> closed to within a mile and a half, when they opened fire on me, the explosions taking place about 200 feet away. When Trewin had got the disposition of the enemy and was making his report, I observed our fleet. The picture of the battlecruisers and of the 'Queen Elizabeth' battleships, with their attendant light cruiser screen and destroyers, rushing forward to cut off the enemy can never be forgotten. At 1545 a petrol pipe broke, my engine revolutions dropped and I was forced to descend and be hoisted in.

Since this was the first time that a heavier-than-air machine was used in a fleet action, one must regret that Rutland and Trewin's good work was wasted; their reports reached the *Engadine*, but she was unable to relay them to the *Lion*. Nor were her planes used again during the battle because the swell prevented any more of her machines taking off. Beatty had to depend on Alexander-Sinclair's reports as the 1st LCS drew the enemy to the north-west, whilst the British battlecruisers turned to E at 1500, and to NE at 1513 – when, by cutting corners, Evan-Thomas reduced his distance to some six miles on Beatty's port quarter. To quote Jellicoe: 'There was now an excellent opportunity for Beatty to concentrate his forces. The enemy was steering towards our Battle Fleet so that the loss of two or three miles by the battlecruisers was immaterial. But the opportunity was not taken.'

The signal, 'Assume complete readiness for action', had already gone to the *Lion*'s masthead, to be answered by battle ensigns hoisted at the yard arms of the *Princess Royal*, *Queen Mary*, *Tiger*, *New Zealand* and *Indefatigable* as, in that order, they followed their leader. Turret crews responded to the order: 'Load! Load! Load!' with no more fuss than they had shown at drill, whilst on the bridge of the *New Zealand* Captain J. F. Green donned his *piu-piu*, the Maori garment that superstition required him to wear in battle. Aboard the German battlecruisers drums likewise beat their crews to quarters as they followed Boedicker to the north-west at 25 knots in the order *Lützow*, *Derfflinger*, *Seydlitz*, *Moltke* and *Von der Tann*, whose Admiral now expected to cut off more light cruisers than Sinclair's because Napier's 3rd LCS had moved to Sinclair's support – leaving a gap in Beatty's look-out screen. So the *Lion*, which had just altered course to E, received no prior warning of Hipper's five battlecruisers before sighting them at 1531, 'faintly distinguishable a very long distance away'. It was fortunate that they were still outside gun range because, whilst Hipper suffered a like disadvantage through having fewer cruisers for his screen, the lighter western horizon had enabled him to sight the British battle-cruisers some ten minutes earlier.

On learning this, Scheer increased his battleships' speed to 16 knots – the maximum at which Mauve's pre-dreadnoughts could maintain station; whilst Hipper, realizing his own dangerous position, recalled Boedicker's squadron and swung his battlecruisers round to SSE, intending to lead his more powerful opponent towards Scheer's Battle Fleet. In this he succeeded; at 1545, on hearing from the *Galatea* and *Falmouth* that the German force had turned to SSE, Beatty altered to the converging course of ESE. Four minutes later, with the range down to 15,000 yards, Hipper's ships opened fire, followed almost immediately by Beatty's.

> The German salvoes gradually came closer until, just as we in the *Princess Royal* saw the burst of one of our shells hitting the *Lützow*, the *Lion* was struck amidships, and we were hit by two shells which knocked out our rangefinder tower. At 1556 the enemy was about ten degrees abaft our beam, steering approximately S, both squadrons firing at each other with a determination that made one expect something big to happen.

A second hit on the *Lion* warned Beatty that 12,000 yards was too close, and he turned two points away just as Hipper altered to SE for the same reason. Aboard the *New Zealand*, near the rear of Beatty's line, 'it was hard to believe that a battle was actually commencing: it was so like an exercise', but the bloody reality was soon brought home to the British vessels. With the advantage of the light and the lee position, so that their targets were clearly visible against the brighter western sky and less obscured by smoke blowing across the range, German gunnery was better. Moreover, notwithstanding the lesson of Dogger Bank, the *Derfflinger* was left unfired at for ten minutes before the *Queen Mary* shifted to her. Nonetheless, although the *Lion*, *Tiger* and *Princess Royal* were all hit, so too were the *Lützow*, *Derfflinger* and *Seydlitz*, the last of these having one of her turrets put out of action. These British successes did not, however, compare with one by the Germans on Beatty's flagship.

> At about 1600 [wrote Lieutenant W. S. Chalmers] a blood-stained sergeant of marines appeared on the bridge, hatless, his clothes burnt. I asked what was the matter: he replied: 'Q turret has gone, sir. All the crew are killed, and we have flooded the magazine.' I looked aft: the armoured roof had been folded back like an open sardine tin, thick yellow smoke was rolling up from the gaping hole, and the guns were cocked up awkwardly in the air.

A shell from the *Lützow* had done more than pierce the roof of the *Lion*'s midship turret, detonating inside. As in the *Seydlitz* at the Dogger Bank, the explosion ignited cordite charges in the working chamber, the flash passing down the trunk to the magazine handing room. But the officer-in-charge,

> Major F. J. W. Harvey, RMLI, with his dying breath, gave the order to close the magazine doors; some were found afterwards with their hands on the clips, but their work was done.

All but two of Q turret's 100 officers and men died in this disaster, but Harvey's splendid presence of mind, which earned him the Victoria Cross, saved his ship from the fate that overtook another of Beatty's force just four minutes later. The *New Zealand* saw

> the *Indefatigable* hit by two shells from the *Von der Tann*, one on the fore turret. Both appeared to explode on impact. Then there was an interval of thirty seconds; at the end the ship blew up. Sheets of flame were followed by dense smoke which obscured her from view. All sorts of stuff was blown into the air, a 50-foot steamboat to about 200 feet, apparently intact.

Since no one in the *Indefatigable*'s A turret closed the magazine doors, all her crew of 1,000 officers and men lost their lives, except for two who were picked up by torpedoboat *S16* whose Captain wrote:

> The rescued men were observers in the spotting top. They had been a long time in the water and claimed that initially they had held up the Captain [C. F. Sowerby] of the ship, who had an arm and a leg torn off, until finally the badly wounded man sank from them.

With his battlecruisers reduced to the same number as his opponent, Beatty again turned away to open the range, and give his ships a chance to extinguish fires caused by enemy hits. This was Evan-Thomas's chance; in the 20 minutes that had passed since the battlecruisers opened fire, he had done everything possible to bring his 5th BS into action; now he was able to cut one more corner, and shortly after 1600 his four ships joined the action. The range was as much as 19,000 yards, yet, to quote Scheer: 'The fire of the English battlecruisers had resulted in no serious damage to our battlecruisers, but the ships of the "Queen Elizabeth" class created an excellent impression.' The *Von der Tann* was quickly damaged below the waterline and flooded with 600 tons of water, and another of the *Seydlitz*'s turrets was put out of action. Against this advantage, Beatty had to offset the destruction of the *Lion*'s W/T transmitter at 1610; henceforward his signals to Jellicoe suffered the delay of having to be relayed by searchlight through the *Princess Royal*. A couple of minutes later Beatty turned his battlecruisers four points towards the enemy, when the 5th BS closed the gap still further. He was not, however, to keep his margin of nine ships over his opponent's five as both sides held their SSE course. Commander von Hase thought that

> the enemy was shooting superbly. Twice the *Derfflinger* came under their infernal hail and each time she was hit. But the *Queen Mary* was having a bad time; engaged by the *Seydlitz* as well as by the *Derfflinger*, she met her doom at 1626. A vivid red flame shot up from her forepart; then came an explosion forward which was followed by a much heavier explosion amidships. Immediately afterwards she blew up with a terrific explosion, the masts collapsing inwards and the smoke hiding everything,

leaving only a handful of survivors from Captain C. I. Prowse's crew of 1,000 officers and men to be rescued by the destroyer *Petard*.

Beatty's classic understatement to Chatfield on seeing a second battlecruiser so catastrophically destroyed has become a part of the Royal Navy's immortal tradition: 'There seems to be something wrong with our bloody ships today.' As calmly he ordered a further alteration of course to enable his ships to 'engage the enemy more closely', and at 1628 had the satisfaction of seeing the enemy alter sharply away; the Germans were no longer able to stand up to the greater weight of British shell. 'It was nothing but the poor quality of their bursting charges that saved us from disaster,' wrote Hipper.

28 Admiral Jellicoe

29 Admiral Beatty, with
Captain Chatfield

30 HM ships leaving Port Stanley

31 *Inflexible* at the Falkland Islands battle

32 *Inflexible* picking up survivors from the *Gneisenau*

33 Destroyers with the Grand Fleet

34 Wreck of the battle-cruiser *Invincible*

35 German battle-cruiser *Moltke*

36 Rear-Admiral Tyrwhitt   *Both from paintings by Glyn Philpot*   37 Vice-Admiral Keyes

38 Rear-Admiral Evan-Thomas   *Both from drawings by Francis Dodds*   39 Rear-Admiral Goodeno

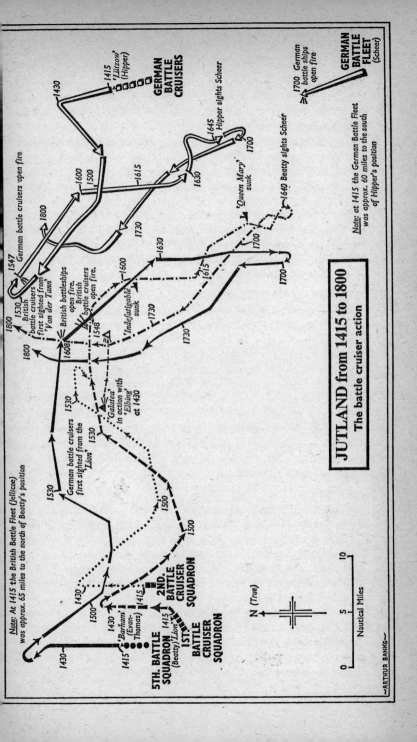

Note: At 1415 the British Battle Fleet (Jellicoe) was approx. 65 miles to the north of Beatty's position

German battle cruisers open fire

1547 German battle cruisers open fire

1430

1415 'Lützow' (Hipper)

GERMAN BATTLE CRUISERS

1800

1600

1500

1615

1730

1645 Hipper sights Scheer

1700

1530 British battle cruisers first sighted from 'Von der Tann'

1800

1800

1800

1630

'Queen Mary' sunk

1640 Beatty sights Scheer

1700

GERMAN BATTLE FLEET (Scheer)

1700 German battle ships open fire

1700

Note: at 1415 the German Battle Fleet was approx. 60 miles to the south of Hipper's position

British battleships open fire. British battle cruisers open fire.

1608

1800

1600

1548

'Indefatigable' sunk

1730

1615

1700

1730

1730

1530

1530

German battle cruisers first sighted from the 'Lion'

1530

'Galatea' in action with 'Elbing' at 1430

1530

1430

1500

1500

1500

JUTLAND from 1415 to 1800
The battle cruiser action

N (True)

0   5   10
Nautical Miles

1430

1500

1500

1430

1415 'Barham' (Evan-Thomas)

1415

1415 'Lion' (Beatty)

5TH. BATTLE SQUADRON

2ND. BATTLE CRUISER SQUADRON

1ST. BATTLE CRUISER SQUADRON

—ARTHUR BANKS—

It was also Evan-Thomas's ships that saved Beatty's battlecruisers. The latter had scored only ten hits whilst suffering as many as 40, but they sustained no more during the next quarter of an hour in which the guns of the 5th BS smote the *Moltke* and the *Von der Tann* again and again.

Hipper had another reason for altering course. Beatty's swift pursuit had made it difficult for his destroyers to gain a position ahead of his battlecruisers; but when the 13th DF at last achieved this, Captain J. U. Farie received the signal: 'Opportunity appears favourable for attacking.' At 1615 he released his eight destroyers; reinforced by four of Commander M. L. Goldsmith's, they headed for Hipper's battlecruisers in three divisions, led respectively by the *Nestor*, Commander the Hon. E. B. S. Bingham, the *Obdurate*, Lieutenant-Commander C. H. Sams and the *Narborough*, Lieutenant-Commander G. Corlett.

> We led out at 34 knots [wrote one of the *Nicator's* officers]. Almost simultaneously we saw enemy torpedoboats [Commander Goehle's 9th TBF] coming out from the German line. When we reached a position on the enemy battlecruiser's bow we turned and fired our first torpedo at 9,000 yards. By this time we were within range of the enemy torpedoboats approaching at about 30 knots, so we went into 'rapid independent' and scored a gratifying number of hits. Two of them stopped, one with a distinct list to starboard [the *V27* and *V29* which sank], whilst the firing of the remainder was very wild. The *Nicator* was not hit at all, but the *Nomad* was disabled in her engine room and we had to leave her. All this time we were under hot fire from the German battlecruisers' secondary armaments and it seemed nothing short of a miracle that we escaped.

Both the British and German attacks were spoiled by this fierce clash. Beatty and Evan-Thomas avoided all 18 torpedoes fired by Goehle's boats by turning their ships two points away. But though Hipper made a much larger turn to evade the 20 fired by Farie's destroyers, one from the *Petard*, Lieutenant-Commander E. C. O. Thomson, struck and flooded the *Seydlitz*, though not enough to drive her out of the line.

By 1620 Goodenough's 2nd LCS had gained a position from which to scout ahead of the British battlecruisers. Having steamed some 50 miles towards the Horn Reefs since first sighting the enemy without finding more than Hipper's ships, Beatty had every reason to believe the Admiralty's intelligence that these were the only enemy force at sea. If, on the other hand, Scheer had held his NW course at 16 knots, Beatty would have sighted him already. The German C-in-C delayed their meeting by steering W for a time, so that the British battlecruisers might be caught between his battleships and Hipper's force — until the *Frankfurt* reported the 5th BS. The German battle fleet, in a long single line headed by Behncke's 3rd BS, was then turned back to NW to support Hipper as quickly as possible. 'We were about 1,500 yards ahead of our battle-cruisers and 13,000 from the enemy,' recalls one of the *Notting-ham*'s officers, 'when suddenly out of the mist on the port bow a line of big ships appeared. We stood on towards them with the rest of our squadron so as to be able to tell the C-in-C and the *Lion* exactly who was there.' At 1638 Jellicoe's and Beatty's illusion that Scheer's ships were in the Jade was dispelled by the *South-ampton*'s electrifying news: 'Have sighted enemy battle fleet bear-ing SE, course N.' Beatty then knew that he had been led into a trap. Despite the loss of two battlecruisers, he had been justly con-fident that his remaining four, plus the 5th BS, would destroy Hipper's five; now he had to escape from overwhelming force, and lead the Germans north until Scheer, in his turn, was trapped by Jellicoe's superior battle fleet, which was only 50 miles away.

Beatty reacted to Goodenough's report by ordering his battlecruisers to reverse course, though he delayed the turn until 1640 when he had seen Scheer's dreadnoughts for himself 11 miles SE. As before, he turned his ships in succession, although this risked bringing the *Princess Royal*, *Tiger* and *New Zealand* dangerously close to the enemy. Fortunately, Hipper was otherwise occupied with Evan-Thomas's ships, and the *New Zealand* finished turning before the head of the German battle fleet came within range. It was a different story with the 5th BS. At 1640 Seymour hoisted Beatty's alter course signal by flags only, which could not be seen by the *Barham*, some seven miles away. Again refusing to act without orders, Evan-Thomas continued to head for the enemy. Six minutes after the *Lion* had turned, Seymour repeated Beatty's signal, again by flags which were not read by the *Barham* until she was abeam of the battlecruisers. But if this second failure in communications be-tween the *Lion* and the *Barham* can be attributed to Beatty's flag lieutenant, not so the method by which the 5th BS was required to alter course. This should have been left to Evan-Thomas to decide; in any case it should have been to *port together*. By specifying to *starboard in succession* Beatty courted disaster. His battlecruisers had suffered so much punishment that he wanted the 5th BS to be the main target for Hipper's gunfire; but by the time the *Barham* turned at 1657, she was within range of Scheer's battle fleet: the fire of the German 3rd BS was concentrated first on her, then on the *Valiant*, then on the *Warspite*, as each swung round the same turning point. Captain M. Woollcombe's ship escaped damage, but both Craig's and Captain E. M. Phillpotts' received considerable punishment, and 'when it was time for the *Malaya* to turn, it was a very hot corner, and it is doubtful if we could have got through if Captain the Hon A. D. E. H. Boyle had not used his initiative and turned the ship early'.

Hipper resumed his southerly course, after making his drastic turn to avoid the 13th DF's torpedoes, until Scheer's battle fleet was sighted from the *Lützow*'s bridge at 1645. And some ten minutes later, and almost simultaneously with the 5th BS, he made the same mistake of turning the 1st SG 16 points *in succession*, when his battlecruisers sustained further damage from the *Barham*'s and the *Valiant*'s accurate fire. They would have suffered more if the *Warspite* and *Malaya* had not turned their guns on the head of Scheer's line, scoring hits on the *König*, *Grosser Kurfürst* and *Markgraf*.

> Very soon after the turn [noted the *Warspite*'s executive officer] I saw on our starboard quarter the masts, funnels and an endless ripple of orange flashes from the whole of the High Seas Fleet. The noise of their shells over and short was deafening. Two of our salvoes hit the leading German battleship: sheets of flame went right over her masthead, and she looked red fore and aft like a burning haystack.

On sighting Scheer's battle fleet, Beatty recalled Farie's destroyers.

> On the way back the *Nestor* and *Nicator* passed the *Nomad*, stopped and helpless. We offered assistance but Lieutenant-Commander P. Whitfield told us to go on. Seeing a line of battleships on our port bow, I exclaimed: 'Now we're all right, here is the 5th BS', but closer investigation showed they were German and very soon we were in the thick of a hair-raising bombardment at 3,000 yards: *Nestor* was going to make certain of this attack. But just as the *Nicator*'s sights were coming on to an enemy battleship, the *Nestor* was hit and we had to put our helm hard-a-port to prevent ramming her. Realizing he was out of action, *Nestor* ordered us to rejoin the *Champion*.

But the damaged *Nestor* and *Nomad* could not escape.

A whole German battle squadron was apparently using the *Nomad* as a target: we were only 2,000 yards from the leading one when we fired our last torpedo. We started sinking by the stern, but all the men were got clear and a German torpedoboat picked us out of the water, to be the Kaiser's 'guests' for the next two-and-a-half years,

in which Bingham, who gained the VC for leading his division with such spirit, thus described the *Nestor*'s end to his wife:

Whitfield and I were left like lambs in the path of the High Seas Fleet, the enemy masses looming nearer and nearer and not a friend in sight. It was a relief when the shells arrived. I could not retaliate, my guns were too small. In a few minutes I had to give the order: 'Every man for himself'. We took to the boats: the *Nestor* sank a few seconds after. We gave three cheers as she went down, then sang 'Tipperary' and 'The King'. Later a division of the 5th TBF picked us up, 75 out of 83, who spent the rest of the battle like rats in a hole, quite sure that British destroyers would sink us. However, the German officers were very kind to us and nature came to my rescue and I slept.

Goodenough turned a blind eye to Beatty's signal to reverse course: the 2nd LCS stood on to the SE until 1700 when the *Southampton* could report the details of Scheer's battle fleet from a range that was closer than seven miles. The Commodore was to do more than this classic piece of cruiser work before the day was done to wipe from the slate the mistakes he had made in 1914. Tyrwhitt, some 300 miles away in Harwich Harbour, reacted to his report with a pointed request to the Admiralty for 'instructions'. He was ordered to do no more than complete with fuel because, 'you may have to relieve light cruisers and destroyers in Battlecruiser Fleet'. In truth, he was held back by the First Sea Lord lest Scheer should detach part of his fleet to raid the Thames Estuary. But this order crossed further word from Tyrwhitt; at 1715, unable to restrain his eagerness to support Beatty, he signalled: 'Am proceeding to sea.' His chagrin when the Admiralty retorted 20 minutes later, 'Return at once,' was, however, as nothing to his feelings when he was eventually allowed to sail after dawn on 1 June – too late for his five light cruisers and 19 destroyers to play any part in the battle.

On receiving the *Galatea*'s first enemy report of the *Elbing*, Jellicoe ordered steam for full speed, which allowed his battle fleet to increase to 18 knots at 1455, and to 20 by 1600. This was all he could do to close the distance separating him from Beatty, which was some 12 miles more than intended because Jellicoe had also been delayed searching trawlers suspected of using W/T to report British warships to Germany. However, to compensate for this, the C-in-C ordered Arbuthnot's and Heath's cruiser squadrons to increase their distance ahead of the *Iron Duke* to 16 miles, as the 3rd BCS, with its accompanying light cruisers *Chester* and *Canterbury* and four destroyers, pushed on to join the Battlecruiser Fleet. And aboard the British battleships officers and men were at their action stations by the time the *Iron Duke* received Goodenough's unexpected but very welcome report that Scheer was only 50 miles away.

To allow Jellicoe to make contact, and to ensure that the German Battle Fleet would not elude the Grand Fleet, as it had so often done before, Beatty knew that he had to get far enough ahead of Hipper to force the 1st SG round to the east, thus preventing it from giving warning of the British Battle Fleet's approach. To this end, he maintained a speed of 25 knots, after turning to NNW, so that by 1710 his battlecruisers had drawn out of range of Hipper's force. The slower 5th BS was in action for another 20 minutes with both Hipper's battlecruisers and with the German 1st and 3rd BS, which had increased to 20 knots, leaving Mauve's pre-dreadnoughts behind. But, though these four British battleships were targets for German dreadnoughts for nearly half an hour, Scheer's 'hope that one would be so damaged as to fall a prey to our main fleet' was not fulfilled; none fared worse than the *Malaya* which had two holes below the waterline and her starboard 6-inch battery wrecked, whilst their 15-inch guns scored effective hits on the *Grosser Kurfürst*, *Markgraf*, *Seydlitz*, *Derfflinger* and the already crippled *Lützow*. Assuredly Evan-Thomas's ships were stoutly built and manned, but Scheer's failure to do them more damage is a reflection on his battle fleet's gunnery; Behncke's and Schmidt's squadrons did not show the same skill as Hipper's.

The 5th BS was a brave sight [wrote Lieutenant Stephen King-Hall of the *Southampton*]. They were receiving the concentrated fire of some 12 heavy ships though it did not seem to worry them. But our position was not pleasant: the battleships at the tail of the German line began to do target practice on our squadron. In the after control we crouched down behind the tenth-of-an-inch plating and ate bully beef; but it seemed rather a waste of time. Surely one of those 11-inch shells would get us; they couldn't go on falling just short and just over indefinitely.

But Goodenough's ships avoided being hit by frequent alterations of course towards each enemy salvo, on the sound principle that it was most unlikely that two successive ones would fall in the same place, while two much smaller ships harried the German battle fleet. Released from screening the *Engadine*, Lieutenant-Commander J. C. Tovey,* in the destroyer *Onslow*, led the *Moresby* in for an attack. Engaged by Reuter's 4th SG, Tovey was compelled to retire; but the *Moresby* managed to fire a torpedo at the *Kronprinz*, third ship in Scheer's line, at a range inside 9,000 yards, a gallant failure from which Lieutenant-Commander R. V. Alison's ship was lucky to emerge unscathed.

At 1730 Beatty, with Hipper no longer in sight from the *Lion*'s bridge, swung his battlecruisers round to NNE. At the same time Scheer, believing his opponent to be escaping, ordered his battle-cruisers to chase; and by altering to NW they were soon in action again. But the eight British heavy ships, which now had the advantage of the better light, inflicted so much fresh damage on the German battlecruisers that Hipper was compelled to turn right away from his doughty opponents. By 1800, when he was as much as six miles on Scheer's starboard bow, because the latter had reduced speed to 15 knots to allow Mauve's squadron to catch up, the 1st SG was in full flight to the east.

How much had Beatty and Hipper achieved so far? The initial advantage had gone to the latter: he had lured a superior British force within range of Scheer's Battle Fleet, and sunk a third of its battlecruisers. Beatty had committed two tactical mistakes, made the worse by signal errors, the one denying him the support of the 5th BS, the second needlessly endangering Evan-Thomas's ships. These vessels had, however, used their 15-inch guns to such effect that Hipper's battlecruisers had suffered heavier damage than the surviving British ones. As important, Beatty had done more than elude Scheer's Battle Fleet; he had out-manœuvred Hipper so that Scheer was, without premonition of his fate, about to meet the superior force which he aimed to avoid. There is, therefore, no question but that, by 1800, the advantage lay with the British. Whether this would result in victory remained to be decided by

* Who was destined to be C-in-C Home Fleet in the Second World War and to become Admiral of the Fleet Lord Tovey.

Jellicoe and Scheer, whose battle fleets were just over the horizon from each other. The former had the more powerful force, but over its prospects hung a cloud more menacing than the mist and smoke of battle that limited the visibility to less than six miles. Because the two fleets had not made initial contact until half-way through the afternoon, less than three hours remained before the darkness of a summer night would close over the North Sea.

10

Jellicoe versus Scheer

Suddenly the German van was faced by the belching guns
of an interminable line of heavy ships.

Der Krieg zur See

So much of consequence occurred around 1800 on 31 May 1916
that it is not easy to present a coherent account of the next
phase of the action that was destined to be known as Jutland to the
British, Skagerrak to their foes. Dreadnoughts could only bring the
maximum number of heavy guns to bear if their 'A arcs' were open
(i.e. if the enemy was between about 50 degrees before and 50
degrees abaft the beam); and since a fleet could, likewise, only
develop its full weight of fire if individual ships avoided masking
each other's 'A arcs', its 'order of battle' had to approximate to
line ahead. But for cruising this formation had disadvantages:
battleships in a long single line could not be easily manœuvred, nor
given an adequate destroyer screen. Jellicoe's battle fleet was,
therefore, approaching Scheer's in six coloumns, each of four ships
in line ahead, with their leaders disposed abeam. Jerram led the
port wing column in the *King George V*; the other half of the 2nd
BS formed the next column under Rear-Admiral A. C. Leveson in
the *Orion*. Jellicoe headed the third column in the *Iron Duke*; four
more ships of the 4th BS, led by Sturdee in the *Benbow*, comprised
the fourth. The fifth column was under Rear-Admiral E. F. Gaunt in
the *Colossus*; Burney in the *Marlborough* led the rest of the 1st BS
on the starboard wing.

Much thought and many exercises had been devoted to the problem of how best to deploy this compact body into a single line
before the enemy opened fire. When actions were fought at 4,000–
6,000 yards, there was time for an admiral to make this decision
after he had sighted the enemy. With ships able to fire at near-
horizon range, Jellicoe had to deploy his fleet whilst the enemy
was outside this distance. For this he was dependent on his ad-

vanced forces for the enemy's bearing and distance, formation, course and speed. But here his admirals and his captains failed him. After Sinclair's initial report around 1430, the British C-in-C heard nothing until Napier's just after 1500. Moreover, no further news of Hipper's ships reached him until Beatty, Goodenough and Napier signalled reports around 1540. Fifteen minutes later Beatty added that he was in action, but Evan-Thomas remained silent so that Jellicoe had to radio him at 1617: 'Are you in company with Senior Officer Battlecruiser Fleet?' to which he received the ambiguous reply: 'I am engaging the enemy.' None of this, for which both Beatty and Evan-Thomas had the excuse that their flagships' W/T was out of action, was, however, of importance when Scheer's battle fleet had not been sighted. It was a very different matter when Goodenough made his report at 1638, followed by Farie and Beatty, whereby Jellicoe first learned that, contrary to the Admiralty's intelligence, the German Battle Fleet was only 50 miles away. He was left with very little time to decide on which column and on what course he should deploy. But, after Goodenough's report at 1700, he heard nothing for 40 minutes, except for W/T bearings of the enemy signalled by the Admiralty at 1700, and again at 1745, which suggested that he would sight the enemy ahead. Scheer's bearing and distance from the *Iron Duke* remained far from clear when the two battle fleets were closing at a combined speed of some 40 knots.

At 1730, as Beatty swung his force round to NNE to lead Hipper away from the British Battle Fleet, the *Falmouth*, four miles to the north of the *Lion*, sighted the *Black Prince* on the starboard wing of Jellicoe's cruiser screen. This visual contact between the two British forces should have given Jellicoe the information he needed, but Napier signalled no more than, 'Battlecruisers engaged to SSW', which the *Black Prince* passed to the *Iron Duke* in the inaccurate form 'Enemy battlecruisers bearing S five miles'. Subsequent reports from the *Southampton* and *Defence* were no more helpful, so that Jellicoe remained in suspense until 1750 when Burney sighted the *Lion* and *Barham* and reported their bearings from the *Marlborough*. This disclosed the disturbing fact that, through differences in navigational reckoning, the *Lion* was 11 miles nearer the *Iron Duke*, and on a more westerly bearing, than the C-in-C had supposed her to be. He would therefore sight Scheer's battle fleet 20 minutes earlier than he had expected. He had that much less time in which to deploy when he still lacked the bearing of his opponent's flagship.

'Large masses of smoke from the hundreds of ships making at

full speed for the scene of the battle lay between the lines forming an impenetrable pall,' wrote the German historian. The 3rd BCS, which had been pressing ahead since 1510, did nothing to pierce this fog because Hood elected to steer SSE to cut off any enemy force which tried to escape into the Skagerrak. This took him to the east of Hipper's ships until, at 1730, Captain R. N. Lawson in the light cruiser *Chester*, six miles to starboard of the *Invincible*, sighted gun flashes to the SW and turned to investigate.

> In a very short time we sighted light cruisers steering NNW, and almost immediately saw the flash of gunfire ripple along the side of the *Frankfurt* [in which Boedicker was leading the 2nd SG ahead of Hipper's battlecruisers]. The enemy's first salvo fell beyond us, the second short, and most of the third came onboard. Our first salvo was also our last, the majority of the guns' crews being smashed up by the enemy salvo. With a whole squadron concentrating on us, the odds were more than we could stand. We altered to NE, which brought our opponents astern and zig-zagged to dodge their salvoes. Fortunately the engine room and boilers were not damaged, and by working up to 28 knots, we gradually increased the range and passed ahead of the *Invincible*. The number of direct hits received was 18, but we were also hit by a large amount of splinters.

The *Chester*'s casualties included the sightsetter of the forecastle gun, Boy First Class John Travers Cornwell.

> Mortally wounded early in the action, he remained standing alone at a most exposed post quietly awaiting orders, with the gun's crew dead and wounded all round him. His age was under $16\frac{1}{2}$ years. I regret that he has since died, but I recommend his case for special recognition in justice to his memory and as an acknowledgement of the high example set by him.

Beatty's well-earned tribute gained for Cornwell a posthumous Victoria Cross, the youngest ever awarded.

Hood brought his battlecruisers to the *Chester*'s rescue. 'At 1755 the *Invincible* opened fire and was followed five minutes later by the *Inflexible* and *Indomitable*. We could see the *Chester* off the port bow heavily engaged with a squadron of enemy light cruisers. Closing to 8,000 yards we steamed between her and the enemy and severely handled them.' The *Wiesbaden* was reduced to a smoking wreck, the *Pillau*'s speed cut to 24 knots, the *Frankfurt* severely damaged. Boedicker's squadron was only saved from annihilation

by the appearance of Hipper's battlecruisers being headed clear of
Jellicoe's battle fleet by Beatty's ships. Hipper did not, however,
engage the *Invincible* and her sisters: accepting Boedicker's belief
that they were a division of battleships, he ordered his torpedoboats to attack them, and swung the 1st SG away to SW, whereby
he came in sight of Behncke's 3rd BS steering NNE, and was able to
turn into his station ahead. The 3rd BCS was attacked by the
Regensburg and the 2nd, 6th and 9th flotillas: but Heinrich's boats
fired only 12 torpedoes, which the British ships avoided by turning
away, before Hood's four destroyers delivered their counter-attack,
as vividly described by 'Bartimeus':

Led by Commander Loftus Jones in the *Shark*, the division hurled
itself at the German force, opening fire with every gun that would
bear. In spite of their numerical superiority the German torpedoboats turned away in the face of this determined onslaught. But
three enemy battlecruisers appeared out of the mist, and the
gallant division came under a deluge of shells. One struck the
Shark's wheel, shattering it and wounding the coxswain. The
Captain ordered the after wheel to be manned and followed the
coxswain down the ladder to the shell-torn upper deck. Wounded
in the thigh and face, Loftus Jones found that a shell had disabled the main engines. Lieutenant-Commander J. O. Barron
brought the *Acasta* between her and the enemy's fire, and asked
if he could be of assistance. The Captain of the *Shark* replied:
'No. Tell him to look after himself.' So the *Acasta* followed in
the wake of the other two boats as they rejoined our battlecruisers.

The enemy then closed in on the *Shark* which was shuddering
with the impact of fresh hits. The wounded crawled into the lee
of the casings and funnels in a pitiful attempt to find shelter.
The midship gun maintained a steady fire with the crew reduced
to two men. When one of them dropped from loss of blood, the
Captain took his place: a moment later a shell took off his right
leg above the knee. As his strength ebbed, Commander Loftus
Jones feared lest his ship should fall to the enemy. When he asked
what had happened to the flag, a man tending him replied that it
had been shot away. In great distress he ordered another to be
hoisted.

But the end was near: the bows of the *Shark* had sunk until
the waves were lapping over the waterlogged hull, and when two
German destroyers approached to administer the *coup de grâce*,

Loftus Jones gave his last order: 'Save yourselves!'. He was helped into the water and floated clear supported by a lifebelt whilst the rest of the crew, about a score, swam to the rafts. The *Shark* sank with colours flying an hour and a half after firing her first shot. Seeing battlecruisers sweep past in pursuit of the enemy, her Captain asked if they were British. Informed that they were, he said, 'That's good!' Then his head fell forward and his gallant spirit fled.

A few weeks later the body of Loftus Jones, whose heroism was recognized by the Victoria Cross, was washed ashore on the coast of Sweden, to be buried, Viking fashion, in a village churchyard there.

In contrast to Boedicker's and Hipper's signals to Scheer, none of this activity was reported to Jellicoe. He was left wondering whether the sound of the 3rd BCS's gunfire on his flagship's port bow could be the bearing of Scheer's battle fleet, until 1801. The *Lion* then appeared out of the mist on the *Iron Duke*'s other bow, leading her consorts in action with an invisible enemy on their further side. Immediately Jellicoe flashed: 'Where is the enemy battle fleet?' Beatty, having lost touch with Scheer, answered: 'Enemy battlecruisers bearing SE'. So Jellicoe repeated his query. Fortunately the mist to the south of the *Lion* then lifted a little, enabling Beatty to answer: 'Have sighted enemy battle fleet bearing SSW'. At last Jellicoe had the information he needed, that the enemy was on his starboard bow, but so close that he could lose no time over his deployment.

He looked at the magnetic compass, as cool and unmoved as ever [wrote Dreyer] before breaking the silence with the order, 'Hoist equal speed pendant south-east.' The Fleet Signal Officer said: 'Would you make it a point to port, sir, so that they will know it is on the port wing column?' Jellicoe replied: 'Very well. Hoist equal speed pendant south-east-by-east,' which was made by W/T at the same time, 1815.

This required Jerram in the *King George V* to lead his column a few degrees to port. The other leaders, by swinging some 70 degrees to port together, led their columns round to form the fleet into line ahead, a further turn in succession to starboard in Jerram's wake, bringing it on to a course of SE by E. Jellicoe was 'guided in my deployment by two factors, one, to "cross the T"; two, to get the best light for gunnery'. But his clear brain achieved more than this;

he put the British Battle Fleet between the High Seas Fleet and its base.

His battleships were in line ahead by 1820, albeit with a 110-degrees bend in it, but concave to the enemy so that all ships could bring their guns to bear. The only alternative available to him, deployment on his starboard wing, would have produced a bend convex to the enemy (unless he had sacrificed the advantage of the easterly position), masking the fire of many British ships for 20 vital minutes. Deployment on a centre column, putting the *Iron Duke* in the lead, would have achieved Jellicoe's aims *and* allowed him to engage Scheer at a more effective range. But this was not possible: such a method had been rejected before the war, because an admiral could control his battle fleet so much better from the centre than the van. 'If I had been in command of the Grand Fleet, I hope I would have had the good sense to make the same deployment as Jellicoe did,' was Admiral of the Fleet Lord Cunningham's verdict. But, to quote Admiral Richmond, 'the battle did not hinge on whether Jellicoe deployed on the starboard or port wing, but on how firmly his determination was set on destroying the enemy and obtaining a decisive victory'.

Much had, meantime, happened in the rapidly narrowing area between the two fleets, in which the numerous battlecruisers, cruisers and destroyers of both sides, together with the 5th BS, manoeuvred at high speed amidst such a hail of shell that the Grand Fleet named it 'Windy Corner'. Shortly before 1800, Napier's 3rd LCS engaged the crippled *Wiesbaden*. So, too, did the *Onslow* before Tovey

saw that he was in an ideal position for a torpedo attack on the enemy battlecruisers. He closed and, when 8,000 yards from the leading vessel, turned to bring the sights on. Unfortunately his ship was struck amidships and enveloped in clouds of steam; and in the confusion only one torpedo was fired. The Captain sent the Sub-Lieutenant aft; finding three torpedoes left, he fired one at the *Wiesbaden* which hit. On returning to the bridge, the Sub. reported two torpedoes left, so Tovey went in again and delivered an attack on the enemy's battle line as it reappeared out of the mist. He then retired until two shells exploded in No 2 boiler room and the ship stopped. Fortunately the battle was surging away from him and soon the two fleets were out of sight. At 1915 the *Defender* appeared: she was also a lame duck, so Tovey accepted her offer of a tow.

But it was 48 hours before 'the Cripple' and 'the Paralytic', as

Kipling called them, reached Aberdeen. With as much gallantry, the *Acasta*, which had become detached from her flotilla, pressed home an attack on the *Seydlitz*.

Shortly before 1800 the 1st CS sighted Boedicker's 2nd SG returning from its unequal combat with the 3rd BCS. Having no accurate knowledge of Scheer's movements, Arbuthnot, who had missed his 'golden moment' on 10 December 1914, turned in pursuit. Two minutes later Hipper's battlecruisers and Behncke's 3rd BS loomed out of the haze only 7,000 yards away and opened fire on the four British cruisers.

The *Defence* was heavily engaged, salvoes dropping all around her. At 1815 a salvo hit her abaft the after turret and a big red flame flashed up. The ship heeled, then quickly righted herself and steamed on. But almost immediately another salvo struck between the forecastle turret and foremost funnel, and she was lost to sight in an enormous black cloud which, when it cleared, showed no signs of a ship at all.

In that devastating explosion Arbuthnot was lost, together with Captain S. V. Ellis and all 900 of his crew. Captain V. B. Molteno's *Warrior*

was now between the enemy battle fleet and our 5th BS. So, after giving the *Wiesbaden* two final salvoes from my starboard guns, I withdrew. The *Warspite* was about two miles astern of her squadron, having made a large circle towards the enemy because her steering gear had jammed. As she came between the *Warrior* and the enemy battle fleet she drew all their fire upon herself, which undoubtedly saved us from being sunk.

The *Warrior* was, nonetheless, in a sorry state. Hit by 15 heavy projectiles, she had more than 100 killed and wounded: she was on fire aft, her upper deck was a shambles, she had a list to starboard, and had lost steam for her engines. However, by 1900 she was clear to the west where she sighted the *Engadine*, and two hours later Robinson's seaplane-carrier had Molteno's disabled cruiser in tow.

But during the night the weather worsened and her stern sank low in the water. At daybreak preparations were made to abandon her. There was a fair sea running, but the *Engadine* was a cross-Channel steamer fitted with a huge rubbing strake to facilitate going alongside. The two ships were working heavily, the noise of rending steel was terrific, and the *Engadine* was holed in several places. Our officers and men grabbed each man as he came across, the wounded being passed over on stretchers. The last of these slipped out and fell between the two ships. Several officers and men jumped on bulwarks as though to go after him, but the Captain shouted that no one was to go over the side. The poor fellow had fetched up on the remains of a fender, but it would be only seconds before he fell through it. Then I saw that he had drifted far enough ahead to be rescued without any real risk. I grabbed a rope with a bowline, went down it, swam to the man, and, holding him in my arms, ordered those on deck to heave away.

For this selfless act Rutland added the Albert Medal to the DSO which he was awarded for his reconnaissance flight earlier in the day. Molteno and his crew gave three cheers as Robinson left the sinking *Warrior* and headed for Rosyth.

The *Black Prince* came to a more fearful end. Seriously damaged by heavy shell, she also withdrew from the action; but because she could still steam at 12 knots, Captain T. P. Bonham unwisely followed in Jellicoe's wake. Around midnight his ship was sighted by the *Thüringen* in Scheer's battle line, and under the concentrated fire of five battleships the *Black Prince* blew up and sank with all her crew. So the *Duke of Edinburgh* was the only ship of Arbuthnot's squadron to escape destruction, Captain H. Blackett gaining the cover of Jellicoe's battle fleet, and joining Heath's 3rd CS.

The visibility around Windy Corner was such that, though Burney sighted the *Barham* at 1750, Evan-Thomas did not see the *Marlborough* until after 1800. Supposing the former's flagship to be leading a battle fleet that had already deployed, Evan-Thomas tried to take the 5th BS into station ahead of her. When he realized his mistake, he decided against leading across the front of Jellicoe's battleships because this would mask their fire: he steered for the rear of the line, which made it impracticable for his ships to use their speed as the *Grand Fleet Battle Orders* envisaged. It also involved the 5th BS in a large turn to port, when it suffered further punishment from Scheer's battle fleet, jamming the *Warspite*'s helm.

We swung under the *Valiant*'s stern and continued round towards the enemy, getting very close to them until Phillpotts managed to steady the ship by working the screws. The whole leading enemy division concentrated on us during this circling and we were

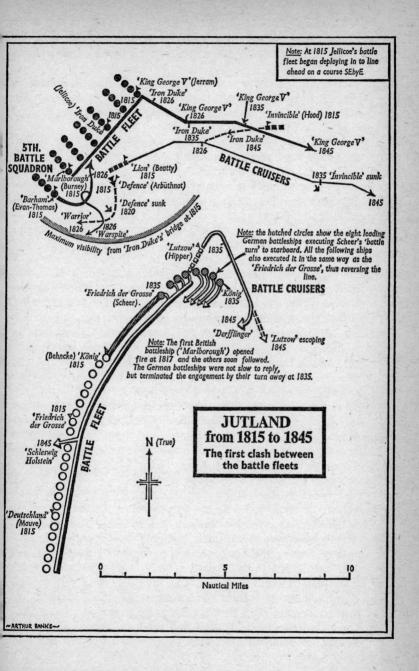

Note: At 1815 Jellicoe's battle fleet began deploying in to line ahead on a course SEbyE

(Jellicoe) 'Iron Duke'

'King George V' (Jerram)
'Iron Duke'
1815   1826
1815   'King George V'
1815   1826   'King George V'
                                         1835
BATTLE FLEET   'Invincible' (Hood) 1815

5TH.
BATTLE
SQUADRON   'Iron Duke'
                          1835   'Iron Duke'
                                        1845   'King George V'
                            1826   1845
'Marlborough'   1826
(Burney)
1815   1815   'Lion' (Beatty)   BATTLE CRUISERS
1815   1815   1835 'Invincible' sunk
'Barham'
(Evan-Thomas)   'Defence' (Arbuthnot)
1815
            'Warrior' 1826   'Defence' sunk   1845
              1826   1820
                    'Warspite'
Maximum visibility from 'Iron Duke's bridge at 1815

                              'Lutzow'   1835
                              (Hipper)
                                              Note: the hatched circles show the eight leading
                                              German battleships executing Scheer's 'battle
                                              turn' to starboard. All the following ships
                        1835   also executed it in the same way as the
                                              'Friedrich der Grosse', thus reversing the
'Friedrich der Grosse'   'König'   line.
(Scheer).   1835   BATTLE CRUISERS

                                 1845
                            'Derfflinger'   'Lutzow' escaping
                                                1845
(Behncke) 'König'   **Note:** The first British
1815   battleship ('Marlborough') opened
                      fire at 1817 and the others soon followed.
1815   The German battleships were not slow to reply,
'Friedrich   but terminated the engagement by their turn away at 1835.
der Grosse'

1845   N (True)
'Schleswig
Holstein'   **JUTLAND**
                                          from 1815 to 1845
                      BATTLE FLEET   **The first clash between**
                                              the battle fleets

'Deutschland'
(Mauve)
1815

          0   5   10
                        Nautical Miles

~ARTHUR BANKS~

heavily hit; everybody thought we had gone. Luckily the Huns could not see us for splashes, spray and smoke, and ceased firing.

The *Warspite*'s standby steering engine was accidentally connected with ten degrees of helm on, so that she made a second circle within 10,000 yards of the head of Scheer's line before her Captain could regain control. But these involuntary turns saved the *Warrior* from the catastrophe which cost Arbuthnot his flagship and his life, albeit after the *Warspite* had sustained 13 fresh hits. And when her steering gear gave further trouble, Evan-Thomas ordered her to return to Rosyth, which left Scheer with the mistaken belief that his ships had sunk her. In fact, she reached port safely, notwithstanding attempted torpedo attacks by *U51* and *U63*.

For all this time the German C-in-C remained wholly unaware of the approach of the British battle fleet, whose deployment was cloaked by the pall of smoke over the battleground. In the hope of damaging a part of the Grand Fleet, because Hipper had reported Hood's 3rd BCS as four battleships, he allowed the head of his line to alter two points to starboard before his illusion was shattered. At 1817 the *Marlborough* opened fire on Behncke's flagship, and was followed by the *Agincourt* with all fourteen of her 12-inch guns, by the *Revenge* with her eight 15-inch, and by many more, some engaging Hipper's battlecruisers, others the unfortunate *Wiesbaden*. At last, after nearly two years of waiting, Jellicoe had brought the High Seas Fleet to battle. Moreover, he had surprised Scheer: obliged to make the passage up the swept channel from the Jade with his three battle squadrons in line ahead, the German C-in-C had no chance to turn to a course of tactical advantage: Jellicoe's battle fleet was 'crossing his T'. The *Lützow* and *Derfflinger*, the *König*, *Grosser Kurfürst* and *Markgraf* were all hit, whilst Scheer's gunners were unable to score on their opponents.

On the other hand, Hipper's squadron gained one more dramatic success. As the *Lion* led her three consorts to the van of the 2nd BS, Hood manœuvred his ships to join Beatty. All seven British battlecruisers were then heavily engaged with Hipper's five, scoring nine hits on the *Lützow* and four on the *Derfflinger*. 'It was clear,' wrote von Hase, 'that the enemy could now see us much better than we could see him. But at 1829 the veil of mist divided. Sharply silhouetted against the horizon we saw the *Invincible*, and at 1831 the *Derfflinger* fired her last salvo at that ship.' One shell struck the *Invincible*'s Q turret and, after an interval of seconds, Q magazine, followed by P, blew up. Since she was 567 feet long and sank in less than 30 fathoms, an officer on the *Indomitable* 'saw her two ends standing perpendicularly above water, the ship appearing to have broken in halves, each resting on the bottom. The survivors were clinging to the floating wreckage; I have never seen anything more splendid than these few cheering as we raced by.' Six only were rescued by the destroyer *Badger*; but the gallant Admiral, Captain A. L. Cay, and more than 1,000 officers and men did not sacrifice their lives in vain: they left four of Hipper's ships in a worse state than the surviving British battlecruisers. The *Lützow* 'received numerous heavy hits, which put B turret and the W/T station out of action and caused flooding of the torpedo rooms, while the gunnery control and communications stations were filled with water. The ship could only proceed at slow speed. I [Hipper] had to transfer aboard torpedoboat *G39*,' after he had extricated his ships by turning SW into the enveloping mist, and instructed Captain Harder to make his own way back to harbour – without much confidence that he would arrive. Captain Hartog in the *Derfflinger*, though handicapped by water streaming through a large gap in his ship's bows, with his W/T out of action, and 180 killed and wounded from 20 hits by heavy shell, led the remaining German battlecruisers, whilst Hipper tried to board the *Seydlitz*, only to find that Captain von Egidy's ship was too badly damaged for him to hoist his flag in her. Since Captain Zenker's crew had been unable to repair the *Von der Tann*'s turrets, only the *Moltke* remained fit for action, but some time was to elapse before Hipper managed to board her.

Behncke's battleships might have suffered comparable damage. A turn away in succession would have invited disaster; a normal turn together was not feasible when the German line was bent round in an arc. Fortunately, they had practised an alternative manœuvre, the *Gefechtskehrtwendung*, in which the rear ship turned first, the others putting their helms over in succession as soon as each saw her next astern begin to turn. Realizing that Jellicoe had caught him at a tactical disadvantage, Scheer ordered this 'battle turn' to starboard at 1835, under cover of smoke from his torpedoboats, and in four minutes his whole battle fleet was steaming W, directly away from its opponents. Except for the *Lützow*, which steered S, Hipper's battlecruisers conformed; so did Boedicker's and von Reuter's light cruisers with the result that, by 1845, the High Seas Fleet had disappeared into the mist, except for the crippled *Wiesbaden* and the 3rd TBF. But although Commander Hollmann was in a favourable position to attack, his boats fired only six torpedoes at Beatty's battlecruisers before Michelsen hoisted their recall.

Nothing exemplifies more the difficulties with which Jellicoe had to contend than the brevity of this first clash between the battle fleets. Despite the skill with which the British C-in-C had enmeshed the High Seas Fleet, poor visibility allowed Scheer to extricate his ships from a potentially disastrous position after the *Iron Duke* had fired only nine salvoes. But Jellico had no reason to be despondent; the Grand Fleet was where it could prevent the High Seas Fleet escaping through the Skagerrak or back to the Jade – whereas Scheer's only compensation was that less than two hours remained before nightfall.

The only effective counter to Scheer's turn was a resolute chase, but although many of the British vessels saw it, no captain reported it to his C-in-C. Jellicoe had to rely on what he could see for himself; and because the poor visibility limited his view to four of Scheer's battleships, he first supposed the enemy's disappearance to be due to the mist thickening. Minutes later he thought that Scheer must have made a small alteration of course, and turned his battle fleet by divisions to SE at 1844. Not for another eleven minutes did he judge that Scheer had made a large turn, when he altered again, but only as far as S which was 90 degrees off the enemy's course. Jellicoe was not risking his battleships by following so closely after a retiring enemy whom he believed might launch a massed torpedoboat attack and sow mines in his wake. This possibility gained support at 1855 when a torpedo from the crippled *Wiesbaden* struck the *Marlborough*, Captain G. P. Ross, flooding a boiler room and reducing her speed to 17 knots. Because this might have been a mine, Jellicoe waited a further ten minutes before turning his fleet so far as SW by S, half an hour after Scheer ordered his *Kehrtwendung* to W, a period of time in which more ships than Jellicoe's cruisers failed to tell him what had happened to the enemy, and Beatty's battlecruisers were delayed in their pursuit by a gyro compass failure that caused the *Lion* to lead round in an involuntary circle.

None of this was, however, of much importance because Scheer made a decision for which there is no comparable justification. Instead of continuing to the west to avoid a further engagement before nightfall, he ordered Schuur's and Goehle's flotillas to attempt a torpedo attack; then, at 1855, he reversed his battle fleet's course by a further *Kehrtwendung*, so that it was again steering straight for Jellicoe's line. For what was tantamount to suicide, the German C-in-C gave this explanation in his report on the battle:

The enemy was in a position to do with us what he pleased before nightfall, taking the initiative from us, and barring our retreat to the German Bight. There was only one way to forestall this; to strike a second blow at the enemy with a second ruthless onslaught, and to bring the torpedoboats against him with full force. This would surprise the enemy, throwing his plans into confusion for the rest of the day, and, if the blow fell heavily enough, would make easier disengagement for the night. It also offered the possibility of a final attempt to bring assistance to the hard-pressed *Wiesbaden*, and to rescue her crew.

It is more likely that a report from the *Moltke* giving the British battle fleet's bearing as E by S at 1845, coupled with Scheer's belief that the 3rd BCS comprised four battleships, led him to suppose Jellicoe's line to be further to the south than it was, so that an alteration to E would allow the High Seas Fleet to 'cross the T' of its rear. Certainly his cruisers, especially Boedicker's 2nd SG, which made a half-hearted reconnaissance to the eastward, failed him as badly as Jellicoe's. But to his Chief of Staff, Captain von Trotha, Scheer admitted: 'If I had done this in a peace exercise, I should have lost my command.'

On the British side there was one splendid exception to the cruisers' failure to act as 'the eyes of the fleet'. Goodenough had followed the retiring Scheer and, at 1904, was able to give Jellicoe the German battle fleet's position and to tell him that it had reversed course. This news, coupled with gunfire to the rear – from Gaunt's battleships driving off an attack by Hollmann's 3rd TBF – and the approach of Schuur's and Goehle's flotillas, was enough for Jellicoe to turn his battle fleet back into line ahead, steering S at 1909. A minute later Hipper's battlecruisers and Behncke's battleships appeared out of the mist to starboard, and the British C-in-C knew that he was again crossing his opponent's T. At 1912 his fleet 'presented a marvellously impressive spectacle as salvo after salvo rolled out along the line'. The unlucky *Wiesbaden* suffered once again, to sink during the coming night with all her crew save one. 'The *Colossus* and *Collingwood* concentrated on the *Lützow*, and we fired five salvoes at her, the range being about 8,500 yards. She burst into flame, listed and turned away,' so badly crippled that some hours later her escorting torpedoboats hastened her end with a torpedo, after rescuing her crew. But more of the British battleships' targets were at the head of Scheer's battle fleet; the *Marlborough* 'sighted three ships of the *König* class and opened fire at one of them at

10,750 yards. The sixth, twelfth, thirteenth and fourteenth salvoes were all distinct hits.' Beatty's ships, three miles ahead of Jerram's flagship, joined in; at 1920 the *Indomitable* 'reopened fire at the enemy battlecruisers at 14,000 yards, our squadron making splendid practice. Time after time a dull orange glow appeared onboard one or another of their ships. One turned out of the line, her after part enveloped in flame.' The Germans replied to this onslaught with little effect. Only one of Jellicoe's battleships was struck, the *Colossus* by a salvo of three 12-inch shells, but the damage to Captain Dudley Pound's ship was slight, only five men being wounded.

On the other hand, many of the German dreadnoughts suffered considerably, especially the *König* in which Behncke was wounded, and the *Grosser Kurfürst*, before Scheer, in an attempt to extricate his ships from such a vulnerable position, decided to sacrifice his battlecruisers. 'Close the enemy and ram,' he signalled. Although seriously damaged, and without Hipper to lead them, the four ships of the 1st SG

> hurled themselves against the enemy. A dense hail of fire swept them. Hit after hit struck the *Derfflinger*. A 15-inch shell pierced the armour of Caesar turret, setting on fire two charges from which the flames spread to the working chamber where they set fire to four more, and from there to the handing room where four more were ignited. But they only blazed; they did not explode. This saved the ship, but killed all but five of the 70 men inside the turret. A few minutes later a 15-inch shell pierced the roof of Dora turret and the same horrors ensued: 80 men were killed instantly.

The *Seydlitz* and *Von der Tann* were also stricken, but the German battlecruisers were not required to complete their death-ride; at 1917 Scheer changed his order to, 'Operate against the enemy's van', so that they might cover his battle fleet's withdrawal at a less dangerous range. However, Hartog then manœuvred the 1st SG so close to the head of the German battle fleet that the *König* was compelled to alter course. 'As a result the ships of the 3rd BS were bunched so close together that several were forced to sheer out to starboard to avoid collisions. Despite reducing to slow speed, the *Kaiserin* came under the lee of the *Prinzregent Luitpold*, and in the wake of the *Kaiser*. This piling up of so many ships under the heaviest enemy fire was so unfavourable that during this short period the enemy registered the greatest number of hits.' Scheer was, nonetheless, able to extricate his fleet by a third battle turn of 16 points

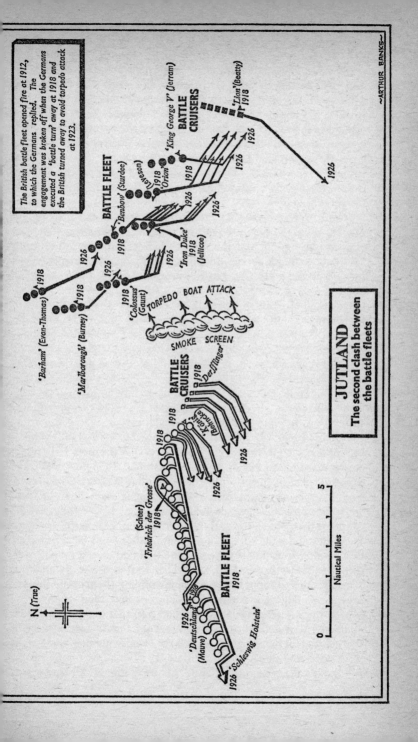

JUTLAND
The second clash between
the battle fleets

The British battle fleet opened fire at 1912, to which the Germans replied. The engagement was broken off when the Germans executed a "battle turn" away at 1918 and the British turned away to avoid torpedo attack at 1923.

N (True)

BATTLE CRUISERS
'Iron' (Beatty)
1918

'King George V' (Jerram)
1918
'Orion'
'Jerson'
BATTLE FLEET
'Benbow' (Sturdee)
'Iron Duke' 1918 (Jellicoe)

'Barham' (Evan-Thomas) 1918
'Marlborough' (Burney) 1918
'Colossus' (Gaunt)
1918

TORPEDO BOAT ATTACK

SMOKE SCREEN

BATTLE CRUISERS
'Derfflinger'
'King' (Behncke)

'Friedrich der Grosse' (Scheer) 1918

BATTLE FLEET
1918

'Deutschland' (Mauve)
'Schleswig Holstein'

Nautical Miles
0   5

~ARTHUR BANKS~

to starboard, thanks largely to the individual initiative of his captains. The *Friedrich der Grosse*, for example, made her turn to port, whilst both the *Markgraf* and the *Ostfriesland* put their helms over without waiting for the *Kaiser* and the *Thüringen*. By 1935 all were again heading W at the maximum speed of Mauve's pre-dreadnoughts, followed by the four German battlecruisers which had survived their sacrificial ordeal. After an engagement that had lasted for just fifteen minutes, compared with twenty-five on the first occasion, the German heavy ships disappeared into the mist, and the British ceased fire.

Scheer ordered his flotillas to cover this turn, but the 3rd, 5th and 7th TBF were too far to the northward, and Schuur's boats were so slow in moving out that they had to be recalled. The 6th and 9th TBF were engaged by the British battleships and counter-attacked by Le Mesurier's 4th LCS and Hawksley's 11th DF; nonetheless, 20 boats closed to under 8,000 yards and fired 31 torpedoes, of which ten reached the British line with an effect out of all proportion to their number. With justification, since Beatty gained the same impression, Jellicoe believed his battle fleet was threatened by many more, and both British and German protagonists of this new weapon believed that at least 30 per cent would hit unless drastic avoiding action was taken. The *Grand Fleet Battle Orders* stressed that the best countermeasure was to turn away by divisions, so that ships would outrun the torpedoes' range; and nothing prior to Jutland had shown that, in poor visibility, this would have a greater disadvantage than temporarily increasing gun range by 3,000–4,000 yards — that of losing contact with the enemy — so that the more risky alternative of turning towards might be justified. Though Sturdee had expressed disagreement with 'the whole line having to turn away from a torpedo threat; a turn towards in some cases might be more efficacious', it was not until long after the battle that Jellicoe admitted that 'a turn towards might sometimes be a useful counter'. At 1923, coincident with Scheer's third battle turn, he ordered his fleet to alter four points away: as the Germans swung round to W, the Grand Fleet turned to SE, which hastened the moment of Scheer's ships' disappearance without avoiding the torpedo danger. Several of Jellicoe's battleships had to comb their tracks: the *Marlborough* 'altered course to starboard so that one passed ahead, number two passed so close astern that we should have been hit if she had not been swinging under helm, whilst number three went right under the ship'.

Jellicoe's decision to turn away was not of itself the reason why he lost contact with his opponent: he thought that the enemy's 'temporary disappearance was due to a thickening of the mist, and no report of this German movement reached me', although it was seen by several battleships at the rear of his line. When he judged the torpedo threat to be over, at 1935, the British C-in-C supposed an alteration of five points – one more than his turn away – would bring his ships back into range; but Scheer had altered to the three-point diverging course of SW. And even Goodenough, who saw Scheer on this course, failed to report it. However, at 1940, a signal from the *Lion* told Jellicoe that his turn had not been enough and he altered again, but only as far as a parallel course. And five minutes later Beatty, who had turned to starboard to engage the German battlecruisers, reported the bearing of the head of Scheer's battle fleet, and, more important, its course. Unfortunately, Goodenough made an erroneous report of an unknown number of enemy ships detached to the NW, which confused his C-in-C. Not until 2000, when Scheer was some 15 miles away, did Jellicoe take the drastic action needed to regain contact by turning his Battle Fleet to W. Even so, he did not increase speed to more than the damaged *Marlborough* could manage. One minute more, and he received a signal from Beatty, originated at 1947: 'Submit van of battleships follow battlecruisers. We can then cut off whole of enemy's battle fleet.' towards which he had sent his light cruisers to keep in touch; an entirely proper signal, though Beatty's denigrators were later to criticize it as insubordinate. But to this message's transit delay Jellicoe added another: he waited 15 minutes before ordering Jerram to 'follow our battlecruisers', with no sense of urgency and without indicating why, by which time Beatty's ships were no longer in sight from the *King George V*. Jerram steered for the direction in which he had last seen Beatty, without increasing speed, and not knowing that he had turned two points away from the enemy.

The two fleets were, nonetheless, still converging. Concerned at being headed so far away from his base, Scheer had altered to S at 1945 when the *Iron Duke* was only 12 miles to the east.

Should we succeed in checking the enemy's enveloping movement and reaching the Horn Reefs before them [he wrote], we should retain the initiative for next morning. To this end, all flotillas had to attack during the night, at the risk of doing without them in new engagements at dawn. The German Battle Fleet had to make for the Horn Reefs by the shortest route, maintaining this course against all attacks by the enemy.

One result of this was the last contacts between the two fleets before nightfall. Around 2025 the German battlecruisers, which were trying to get into station ahead of Scheer's Battle Fleet, were subjected to heavy fire from Beatty's force, without being able to make any effective reply. Since all but two of the *Derfflinger*'s 12-inch guns were out of action and her hull was flooded with more than 3,000 tons of water, Hartog swung the 1st SG away to a position on Scheer's disengaged side. This brief action coincided with Hipper's attempt to board the *Moltke*, so that he was prevented from regaining control of his squadron until after 2100.

Napier's cruisers were

> ordered to sweep to the westward to locate the head of the enemy's line. We were in the process of spreading when, at 2020, five enemy light cruisers were observed bearing NNW. We engaged them at 7,000 yards. Their salvoes were all short, and ours may have been as bad because it was impossible to spot under such hopeless light conditions.

Next, Beatty's ships turned their guns on Mauve's pre-dreadnoughts which were now leading the German battle fleet, when hits on the *Schleswig-Holstein*, *Pommern* and *Hessen* deflected this squadron away to the SW where it disappeared from view. Le Mesurier and Hawksley also saw it but, 'observing that the *King George V* had altered course away, we deemed it necessary to follow her so as not to lose touch with our own fleet'. No wonder Beatty revised his fighting instructions after the battle to stress that his cruisers' only duty, so long as enemy heavy ships remained afloat, was to 'locate and report, attack and destroy'.

A little earlier than this, at 2010, Hawksley sighted Heinecke's 5th TBF to the east of the rest of Scheer's fleet, and led his destroyers in for an attack on them, supported by the 4th LCS. This brought the British ships within range of Behncke's squadron, at the rear of Scheer's line. Hawksley missed his opportunity for a torpedo attack, but Le Mesurier's ships

> closed to about 8,500 yards. We were not fired at previous to turning, possibly because they could not make us out as friend or enemy, but they then rectified the error and got our range quickly. Having fired torpedoes, we proceeded east at full speed to join our own fleet. We were in sight of the German battleships for ten minutes and were hit five times. High speed and zigzagging saved us from annihilation.

Although damage to Le Mesurier's flagship prevented him signalling a report, Jellicoe saw something of this engagement for himself and at 2038 flashed to the *Comus*: 'What are you firing at?' From Captain A. G. Hotham's reply, 'Enemy battle fleet', the C-in-C believed he was closing the enemy, which seemed to be confirmed a moment later by gunfire towards the British rear where Goodenough's squadron had a short action with the 2nd TBF. But not until 2100 was the situation made reasonably clear by reports from the *Lion* and *Falmouth*.

A third, more crucial, encounter followed. The *Caroline* and *Royalist*, stationed ahead of the *King George V*, in which Jerram was still trying to follow Beatty's unseen ships, sighted Scheer's line. Captains H. R. Crooke and the Hon H. Meade turned to attack Mauve's pre-dreadnoughts with torpedoes as they reported this to Jerram. Largely because his navigating officer assured him that the ships sighted were British battlecruisers, Jerram negatived the attack. When Crooke repeated that they were the enemy, Jerram answered, 'If you are quite sure, attack,' whereupon the *Caroline* and *Royalist* fired their torpedoes. Hawksley also sighted these ships, identified them as enemy, and turned towards, expecting the 2nd BS to open fire – but Jerram remained convinced that they were Beatty's ships. Not everyone agreed with this; Leveson's flag lieutenant in the *Orion* went so far as to say: 'Sir, if you leave the line now and turn towards, your name will be as famous as Nelson's.' But, like Evan-Thomas, the Rear-Admiral had been schooled to obey; he answered: 'We must follow our next ahead.' As Scheer's ships turned again to the west before resuming their southerly course, Jerram continued to lead the British battle fleet on a parallel course instead of a closing one.

This was the last meeting between the two fleets before night closed over the North Sea. Despite losses, for which much of the credit was Hipper's and his battlecruisers', the Grand Fleet remained in command of the situation. Scheer had twice fled from the thunderous cannonade of a force which now stretched for more than ten miles between the High Seas Fleet and the safety of its harbours. Although there had been no Trafalgar on 31 May, in large measure because contact had been made so late in the day, because Scheer was intent on avoiding action and because of the mist, Jellicoe could have high hopes of another 'Glorious First of June' when the sun rose on a new day in five hours' time.

Appendix F

The British Grand Fleet at Jutland

THE BATTLE FLEET

Battleships
(from van to rear when deployed)

Completed: 1909–16. *Displacement:* 18,600–28,000 tons. *Armour:* 9 to 12″ belt; 9 to 13″ turrets. *Designed speed:* 21 knots (*Canada* 23). *Armament:* ten 12″ guns (9 ships); fourteen 12″ guns (*Agincourt*); ten 13·5″ guns (11 ships); ten 14″ guns (*Canada*); eight 15″ guns (2 ships); sixteen–eighteen 4″ *or* twelve–twenty 6″ guns; three–four 21″ (in three ships, three 18″) torpedo tubes.

SECOND BS

King George V	Captain F. L. Field*
	(*Flagship of* Vice-Admiral Sir Martyn Jerram)
Ajax	Captain G. H. Baird
Centurion	Captain M. Culme-Seymour
Erin	Captain the Hon V. A. Stanley
Orion	Captain O. Backhouse
	(*Flagship of* Rear-Admiral A. C. Leveson)
Monarch	Captain G. H. Borrett
Conqueror	Captain H. H. D. Tothill
Thunderer	Captain J. A. Fergusson

FOURTH BS

Iron Duke	Captain F. C. Dreyer
	(*Flagship of* Admiral Sir John Jellicoe)
Royal Oak	Captain C. MacLachan
Superb	Captain E. Hyde-Parker
	(*Flagship of* Rear-Admiral A. L. Duff)
Canada	Captain W. C. M. Nicholson
Benbow	Captain H. W. Parker
	(*Flagship of* Vice-Admiral Sir Doveton Sturdee)

* Later Admiral of the Fleet Sir Frederick Field, First Sea Lord 1930–2.

Bellerophon	Captain E. F. Bruen
Téméraire	Captain E. V. Underhill
Vanguard	Captain J. D. Dick

FIRST BS

Marlborough	Captain G. P. Ross
	(*Flagship of* Vice-Admiral Sir Cecil Burney)
Revenge	Captain E. B. Kiddle
Hercules	Captain L. Clinton-Baker
Agincourt	Captain H. M. Doughty
Colossus	Captain A. D. P. R. Pound*
	(*Flagship of* Rear-Admiral E. F. A. Gaunt)
Collingwood	Captain J. C. Ley
Neptune	Captain V. H. G. Bernard
St Vincent	Captain W. W. Fisher

Battlecruisers

(temporarily attached)

Completed: 1908–9. *Displacement:* 17,250 tons. *Armour:* 6″ belt; 7″ turrets. *Designed speed:* 25·5 knots. *Armament:* eight 12″ guns; sixteen 4″ guns; four 18″ torpedo tubes.

THIRD BCS

Invincible	Captain A. L. Cay
	(*Flagship of* Rear-Admiral the Hon. H. L. A. Hood)
Inflexible	Captain E. H. F. Heaton-Ellis
Indomitable	Captain F. W. Kennedy

Armoured Cruisers

Completed: 1905–8. *Displacement:* 10,850–14,600 tons. *Armour:* 6″ belt. *Designed speed:* 22–23 knots. *Armament:* four 9·2″ and ten 7·5″ guns (3 ships); six 9·2″ and four 7·5″ guns (2 ships); six 9·2″ and ten 6″ guns (2 ships); four 7·5″ and six 6″ guns (1 ship); two-five 18″ torpedo tubes.

FIRST CS

Defence	Captain S. V. Ellis
	(*Flagship of* Rear-Admiral Sir Robert Arbuthnot)
Warrior	Captain V. B. Molteno
Duke of Edinburgh	Captain H. Blackett
Black Prince	Captain T. P. Bonham

* Later Admiral of the Fleet Sir Dudley Pound, who was First Sea Lord during the greater part of the Second World War.

SECOND CS

Minotaur	Captain A. C. S. H. D'Aeth
	(*Flagship of* Rear-Admiral H. L. Heath)
Hampshire	Captain H. J. Savill
Cochrane	Captain E. La T. Leatham
Shannon	Captain J. S. Dumaresq

Light Cruisers

Completed: 1909–16. *Displacement:* 3,300–3,750 tons (*Chester* 5,200). *Designed speed:* 26 knots (5 ships); 29 knots (6 ships). *Armament:* Six–ten 4″ guns (4 ships); ten 5·5″ guns (*Chester*); two 6″ and six 4″ guns (*Royalist*); four 6″ guns (5 ships); two 21″ torpedo tubes (5 ships); eight 21″ torpedo tubes (6 ships).

FOURTH LCS

Calliope	Commodore C. E. Le Mesurier
Constance	Captain C. S. Townsend
Caroline	Captain H. R. Crooke
Royalist	Captain the Hon H. Meade
Comus	Captain A. G. Hotham

ATTACHED: (chiefly for repeating visual signals between units of the Battle Fleet)

Active	Captain P. Withers
Bellona	Captain A. B. S. Dutton
Blanche	Captain J. M. Casement
Boadicea	Captain L. C. S. Woollcombe
Canterbury	Captain P. M. R. Royds
Chester	Captain R. N. Lawson

Destroyers

Completed: 1912–16. *Displacement:* 1,000 tons (approx). *Designed speed:* 28–30 knots. *Armament:* three 4″ guns; two–four 21″ torpedo tubes. (*Castor* as 4th L CS above).

FOURTH DF

Tipperary (Captain C. J. Wintour), *Acasta, Achates, Ambuscade, Ardent, Broke, Christopher, Contest, Fortune, Garland, Hardy, Midge, Ophelia, Owl, Porpoise, Shark, Sparrowhawk, Spitfire, Unity*

ELEVENTH DF

Castor (light cruiser: Commodore J. R. P. Hawksley), *Kempenfelt, Magic, Mandate, Manners, Marne, Martial, Michael, Milbrook, Minion, Mons, Moon, Morning Star, Mounsey, Mystic, Ossory*

TWELFTH DF

Faulknor (Captain A. J. B. Stirling), Maenad, Marksman, Marvel, Mary
Rose, Menace, Mindful, Mischief, Munster, Narwhal, Nessus, Noble, Nonsuch,
Obedient, Onslaught, Opal

Miscellaneous

Abdiel (Minelayer)
Oak   (Destroyer tender to fleet flagship)

THE BATTLECRUISER FLEET

Battlecruisers
(from van to rear)

Completed: 1912–14. Displacement: 26,350–28,500 tons. Armour: 9″ belt and
turrets. Designed speed: 27–28 knots. Armament: eight 13·5″ guns; sixteen
4″ (Tiger twelve 6″) guns; two (Tiger four) 21″ torpedo tubes.

Lion   Captain A. E. Chatfield*
                        (Flagship of Vice-Admiral Sir David Beatty)

FIRST BCS

Princess Royal   Captain W. H. Cowan
 —   (Flagship of Rear-Admiral O. de B. Brock)
Queen Mary   Captain C. I. Prowse
Tiger   Captain H. B. Pelly

Completed: 1911–12. Displacement: 18,750 tons. Armour: 6″ belt; 7″ turrets.
Designed speed: 26 knots. Armament: eight 12″ guns; sixteen 4″ guns; three
21″ torpedo tubes.

SECOND BCS

New Zealand   Captain J. F. E. Green
                        (Flagship of Rear-Admiral W. C. Pakenham)
Indefatigable   Captain C. F. Sowerby

Fast Battleships
(temporarily attached)

Completed: 1915–16. Displacement: 27,500 tons. Armour: 13″ belt and turrets.
Designed speed: 25 knots. Armament: eight 15″ guns; fourteen 6″ guns; four
21″ torpedo tubes.

* Later Admiral of the Fleet Lord Chatfield, First Sea Lord 1932–5, and subsequently Minister for Coordination of Defence until 1940.

FIFTH BS

Barham	Captain A. W. Craig
	(*Flagship of* Rear-Admiral H. Evan-Thomas)
Valiant	Captain M. Woollcombe
Warspite	Captain E. M. Phillpotts
Malaya	Captain the Hon A. D. E. H. Boyle

Light Cruisers

As 4th LCS above.

FIRST LCS

Galatea	Commodore E. S. Alexander-Sinclair
Phaeton	Captain J. E. Cameron
Inconstant	Captain B. S. Thesiger
Cordelia	Captain T. P. H. Beamish

Completed: 1911–14. *Displacement:* 4,800–5,400 tons. *Designed speed:* 25·5 knots. *Armament:* eight 6″ guns (4 ships); nine 6″ guns (2 ships); two 6″ and ten 4″ guns (1 ship); ten 5·5″ guns (1 ship); two 18″ or 21″ torpedo tubes.

SECOND LCS

Southampton	Commodore W. E. Goodenough
Birmingham	Captain A. A. M. Duff
Nottingham	Captain C. B. Miller
Dublin	Captain A. C. Scott

THIRD LCS

Falmouth	Captain J. E. Edwards
	(*Flagship of* Rear-Admiral T. D. W. Napier)
Yarmouth	Captain T. D. Pratt
Birkenhead	Captain E. Reeves
Gloucester	Captain W. F. Blunt

Destroyers

Completed: 1912–16. *Displacement:* 1,000 tons (approx). *Designed speed:* 30–34 knots. *Armament:* three 4″ guns; two–four 21″ torpedo tubes (*Fearless* and *Champion* as 4th LCS above).

FIRST DF

Fearless (light cruiser: Captain D. C. Roper), *Acheron, Ariel, Attack, Badger, Defender, Goshawk, Hydra, Lapwing, Lizard*

NINTH AND TENTH DF (combined)

Lydiard (Commander M. L. Goldsmith), *Landrail, Laurel, Liberty, Moorsom, Morris, Termagent, Turbulent*

THIRTEENTH DF

Champion (light cruiser: Captain J. U. Farie), *Moresby, Narborough, Nerissa, Nestor, Nicator, Nomad, Obdurate, Onslow, Pelican, Petard*

Seaplane-Carrier

Engadine

Appendix G

The German High Seas Fleet at the Skagerrak

THE BATTLE FLEET

Battleships
(from van to rear)

Completed: 1909–14. *Displacement:* 18,875–25,800 tons. *Armour:* 12 to 14″ belt; 11 to 14″ turrets. *Designed speed:* 19–21 knots. *Armament:* ten 11″ guns (8 ships); twelve 11″ guns (4 ships); twelve 12″ guns (4 ships); twelve–fourteen 5·9″ guns; five–six 17·7″ or 19·7″ torpedo tubes.

THIRD BS

König	Captain Brüninghaus
	(*Flagship of* Rear-Admiral Paul Behncke)*
Grosser Kurfürst	Captain E. Goette
Kronprinz	Captain C. Feldt
Markgraf	Captain Seiferling
Kaiser	Captain Freiherr von Keyserlingk
	(*Flagship of* Rear-Admiral H. Nordmann)
Kaiserin	Captain Sievers
Prinzregent Luitpold	Captain K. Heuser

FIRST BS

Friedrich der Grosse	Captain T. Fuchs
	(*Flagship of* Vice-Admiral Reinhard Scheer)
Ostfriesland	Captain von Natzmer
	(*Flagship of* Vice-Admiral E. Schmidt)
Thüringen	Captain H. Küsel
Helgoland	Captain von Kameke
Oldenburg	Captain Höpfner
Posen	Captain R. Lange
	(*Flagship of* Rear-Admiral W. Engelhardt)

* Subsequently Chief of the German Naval Staff, 1920–4, for the small Fleet which the Treaty of Versailles allowed Germany to retain.

Rheinland	Captain Rohardt
Nassau	Captain H. Klappenbach
Westfalen	Captain Redlich

Completed: 1903–5. *Displacement:* 13,200 tons. *Armour:* 10″ belt; 11″ turrets. *Designed speed:* 17 knots. *Armament:* four 11″ guns; fourteen 6·7″ guns; six 17·7″ torpedo tubes.

SECOND BS

Deutschland	Captain H. Meurer
	(*Flagship of* Rear-Admiral F. Mauve)
Hessen	Captain R. Bartels
Pommern	Captain Bölken
Hannover	Captain W. Heine
	(*Flagship of* Rear-Admiral Freiherr von Dalwigk zu Lichtenfels)
Schlesien	Captain F. Behncke
Schleswig-Holstein	Captain Barrentrapp

Light Cruisers

Completed: 1903–8. *Displacement:* 2,500–3,550 tons. *Designed speed:* 21–24·5 knots. *Armament:* ten 4·1″ guns; two 17·7″ torpedo tubes.

FOURTH SG

Stettin	Captain F. Rebensburg
	(*Broad pendant of* Commodore L. von Reuter)
München	Commander O. Böcker
Hamburg	Commander von Gaudecker
Frauenlob	Captain G. Hoffmann
Stuttgart	Captain Hagedorn

Torpedoboats

Completed: 1912–15. *Displacement:* 800–1,000 tons. *Designed speed:* 35 knots. *Armament:* two 3·5″ or 4·1″ guns; four–six 19·7″ torpedo tubes. (*Rostock: Completed:* 1913. *Displacement:* 5,500 tons. *Designed speed:* 27 knots. *Armament:* twelve 4·1″ guns; four 19·7″ torpedo tubes).

Rostock (light cruiser)	Captain O. Feldmann
	(*Broad pendant of* Commodore A. Michelsen)

FIRST TBF (half)

4 boats under Commander C. Albrecht in *G39*

THIRD TBF

7 boats under Commander Hollmann in *S53*

FIFTH TBF

    11 boats under Commander Heinecke in *G11*

SEVENTH TBF

    9 boats under Commander von Koch in *S24*

THE BATTLECRUISER FORCE

Battlecruisers

Completed: 1910–15. *Displacement:* 19,370–26,740 tons. *Armour:* 10 to 12″ belt; 9 to 10½″ turrets. *Designed speed:* 25–27 knots. *Armament:* eight 11″ guns (1 ship); ten 11″ guns (2 ships); eight 12″ guns (2 ships); ten–fourteen 5·9″ guns; four 17·7″ or 19·7″ torpedo tubes.

FIRST SG

Lützow	Captain Harder
	(*Flagship of* Vice-Admiral Franz Hipper)
Derfflinger	Captain Hartog
Seydlitz	Captain M. von Egidy
Moltke	Captain von Karpf
Von der Tann	Captain W. Zenker*

Light Cruisers

Completed: 1915–16. *Displacement:* 4,350–5,300 tons. *Designed speed:* 28 knots. *Armament:* eight 5·1″ or 5·9″ guns; two or four 19·7″ torpedo tubes.

SECOND SG

Frankfurt	Captain T. von Trotha
	(*Flagship of* Rear-Admiral F. Boedicker)
Wiesbaden	Captain Reiss
Pillau	Captain K. Mommsen
Elbing	Captain Madlung

Torpedoboats

Completed: 1914–15. *Displacement:* 900–1,850 tons. *Designed speed:* 35 knots. *Armament:* three 3·5″ or four 4·1″ guns; six 19·7″ torpedo tubes. (*Regensburg* as *Rostock* above).

    Regensburg (light cruiser) Captain Heuberer
                     (*Broad pendant of* Commodore P. Heinrich)

* Subsequently Chief of the German Naval Staff. 1924–8.

SECOND TBF

   10 boats under Captain Schuur in *B98*

SIXTH TBF

   9 boats under Commander M. Schutlz in *G41*

NINTH TBF

   11 boats under Commander Goehle in *V28*

Scheer's Escape

Jutland: the night actions

The German Battle Fleet, aided by low visibility, avoided prolonged action with our main forces, and soon after these appeared on the scene returned to port.

Admiralty communiqué, 2 June 1916

Scheer was so determined to gain the sanctuary of the Horn Reefs swept channel, leading south through the German minefields to the Jade, that he accepted the hazards of an engagement with the Grand Fleet during the night, for which his own ships were equipped and trained. Conversely, and in accordance with accepted British policy, Jellicoe 'rejected the idea of a night action as leading to possible disaster, first owing to the presence of torpedo craft in large numbers and, secondly, to the impossibility of distinguishing between our own and enemy vessels' – his own having neither adequate searchlights nor starshell to illuminate their targets. He also thought that, since Scheer had twice turned away from the British Battle Fleet during the day, he would not risk running into it during the night by making for the Horn Reefs. Two other swept routes to the Jade being available, Jellicoe decided 'to steer to the southward where I should be in a position to renew the engagement at daylight, and should be favourably placed to intercept the enemy should he make for Heligoland or the Ems'.

At 2117 the British C-in-C closed up his battle fleet into its night cruising order of four columns in line ahead disposed abeam. Jerram's 2nd BS was nearest the enemy; next to the east came Sturdee's 4th, led by the *Iron Duke*; then Burney's 1st, with Evan-Thomas's three 'Queen Elizabeths' occupying the port wing. Jellicoe signalled no 'night intentions'; his captains were left to assume that the dark hours would be relatively quiet before the battle was renewed after dawn on 1 June. Beatty was of the same mind:

I assumed the enemy to be to the NW, and that we had established ourselves between him and his base. On receiving Jellicoe's signal that the course of the fleet was S, in view of the damaged condition of my battlecruisers, and our position being such as to make it certain we should locate the enemy at daylight under favourable circumstances, I did not consider it desirable or proper to close him during dark hours. I concluded that I should be carrying out the C-in-C's wishes by turning to the course of the fleet, my duty being to ensure that the enemy could not regain its base by passing round our southern flank.

With this object, Beatty began to lead his ships, which were accompanied by Alexander-Sinclair's and Napier's light cruisers, into station 15 miles WSW of the *Iron Duke* at 2124. Goodenough's 2nd LCS had already taken station astern of Burney's 1st BS, while Heath's and Le Mesurier's squadrons went to the east of Evan-Thomas's 5th BS, although this was the side away from the enemy.

Jellicoe did not ignore the possibility that Scheer might try the Horn Reefs route. First, at 2127, his destroyer flotillas were ordered to follow five miles astern of his battle fleet where

they would fulfil three conditions. They would be in an excellent position for attacking the enemy should he turn to regain his base during the night. They would be in a position to attack enemy torpedoboats should the latter make a night attack on our heavy ships. Finally, they would be clear of the danger of attacking our battleships in error, or of our battleships firing on them.

But, as with his battle fleet, Jellicoe gave them no such instructions: his destroyers' captains were left to suppose that, in accordance with the *Grand Fleet Battle Orders*, their prime task was to keep in touch with their own battle fleet so as to be available for action next day. Secondly, at 2205, Jellicoe detached the *Abdiel* to lay her mines off the Horn Reefs light vessel, which she did without incident before 0200.

To be fair to Jellicoe, such news as he gleaned from his ships around 2130, notably Jerram's rejection of the *Caroline*'s report (p 193), and a signal from Beatty giving the enemy's course as WSW, led him to believe the High Seas Fleet to be well to the NW of the *Iron Duke*. In reality it was as little as eight miles away because Scheer had altered to SSE at 2114, since when he had been converging on Jellicoe at an acute angle at 16 knots. This course 'is to be maintained', he told his captains, because it led straight for the Horn

Reefs where, at 2106, he radioed for a morning zeppelin reconnaissance. Mauve's pre-dreadnoughts were also ordered to the rear so that the German battleships would be led by the undamaged 1st BS, headed by Captain Redlich's *Westfalen*. The 2nd BS was about to comply when the *Schleswig-Holstein* sighted one of Goodenough's light cruisers. Much more important, the 2nd and 4th SG, which were on the side of their battle fleet nearest the enemy, saw the *Lion* flash to the *Princess Royal*: 'Please give me challenge and reply now in force as they have been lost' – an error of judgement on Chatfield's part – to which Cowan gave the answer, with the unfortunate consequence that the High Seas Fleet acquired the current British secret recognition signals. Captain Barrentrap, Boedicker and von Reuter were at one in deciding against revealing themselves by opening fire, and Mauve waited until the 2nd LCS had disappeared before turning his ships. Scheer's Battle Fleet did not, therefore, attain its night disposition until 2200, by which time Hipper's battlecruisers had been ordered to the rear.

Two hours earlier than this, Scheer decided on an offensive move to assist his fleet's escape: Michelsen, in the *Rostock*, would conduct night attacks on the Grand Fleet with all available torpedoboats. But, though the Germans, unlike the British, were trained in such tactics, they had not appreciated the need for a searching force to locate the enemy. Moreover, Michelsen soon found that Heinrich, in the *Regensburg*, had forestalled Scheer's orders at 2045: selecting those boats which had more than one torpedo left – Schuur's 2nd TBF and three of Schultz's 6th – he ordered them to attack, in the sector ENE to ESE where he believed the British battle fleet to be, whilst the rest of Schultz's boats and Goehle's 9th TBF went to screen Scheer's battle squadrons or to join Michelsen. The latter decided to allow his colleagues' arrangements to stand, and sent his own good flotillas, Heinecke's 5th and Koch's 7th, to attack in two sectors more to the south.

The 2nd TBF approached too soon: there was still enough light for it to be driven off by Goodenough's cruisers and Hawksley's 11th DF. Half an hour later Schuur tried again, but he was too far astern of the British battle fleet to achieve anything. Joined by Hollmann's 3rd TBF, which had become detached from Michelsen's group, he set course for the Skaw, some 20 torpedoboats returning to Kiel by this route, having taken no further part in the battle – a failure for which Schuur was subsequently made the scapegoat and relieved of his command. Koch's boats were fired on by Behncke's 3rd BS soon after 2130, albeit without serious consequences. More-

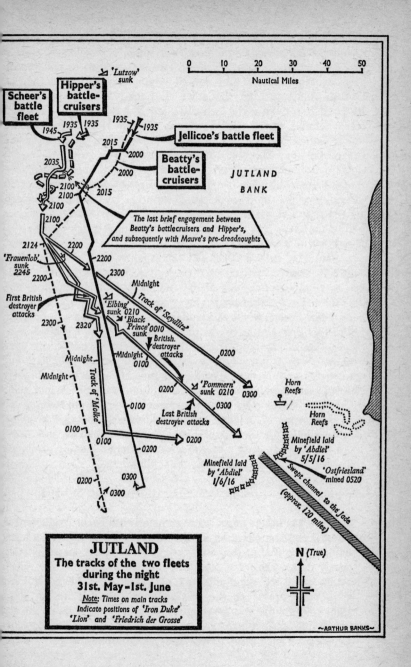

JUTLAND
The tracks of the two fleets
during the night
31st. May – 1st. June
Note: Times on main tracks
indicate positions of 'Iron Duke'
'Lion' and 'Friedrich der Grosse'

0 10 20 30 40 50
Nautical Miles

'Lutzow' sunk

Scheer's battle fleet

Hipper's battle-cruisers

Jellicoe's battle fleet

Beatty's battle-cruisers

JUTLAND
BANK

1945 1935 1935
1935 1935
2015
2000
2035 2000
2015
2100 2100
2100
2100
2124
2200 2200
'Frauenlob' sunk 2245
2200
2300

The last brief engagement between
Beatty's battlecruisers and Hipper's,
and subsequently with Mauve's pre-dreadnoughts

Midnight
Track of 'Seydlitz'

First British destroyer attacks

2300
2320
Midnight
Midnight
Track of 'Moltke'

'Elbing' sunk 0210
'Black Prince' sunk 0010
British destroyer attacks

'Pommern' sunk 0210
Last British destroyer attacks

0100
Midnight
0100
0200
0200
0300
0200
0100
0100
0200
0300
0300
0200
0200
0300
0300

Horn Reefs

Horn Reefs

Minefield laid by 'Abdiel' 5/5/16

Minefield laid by 'Abdiel' 1/6/16

'Ostfriesland' mined 0520

Swept channel to the Jade
(approx. 120 miles)

N (True)

~ARTHUR BANKS~

over, for fear that funnel sparks would disclose their approach, both his flotilla and Heinecke's limited their speed to 18 knots whereby they made contact with Jellicoe's destroyers instead of his battle fleet. At 2150 the 5th TBF sighted Wintour's 4th DF steering N towards its station for the night. Supposing it to be screening Jellicoe's heavy ships, the Germans fired four torpedoes – without result because, at the crucial moment, the 4th DF chanced to turn to the Grand Fleet's course of S. The *Garland* saw the enemy and opened fire, but Wintour decided against pursuit, which allowed Koch to attempt another attack. But by this time his boats were too far to the rear; like Schuur's, they passed astern of the Grand Fleet, then steered for the Horn Reefs. Thereafter, 'it is much to be regretted that throughout the whole night our torpedoboats, searching for the great British fleet, failed to find it, although they knew exactly where it was last seen'.

Around 2140 the *Frankfurt* and *Pillau* sighted the *Castor* and the 11th DF, likewise moving to their station for the night; but the British vessels saw nothing of the 2nd SG as it fired torpedoes at six cables, then altered course away without opening fire. Half an hour later Boedicker's light cruisers closed the *Castor*'s flotilla again. This time Hawksley saw their shadowy shapes, but supposed them to be friendly because they flashed the British challenge: the Germans were able to come to within a mile before switching on searchlights and opening a murderous fire, from which the *Castor* suffered considerable damage and numerous casualties before she could reply. 'Of the eight destroyers astern of her,' wrote Hawksley, 'two fired torpedoes, of which one passed under the *Elbing*, but some were so blinded by the *Castor*'s guns that they could see nothing, and others were so certain that they were being fired on by our own ships, that they decided not to fire their torpedoes.'

This engagement was followed by one between Goodenough's and von Reuter's squadrons. According to Lieutenant King-Hall,

at about 2215 there appeared on our starboard beam, 1,500 yards distant, five ships steering in the same direction. The next few minutes were full of suspense; then the two squadrons simultaneously decided that the other was hostile and opened fire. The action lasted three-and-a-half minutes. The four leading German ships concentrated on the *Southampton*, the fifth fired at the *Dublin*. The range was amazingly close: there would be no missing. A great deal of high explosive burst along the *Southampton*'s upper deck which was strewn with dead and wounded.

The damage inflicted on the *Dublin*, though not so serious, was enough for Captain A. C. Scott to lose touch with his squadron; so did Captain A. A. M. Duff's *Birmingham*. But von Reuter's squadron suffered worse; the *Stettin* had several guns put out of action: more important, King-Hall had 'passed down an order to the torpedo flat and fired at a group of hostile searchlights. They suddenly went out and the enemy vessel, the *Frauenlob*, sheered off to starboard'. To quote one of the five survivors from Captain Hoffmann's crew:

> About 2240 I noted a heavy shock to the ship, the electric light went out and the ammunition hoists stopped, the supply being continued with hand tackles. The emergency lighting worked well, so that for a while there was no real trouble, but after a short time the ship heeled far over to port, and the executive officer ordered us to leave the magazine. When I reached the forecastle deck the guns had been abandoned, and the ship was listing so far that I jumped overboard. As I surfaced I heard the Captain call for three cheers for the Kaiser. Only the bow of the *Frauenlob* was visible; apparently the ship had capsized and now went down stern first. After drifting on a raft for 12 hours I was rescued by the Dutch escort vessel *Thamos*.

These actions were reported to Scheer who also saw something of them for himself whereby, because the German W/T intercept service had informed him that the British destroyers were stationed five miles to the rear, he knew that his Battle Fleet's course would take it across Jellicoe's wake. Except for encounters with British light forces, the High Seas Fleet should reach the safety of its minefields shortly before dawn. When the *Westfalen* altered to S to avoid the action between Goodenough's and von Reuter's squadrons, Redlich was ordered back to SE by S, at 2234, and to 'stand on', an exhortation which Scheer repeated whenever a British attack turned his ships from the direction of the Horn Reefs.

Jellicoe had also seen and heard these engagements; from the *Garland*'s and *Castor*'s reports he concluded that they were enemy light forces searching for his Battle Fleet, because at 2155 the Admiralty radioed the substance of Scheer's instructions to Michelsen's torpedoboats (p 206). Whitehall made other attempts to help. At 2123 Jellicoe received the 2100 position of the rear ship of Scheer's line: this being to the SW of the *Iron Duke*, he rejected it: 'I should not for a moment have relied on Admiralty information in preference to reports from ships which had actually sighted the enemy to the NW.' (Room 40 had obtained the position from a signal made by the *Regensburg*; unfortunately she was 14 miles out in her reckoning.) This experience led him to doubt the accuracy of the Admiralty's next intelligence: between 2155 and 2210 Room 40 deciphered four messages from Scheer, the War Room combining three of these into a signal received by Jellicoe at 2330: 'German Battle Fleet ordered home at 2114. Battlecruisers in rear. Course SSE¾E. Speed 16 knots.' Most of this agreed with the British C-in-C's appreciation, but he rejected the course because it meant that the German Battle Fleet must be very near his rear, when reports from Goodenough (of his action with the 4th SG) and the *Birmingham* supported his belief that the High Seas Fleet was to the NW. (Duff's report was, by an unlucky chance, misleading; he had a momentary sighting of Hipper's battlecruisers shortly after 2315 when, for reasons to be related (p 212), the High Seas Fleet had temporarily altered away to W by S). This should, however, have been of small importance because the fourth message intercepted by Room 40 was Scheer's request for a zeppelin reconnaissance (p 206), which gave a clear indication of the way the High Seas Fleet was returning home. But it was not passed to Jellicoe: according to Admiral James, 'the Chief of Staff [Oliver] had left the War Room to snatch much-needed rest, and had left in charge an officer [Captain Jackson, whose arrogant contempt for the work of Room 40 had so misled Jellicoe and Beatty earlier in the day], who had no experience of German operational signals and was unaware of the significance of this one'. To quote Jellicoe: 'Of course, if the Admiralty had given me the information as to the airship reconnaissance at the Horn Reefs, I should have altered in that direction during the night.' As it was, the British Fleet held its course, whilst the C-in-C, reasonably assured that he would achieve a decisive victory by a gunnery duel with the enemy beginning soon after dawn, retired to his shelter at the back of the *Iron Duke*'s bridge to take what rest he could during the period of darkness that remained.

These three hours did not pass without his being disturbed. More signals, bursts of gunfire and the glare of searchlight beams were reported to the British C-in-C; but not all was reported that should have been, either by the Admiralty or by his own admirals and captains. He did not know that Boedicker's remaining ships clashed with the most westerly of the British flotillas, Wintour's 4th.

The flotilla was in line ahead, Captain (D) leading in the *Tipperary*, followed by the *Spitfire*, *Sparrowhawk* and some eight other destroyers. The night was dark, and we had absolutely no idea of where the enemy were, and only a very vague idea of the position of our own ships. About 2315 we distinguished three cruisers steaming at high speed on our starboard quarter. When they were in to 700 yards the *Tipperary* made the challenge. In reply the *Frankfurt*, *Pillau* and *Elbing* switched a blaze of search-lights on our unfortunate leader, and in less than a minute she was hit and badly on fire forward.

The enemy's second salvo cut one of the *Tipperary*'s main steam pipes, bringing her turbines to a standstill, the majority of her crew including Wintour were killed, and she was set on fire forward. The *Spitfire*, Lieutenant-Commander C. W. Trelawney, followed by the two boats astern of her, and the *Broke*, Commander W. L. Allen, turned and fired torpedoes. 'Much to our joy one was seen to get the second enemy ship between the after funnels and the mainmast, and she seemed to stop firing, heel over and all her lights went out.' The smitten ship was the *Elbing*, which had fired the first shot in the battle. Madlung, and his two squadron mates, tried to escape by steering through the head of Scheer's battle fleet: Captains Trotha and Mommsen reached the protective lee of the 1st BS, but the *Elbing* was rammed by the *Posen*, Captain Lange, flooding her engine room and depriving her of all steam. The leading ships of the 4th DF came under heavy fire from the *Westfalen*, *Nassau* and *Rheinland*, but the German shooting was poor. Although the *Westfalen* fired nearly 150 rounds from her 5·9-inch and smaller-calibre guns in four minutes at point-blank range, only one destroyer suffered seriously in a fight in which the British vessels' 4-inch guns did appreciable damage to the upper works of their massive opponents. Trelawney, having discovered that the *Spitfire* had no torpedoes left,

decided to return to the burning *Tipperary*. As we neared her the *Nassau* tried to ram us at full speed. The two ships met bow to bow in a fearful crash that rolled the *Spitfire* over to starboard as no sea ever made her roll. The German battleship also opened fire with her 11-inch guns, whose blast cleared everything before it. Our foremast came tumbling down, and the foremost funnel was blown back like the hinged funnel of a river steamboat. The enemy surged down our port side clearing everything before her; but none of her shells hit us. When the *Nassau* disappeared, we were still afloat, but about 60 feet from our port side had been torn away, and the enemy had left 20 feet of her upper deck inside our messdeck. However, the engineers decided that we could steam with three out of four boilers, and the bulkheads were holding, so we shaped course W, speed six knots.

The brunt of this clash was borne by the leading British destroyers because those to the rear believed Boedicker's ships to be British cruisers making a disastrous mistake, until stray searchlight beams illuminated the unmistakable shapes of 'Helgoland' dreadnoughts. Yet neither Allen of the *Broke*, now senior officer of the flotilla, nor any other destroyer, wirelessed this vital news to Jellicoe – even when their attack drove the head of Scheer's line away to W by S (as mentioned on p 210). Collecting eight of his scattered flotilla, Allen set a southerly course to regain station on Jellicoe's battle fleet. But soon after midnight,

the hull of a large ship was sighted on the starboard bow not more than half a mile away. The Captain gave the order to challenge, but as he spoke the stranger switched on a string of coloured lights, an unknown signal in our Service. 'Starboard twenty; full speed ahead both; starboard foremost tube fire when your sights come on; all guns green four oh, a battleship' – but we were too late. The *Westfalen* switched on a blaze of search- lights, then shells could be heard screaming over our heads.

The sub-lieutenant of the *Sparrowhawk* continues the story of this the 4th DF's second clash with the head of Scheer's line.

The helm was put over and orders passed to fire the remaining torpedo. The *Broke*, ahead of us, had also put her helm over but, just as we were both turning, she was hit forward, and when she should have eased her helm and steadied to fire a torpedo, as we were doing, I saw that she was still swinging to port with her helm jammed, and coming straight for our bridge at 28 knots. I remember shouting a warning to everyone to hold on, and to the forward gun's crew to clear the forecastle, just as she hit us.

The five following destroyers managed to avoid these two cripples, but Lieutenant-Commander E. G. H. Masters of the *Contest* failed to see Lieutenant-Commander S. Hopkins's ship in time, and sliced off the *Sparrowhawk*'s stern.

The *Broke* was badly damaged, with 42 dead and 34 wounded. Fortunately her foremost boiler-room bulkhead held, allowing Allen to set course to the north at slow speed. An hour later he sighted two torpedo-boats, but 'the Germans appeared even more scared than we were. On approaching to 500 yards their leader opened fire with her bow gun. We replied with our remaining one, and to our joy both ships put their helms over and disappeared into the early morning mist.' Allen continued his slow passage until 0600 on 2 June, when he feared that his ship's bulkheads would not stand up to punching into a considerable sea from the NW, and was compelled to turn her stern to it and steer towards Heligoland. Fortunately, the wind and sea moderated towards sunset, allowing him to reach the Tyne some 24 hours after the *Spitfire*. The crippled *Sparrowhawk* lay where she was, unable to steam and lit by the flames of the burning *Tipperary*, until she was seen around 0200 by a German torpedoboat which closed to 100 yards, before making off to the east without opening fire. The *Tipperary* then sank, extinguishing her unwelcome flames; but Hopkins and his crew had another disturbing moment as the new day dawned, when a German light cruiser appeared. The *Sparrowhawk*'s crew prepared to engage with their remaining gun, but the enemy did not open fire; on the contrary, at 0340 'she settled down forward, then stood on her head and sank'. She was the crippled *Elbing* in which Madlung had been trying to reach the Danish coast. At 0610 a submarine alarm turned out to be a Carley raft with 15 of the *Tipperary*'s crew. An hour later three British destroyers hove in sight and the *Marksman*, Commander N. A. Sulivan, took the battered *Sparrowhawk* in tow. But when both hawsers parted, Sulivan was ordered to sink the wreck, after taking off the surviving members of Hopkins's crew and the fortunate few whom he had saved from the *Tipperary*.

Neither Allen nor Hopkins was left with a serviceable W/T transmitter to report this action to Jellicoe: but Commander R. B. C. Hutchinson of the *Achates*, who now assumed command of what was left of the 4th DF did not do so either, leaving the C-in-C in ignorance of the fateful truth, that Scheer's Battle Fleet was crossing his wake. But if this be criticism, there can be nothing but praise for the tenacity with which these six British destroyers opposed the enemy. Before they could be chased away to the NE, the *Achates* and two others fired their torpedoes of which one struck the *Rostock*. 'Both turbines stopped, the electric power failed, and the steering engine turned hard-a-starboard, and a collision with the ships ahead and astern was only avoided because the line turned away. The hand steering was connected and manned. Shortly there came the report that the engines could be run at 17 knots,' though it was not long before steam failed and Michelsen's flagship had to be taken in tow. The *Fortune*, Lieutenant-Commander F. G. Terry, was sunk, and the *Porpoise*, Commander H. D. Colville, damaged by a heavy shell, but Lieutenant-Commander G. A. Marsden attacked

> a big ship steaming on the opposite course. Before I could judge the effect of our torpedoes, the enemy switched on searchlights, and I became aware that the *Ardent* was taking on a division of German battleships. Shell after shell hit us, and we stopped. Our three guns ceased firing, and I was wounded. I could feel the ship sinking and told my first lieutenant to get out the boats and rafts. But the enemy poured in five more salvoes at point-blank range, and the *Ardent* gave a big lurch, and heeled right over. I flopped into the sea, where there was no support beyond lifebuoys for the forty or fifty survivors, and I saw most of them die one by one. After the sun came up, I found a skiff's oar, put it under my arms and dropped off to sleep. I woke to find the *Marksman* close alongside, then relapsed into unconsciousness so that I have no recollection of being got onboard just after 0600.

To his crew, of whom only one survived besides himself, Marsden paid this heartfelt tribute: 'All hands fought the ship with the utmost gallantry till she sank, then met their death in that composed and happy spirit that comes to all who do their duty to the end.' There were many more in both fleets who earned a like epitaph.

These hard-fought encounters between the 4th DF and Scheer's Battle Fleet cost Germany two light cruisers against the loss of four British destroyers plus three badly damaged. But Scheer's determination to reach the Horn Reefs before dawn was only momentarily checked: moreover, although the darkness had been rent by heavy gun flashes time and again during the best part of an hour, not so much as a whisper of what was happening reached Jellicoe. That none of the British destroyers which were so hotly engaged made an enemy report may be understandable; but between 2315 and 0015 there were others which could have told their C-in-C that the High Seas Fleet was crossing the wake of his battle fleet, for which there is no comparable excuse. Unable to maintain 17 knots the torpedoed *Marlborough* and her division, together with the 5th BS which was keeping station on her, had dropped astern. So Scheer's converging course crossed only three miles to the rear of these seven battleships which were in a position to see more of the 4th DF's action than the rest of the British battle fleet. At 2340 the *Malaya* observed 'three points abaft starboard beam an attack by our destroyers on some enemy ships steering the same way as ours.

40   Jellicoe's flagship HMS *Iron Duke*

41   A salvo from a 'Revenge' class battleship

42 Admiral von Hipp

43 Admiral Scheer

44 German battle-cruiser *Seydlitz* on fire

45 British 15-inch gunned cruiser *Glorious*

46 Cruiser *Furious* as an aircraft-carrier

47 British battle-cruiser *Repulse*

48 U-boat torpedoes a British merchant ship

49 British submarine E11

50 Small UB-type submarine and U35

51 Blockships in the Channel at Zeebrugge

52 HMS *Vindictive* after Zeebrugge raid

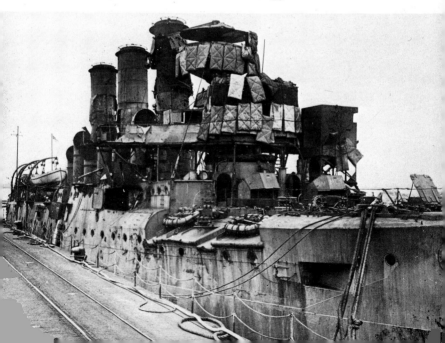

53 German dreadnought *Bayern* in Scapa Flow

54 Scuttled German battle-cruiser *Hindenburg*

Leading ship had two masts, two funnels and a conspicuous crane — apparently "Westfalen class".' She *was* the *Westfalen*, leading Scheer's line: and the *Malaya*'s gunnery officer trained his turrets on her and asked permission to fire. But Boyle refused: like Arbuthnot in December 1914, he argued that what he could see must be visible in the *Barham*; the *Malaya* must await orders from Evan-Thomas. For the same reason Boyle made no enemy report. In fact, neither the *Barham* nor the *Valiant*, nor Burney's ships, saw more than what appeared to be 'constant attacks by torpedo craft on ships which they could not identify, first to the westward and then to the northward'.

At about the same time, Farie, whose 13th DF was next to port of the 4th, saw heavy firing on the *Champion*'s starboard beam — which impelled him to increase to high speed, and 'haul out to the east because I was unable to attack whilst our own forces were between me and the enemy'. By doing this without signal, when leading a flotilla which was showing no lights, Farie lost touch with all his destroyers except the *Moresby* and *Obdurate*. He also obliged the British flotillas to the east of him to move farther in that direction, which opened a road for the German fleet, whilst his own rear ships, the *Menace* and *Nonsuch*, were nearly rammed and sunk by the *Frankfurt* and *Pillau*. There were, however, worse examples of missed opportunities than this one. Soon after the German battle-cruisers had moved to the rear of Scheer's Battle Fleet, von Egidy reported that the damaged *Seydlitz* could not maintain 16 knots and was ordered to make his own way to the Horn Reefs. Next, the *Moltke*, Hipper's flagship, lost touch and also steered to the east. As a result, both these lone battlecruisers ran into Jellicoe's battle fleet. At 2230 Captain von Karpf's ship was seen by the *Thunderer* at the rear of Jerram's 2nd BS; but Captain J. A. Fergusson neither reported the *Moltke* nor opened fire, 'as it was inadvisable to show up our battle fleet'. Thus allowed to veer away to the west, Karpf resumed his old course too soon, and sighted Jerram's ships again at 2255. This time, however, none saw Hipper's flagship, so that she was able to elude them for a second time. When von Karpf again turned towards the Horn Reefs, and was frustrated for a third time at 2320, Hipper told him to steer S whereby, around 0130, the *Moltke* passed clear ahead of the Grand Fleet, and so reached safety. Her W/T being out of action, no reports of these encounters reached Scheer until Hipper fell in with torpedoboat *G39* at 0227, when they were too late to be of use.

The *Seydlitz* had a more remarkable escape. She was sighted

around midnight by the *Marlborough* when Burney and Ross identified her as 'a large ship', but did nothing; by the *Revenge*, where
Captain E. B. Kiddle was satisfied by the wrong reply to his challenge; and by the *Agincourt* whose Captain, H. M. Doughty, 'did not
challenge her so as not to give our division away'. The light cruisers
Boadicea and *Fearless* also saw the *Seydlitz* but followed the example
of Burney's captains, 'it being too late to fire a torpedo when she
could be identified'. With thousands of tons of water in his ship's
battered hull, von Egidy was allowed to wander safely past four
British battleships, not to mention a flotilla of destroyers, to reach
the Horn Reefs in the morning, even though his ship was so much
down by the bows that her speed was reduced to seven knots.

The head of Schmidt's 1st BS was to the east of Jellicoe's Battle
Fleet by 0030, but three groups of British destroyers remained between Scheer's Battle Fleet and safety. The most westerly of these
should have comprised no more than the seven boats of the merged
9th and 10th DF's, which would have passed ahead of the converging German line. However, unknown to Goldsmith in the *Lydiard*,
the six boats of the 13th DF, which had lost touch with the
Champion, had extended his line, so that its four rear ships sighted
the German 1st BS. They identified their opponents too late to attack, and the *Petard*, coming next,

> had fired all her torpedoes, so there was nothing we could do but
> get away [recalled her captain, Lieutenant-Commander E. C. O.
> Thomson]. But as soon as we passed ahead of the *Westfalen* she
> switched her searchlights on us; and we saw the flashes of her
> secondary armament, felt the ship tremble slightly, and guessed
> we had been hit aft. The second ship in the line joined in and a
> salvo struck us forward. German searchlights were then trained
> on the *Turbulent*, my next astern, and she was rammed and sunk
> by the *Westfalen*. Lieutenant-Commander D. Stuart and his whole
> crew were lost, but we escaped without further incident, having
> been hit six times, one killing or severely wounding the crew of
> the after 4-inch gun.

For most of the 11 British destroyers which emerged unscathed
from this encounter, 'it all happened so suddenly that we hardly
realized what was taking place. It did not strike us in the *Nicator*
that this was the German fleet breaking through the line at the
weakest point.' The failure of the *Petard* and her sisters to radio an
enemy report is less easy to understand. Be this as it may, Jellicoe
learned no more of what was happening than Captain E. F. Bruen

of the *Bellerophon*, stationed three ships from the rear of Sturdee's 4th BS, who recorded: 'During the first watch there was quite a lot of firing to the NE and a cruiser seemed to be on fire. At about 2340 there was further firing astern, and for the first hour or so of the middle watch there was intermittent firing on the port quarter. Otherwise the night passed without incident.' In the *Lion*, some five miles further ahead, Chatfield 'expected any moment to be attacked by torpedoboats, but no exciting incident occurred with the exception of many indications that other portions of the fleet were not having such a peaceful time as we were'. But, according to Dreyer in the *Iron Duke*, no one supposed this to be more than 'German cruisers and destroyers trying to break through our destroyer screen to attack our battle fleet'.

Another tragedy was enacted in the Admiralty. At 2315 Room 40 deciphered two signals, made at about 2230; the first, from Scheer, read: 'Main fleet steering SE by S', which was not significantly different from the course the War Room had already passed to Jellicoe. But when read in conjunction with the second, from Michelsen to his torpedoboats, 'Be assembled by 0200 at Horn Reefs or course round Skaw', the War Room held vital intelligence (despite Room 40's accidental omission of the words 'with our main body' after 'assembled') that could have reached Jellicoe by midnight and enabled him to intercept Scheer at dawn. Fate decreed otherwise; Thomas Jackson did nothing with it. Nor were three subsequent messages relayed to Jellicoe, in which Scheer gave the position and course of his Battle Fleet at 2306, and small adjustments to its course. With a like contempt for Room 40's work, Jackson also failed to pass to the *Iron Duke* messages deciphered at 0120 and 0125, giving Scheer's position at 0043 and 0103, which might have reached Jellicoe in time to influence events. One is left to wonder why, at 0148, the Director of Operations troubled to tell the C-in-C that U-boats were coming out of German ports, and to give him the position of the sinking *Lützow*, followed at 0312 by the position in which the *Elbing* had been abandoned.

Goldsmith's ships had so nearly passed clear ahead of the German Battle Fleet that the 12th DF, led by Captain Stirling in the *Faulknor*, must have done so but for the chance that it was keeping station on Burney's lagging squadron.

At 0143, as daylight was appearing, a line of ships was sighted on the *Obedient*'s starboard beam, steering ESE. Owing to the mist we could not determine whether they were enemy until one of them challenged us incorrectly, when our Captain, Commander G. W. Campbell, decided to attack. We altered to starboard to do so, then saw that the enemy had turned six points away. They were now clearly visible, dreadnoughts leading and pre-dreadnoughts following. Conditions were nearly ideal, as it was too light for searchlights, yet sufficiently dark to make gunlaying difficult. At 0205 we fired our first torpedo at the fourth ship of their line, at 2,000 yards, when she opened fire on us from all calibres of guns. Just as it seemed we must be hit, and our torpedo to have missed, came our reward. A dull red ball appeared amidships in the *Pommern* which spread fore and aft and flared up the masts in red tongues of flame. Then the ends of the ship came up, as though her back was broken, before the mist shut her from view. A heavy fire continued to be directed at us, the *Nessus* and *Onslaught* being hit, but we increased speed and commenced to zigzag which saved us. Further torpedoes were fired by the *Maenad*'s division, but nothing could be seen of the result.

Stirling's attack was the most skilfully conducted in the whole battle, even though only six of his destroyers fired a total of 17 torpedoes, the others being driven off by accurate German gunfire. It cost Scheer one of his pre-dreadnoughts, with Captain Bölken and all his company. Moreover, Stirling made three enemy reports; but for no certain reason — perhaps a damaged aerial in the *Faulknor*, perhaps enemy jamming — no ship received the first two, and the third was read only by the *Marksman*, one of Stirling's own flotilla.

Had Jellicoe received these signals, he could have reached a position near the German minefields from which to open fire on Scheer's battle fleet at 10,000 yards by 0330. As it was, the long-drawn-out battle was almost over; Jellicoe's expedient of using his flotillas to prevent the High Seas Fleet crossing his stern had failed, not least because, to quote a German report, 'all the English destroyer attacks betrayed lack of training in night attack procedure. All were made singly.' Hawksley had been appointed first Commodore Grand Fleet Flotillas too recently to teach them the technique of coordinated attacks, whether by day or night. Jellicoe had also been left in ignorance of the fact that the enemy had eluded his grasp; that Scheer's unshakeable resolve had taken his fleet across the path of the Grand Fleet at no greater cost than the loss of one pre-dreadnought and three light cruisers.

Scheer's fleet was, however, anything but ready for another battle with his more powerful opponent. At 0230, when he had very few torpedoboats still in company,

> reports showed that the 1st SG could not sustain a serious fight. The leading ships of the 3rd BS could not have fought for any length of time owing to shortage of ammunition. The *Frankfurt*, *Pillau* and *Regensburg* were the only light cruisers available. In such misty weather there was no depending on aerial reconnaissance. There was, therefore, no certain prospect of defeating the enemy; so I abandoned further operations and ordered a return to port.

Conversely, on board HMS *Neptune*, 'at 0200 we were all back at our action stations. The visibility gave promise of a better day. We had plenty of ammunition left and felt that, given the chance, we could make short work of what remained of the enemy.' Jellicoe still supposed the enemy Battle Fleet to be to the NW, even when dawn disclosed no German vessel in sight. His first concern was, however, the extent to which his squadrons and flotillas had become scattered during the few hours of dark. Seven battleships had dropped well astern; except for Le Mesurier's 4th LCS, his battle-cruisers and cruisers were out of sight ahead; and he had no destroyers to deal with torpedoboat attacks or, potentially more menacing, with U-boats. 'All this,' he wrote, 'rendered it undesirable to close the Horn Reefs. It was necessary to collect the battle fleet and the destroyers before renewing the action.' At 0230, he reversed course and deployed into single line ahead, after wirelessing his position and intentions to Beatty and other senior officers and ordering them to conform.

The High Seas Fleet would, therefore, have avoided further action but for Farie's 2330 decision to turn away to the east. Because daylight made it possible to distinguish friend from foe, the *Champion* altered towards the sound of Stirling's dawn engagement. With the *Moresby* and *Obdurate* augmented by the *Marksman* and *Maenad* from the 12th DF, Farie sighted the rear four 'Deutschlands' of Scheer's line at 0230. He did not, however, attack them: he again turned the *Champion* away. But Lieutenant-Commander R. V. Alison of the *Moresby* 'considered action imperative and hauled out to port, firing a torpedo at 0237. A concussion shook the ship two minutes later.' Such initiative deserved to achieve more than

> a violent explosion in torpedoboat *V4*, with a high black column of water. The entire fore part was bent around to port, broke off

and sank, to rise briefly to the surface behind the stern of the boat. V2 and V6 closed. V2 lowered boats, threw lines and buoys and finally laid her forecastle alongside the stern of the boat, now rearing high out of the water, so that her crew could jump directly aboard. Others swam across, the cutter bringing the wounded alongside. Altogether 64 were saved. Since our main body was now passing, I directed the Captain of V6 to destroy the wreck, which he did with a torpedo after gunfire proved ineffective.

This was the last that any British ship saw of a major German unit before the head of Scheer's line reached the Horn Reefs light at 0330. But not all the High Seas Fleet gained the Jade without further incident. At 0330 the *Champion* and her four destroyers sighted four enemy torpedoboats carrying the crew of the sunken *Lützow*. Closing to 3,000 yards both sides opened fire, the *G40* being quickly disabled. As quickly Farie lost his opponents in the morning mist so that they were able to take their crippled sister in tow. Reinforced by the *Regensburg*, this German force was sighted 40 minutes later by the damaged *Dublin*, which had had the alarming experience of passing alone through the High Seas Fleet during the night, fortunately without being detected. However, before Scott or Heinrich could open fire, the mist closed over them, and the luckless *G40* was able to reach harbour. The crippled *Rostock* was less fortunate; whilst being towed towards the Horn Reefs, her escorts were sufficiently alarmed by a zeppelin report of the proximity of British battleships to scuttle her after taking off Michelsen and his flagship's crew. At 0520 Schmidt's flagship, the dreadnought *Ostfriesland*, struck one of the *Abdiel*'s mines, fortunately for Captain Natzmer without doing serious damage. Nor did this incident deter Scheer from holding on for the Jade where, with a sense of relief shared by all but a few of his officers and men, he arrived early in the forenoon. (They passed safely over three British submarines lying off the Vyl lightship, because these had been sent there as part of Jellicoe's original plan for drawing the enemy out, with orders to remain on the bottom until 2 June, so that they knew nothing of Jutland until they returned to Yarmouth on 9 June.) Behncke's flagship, the *König*, was drawing so much water forward that she was delayed until a rising tide allowed her to clear the Amrum Bank. The *Seydlitz*, with a draught as deep as 42 feet forward, grounded off the Horn Reefs. Von Egidy managed to clear this obstacle before any British vessel could come within range; but his ship subsequently stuck fast on the Amrum Bank, where the *Pillau* and salvage steamers had a 32-hour struggle before she was eventually towed into the Jade stern first and near to cap- sizing.

Five zeppelins had left their sheds for a reconnaissance at 1130 on the 31st; but, despite much prompting by W/T after the *Elbing* sighted the *Galatea*, none was nearer than 30 miles of the British or German fleets before they were recalled at 1800. Scheer's request for a dawn reconnaissance on the 1st was not received by his air- ship commander. However, Captain Strasser sent six zeppelins out at midnight, of his own initiative. Four of these achieved no more than on the previous day. *L24* confused matters by reporting that there were British (phantom) battleships in Jammer Bay on Den- mark's north-west coast. Only *L11* achieved anything; at 0319,

> a zeppelin suddenly appeared out of the morning haze and steered towards the *Neptune*. An order was passed to X turret to fire one round at the maximum elevation. Our next ahead fired a whole salvo and other ships started in. The airship lifted its nose to the morning breeze and disappeared, and a signal was received order- ing us not to waste ammunition.

L11 continued to shadow for more than an hour, approaching so close to the *Indomitable* at 0340 that she received a 12-inch salvo, but her reports only confirmed Scheer's decision to return to har- bour without renewing the battle. The U-boats that left Borkum Roads at 2045 on the 31st achieved even less: only *U46* made an unsuccessful attack on the *Marlborough* as she was being escorted home, after Burney had transferred his flag to the *Revenge*.

Since Beatty had not received even the limited intelligence that the Admiralty had radioed to Jellicoe during the night, and was too far ahead to see the destroyer actions, he did not share his C-in-C's belief in Scheer's whereabouts. He thought the enemy would have made such speed towards one of his southern routes to the Jade, that he would now be to the SW. So the Battlecruiser Fleet held on until shortly after 0300 before conforming with the Battle Fleet's turn to N. Even then, at 0404, Beatty signalled Jellicoe: 'Submit I may sweep SW to locate enemy.' Jellicoe had, however, already received news that dashed all his hopes: from a signal sent by the Admiralty at 0330, he learned that the German Battle Fleet was only 16 miles from the Horn Reefs at 0230 – 30 miles to the NE of the *Iron Duke* – steering SE by S at 16 knots. Since an hour and a half had elapsed since then, he could only answer Beatty with the bitter pill: 'Enemy fleet has returned to harbour.' And to all the Grand Fleet's officers and men came 'the gradual realization, the maturing disappointment, that we should not see the High Seas Fleet that day: there was to be no completion of yesterday's work'.

At 0415 Jellicoe re-formed his battleships into their day cruising order. Both he and Beatty, who was in visual touch by 0520, hoped that they might yet locate the damaged *Lützow* or *Elbing*. But 'the only signs of the enemy were hundreds of drowned bluejackets in their lifesaving waistcoats, floating near the great smears of oil and wreckage that marked the grave of some ship'. There were as many tell-tale relics of the British vessels which had been sunk, but nothing more. At 1100 Jellicoe told the Admiralty that the Grand Fleet was returning to harbour; and as its ships steamed towards Scapa and Rosyth, many enacted the last poignant scene. Onboard the *Lion*

> the removal of the charred bodies from Q turret was a very sad sight. For the burial, the Admiral, Flag Captain, and all available officers and men were on the quarterdeck. There were two parties of bearers, and planks, port and starboard, on which the bodies were placed in turn under the Union Flag, to be slid off on to the sea. There were 95 mutilated forms in their hammocks, shotted at the feet, including those of six officers. The band played hymns and the Dead March during the half-hour the ceremony lasted.

'I mourn the loss of brave men, many of them personal friends, who have fallen in their country's cause,' King George V signalled to Jellicoe on 3 June. 'Yet even more do I regret that the German High Seas Fleet was enabled by the misty weather to evade the full consequences of an encounter they have always professed to desire, but for which, when the opportunity arrived, they showed no inclination.'

12

Who Won?

---

*The raids on the Scandinavian convoys –
The action of 17 November 1917*

That terrible day when we might have accomplished so much.

Admiral Sir David Beatty

The British casualties at Jutland were much heavier than the German: 6,097 out of some 60,000 officers and men serving in the Grand Fleet lost their lives; in contrast the High Seas Fleet lost only 2,551 out of 36,000. But the casualty list is not the yardstick by which a naval action is judged.

The ships sunk are best tabulated:

	British	*German*
Battleship (pre-dreadnought)	—	1
Battlecruisers	3	1
Armoured cruisers	3	—
Light cruisers	—	4
Destroyers/Torpedoboats	8	5
	14	11
out of approx	151	99

From these figures, especially the Grand Fleet's loss of three battle-cruisers and three armoured cruisers, Germany claimed a victory. But as soon as 2 June Jellicoe had available 31 dreadnoughts, seven battlecruisers and 30 cruisers, against which Scheer could match only 18, four and nine. More important, within 12 hours of returning to harbour, the British C-in-C reported 26 dreadnoughts and six battlecruisers ready for sea and action. Scheer, with four of his dreadnoughts and all his battlecruisers in need of heavy repairs, made no such claim. The last of these was not back in service until the end of 1916, whereas even the torpedoed *Marlborough* returned to Scapa by the beginning of August.

The British losses were so much heavier because the *Queen Mary*, *Indefatigable* and *Invincible* were each destroyed by a single salvo. The key to these three catastrophes was quickly found in the *Lion*'s burnt-out Q turret. The Germans had had the advantage of this salutary lessons at the Dogger Bank action (p 146); although no fewer than nine turrets in Hipper's battlecruisers were pierced by British heavy shell at Jutland, their magazines were not endangered. But the Admiralty had retained their confidence in the working chamber as a safeguard against the flash from a cordite fire passing down the turret trunk, notwithstanding such related incidents as the near-loss of the *Kent* at the Falkland Islands (p 110).

The *Seydlitz* and *Derfflinger*, *König* and *Grosser Kurfürst*, to name the worst damaged of the German heavy ships, also survived the battering to which they were subjected for other reasons. First, Fisher required his dreadnoughts to be armed with the largest possible gun; the *Dreadnought*'s 12-inch grew into the 15-inch of the 'Queen Elizabeths'. But he would spend no money on new docks: Britain's dreadnoughts had to be designed to fit those already available. Von Tirpitz intended his dreadnoughts to be unsinkable gun platforms: he accepted smaller-calibre weapons, 11-inch at first, 12-inch later, and widened Germany's docks, which allowed her dreadnoughts and battlecruisers to carry a greater weight of armour than the British, e.g.

	Iron Duke	König	Lion	Derfflinger
Displacement (*tons*)	25,000	25,390	26,350	26,180
Beam (*feet*)	90	97	88	95
Main armament	10–13·5″	10–12″	8–13·5″	8–12″
Armour (*sides*) (*max*)	12″	14″	9″	12″
(*turrets*) (*max*)	11″	14″	9″	11″

Second, when battles were fought at point-blank range, ships were best protected by armouring their sides, and although deck armour against plunging projectiles acquired a comparable importance when ranges increased, this was so little appreciated that neither British nor German decks exceeded 2½ inches in thickness. But this was more to the Grand Fleet's disadvantage than the High Seas Fleet's because of deficiencies in British gunnery, notably the poor shooting by Beatty's battlecruisers. Thus:

	Rounds fired 12-inch and above	Hits obtained	Rounds fired to obtain one hit
British battlecruisers	1,650	26	64
British battleships	2,626	98	26

with this consequent poor comparison between the standards of the two fleets:

	Guns, 11-inch and above	Hits obtained	Hits per gun
British	344	124	0·36
German	244	120	0·53

when there was, in fact, little difference between the achievements of their battleships:

	Guns, 11-inch and above	Hits obtained	Hits per gun
British	296	110	0·37
German	200	80	0·4

Third, there was the undoubted tendency of British shells to break up on impact, instead of penetrating, as the Germans had noted in the first action of the war (p 133). When Controller, Jellicoe realized the need for armour-piercing shells that would be effective at the oblique trajectory of long-range fire, but he left the Admiralty too soon to ensure that they were provided. Not until Jutland was this lesson learned.

To admit these faults in the design of the British fleet does not, however, determine the victor in its only major clash with the High Seas Fleet. To quote Lord Hankey: 'Victory is measured not by a comparison of casualties and losses, not by tactical incidents in the battle, but only by results.' Scheer's purpose was to weaken a stronger enemy by engaging a part of his fleet, Jellicoe's to damage the High Seas Fleet without subjecting his own to undue risk, especially from underwater attack. The first round went to Scheer because Hipper's force, having made chance contact with the Battle-cruiser Fleet, enticed it within range of the German Battle Fleet. The second was Jellicoe's because Beatty lured an unsuspecting High Seas Fleet north until it was surprised by the British Battle Fleet, an achievement that is sufficient answer to those who assert that he was decisively defeated during the first phase of the battle. Points were equal in the third round; although Jellicoe engaged on a course that cut Scheer off from his base, he twice failed to follow his opponent when he recoiled, the second time being after the German C-in-C's ill-judged return to the east. But Scheer's escape during the night from the trap into which he had fallen, to reach safety by dawn, gave him the fourth round.

So much – two rounds to one – stands to the German Navy's

credit. Though a recent creation, its ships and equipment had proved superior to the British, whilst its captains, officers and men were as well – in some ways better – trained. They had, moreover, a C-in-C who was a determined fighter and Jellicoe's equal as a tactician; whilst in von Hipper (he was ennobled for his part in the battle, an honour which Scheer declined) they had the ablest admiral on either side in the whole war. What, then, of Jellicoe's purpose, for which his officers and men fought with so much courage? One of his captains might write: 'We had them stone cold and we let them go. To wait all that time and then turn away from them instead of towards was sickening. They gave us our chance and we weren't allowed to take it.' But Jutland was not limited to four rounds; there was a fifth, of which Hankey justly said: 'On the morning that followed the battle Jellicoe found himself in undisputed possession of the North Sea without a sign of an enemy, and to all intents and purposes this state of affairs continued.' In the telling words of the *Berliner Tageblatt*: 'Germany narrowly escaped a crushing defeat. It was clear to every thinking person that this battle must, and would be the last one.' And neutral opinion was effectively epitomized by a New York newspaper: 'The German Fleet has assaulted its jailor, but it is still in jail.'

Scheer was quick to realize that, though the Kaiser might deceive the German people into believing that their Fleet had gained a victory at Jutland, his officers and men were not so gullible. The British might have lost more ships, but at Kiel and Wilhelmshaven they could see the heavy damage suffered by so many of their own. This evidence that their Battle Fleet had failed to stand up to Jellicoe's broadsides undermined their morale. To restore it, Scheer sortied as soon as the middle of August 1916, for a dawn bombardment of Sunderland by von Hipper's 1st SG, comprising his two serviceable battlecruisers and three dreadnought battleships supported by a battle fleet of 16 other dreadnoughts. Forewarned by Room 40, the Admiralty ordered the Grand Fleet to sea, 29 dreadnoughts and Beatty's six battlecruisers sailing in ample time to intercept. And by 1400 on the 19th Jellicoe was so confident of making contact that he readied his ships for action. But the chance of the devil denied him the battle for which he hoped. Scheer's zeppelins were spread across his line of advance; this time, too, the Harwich Force was out; and shortly after noon zeppelin *L13* sighted Tyrwhitt's light cruisers and destroyers 75 miles ENE of Cromer and made the mistake of reporting them as battleships.

Believing that he had a detachment of the British battle fleet within reach, Scheer turned his whole fleet SE towards them, away from the Grand Fleet; and by the time he discovered that he was chasing phantoms, *U53* had sighted Jellicoe's ships and revealed how nearly the High Seas Fleet had been trapped by overwhelming force. Tyrwhitt located the German fleet heading for home at 1745, but abandoned plans for a torpedo attack when he found that he could not gain the requisite position ahead of the enemy until after dark, when he judged the attempt would be suicidal, Jellicoe having already signalled that the Grand Fleet was too far off to come to his support.

For this abortive operation, Scheer deployed as many as 24 U-boats in positions for attacking the Grand Fleet, to which two of Jellicoe's light cruisers fell victims. The *Nottingham* was sunk by *U52* in the morning watch on the 18th; the *Falmouth* was disabled by *U63* at 1652 on the 19th, and sent to the bottom next day by *U66* as she was being towed towards the Humber. The Admiralty also disposed 25 submarines in the southern part of the North Sea; and at 0505 on the 18th, Lieutenant-Commander R. R. Turner in *E23* put a torpedo into the dreadnought *Westfalen*, when Scheer ordered her back to the Jade. The Admiralty reacted by again endorsing Jellicoe's cautious strategy. The Grand Fleet, in which it would take a year to remedy the material deficiencies revealed by Jutland, was the keystone of the Allied cause. The High Seas Fleet was of secondary importance to Germany and might accept greater risks. Only in special circumstances – such as a threatened invasion, or an attack on the Thames – was the British Battle Fleet to venture south of the Horn Reefs. Moreover, when Room 40 next warned that Scheer intended a sortie, the Grand Fleet was not immediately ordered out, to risk possible U-boat attack; on 18 October 1916 it was brought only to short notice for steam. Nor, in the event, was it required to sail; a few hours after the High Seas Fleet left the Jade, Lieutenant-Commander J. de B. Jessop put one of *E38*'s torpedoes into the light cruiser *München*. Scheer, fearing a submarine trap such as he was accustomed to lay, hurried back to harbour.

From the failure of these two post-Jutland operations, the German C-in-C realized that his chances of trapping a part of Jellicoe's Battle Fleet were too slender to justify further major sorties by the High Seas Fleet. He had a further set-back in November: sailing the *Moltke* and a division of dreadnoughts to cover the rescue of *U20* and *U30* after they had stranded on the Danish coast, he nearly lost both the *Grosser Kurfürst* and the *Kronprinz* to torpedoes from Commander Noel Laurence's submarine *J1*. However, two raids on the Straits of Dover were more successful, with repercussions on the Grand Fleet. On the night of 28 October, torpedoboats from Zeebrugge sank a British destroyer and six drifters; and on 23 November they fired on defenceless Margate. This revived the virulent criticism of the Admiralty that had followed the earlier bombardments of the British east coast and, together with the growing need to find an effective defence against Germany's U-boats, decided Balfour to find a new, more vigorous First Sea Lord. At the end of November Jellicoe 'turned over to Beatty the most efficient fighting machine the world has ever seen', and took Jackson's place in Whitehall. By the irony of politics, Balfour was himself replaced a week later; on becoming Prime Minister, Lloyd George chose the erstwhile champion of Ulster, Sir Edward Carson, to be his First Lord.

Beatty was Jellicoe's natural successor as C-in-C Grand Fleet, but his aggressive handling of the battlecruisers did not lead to any significant change in strategy. The blockade of Germany was not to be hazarded by attrition by U-boat attack, even when the destruction of the dreadnought *Vanguard* in Scapa Flow by the explosion of unstable cordite, on 9 July 1917, was more than compensated by a squadron of American dreadnoughts. But he made one significant innovation: he began to run the Scandinavian trade, for whose protection the Grand Fleet was responsible, in convoys with an anti-submarine escort of destroyers and armed trawlers. He realized that this made the trade an attractive target for a tip-and-run raid by surface craft, but believed the risk to be acceptable; and when six months elapsed without untoward incident it seemed he was justified. In truth, Scheer was otherwise occupied. The High Seas Fleet was convulsed by mutinies that summer, the consequence of inactivity, short rations, the callous attitude of its officers towards their men, and subversive propaganda by the supporters of the Social Democrats in the Reichstag who were clamouring for peace. The Allies might be powerless to break the German Army's stranglehold on Flanders, but at home the British Navy's blockade was sapping the German people's will for war. By shooting two ringleaders and by other stern measures, Scheer suppressed this revolt as effectively as the French dealt with similar trouble in their Army in the same year. Then, in September, most of the High Seas Fleet was required to take part in an operation to finish off the war with Russia, the capture of the islands of Dagö and Ösel in the Gulf of Riga (see pages 250–51). So it was October before Scheer could sail the newly completed light cruiser *Brummer*, under Captain Leonhardi, and her sister-ship the *Bremse*, under Captain Westerkamp, for a foray against the Lerwick–Bergen convoy route.

Evading detection by Beatty's North Sea patrols, these new 28-knot, 5·9-inch-gunned ships reached a position 60 miles to the east of Shetland at dawn on the 17th, and surprised an east-bound convoy. The *Brummer*'s second salvo at 3,000 yards disabled the escorting destroyer *Strongbow* which sank with her flag flying, her after gun still firing. With as much gallantry against overwhelming odds, the *Mary Rose* followed her to the bottom. The *Brummer* and *Bremse* then sank nine out of 12 merchant ships, before retiring at high speed to avoid the British forces they expected to hurry to the scene. But since neither the convoy nor its escort radioed an enemy report, Beatty knew nothing of the attack until the surviving ships reached Lerwick many hours later, by which time the raiders were well on their way back to Germany.

This undoubted success encouraged the *Admiralstab* to consider similar raids farther afield, including the possibility of increasing the fuel capacity of the *Brummer* and *Bremse* so that they might operate in the Atlantic. But neither Scheer nor von Hipper would agree to risk their cruisers or battlecruisers in this way, now that the British must have been alerted to the danger. On the other hand, Commodore Heinrich was satisfied that the Scandinavian convoys were still being run with no more than a small anti-submarine escort. So, early on 11 December, he sailed his 2nd TBF, of which four large boats under Captain Heinecke turned west at 1700, leaving the other four, under Lieutenant-Commander H. Kolbe, to continue to the north. That night Heinecke found two stragglers from a southbound convoy off Berwick and sank them. He then attacked a group of trawlers, sinking one, before turning SE for home at 0700, unaware that he was only 20 miles from the convoy itself, and leaving the Admiralty to suppose that his previous victims had been torpedoed by a U-boat. Kolbe's northbound force was slowed by bad weather to nine knots, so that his four boats did not reach the latitude of Bergen until 1800 on 12 December. But five-and-a-half hours later they sighted a convoy of six merchant ships, escorted by HMS *Partridge* and *Pellew* and four trawlers. These two British destroyers turned to engage them as the convoy scattered and the trawlers made their escape. Ten minutes after opening fire, Lieutenant-Commander R. H. Ransome's *Partridge* was disabled and sunk, but not before she had cleared an enemy report, and fired a torpedo which hit *V100* but unfortunately failed to explode. The

Pellew, with her port engine disabled, could do nothing to prevent the enemy sinking all six vessels in the convoy, although Kolbe allowed her to gain the safety of Norwegian territorial waters rather than risk meeting the British 3rd LCS as it hurried to the scene in response to the *Partridge*'s report.

The German Navy's justifiable pride in these two raids was subdued by a humiliating reminder of the omniscient strength of the Grand Fleet. Though Beatty adopted Jellicoe's cautious strategy, he was always watching for a favourable opportunity to strike at the enemy. In addition to using his seaplane-carriers for raids on Scheer's zeppelin sheds, he noted that the British minefields which had been laid in the Heligoland Bight as an anti-U-boat measure required the German C-in-C to send his minesweepers as far as 150 miles to seaward of the Jade. And after Tyrwhitt's light cruisers and destroyers had decimated their torpedoboat escort, he was not surprised to learn that Scheer intended to support further minesweeping operations with a covering force of battleships. Since Beatty's Battle Fleet had been strengthened by Rear-Admiral Hugh Rodman's 6th BS, appropriately headed by the *New York*, and his Battlecruiser Force (as it was now more properly named, because it was a part of the Grand Fleet) had been augmented by the *Repulse* and *Renown*, each with six 15-inch guns, and the *Courageous* and *Glorious*, with four 15-inch guns apiece, he could afford the risk of gaining a rich prize by a surprise attack on such a German force.

On 16 November, Scheer sent his minesweepers out escorted by two flotillas of torpedoboats, supported by Rear-Admiral von Reuter's 2nd SG (a new *Königsberg* (flag), the *Frankfurt, Pillau* and a new *Nürnberg*), and covered by the dreadnoughts *Kaiserin*, Captain Grasshoff, and *Kaiser*. Forewarned by Room 40, Beatty sailed his Battlecruiser Force, now commanded by Pakenham, accompanied by Admiral Madden's 1st BS. Shortly after 0730 next day the German minesweepers were surprised by the *Courageous*, Rear-Admiral Trevylan Napier, and *Glorious*, and Alexander-Sinclair's 6th LCS. Slipping their gear, the sweepers fled SE as von Reuter hurried to their rescue — until he came under fire from the *Repulse*, Rear-Admiral Richard Phillimore. The 2nd SG then reversed course and, under cover of a smoke screen, headed for the protective wing of Grasshoff's battleships. There followed a running fight, in which the gunnery conditions were too difficult for either side to score many hits, until 0930, when Napier judged the mine risk too great for the larger British ships to advance any further. But when he hoisted their recall, Phillimore ignored it. As the *Courageous* and *Glorious* turned back, the *Repulse* with Commander Walter Cowan's 1st LCS and the 6th LCS pressed on to sight the *Kaiser* and *Kaiserin* – which had been delayed coming to von Reuter's support by Grass-hoff's inexplicable decision to steer SE, away from the hard-pressed 2nd SG, for a time after receiving their first enemy report, instead of towards them.

On coming under fire from the German battleships, Phillimore swung his force away to the NW, hoping to lead his opponents to where Pakenham's and Madden's squadrons were waiting. But von Reuter was unable to persuade Grasshoff to leave the safety of the German minefields, even though the battlecruisers *Hindenburg* and *Moltke* were hurrying north to his support. So the action came to an unsatisfactory end with no losses on either side, apart from a handful of German minesweepers. Damage was limited to Cowan's flagship, the *Caledon*, which 'got such a punch in the ribs from a 12-inch shell, that I thought she was going to drop in halves', and to the *Cardiff* and *Calypso*; and to the *Königsberg* where two 15-inch hits reduced her speed to 17 knots.

This offensive move by Beatty was nonetheless worth while: by sending heavy ships into waters that the Germans regarded as their own, he disrupted their morale. And Scheer was sufficiently angered by Grasshoff's inept handling of his battleships to relieve him of his command. However, Beatty did not attempt any further similar operation. In January 1918, the War Cabinet concluded that the failure of the previous autumn's offensive in Flanders was of such serious consequence that the Grand Fleet should do nothing to provoke a fleet action, even though it had 43 dreadnoughts and battlecruisers to Scheer's 24. Subject to maintaining the blockade, the Navy's overriding task must be to defeat the U-boats. The rest of the nation's effort must be devoted to enabling their Army, which had suffered appalling casualties, to hold back the Germans, who were now being reinforced from their Eastern Front following Russia's collapse, until the full weight of the American Army could be put into the line in 1919.

A fleet action was, nonetheless, still possible. The two Scandinavian convoy débâcles had obliged Beatty to cover the Lerwick–Bergen trade with a division of dreadnoughts, and these might prove sufficient bait to draw the High Seas Fleet. But whilst the British C-in-C welcomed such a chance to avenge the ships he had lost at Jutland, he feared that the Admiralty might fail to give him enough warning for the Grand Fleet to reach the scene before the covering force was overwhelmed. April 1918 showed that his fears were any-thing but groundless. Scheer had learned, at last, the need to con-ceal his plans by refraining from using W/T to communicate his sailing orders. Room 40 gleaned no news of the High Seas Fleet's sortie from the Jade on 22 April, its quarry a large homeward-bound convoy covered by the 2nd BCS and 7th LCS. The Admiralty and Beatty remained ignorant of the crucial fact that the German Battle Fleet was moving further afield than it had dared to do for the past four years, until it was as far north as the Norwegian coast to seaward of Stavanger. Fortunately for the convoy, Scheer's in-telligence was 24 hours in error: it had already crossed the North Sea and entered the Firth of Forth. And when he ordered von Hipper's battlecruisers to search for it, the *Moltke* chanced to lose a propeller, which flooded an engine-room and brought her to a standstill. This disabling accident obliged Scheer and von Hipper to break W/T silence, which was enough for the Admiralty to order Beatty to sea from Rosyth with 31 battleships, four battlecruisers, 26 cruisers and light cruisers and 85 destroyers early in the afternoon of 23 April. But the High Seas Fleet was already retiring to the south, with the *Moltke* in tow of the *Oldenburg*. By nightfall it had crossed ahead of the Grand Fleet's line of advance, to reach the Jade next morning without incident, except for the near-loss of the *Moltke* to a torpedo fired by Lieutenant-Commander C. Allen's submarine *E42*, which was patrolling near the northern edge of the minefields guarding the Heligoland Bight.

Since the High Seas Fleet did not sortie again until after the war was over six months later, in circumstances to be related in the Epilogue to this book, the curtain is best rung down on this Second Act by attempting to answer two questions; why Jutland was not a clear victory for either side, and whether Jellicoe or Scheer could, or should, have made it so. Germany's principal weapon was a magnificent Army which nearly gained her victory in France; indeed, would have done so if it had not been rashly committed to a war on two fronts. Von Tirpitz's High Seas Fleet comprised ships with-out the endurance to operate against the trade routes: restricted to the North Sea it was never large enough to be sure of victory unless it could bring only a part of the Grand Fleet to action. Even so, it had small chance of breaking the British blockade: rather than risk losses which could not be replaced, it was better kept 'in being' to prevent a closure of Germany's U-boat bases, and to en-sure that the Allies did not attempt an amphibious landing on her north-west coast. That it was Scheer's duty to avoid an engagement with the whole Grand Fleet, coupled with his success in escaping from it during the night of 31 May–1 June 1916, after Hipper had inflicted heavy losses on Beatty's Battlecruiser Fleet, is, therefore, a sufficient answer to both questions from his point of view.

With Jellicoe they need more detailed consideration. The mistakes and signalling errors by his ships; the failure of his admirals and captains to make enemy reports; the lack of cooperation between Room 40 and the Admiralty War Room; the deficiencies in British gunnery and in ship and shell design: none of these is sufficient to explain why a more powerful Grand Fleet failed to decimate the High Seas Fleet on 31 May. There were other fundamental reasons which contain lessons for all time for those whose business is war at sea. On the afternoon of 1 June 1916,

Beatty came into the *Lion*'s chart-house. Tired and depressed, he sat down on the settee and closed his eyes. Unable to hide his disappointment at the result of the battle, he repeated in a weary voice, 'There is something wrong with our ships'; then, opening his eyes, he added, 'and something wrong with our system.'

The development of the broadside-mounted 'great gun' suggested a better alternative to the *mêlée* that characterized naval actions before the Armada: Blake, Deane and Monk fought against the Dutch in line ahead. The *Fighting Instructions* of 1691 forbade any departure from this formation 'till the main body of the enemy be disabled or run'; and the battle fleet, though divided into three squadrons, was rigidly controlled by the admiral in the centre. The actions off Barfleur (1692) and Malaga (1704) might confirm the wisdom of these instructions; but in the Chesapeake battle (1781) they cost Graves the opportunity of destroying De Grasse's fleet. Those who diverged from the now *Permanent Fighting Instructions* to the extent of engaging only a part of the enemy's line, paid the price of failure, notably Mathews after his engagement off Toulon (1744), and Byng after his off Minorca (1756). There were, nonetheless, others who realized their limitations, and sought ways of defeating a French Fleet that was reluctant to stand and fight. Rodney broke the enemy's line at the Saints (1782): Anson at Finisterre (1747), Hawke at Quiberon Bay (1759) and Byron at Grenada (1779) ordered a general chase. These successes, together with Boscawen's at Lagos (1759) and Rodney's at the Moonlight Battle (1780), lifted the dead hand of the *Permanent Instructions*.

With the further advantage of the signal codes developed by Kempenfelt and Popham, Howe broke the enemy's line at many points at the Glorious First of June (1794); Nelson quit the line to forestall a likely enemy escape at St Vincent (1797); Duncan approached in two lines and divided the Dutch into three at Camperdown (1797); and Collingwood's division attacked Villeneuve's rear, while Nelson's broke through his centre, throwing the Combined Fleets into disastrous confusion at Trafalgar (1805).

From all this experience emerged two lessons: the centrally controlled, line-ahead gun-duel was seldom decisive, and 'fighting instructions' must not be regarded as inflexible orders. Nonetheless, once Napoleon was out of the way, rigidity was reimposed in a new set of *Instructions* which re-established the line-ahead gun-duel for the next hundred years. The only accepted solution out of the likely *impasse*, proved by Tsushima but difficult to achieve, was to concentrate a superior force on part of the enemy's line by 'crossing the T'. A few admirals advocated 'divided tactics'; Admiral Sir William May, C-in-C Home Fleet, 1910–11, allowed his battleship division commanders a free hand to manœuvre their ships so as to concentrate a superior force on part of the enemy's line. Coordinating their attacks was, however, found to be so difficult that his successor abandoned them; and though Jellicoe revived the idea, in modified form, for his fast 5th BS, he did little to practise anything but the rigid line. His clinical mind favoured centralized command; he issued battle *orders*, not instructions; and such was the late Victorian Navy's concept of obedience that most of his admirals and captains accepted these 75 pages as dogma. And he actively discouraged those who pressed for changes, notably Sturdee who said after Jutland: 'Had I had the starboard wing position I should have disobeyed the deployment signal and led my squadron to the other side of the Germans.'

Lacking the 'Nelson touch', Jellicoe required his captains to comply with written orders; he could not realize that with so large a fleet, much of it beyond his sight, success would depend on his admirals' and captains' initiative in executing his ideas in the light of prevailing circumstances. Two of these were particularly important at Jutland: the visibility and the few hours of daylight remaining after the Battle Fleets made contact. In the words of one officer: 'Was it likely that the weak and less heavily gunned German fleet would expose itself to destruction in order to conform to our concept of how a battle should be fought?' And Cowan of the *Princess Royal* wrote:

With the Grand Fleet now in sight and within striking distance we felt like throwing our caps in the air – it looked a certainty that we had them. The Germans were confronted by our preponderant battle fleet, itching for blood. Then, however, began that desperate, pompous business of deployment. It had ever been beyond my intellect to grasp its value. We were longing for just *one* of their divisions of eight to tag in astern of our battle-cruisers and give that extra bit of punch which could crumple the head of the German battle line.

Twenty-eight dreadnoughts might have achieved a very different result against 16, plus six older ships, if Jellicoe's 2nd and 4th BS had deployed to the east of the German battle fleet, and the 1st and 5th to the west. Scheer's *Kehrtwendung* would have availed him little; caught between the fires of two forces not significantly inferior to his own, he must have accepted battle or attempted flight, leaving Mauve's slow squadron to its fate. With Tyrwhitt's Harwich Force and Bradford's 3rd BS ahead, only a tithe of his fleet could have regained its harbours by one of the southern routes. It is, however, far easier to suggest this now than it could have been for Jellicoe to order it, or for Burney to do it on his own initiative, on 31 May 1916. 'None of my critics,' wrote Jellicoe, 'appear to have realized the extent to which the absence of information regarding the High Seas Fleet, and the lack of visibility, affected my handling of our fleet.'

The second major reason for Jutland's result was Jellicoe's caution, frankly expressed in his letter to the Admiralty in October 1914 (p 135), and exemplified by his alterations away from enemy torpedo fire, and his slow reaction to Scheer's 'battle turns'. 'The lessons of the fight, written into my [Cowan's] soul, were that if you do not seize your chances when they offer, you will never get them again. Also, that when the chance is offered for a superior fleet to strike, it might be better to forget all about torpedoes: the damage from German torpedo attack that day was trifling compared with what their gunfire achieved.' Jellicoe placed too much emphasis on the hazards of U-boat attack during a fleet action; he had an unwarranted belief that the enemy would sow minefields in his wake; and he attached undue importance to the danger of enemy torpedo-boat attacks. This caution was an amalgam of several factors. One was inherent in his intellectual approach to every problem. For a second, he was, after two years of war, no longer the physically fit and mentally adventurous leader that Fisher had known before

1914. Of the third, Mahan gave warning as early as 1890 when he wrote that in the eighteenth century 'the attention of the Royal Navy's officers was not diverted or absorbed, as that of our day has been, by decisive changes in the instruments with which their ideas were to be given effect'. How much more true was this of the technical inventions that flowered in the decade preceding 1914, with the parallel importance attached to material strength that was embodied in the dreadnought race with Germany, and the consequent neglect of the human element, especially the failure to develop 'captains of war' as well as 'captains of ships'. The fourth factor was one with which no previous British admiral had had to contend since the Armada. To gain their victories Rodney, Howe, Jervis and Nelson hazarded only a third of Britain's battle fleet. The Kaiser's strategy compelled the Admiralty to entrust nearly the whole of it to one man. Had Villeneuve destroyed Nelson's 27 ships-of-the-line, 54 would have been left to keep Britain's moat; Jellicoe would not risk all his country's dreadnoughts 'to gain or lose it all'.

This last justification is epitomized in a quotation from Captain Herbert Richmond's diary:

> It is absolutely necessary to look at the war as a whole; to avoid keeping our eyes only on the German Fleet. What we have to do is to starve and cripple *Germany*, to destroy *Germany*. The destruction of the German Fleet is a means to an end and not an end in itself. If in endeavouring to destroy the German Fleet we run risks which may prejudice the greater object, those risks are too great.

Successive Cabinets had allowed the War Office to commit its small military strength to the Continent, making France the cornerstone of British strategy. With too few soldiers left for amphibious operations, Britain's Fleet was relegated to a secondary role. While the Nation and the Empire poured a generation of young men into Flanders, and employed more of their resources than they could afford in sustaining them, the Fleet was required only to ensure that neither was interrupted, and to deny help to Germany's war potential from overseas. It was not to be hazarded for the sake of destroying an enemy navy whose influence on events in France was supposed to be marginal.

After the first weeks of the war had committed the Allied armies to years of stalemate in France, 'most experienced commanders would probably have acted as Jellicoe did', wrote Chatfield. 'His was a weapon on which the world depended. He was not prepared to take immeasurable risks.' Cyril Falls put it another way: 'He fought to make a German victory impossible rather than a British victory certain'. 'But,' wrote Churchill, 'a perception that a decisive battle is not a necessity in a particular situation, and ought not to be purchased at a heavy risk, should not engender a defensive habit of mind or scheme of tactics.' Beatty did more than recognize one of these reasons for the limited results of Jutland; whilst Jellicoe made a number of amendments to his *Battle Orders* after the action, and stressed the importance of night gunnery practices, his successor as C-in-C undertook a complete revision, issued in the middle of 1917, which was, to quote Richmond,

> a marked advance in tactical thought. The mathematical principles culminating in a battle plan on an established form, disappear, and in their place we have a clear, short exposition of principles marked by a high degree of courage and preparedness to accept risks. If such orders had been in existence on 31 May last year, I make small doubt that the High Seas Fleet would have been destroyed.

The Grand Fleet was also acquiring a more potent striking force. Shipborne seaplanes had proved of value for attacks on Germany's zeppelin sheds, but all too often the weather in the North Sea prevented their use. Beatty's solution was the aircraft-carrier, a ship that could fly off wheeled planes and land them on again. In 1918 the large cruiser *Furious* was so converted: in 1919 she would be reinforced by the *Argus* and the *Vindictive*. With these he could prove the potency of the airborne torpedo, first used successfully in 1915 by Flight Commander Edmonds piloting a Short seaplane from HMS *Ben-my-Chree* against a Turkish vessel off Gallipoli. He could deal a blow against the High Seas Fleet lying in the supposed security of the Jade, as effective as Admiral Cunningham's against the Italians in Taranto and the Japanese attack on the US Fleet in Pearl Harbor were to be a quarter of a century later. But the war did not last into 1919; nor was Beatty given any other chance to prove the value of his more flexible *Battle Orders*. So one question must remain unanswered: if Jellicoe lacked fire in his belly, Beatty had it to excess: if the High Seas Fleet had come out he might have been as reckless in handling the whole Grand Fleet as he was with the Battlecruiser Fleet during the initial stages of Jutland.*

* A note on the prolonged and sometimes bitter post-Jutland controversy in Britain will be found in Appendix H on p 239.

To quote a German critic:

There are those who maintain that the British naval policy of caution was a mistaken one. They claim that failure to use the Allied Fleets aggressively resulted in needless prolongation of the war; that the policy of conservation involved greater risk than would have been incurred by an aggressive strategy and tactics to gain decisive victories at sea. What sea power accomplished should be appreciated; but it should also be appreciated that the navies did not accomplish more. The seat of the trouble was in the system which had rested satisfied with material preparations, and had neglected the study of plans for war and the development of skill in the conduct of naval campaigns.

A dogmatic system of tactics, coupled with a too rigid obedience to orders, formed one chain that bound both Jellicoe and Beatty. Another was a misconceived strategy that failed to use the Royal Navy to turn the flanks of Germany's military might. Neither chain was of their making and, in command of the Grand Fleet, neither had the 'admixture of madness' — Aristotle's definition of genius — to break the one, nor the power to influence the other.

Appendix H
The post-Jutland controversy

For the British people who had waited two years for the Grand Fleet to meet the High Seas Fleet in a battle which they expected to be a triumph comparable with Trafalgar, the action off Jutland on 31 May 1916 was inevitably a grievous disappointment. There were, however, special reasons why the consequent controversy became so acute in the decade after 1918, and why it was sustained for so long. The first was the Admiralty communiqué, hurriedly written by Balfour before Jellicoe could telegraph his first report, to counteract Berlin's claim to victory which was trumpeted to the world as soon as Scheer reached the Jade. The First Lord's uninspired style may be judged from the quotations at the head of Chapters 7 and 8. He likewise wrote that, 'among [the Battle-cruiser Fleet] the losses were heavy', and catalogued them. Conversely, although he said that 'the enemy losses were serious', he lacked the knowledge to specify them, nor could he detail the substantial damage suffered by many of the German ships. As a result, both press and public concluded that the Grand Fleet had been defeated. A longer, reassuring account of the battle was issued as soon as Jellicoe had provided the requisite facts. But already the damage had been done; despite Churchill's incomparable prose, many believed that the Admiralty was concealing the truth of what had happened on that eventful day.

Within the Royal Navy debate was inevitable; the lessons of any battle should be analysed so that steps may be taken to rectify faults. But in this instance the Service was divided between those who championed Jellicoe to the detriment of Beatty and vice versa: to the natural and normally healthy rivalry between those who served in the former's Battle Fleet and those in the Battlecruiser Fleet were added such discords as the older officers' resentment at Beatty's rapid promotion, and their dislike of his flamboyance, both of which had captured the imagination of the younger officers. Soon the press, which had already built up Beatty's *panache* into a heroic image against which Jellicoe's quiet personality counted for little, was distorting Jutland into a victory for the Battle-cruiser Fleet, and ascribing Scheer's escape to Jellicoe's failure to handle his Battle Fleet with comparable skill. And a disappointed nation noted that, although Beatty remained in the Grand Fleet until the High Seas

Fleet surrendered, Jellicoe was First Sea Lord for only a year, and held no further appointment until after the war.

All this led Wemyss (who had not served in the Grand Fleet), when he learned that Jellicoe intended to publish his own account of the battle (*The Grand Fleet, 1914–1916*, which in fact contributed no more to the controversy than Scheer's *Germany's High Seas Fleet in the World War*, both of which appeared in 1919–20), to appoint a small committee under Captain J. E. T. Harper, to compile an official narrative, with diagrams, using all available documentary evidence (i.e. the reports of flag officers and captains, ships' signal logs, track charts, etc). Harper was both thorough (e.g. he had the wreck of the *Invincible* located, to provide an accurate position with which to reconcile the navigational reckonings of the *Iron Duke* and the *Lion*) and careful to avoid making comments on the conduct of the action. Moreover, to ensure that his work would be accepted as unprejudiced and so stifle ill-informed controversy, Wemyss decided against showing it to Jellicoe or Beatty before it was issued. Harper had, however, only just completed his *Record* in October 1919 when Beatty succeeded Wemyss as First Sea Lord. Already as early as July 1916, he had shown himself highly sensitive to any criticism of his part in the battle by a dispute with Jellicoe over the latter's dispatch, when he had gone so far as to demand the right to edit it before publication. Now, he was able to read the proofs of the *Record* and, since this did not show his leadership of the battlecruisers in the same favourable light as the public had come to see it, Harper was required to make a number of alterations to both text and plans. Beatty also added a foreword of his own, emphasizing his part and minimizing Jellicoe's.

Harper accepted many of these emendations, but some he refuted with documentary evidence, maintaining this to be nearer the truth than any individual's recollection of events more than three years old. And when overruled, he made a tactless demand for the inclusion of a note to the effect that he accepted no responsibility for a *Record* which did not wholly accord with the facts. This dispute reached the ears of Jellicoe who then asked to see Harper's work; and so pertinent were his criticisms of Beatty's amendments, so strong his objections to his foreword, that the Admiralty agreed to have the *Record* re-examined. But how to revise it to the satisfaction of both Jellicoe and Beatty placed the Board in such a dilemma that an objection by the prospective publishers of the *Official History* (that its sales would be prejudiced by the earlier appearance of the *Record*) was welcomed as sufficient reason for pigeon-holing the *Record sine die*. This overlooked the fact that the First Lord had already told Parliament that the *Record* was being prepared: caustic questions were asked, especially when Wemyss wrote to *The Times* in December 1920, regretting that it had not yet been issued. And the publication of the *Jutland Dispatches* in the same month ('a vast mass of undigested facts from which the layman cannot possibly disentangle the true history of this great sea fight') did nothing to allay public belief that the Admiralty had something to hide.

The clamour for a reliable and readable account of the battle was, however, largely stilled by the appearance of the *Official History: Naval Operations, Volume III*, in 1923. Sir Julian Corbett did his work so well that the handicaps under which he worked were not appreciated; that he had no access to any detailed German version and, for security reasons, was forbidden to disclose the signals deciphered by Room 40. However, he was allowed to use both the *Harper Record* and a secret *Naval Staff Appreciation of Jutland* which had been specially prepared for distribution only within the Navy. Unfortunately, its joint authors, the brothers Captain K. G. B. and Commander A. C. Dewar, went beyond what was reasonable in their criticisms. No Board could be expected to approve a work which not only condemned many aspects of the British conduct of the action, but virtually ignored the factors that made Jellicoe's and Beatty's tasks so difficult: indeed, they ordered its destruction (a holocaust from which, fortunately for posterity, at least two copies survived). Corbett's too revealing version was not so easily disposed of; the Board hesitated to 'doctor' the work of a historian of repute. Instead, they issued a *Narrative of the Battle of Jutland* which was not only pedantically written but worse than biased in Beatty's favour. Although Jellicoe had been allowed to read it before publication, his numerous objections were met by the discourtesy of relegating them to an appendix, to which were added many dissenting footnotes and the disclaimer, 'where the appendix differs from the *Narrative*, Their Lordships are satisfied that the *Narrative* is more in accordance with the evidence available'. Fuel was added to the resulting fire by *Der Krieg zur See* (the German Official History) which, notwithstanding its attempts to prove a German victory, threw fresh light on the handling of the British forces that was not always favourable to Beatty; by Churchill's misguided criticisms of the battle in *The World Crisis*; and by Admiral Sir Reginald Bacon's *The Jutland Scandal*, whose defence of Jellicoe was heightened by a threat of legal action by those whom the author took to task for their partisan support of Beatty.

The controversy was still a live issue when Beatty was superseded as First Sea Lord by Madden, who had been Jellicoe's Chief of Staff at Jutland. He soon (1927) authorized publication of Harper's *Record of the Battle of Jutland* 'to dispel the idea that there is any mystery, sensational evidence, or criticism contained in it', although, to save expense, the diagrams were omitted. In the same year, Harper (by this time retired) issued *The Truth about Jutland*. And taken together these two works did much to cut the rival arguments down to size; at last, a decade after the war, it seemed possible to make an objective evaluation of the battle.

There the matter rested until the late 1930s, when Corbett's *Naval Operations, Volume III*, was revised. The new edition did more than take into account the German Official History; it disclosed the signals deciphered by Room 40 which made clear that Scheer was returning home by the Horn Reefs, but which were not passed to Jellicoe. But when this appeared in 1940, the British people were too concerned with another battle being fought in the skies over their heads for much to be written of the scant justice accorded to Jellicoe by the Admiralty's refusal to reveal before his death its own significant contribution to Scheer's escape. It should, nonetheless, have put an end to controversy; as revised, Corbett's book, together with *Der Krieg zur See*, revealed all the relevant facts about Jutland (although the former neither was, nor is, easy to obtain because the bulk of the stock was bombed before issue, leaving extant only the few copies already sent to reviewers, etc).

There were, nonetheless, some who still supposed that the whole truth had yet to be disclosed, because it was known that Harper had entrusted certain documents appertaining to the *Record* under seal to the Royal United Service Institution. But, when released in 1963, these were found to amount only to a copy of his typescript, together with proofs of both the text and diagrams on which are marked the alterations that Beatty required but which Harper contested, the relevant Admiralty minutes, etc, covering the dispute, and Harper's subjective and somewhat embittered account of it. These show how Beatty tried to conceal his battlecruisers' poor gunnery by 'manipulating' the *Record* covering the run north (1700–1800), to the disadvantage of the 5th BS; and how he attempted to magnify the small part played by his battlecruisers in repulsing Scheer's ill-judged attempt to force a way through the Grand Fleet after his initial 'battle turn' away, by likewise 'manipulating' the *Record* for the period 1800 to 1850. (A specific example is the involuntary 360-degree turn by the *Lion* due to a compass failure (p 186): notwithstanding much evidence to support this, and despite the fact that he was away from the bridge at the time examining the damage done to his flagship, Beatty insisted that he ordered a turn of 90 degrees to close the enemy which, through a compass failure, became an involuntary one of 180 degrees to starboard, and that this was corrected by a 180-degree turn to port – even though it was clear that, if the initial turn had been intentional, the consequences of the compass failure should have been rectified by a turn to port of only 90 degrees.) The 'Harper Papers' also contain Jellicoe's strong objections to Beatty's never-published foreword to the *Record*, in which he implied that he had successfully faced Hipper with an inferior force (i.e. he ignored the presence of the 5th BS); that Jellicoe was slow in bringing his Battle Fleet to his support; and that even after it had come within range of the High Seas Fleet, it took little part in the action. But this revealed no more than the details of an unhappy incident in the life of a great man; it threw no fresh light on the battle.

In short, the Jutland controversy has been dead since 1940; since then it has been possible to tell the full story, and correctly assess the merits of Jellicoe's and Beatty's handling of their ships. The reputations of these two great admirals could not be charred by raking over the dead embers of a once fierce argument that was kept ablaze for too long by a human weakness in one of them. Beatty may have made use of his position as First Sea Lord to distort the truth about Jutland in his own favour, but lesser men have suffered *folie de grandeur* with smaller excuse. There are aspects of Nelson's life that are open to harsher criticism, but no one questions his right to look down on the heart of London from the summit of a column in Trafalgar Square.

ACT THREE

Under the Sea

13

U-Boats and Q-Ships

British submarine operations – German U-boat warfare

> Pitt was the greatest fool that ever existed to encourage a
> mode of war which those who commanded the seas did
> not want and which, if successful, would deprive them
> of it.
>
> Lord St Vincent

From the time of Archimedes men of every maritime nation
dreamed of building war vessels that could submerge at will and
operate under the sea, so that they might sink the enemy without
forewarning of their presence. John Napier of Merchiston was one
of many who committed their dreams to paper when he published
his description of a 'device' to 'sail under water' in Edinburgh in
1596. And Thomas Day was but one of those who lost their lives
when they tried to turn their dreams into reality, his 'submarine
boat' failing to rise from the bottom of Plymouth Sound in 1774.
But two thousand years elapsed between the death of Archimedes
and the first recorded use of such a craft in combat. In 1778 the
American revolutionaries sent David Bushnell's hand-propelled
Turtle to attack HMS *Eagle*, the 64-gunned flagship of Admiral
Lord Howe, at her berth in New York harbour. Her one-man crew
tried to screw a gunpowder charge, operated by a time fuse, to the
hull of this ship-of-the-line. But he was unable to pierce the *Eagle*'s
copper-sheathed bottom, and had to jettison the explosive to avoid
his own destruction. Twelve years more and Robert Fulton built a
'plunger' in France, where he failed to interest Napoleon in its
possibilities, then brought it to England. And Home Popham employed two of these 21-foot craft, which were propelled by 'a spiral
sculler turned by a crank' in the attack on Boulogne on 2 October
1804. But, to quote Lord Keith, the British commander, 'no very
extensive injury was sustained' by the French ships; and after St
Vincent had condemned them in the percipient words heading this
chapter, they were not used again.

Another 60 years elapsed before the submarine came into its own. On 17 February 1864, the Confederate *Hunley* emerged from Charleston harbour to sink the blockading Federal corvette *Housatonic*. More important were three inventions of this same half-century: the battery-driven electric motor for submerged propulsion, the internal combustion engine (at first using petrol but soon, with much greater success, diesel fuel) for surface propulsion and battery charging, and the Whitehead torpedo for an effective underwater weapon. But the Admiralty showed no enthusiasm when Nordenfelt demonstrated his *Nautilus* of 240 tons in 1887, perhaps because only Lord Charles Beresford's presence of mind saved the entire Board from a watery grave in one of London's docks. It was left to the French Navy to be the first to acquire such a craft, the *Gustav Zédé*, of 270 tons, armed with a single torpedo tube, in 1895. But this lead was soon followed by the US Navy which commissioned the *Holland* in 1900. And although the majority of British naval opinion held to St Vincent's view – Admiral Sir A. K. Wilson went so far as to declare that the crews of all submarines should be treated as pirates – the Admiralty ordered five in the same year, albeit to solve the problem of defence against such craft, not for attack: the superiority of the British Battle Fleet over all others was such that it had no need to resort to such an underhand weapon against an opponent. But to Fisher it was 'perfectly astounding how the very best of us absolutely fail to realize the vast impending revolution in naval warfare that the submarine will accomplish', and there is no better tribute to his perception, and to the enthusiastic drive of Captain R. H. Bacon, the first Inspecting Captain of Submarines, than the simple fact that by August 1914 the Royal Navy had as many as 80 boats in commission.

As with all navies, the early British submarines were restricted, by their small size and limited endurance, to defending their own shores. But the completion of the eight 'D' class in 1910–12 and the first 15 of the 'E' class in 1913–14 (the latter being of 660 tons, with a speed of 15 knots on the surface and ten submerged, and armed with five 18-inch torpedo tubes and a single 12-pounder gun) opened up new possibilities. Based on Harwich, these could operate as far afield as the Heligoland Bight. 'Fisher's toys', as Beresford called them, had developed into weapons of offence which could be used in waters too hazardous for the British Battle Fleet. And such were their achievements that by November 1918 150 more had been built, including the successful 'H' class of only 360 tons; the bigger 'L' class of 890 tons (of which some survived to fight again in the

Second World War); the ill-fated 'K' class of as much as 1,880 tons, which were driven on the surface by steam at 23 knots in pursuit of Jellicoe's misconceived idea that submarines could work with the Battle Fleet, of which no fewer than five out of 17 were sunk in disastrous accidents; and the equally large and likewise ill-fated submersible monitors of the 'M' class, armed with a single 12-inch gun for surprise bombardments of the enemy coast.

The majority of these 230 boats, of which as many as 50 were lost by enemy action or to other hazards of 'the Trade', were used in the southern part of the North Sea. After the Heligoland Bight action had exposed the fallacy of Keyes's concept of flotilla operations controlled by surface craft, they were employed singly, each in its own allotted patrol area, to observe and report sorties by units of the High Seas Fleet and, when opportunity offered, to torpedo them, as mentioned in previous chapters. With a like success, they laid mines in the swept channels leading to the Jade. A handful were, however, deployed in two other seas, and to greater effect because neither could be penetrated by British surface craft.

One of these was the Baltic. Here, at the outset of the war, the Germans compelled the Russian Navy to abandon Libau and withdraw into the Gulf of Finland. This posed two problems: how to prevent the High Seas Fleet maintaining its efficiency by exercising undisturbed in the southern Baltic; and how to disrupt Germany's ore imports from neutral Sweden's mines at Luleå in the Gulf of Bothnia. On learning that Russia's submarines were immobilized for lack of spares, the Admiralty ordered *E1*, Lieutenant-Commander Noel Laurence, *E9*, Lieutenant-Commander Max Horton,* and *E11*, Lieutenant-Commander Martin Nasmith, to penetrate the Kattegat in October 1914, and attempt the passage of the Sound, scene of one of Nelson's trio of immortal victories. Nasmith was unlucky; delayed by an engine defect, he was detected by German patrols in these shallow waters and obliged to turn back; but Horton and Laurence completed the 1,200-mile journey to Reval (now Tallinn). And from there, in the short time that remained before ice froze them in for the winter, *E1* and *E9* proved their worth; by attacking German transports they foiled an enemy attempt to capture Petrograd (long famed as St Petersburg soon to be re-named

* Subsequently Admiral Sir Max Horton, Flag Officer Submarines and later victor of the Battle of the Atlantic when C-in-C Western Approaches, in the Second World War.

Leningrad) by a series of amphibious landings along the southern shore of the Gulf of Finland.

This success decided the Admiralty to reinforce their Baltic flotilla with four more boats. In the summer of 1915, *E8*, Lieutenant-Commander F. H. H. Goodhart, *E18*, Lieutenant-Commander R. C. Halahan, and *E19*, Lieutenant-Commander F. A. N. Cromie, passed safely through the Sound despite increased vigilance by German patrols; but Lieutenant-Commander Geoffrey Layton had the misfortune to run *E13* aground on the Danish island of Saltholm, where she was shelled by enemy torpedoboats. Although the British flotilla was under the operational control of the Russian C-in-C, Vice-Admiral Kanin, and his Commodore Submarines, Podgoursky, its own senior officer, Horton, was chiefly responsible for seeing that it did not lapse into the inactivity that characterized the Russians. And right well he did this, despite the special difficulties that faced submarines in the Baltic: its low salinity made depth-keeping difficult, and the short summer nights allowed little time for charging batteries on the surface under the cover of darkness. *E9* had an early success off Libau in May: attacking a German troop convoy, Horton sank one of the transports, which was enough to send the rest scurrying back to harbour. In the next month he torpedoed another transport and in July he crippled the cruiser flagship, SMS *Prinz Adalbert*. Submarine *E1* was as active but out of luck until August, when Laurence disabled the powerful battlecruiser *Moltke* while she was covering an operation against the Gulf of Riga. Finally, on 23 October, *E8* sent the repaired *Prinz Adalbert* to the bottom before the British flotilla was diverted to interrupting the iron ore traffic from Luleå, a task involving the additional hazard of complying with International Law – the need to give the crew of each intercepted freighter time to take to the boats before sinking her. The many minefields with which the Baltic was sown were another danger, to which *E18* succumbed with all hands. And *E19* nearly met disaster in an anti-submarine net laid across Lübeck Bay before Cromie completed a successful torpedo attack on the light cruiser *Undine* – by which time the Germans had such a respect for the British flotilla that some called the Baltic 'Horton's Sea'.

Horton and Laurence were called home for service in new submarines in January 1916, leaving the mantle of senior officer to Cromie. No better man could have been chosen for the exceptionally difficult task which lay ahead. It was not his fault that his flotilla achieved little this summer: Kanin and Podgoursky were obsessed with the possibility of a further enemy attack on the Gulf of Riga, and restricted the British boats to defensive patrols. But the prospects for 1917 seemed brighter when these officers were relieved by the more enterprising Admiral Nepenin and the energetic Commodore Verderevsky, and the Admiralty sent as reinforcements, by way of Archangel, four 'C' class boats that were small enough to proceed thence by canal and lake to Petrograd, thus avoiding the now too hazardous passage of the Sound. With as many as eight submarines, Cromie expected no difficulty in dominating the greater part of the Baltic. But, in the event, he was faced with a more insidious enemy. The February Revolution broke whilst he was visiting the Russian capital, where he experienced the anger of the mob when it broke into the Astoria Hotel and saw, too, that the mutinous garrison was supported by sailors from Kronstadt. Hurrying back to Reval, the ominous calm onboard the Russian depot-ship was broken soon after his return by the arrival of two members of the Duma to enlist support for the Provisional Government. The *Dvina*'s crew responded to this appeal by breaking ship and joining the workers ashore in demonstrations against the Imperial régime. Fortunately, there was little bloodshed, nothing compared with the mutinies at Kronstadt and Helsinki, where Admiral Nepenin was among more than 100 officers who were butchered. And though Cromie could not prevent the *Dvina*'s company electing a Soviet, which replaced the Russian ensign with the red flag and changed her name back to *Pamyat Azova*, he did persuade them to allow Captain Nikitin to retain his command, and to spare the lives of their more unpopular officers.

Command of the Baltic Fleet now passed, first to Vice-Admiral Maximov who sought to placate his men by wearing a red tie and rosettes, then to Rear-Admiral Verderevsky, before both were succeeded by the much abler Rear-Admiral Rasvozov. But even he was powerless to do much without the agreement of the *Tsentrabalt*; and although this Central Soviet agreed to continue the war, very few of the Russian ships were in a fit condition to fight, after so many of their officers had been murdered. Nor were the British submarines allowed to take the offensive; they had to be conserved against a German advance on Petrograd. The *Pamyat Azova* was moved to Hango, from where the four 'E' class boats patrolled the entrance to the Gulf of Finland, and the 'C' class moved into the Gulf of Riga. Here, soon after the Latvian capital fell in September 1917, enemy minesweeping and bombing from the air made clear that the Germans were about to assault the islands of Ösel, Dagö and Moon, whose guns dominated the entrance. The Russian Navy's attempts to impede this activity proved futile: the crews of two destroyers abandoned ship precipitately as soon as one ran aground and the battleship *Slava* was ignominiously mined in Moon Sound. And it was not until after the Germans had completed an unopposed landing on Ösel on 12 October, where the forts surrendered without a struggle, that Cromie was allowed to send his submarines against the enemy. Lieutenant D. C. Sealy in *C27* sank a torpedoboat and crippled a transport as soon as the evening of the 15th; but *C26*, Lieutenant B. N. Downie, and *C32*, Lieutenant C. P. Satow, were unable to reach the area until after the German fleet had anchored off Moon island. Satow managed to penetrate this anchorage and torpedo a transport, but Downie was not so fortunate. When he chanced to run his boat aground, his struggles to free her brought her to the surface, with the consequence that he and Satow were hunted almost to exhaustion before they managed to escape to Pernu.

The October Revolution, and the opening of armistice talks at Brest-Litovsk, rendered the British flotilla's already unenviable position exceptionally precarious. There was no possibility of escape from the Baltic; even if the Sound had not been so closely patrolled as to make this impracticable, the German delegates at Brest-Litovsk required the Russians to keep Allied ships in port. There was also a strong possibility that the *Tsentrabalt* would turn against the British officers and men, after agreeing to surrender their own fleet. However, after preparing a plan to use his submarines to torpedo the Russian ships should they try to leave harbour, Cromie talked the Bolsheviks out of such treachery, and persuaded them to guarantee the safety of their erstwhile allies. The Admiralty then ordered the British crews to withdraw by way of Murmansk, leaving their submarines at Helsinki in the hands of small care and maintenance parties.

Those that remained included Cromie, who became naval attaché in Petrograd, and Downie who stayed aboard the *Pamyat Azova* to ensure that the British flotilla did not fall into enemy hands. This was in January 1918. But the arrival of German troops at the end of March, to help the Finns in their fight against the Reds, left Downie with no alternative: one by one he took his submarines to sea, and scuttled them. Then he and his little band of men went home by way of Murmansk. Only Cromie remained: 'the young officer who had arrived, thinking of little beside his crew, his equipment and his operations, had become the *de facto* ambassador of Great Britain in Petrograd', wrote Sir Samuel Hoare. 'There for six months he maintained the British front in the face of difficulties and dangers as formidable as any that he had met in the Baltic.' His task was to prevent the Russian fleet falling into German hands, but inevitably he became enmeshed in intrigues with the Whites and more and more suspect by the Reds, so that by August he had outlived his usefulness. The British representative in Moscow, Bruce Lockhart, urged him to leave, but Cromie was reluctant to go and delayed too long. On the day that Lockhart was arrested, the *Cheka* burst into the Embassy. Cromie appeared at the head of the staircase prepared to defy the intruders, shots were fired, and a very gallant officer fell, mortally wounded.

(To this unhappy end to the story of the British flotilla in the Baltic, a postscript must be added. Nearly 40 years later HM Submarine *Amphion* visited Helsinki to mark the centenary of the bombardment of Sveaborg by Dundas's fleet, in which one of her namesakes was the only British ship to sustain a casualty. And to her the Finnish Navy presented the builder's name-plate, of polished brass, mounted on teak, from one of the scuttled 'E' class boats, whose salvage from the approaches to the port had just been completed.)

The other sea in which British submarines operated, with a like success, was a much smaller one at the north-east end of the Mediterranean, the Sea of Marmora. Less than 200 miles from west to east, and a quarter that distance from north to south, this deep Turkish lake, which gave access to the Russian-dominated Black Sea, was entered only by way of the Dardanelles, a channel some 50 miles long, but only four across at its widest point, and under one where it makes a sharp S bend through the Narrows past Chanak. On 13 December 1914, five weeks after Turkey's decision to come into the war on Germany's side, Lieutenant-Commander Norman Holbrook took his eight-year-old submarine *B11*, of only 280 tons, into these treacherous waters. Submerged to avoid detection and destruction by the searchlights and guns on both shores, he cleared five rows of moored mines to sink the 40-year-old battleship *Messudiyeh*. He went on to prove that an underwater speed limited to eight knots was no obstacle to entering the Marmora despite a four-knot current running out through the Straits, before returning to Mudros, a feat for which he was awarded the first naval Victoria Cross of the war.

Holbrook's exploit lit the way for others, though not all shared his success. The French *Saphir* struck bottom near Nagara Point on 15 January 1915, and had to surface, when she was quickly destroyed by

the shore batteries. Britain's *E7* was trapped in nets and had to be
scuttled by her crew. *E15* grounded off Kephez Point on 17 April 1915,
and came under fire which killed her Captain, Lieutenant-Commander
T. S. Brodie. To prevent her being salvaged by the Turks, *B6*, commanded by Brodie's brother, Lieutenant-Commander C. G. Brodie,
tried to torpedo her. So did Holbrook in *B11*. A further attempt by
two destroyers, under Lieutenant-Commander Andrew B. Cunningham,* failed to find the stranded boat. Finally, Lieutenant-Commander Eric Robinson took two battleships' picket boats into the
Dardanelles under cover of night. One was sunk by gunfire from the
forts, but with the other he managed to damage *E15* beyond repair,
earning not only the VC but from a German officer in Constantinople
the tribute: 'I take my hat off to the British Navy.'

The Australian *AE2* was only a shade more fortunate. Although
Lieutenant-Commander H. G. Stoker touched ground on both shores
of the Dardanelles, he passed into the Marmora late in April 1915,
where he torpedoed a Turkish gunboat. But his boat was then hunted
and destroyed by another Turkish vessel, after which Stoker had to
suffer the rigours of a prisoner-of-war camp before becoming a distinguished actor on the London stage after the war. Another to enter
the Marmora was *E20*, but only to meet a new hazard: she was torpedoed by *UB14*, a small submarine that had been brought overland
from Germany to Constantinople. And the French mourned the
Joule, *Mariette* and *Turquoise*.

Such heavy losses were, however, the price that had to be paid for
the triumphs of others in waters so dangerous. On 26 April 1915,
E14 followed *AE2* into the Marmora where, in the course of a three
weeks' patrol, Lieutenant-Commander E. C. Boyle sank two gunboats
and two transports bringing reinforcements for the hard-pressed
Turkish troops on the Gallipoli peninsula. This and further successful patrols gained him the VC. Even more memorable were the exploits of *E11* whose Captain, the handsome Nasmith, was also
awarded this highly prized decoration 'for valour'. His first patrol
did more than atone for his failure to enter the Baltic in the previous
October. Slipping through the Straits on 19 May, to the heart-
stopping rasp of a mine wire scraping his submarine's hull, he
wreaked havoc among Turkish shipping in the Marmora, sinking
most of his victims with demolition charges, after their passengers
and crews had taken to their boats, the former including the correspondent of the *Chicago Herald*, Raymond Gram Swing, who was to

* Later Admiral of the Fleet Lord Cunningham of Hyndhope, C-in-C Mediterranean, and subsequently First Sea Lord, in the Second World War.

become famous for his broadcasts from London to America during the darkest days of the Second World War. Nasmith also set his torpedoes to float at the end of their run so that he could recover those that missed their target, when he performed the dangerous task of removing their firing pistols himself before allowing his men to guide them back into their tubes. But these were run-of-the-mill exploits compared with 25 May, when he dared to take *E11* into the Bosphorus in daylight, past Constantinople (now Istanbul) where he photographed the dome of the mosque of St Sophia through his periscope, before sinking the large transport *Stamboul* at her berth alongside the arsenal at the entrance to the Golden Horn. And not until 6 June, after unsuccessful attempts to torpedo the Turkish battleships *Barbarossa* and *Turgut Reiss,* did he take *E11* out through the Dardanelles again and back to the safety of Mudros.

Nasmith made two further patrols in the Marmora during 1915, of which one lasted for as long as 47 days, bringing his time spent there to more than three months, and raising the total British bag to two battleships, six smaller warships, 16 transports, ammunition and storage ships, more than 30 steam freighters, and nearly 200 sailing ships – plus, unusual game for a submarine, one train. Its fate was sealed by Nasmith's first lieutenant, Guy D'Oyly-Hughes, who swam ashore one night in the Gulf of Ismit and blew up a railway viaduct under the noses of its guards. So it was that, whilst enemy troops remained masters of the heights of Gallipoli, the exceptional skill and courage of a handful of young submarine captains, with crews who were 'all of one company', gripped Turkey by the throat in the Sea of Marmora. Their exploits will always be a jewel that illuminates the otherwise sombre failure of the Gallipoli campaign, even though one vital target eluded these gallant gentlemen of 'the Trade'. To the disappointment of Boyle, Nasmith, and those that followed in their wake, the *Goeben* never offered herself as a target for their torpedoes.

However, notwithstanding this success, and the parallel one in the Baltic, the Royal Navy's submarine offensive, from 1914 to 1918, was never more than ancillary to the operations of the British Battle Fleet. With the Imperial German Navy it was a different story. Handicapped by the need to concentrate his country's resources on building an adequate surface fleet, von Tirpitz was unable to complete *U1* before the end of 1906. So, as late as December 1914, the High Seas Fleet counted only 35 submarines, the largest being of 690 tons, capable of 16 knots on the surface and ten submerged, all armed with four 19·7-inch torpedo tubes and some with a single 3·4-inch gun – very similar to the British 'E' class. But though few in number, these boats were uninhibited by the restrictions which the Kaiser imposed on his Battle Fleet. They were, moreover, presented with a multiplicity of splendid targets by a British Navy that was all too slow in understanding the new danger that lurked beneath the sea on whose surface its ships had held undisputed sway for so long.

'On 17 September, during my visit to the Grand Fleet,' wrote Winston Churchill, 'I heard an expression which arrested my attention. An officer spoke of "the live-bait squadron".' He learned that this referred to the 7th CS, of five 12,000-ton armoured cruisers which were employed patrolling the Dogger area of the North Sea. Returning to the Admiralty, he addressed a minute to Battenburg in which he said, *inter alia*: 'The *Bacchantes* ought not to continue on this beat. The risk to such ships is not justified by any services they can render.' But disaster struck before the First Sea Lord could give effect to the First Lord's wisdom. The *Aboukir*, *Cressy* and *Hogue* were still watching the Broad Fourteens at 0630 on 22 September, steaming at less than ten knots on a steady course, when Lieutenant-Commander Weddigen put one of *U9*'s torpedoes into the *Aboukir*. Twenty-five minutes later she capsized and sank. To quote Churchill again:

> Both her consorts hurried with chivalrous simplicity to the aid of the sinking ship. Both came to a dead standstill within a few hundred yards of her and lowered their boats to rescue the survivors. In this position they in their turn were sunk, first the *Hogue* and then the *Cressy*, by the same submarine. Out of over 2,000 men aboard these three ships, more than 1,400 perished.

Berlin gave Weddigen (who was destined to lose his life very soon on the *Dreadnought*'s ram) a well-deserved hero's welcome. The Admiralty blamed Rear-Admirals Arthur Christian and Henry Campbell, not least for being in harbour at the time, instead of out with this patrol, and Captain John Drummond, the senior officer in the *Aboukir*, and placed all three on half-pay (though they were re-employed later).

Despite this example, further losses followed for which there was as little excuse. On 15 October 1914, the old cruiser *Hawke* was torpedoed, with the loss of all but 21 of her crew, whilst steaming on a steady course to regain station on a patrol line, after she and the *Endymion* had *stopped* to transfer mails by boat. Two weeks later the seaplane-carrier *Hermes* was torpedoed whilst on passage from

Dunkirk to Dover. And, on the night of 31 December–1 January 1915, the pre-dreadnought *Formidable* was sunk with the loss of 547 officers and men. The Admiralty accepted responsibility for failing to provide her with a destroyer screen, but convicted Vice-Admiral Sir Lewis Bayly of negligence in taking his squadron down Channel on a steady course at no more than ten knots, and ordered him to strike his flag (though he more than re-established his reputation in the last year of the war as commander of the Queenstown base where his outspoken personality was much appreciated by the US ships that were based there).

Such skilful attacks on British major warships stand to the credit of the German Navy: though executed without warning, and involving heavy loss of life, they were as much within the rules of war as von Spee's destruction of Cradock's cruisers off Coronel. Nor were they without risks to the attackers: early victims included *U5* and *U11* mined off Zeebrugge, *U15* rammed by the light cruiser *Birmingham*, and *U18* sunk while trying to enter Scapa Flow (p 134). The *Admiralstab* was not, however, content with operations in the North Sea, which hampered the Grand Fleet's blockade to the extent that they compelled Jellicoe to leave his Orkney base for the more distant Loch Ewe and Lough Swilly until Scapa could be adequately defended against a threat in which the Admiralty had refused to believe as late as July 1914. *U21* was sent through the Straits of Gibraltar into the Mediterranean in April 1915, whereby, by sinking the pre-dreadnoughts *Majestic* and *Triumph* in the next month (p 32), Lieutenant-Commander Hersing impelled Fisher to withdraw the recently completed 15-inch-gunned dreadnought *Queen Elizabeth*, first of her class, from de Robeck's bombarding force, lest she suffered a similar fate.

Much more important, however, when Germany's golden dream of a swift victory on land dissolved into the nightmare of prolonged trench warfare, the *Admiralstab* realized that their U-boats could be a potent weapon against the merchant shipping on which Britain was largely dependent for the sinews of war, including much of her food. Against unleashing such a weapon there was, however, the same obstacle as hampered the British submarine campaign against the Luleå iron-ore trade. International Law recognized no distinction between a submarine and a surface warship: both were required to board a merchant vessel to check whether she was carrying contraband, before putting a prize crew onboard, or sinking her after ensuring the safety of her passengers and crew. But the chivalry that so enhanced the reputation of von Müller and the *Emden* was denied to Germany's underwater fleet: the 20–30 minutes needed to comply with these rules were enough to expose a U-boat to destruction by British destroyers and other small craft.

The solution was to defy International Law; to sink without warning, by torpedo or gunfire, despite the likely loss of non-combatant lives. Moreover, if Germany was to attempt such a blockade of Britain, both neutral and Allied shipping must be subjected to this form of warfare. But use her U-boats for such a campaign she must, argued Admiral Bachmann with von Tirpitz's support, because her Battle Fleet had small chance of destroying Britain's command of the surface of the sea. The Chancellor, von Bethmann Hollweg, held a different view: attacks so contrary to International Law must provoke the animosity of the neutral Powers, above all of the USA. As so often, Germany's Supreme War Lord overruled his civilian Minister in favour of his Service advisers. On 16 February 1915, Berlin declared a War Zone round the British Isles in which 'every merchant vessel will be destroyed without it being possible to avoid damage to the crews and passengers', it being 'impossible to avoid attacks being made on neutral ships in mistake for those of the enemy'. Germany's specious excuse was Britain's realization of the extent to which the Declaration of London (1909) – never formally ratified because the House of Lords wisely rejected it, but nonetheless accepted by Asquith's Government at the outbreak of war – restricted her powers of blockade, and the 1915 decision to cast off its shackles by a series of Orders in Council which considerably extended the list of goods classed as contraband.

The Admiralty took a multiplicity of steps to counter this unexpected form of warfare. The local defence flotillas of old destroyers, stationed at ports round Britain's coasts, were augmented by an Auxiliary Patrol of more than 1,000 armed trawlers, drifters and yachts, to which were added, as they could be built, such craft as P-boats (which had the deceptive silhouette of a surfaced submarine), PC-boats (which had the equally deceptive silhouette of a small freighter), motor launches (of which some 500 were mass-produced in the USA) and 'blimps' (small non-rigid airships manned by the RNAS). Hydrophones that could hear a U-boat's propellers were devised by Professor William Bragg (Asdic, later called Sonar, a supersonic method of locating a submarine's hull, was a decade away). Depth charges, of 300 lb of TNT or Amatol detonated by a hydrostatic pistol, were invented: their first victim was the small submarine *UC7* in July 1916 (and no better anti-submarine weapon was devised until the 'hedgehog' or 'squid' were produced half-way through the Second World War). As important, when it became clear that the U-boats' sting was not limited to the few torpedoes they could carry, that they would risk surfacing to sink their quarry by gunfire, Allied merchant ships were themselves defensively armed with a gun at the stern, a measure that not only proved to be a deterrent but which ended several U-boats' short careers.

Seemingly innocent trawlers were also sent out, each with a small submarine in tow, submerged, and connected by telephone. If a U-boat surfaced to attack one of these trawlers, her submarine was released to stalk and sink it. Thus *U40* fell a victim to the *Taranaki* and *C24* off Aberdeen in June 1915. Another deceptive measure was employed on a greater scale: merchant vessels, from small coasters up to 4,000-ton freighters, were equipped with concealed armaments, and set to decoy U-boats to their doom. The first of these 'mystery ships' to score a success was the *Prince Charles* which sank *U36* in July 1915. How another Q-ship, as they were officially known, performed her task is told by one who was there:

A group of small sailing vessels left Falmouth, escorted by the armed trawler *Harlech Castle* and the 'mystery' brigantine *Probus*. Course was set for Brittany with the trawler one mile ahead and the *Probus* four miles astern. Shortly after noon two days later, the *Probus* sighted a ketch-rigged vessel on her starboard quarter, steering the same course. But when the stranger was seen to be overhauling the *Probus*, the latter's Captain suspected that she was propelled by more than sails, a suspicion proved well founded when, at 1430, the 'ketch' suddenly opened fire. The *Probus* was at once hove-to, her crew sent to action stations, her guns cleared away, and her boat made ready, whilst the U-boat, for such it was, kept up a rapid fire, though most of her shells fell short. When it was clear that the enemy might attack the unarmed sailing vessels before the trawler could turn back the *Probus*'s Captain ordered: 'Up starboard 12-pounder. Hoist white ensign.' The Q-ship's first shot at a range of 3,500 yards fell 500 yards short: nonetheless the Germans immediately left their gun and made for the conning-tower. And the *Probus*'s second shot was a direct hit amidships. The British ship's port 12-pounder was then brought into action, its fourth shot bringing down the mast and sails of the enemy's disguise. Thirteen more rounds and the U-boat ceased fire, to settle by the stern, turn over to port and sink.

Commander Goetting of *U153* describes another action, albeit dated as late as 25 April 1918:

1125. Off Cape Blanco. W/T message from *U154*, Commander Gercke, giving her position. Steamer visible WNW, 11 miles, steering S. After *U153* had attained favourable intercepting position, opened fire with both 5·9-inch guns at 11,000 yds. Steamer made smoke and zigzagged in a north-westerly direction, as she replied with a 4-inch gun, and simultaneously fired to the north. Soon the flashes of *U154*'s two guns were seen: she also had the steamer under fire. When *U153* closed to 8,300 yards the first hit was obtained on her stern. After five more hits, the now fiercely burning vessel hove to and lowered her boats. *U153* approached to interrogate their occupants. *U154* requested medical assistance: she had eight dead and five severely wounded: *U153*'s doctor was sent across. The steamer, which proved to be the Q-ship *Willow Branch* of 3,314 tons, armed with one 4-inch gun at the stern and a 12-pounder each side forward, was sunk by a torpedo from *U153*. In the evening the two U-boat Captains discussed further joint operations before proceeding towards the Canary Islands. At 1825 on 11 May, off Cape St Vincent, *U154* suddenly vanished in a tall column of water and a dark cloud of smoke: she had been torpedoed by the British submarine *E35*,

which had been ordered to intercept on the basis of intelligence garnered by Room 40, whose cryptographic experts did as much to help the battle against the U-boats as they did to warn the Grand Fleet of enemy sorties from the Jade.

Many similar stories can be told of how the captains and volunteer crews of these Q-ships risked their lives as 'live bait to catch unsuspecting prey'. Not a few richly earned the VC, notably Commander Gordon Campbell of the *Dunraven*. It must, however, be admitted that they lost much of their value once the Germans had learned their secret. After 1916, U-boats were too wary for Q-ships to score many successes: indeed, their total bag amounted to only 11 U-boats against which had to be set the loss of 27 out of nearly 200 such decoys. (An attempt to use them again in the Second World War proved as costly and ineffective and was soon abandoned.)

Fortunately for the Allies, Germany's first unrestricted U-boat campaign did not last for much longer than six months. Von Bethmann Hollweg's fears proved well founded. Initial neutral protests were as nothing to the outcry that followed *U20*'s successful attack on the *Lusitania*, off Queenstown on 7 May 1915, which not only sank this 30,000-ton liner but cost the lives of as many as 1,198 of her passengers and crew. When the world raised its voice in scandalized horror at an act of inhumanity such as no civilized belligerent had previously dared to perpetrate, Germany tried to justify Lieutenant-Commander Schwieger's action with the specious argument that the *Lusitania* was carrying a small quantity of small-arms ammunition. Nonetheless, the Kaiser banned further attacks on large passenger liners that made no offensive move. This small restriction was, however, not enough to prevent another serious incident: on 19 August, Lieutenant-Commander Schneider in *U24* interpreted the White Star liner *Arabic*'s zigzag course as an offensive manœuvre, and sent her to the bottom of the Irish Sea. This time President Wilson's protest was so strong that von Bethmann Hollweg's counsel prevailed. Since the *Admiralstab* could claim only a qualified success for unrestricted U-boat warfare – although Britain had lost 900,000 tons of shipping, her building yards had completed 2,000,000 tons of new vessels; moreover, Germany had lost 15 U-boats against only 10 new ones completed – Bachmann was superseded by Admiral von Holtzendorff. And on 5 October 1915, he issued the order 'to cease all forms of submarine warfare on the west coast of Great Britain and in the Channel'.

The *Admiralstab* did not, however, lose faith in the potential value of an effective U-boat blockade of Britain. In 1916 the Imperial German Navy would reap the harvest of a building programme begun a year before, which was destined to augment its underwater fleet by more than 100 U-boats (some as large as 1,500 tons, some armed with six tubes, others to lay mines, a few, like the *Deutschland*, adapted to carry freight across the Atlantic), by 136 UB-boats ranging from 130 to 520 tons, and by 94 UC-boats of 170 to 490 tons, bringing the total number used during the war up to a figure little short of 400. And with the generals' growing demands for a naval offensive that would help the German Army to achieve a breakthrough on the Western Front came a note from the USA to all belligerents, dated 18 January 1916, which seemed to provide the Kaiser with a solution to the contradictory advice of his civilian and Service advisers. Since the British Government rejected Wilson's suggestion that merchant ships should no longer be armed for their own defence, Berlin supposed that Washington would adopt retaliatory measures to compel London's compliance; and, by curiously tortuous thinking, that it would be safe to renew U-boat warfare against merchant shipping provided that passenger ships were exempt from attack.

This restriction was too much for the bellicose von Tirpitz, who tendered his resignation. To his successor, Admiral von Capelle, nemesis came quickly: on 24 March 1916, Lieutenant Pustkuchen in *UB29* torpedoed the cross-Channel steamer *Sussex*, while she was carrying a number of American passengers, on the pretext that she was a troop transport. Washington retorted that, unless Germany abandoned 'submarine warfare against passenger and freight-carrying vessels, the Government of the United States can have no choice but to sever diplomatic relations'. This threat was enough for the Kaiser to restrict his U-boats to legitimate targets. For the next nine months they were used chiefly to support such operations as Scheer was authorized to undertake with his Battle Fleet. But Jutland, and the failure of Scheer's subsequent sorties, persuaded the Kaiser to change his mind once more. Accepting his naval C-in-C's contention that 'a victorious termination of the war can only be attained by destroying the economic existence of Great Britain by the employment of submarines against commerce', he ordered unrestricted U-boat warfare to begin again on 1 February 1917, this time with as many as 60 available for patrol compared with less than half that number two years before. Holtzendorff prophesied that five months of such warfare would compel Britain to ask for terms. Von Capelle was almost as optimistic, his assessment being six months.

Of the many attacks made on shipping in the next two years the story of one, which involved three U-boats, must suffice. To quote first from the report of Lieutenant von Schrader of *UB64*:

19 July [1918] At 1350 [GMT], about 27 miles S of Barra Head, carried out submerged attack. One torpedo hit port side of armed English steamer *Justicia*, 32,234 tons. Dived deep whilst 35 depth charges were dropped by destroyers. Came to periscope depth at 1520. Steamer lay stopped. At 1615 fired double bow shot at her port side. Scored two hits. Dived deep to avoid depth charges. Commenced third attack at 1703. Fired single bow shot at 1948 which hit steamer's starboard side. Then dived deep to avoid 11 depth charges and left area to charge batteries. Surfaced at 2228 to see ship still afloat and in tow. Kept contact during night. At 0337 attacked once more with single bow shot, but no explosion detected because of depth charges. At 0640 surfaced, after reloading torpedoes. Proceeded to position ahead of steamer. At 0930 saw two tall columns of water alongside steamer, which must have come from two torpedo hits by another U-boat.

It was at 0840 that morning that *U54* sighted the damaged *Justicia*. Closing his prey, Lieutenant-Commander Ruckteschell dived.

> Arriving under the escorting vessels, *U54* was greeted by loud propeller noises and a drum-fire of depth charges, which compelled her to go down to 25 fathoms. This delayed her arrival at the best firing position. On returning to periscope depth, her Captain found that *U54* had no time to turn back and make a bow approach, but would have to use her stern tubes. Fifteen seconds after these had been fired at 0932, there was an explosion which was assumed to be a hit. *U54* then went deep to the accompaniment of a fresh hail of depth charges. Since her batteries were practically discharged, she had to escape to such a distance from the escorts as would allow her to surface and recharge. The effect of *U54*'s two torpedoes was confused by the coincidental arrival of *UB124* on the scene.

The latter's Captain, Lieutenant-Commander Wutsdorff, sighted the *Justicia* around 0700 and

> fired two torpedoes at her port side from a distance of 2,500 yards. No explosion was observed, but one was clearly heard. Due to a mistake by one of the crew, water entered the boat when she dived deep, so that she went to the bottom in 45 fathoms where British destroyers' 65 depth charges did no damage. Towards 1600, her Captain decided to rise to periscope depth. This proved difficult but eventually, by using compressed air on all tanks, the boat shot to the surface with a marked angle down by the stern, so that the water in the bilges flooded both electric motors, rendering them useless. Three destroyers immediately opened fire and, since *UB124* could no longer submerge, her Captain decided to scuttle the boat which sank at 1625. The crew were picked up by HMS *Marne*.

On this unusual action the German official historian added this crisp comment:

> *U54* fired two torpedoes at the port side of the *Justicia* at 0932, apparently later than *UB124*. But English sources, together with the reports of the two U-boat commanders, lead to the conclusion that the two hits must be credited to *UB124*, the explosion heard after the first shots being from depth charges.

More important, Wutsdorff did not lose his submarine to no purpose: at 1240, nearly three-and-a-half hours after his attack, the
Justicia sank.

To meet this recrudescence of unrestricted U-boat warfare, the
Admiralty intensified all its anti-submarine measures, only to find
that it was fighting a losing battle. Patrolling the waters round the
British Isles, into which so much overseas and coastal shipping was
funnelled, could not prevent this new form of blockade. The vessels
so employed might number several thousand, but it would have
needed many times that figure so to swamp these seas that U-boats
would be unable to sink their victims, except at the risk of an immediate counter-attack. As often as not, half an hour or more elapsed
before the nearest patrol reached the position where a merchant ship
had been torpedoed, with small chance of destroying her assailant
when there was no adequate underwater detection device, and the
only weapon one so imprecise as the depth charge. By the end of
April 1917 Britain had lost a further $1\frac{1}{4}$ million tons of merchant
shipping, a figure which rose to another $1\frac{1}{2}$ million tons in the next
four months, a rate which all her shipbuilding resources could not
hope to match.

The consequences were critical. Despite the belated introduction
of stringent rationing, the country's reserves of essential foods
dropped to a bare six weeks' supply. So, too, with the sinews of war;
to give one example, for shortage of oil the Grand Fleet's exercises
had to be curtailed. 'Is there no solution?' asked Rear-Admiral Sims,
who was in charge of the US Naval Mission in London. 'Absolutely
none that we can see,' was Jellicoe's pessimistic answer. And the
First Sea Lord was not the only man who feared that Britain was
near to being defeated by a weapon against which all her immense
naval strength, epitomized in Beatty's Grand Fleet, seemed powerless.

14

Twisting the Dragon's Tail

Convoys – The raids on Zeebrugge and Ostend

> You have written a glorious page for us, straight back to
> the old, splendid, Nelson days. It has done more for the
> honour and reputation of the Navy than anything else in
> this war.
>
> *Rear-Admiral Walter Cowan to*
> *Vice-Admiral Sir Roger Keyes*

Centuries ago, when there was no distinction between ships of war
and cargo carriers, when most vessels were armed against attack,
safety was found in numbers: when danger threatened, these mer-
chant-cum-warships gained mutual protection by sailing together.
And this lesson was not discarded when it became impracticable to
equip vessels with an adequate armament and retain their carrying
capacity; when in the seventeenth century Britain acquired a Royal
Navy of ships-of-the-line. In her wars with France, Britain's merchant shipping sailed in convoys, escorted by squadrons of warships
in the broad oceans, with a fleet to cover them in more dangerous
waters. And the Napoleonic wars afforded a wealth of evidence to
prove the efficacy of this method of protecting seaborne trade. To
cite one example, Howe was covering outward- and homeward-bound
convoys when he worsted Villaret on the Glorious First of June
1794.

Half a century after Napoleon's banishment to St Helena, so much
valuable experience was abandoned. The Crimean War revealed an
awkward difference between the French and British definitions of
contraband. The Declaration of Paris (1856) did more than resolve
this: privateering was also outlawed. No longer were nations to
license private individuals to arm vessels at their own expense to
prey on enemy shipping, as Queen Elizabeth I had encouraged Sir
Francis Drake to do. With this reduction in the hazards to which
merchant vessels were subject in war, the Admiralty succumbed to
the Victorian dogma of *laissez-faire*; that in war, as in peace, ship-

owners should be allowed to sail their ships as they wished; indeed, that with the advent of steam vessels, no Government interference with their movements was economically acceptable. When three admirals, in their critique on the naval manœuvres of 1888, reported that 'convoys for commerce are wanting', the Admiralty replied, 'The days of convoys are passed.' By August 1914, it was accepted that only troopships would be so sailed; all other shipping was to be protected by cruisers patrolling the trade routes, especially the focal areas. And since this proved adequate in the first six months of the war, largely because Germany deployed no more than a handful of cruisers overseas, the Admiralty saw no reason to change its policy.

In July 1914 the *Strand* magazine chanced to publish *Danger*, a story by Arthur Conan Doyle which told of a British defeat by a submarine blockade. To the chorus of derisive adjectives which greeted this prophecy, one admiral added: 'No nation would permit submarine attacks on merchant ships. All officers who did it would be shot.' But though the first unrestricted U-boat campaign went a long way to justify Conan Doyle's warning, its results were insufficiently conclusive for its real lesson to be learned: that the U-boats were the old privateers in new guise, against which there was only one protection, the old and well-proven convoy system, whose manifold advantages included that of ensuring that warships were always on the spot ready to make immediate counter-attacks. That this defensive-offensive strategy might be worth trying had to await Jellicoe's formation of an Anti-Submarine Division of the Naval War Staff under Rear-Admiral A. L. Duff in December 1916, and the recrudescence of unrestricted U-boat warfare at the outset of the following year.

Unfortunately the First Sea Lord was too ready to listen to those who argued that merchant ships would be unable to keep station in convoy, especially when darkened at night. He was overawed by the magnitude of the world-wide organization for shipping control that would have to be set up. Above all, he contended that Britain lacked the destroyers to provide escorts after the paramount needs of the Grand Fleet had been met. Not until May, a month after the entry of the USA into the war removed this last objection, did Jellicoe bow to Prime Minister Lloyd-George's pressure and allow a trial convoy to be run from Gibraltar, followed two weeks later by one from Hampton Roads. And another three months passed before all shipping was run in convoy through the War Zone. So it was only in the last four months of 1917 that the system became effective, with the visible result that the steep rising graph of merchant shipping lost was reversed, the tonnage sunk in this period falling below a million tons.

Lloyd George wrote after the war: 'By the end of 1917 we knew that the German effort to blockade us would not succeed.' But by this time Jellicoe was no longer at the Admiralty: as he wrote on 28 December, a few days after leaving office, to Admiral the Hon Sir Alexander Bethell, who commanded the Channel Fleet in the first months of the war and was now C-in-C Plymouth:

> I was dismissed by letter at a moment's notice without being given any reason at all. No doubt it will be said that I was war-weary, that I wanted a rest, or that I am too old and lack the true aggressive spirit. But I think the real reason is that I have had occasion lately to take exception to the autocratic attitude of the First Lord in his dealings with various flag officers both afloat and at the Admiralty.

Jellicoe *was* a tired man. There were, too, good grounds for his objection to Sir Eric Geddes: the latter had, for example, usurped Beatty's authority as C-in-C Grand Fleet by dictating the composition of the court of inquiry into the German attacks on the Scandinavian convoys. But the First Sea Lord was, in truth, dismissed for his failure to introduce the convoy system earlier in the year. Lloyd George required a scapegoat for the disasters that all but overwhelmed the Allies on land and sea in the latter half of 1917, but felt powerless to remove Haig from his command in France in the face of the royal favour and popular support that he enjoyed. So the Prime Minister chose the dictatorial Geddes to relieve Sir Edward Carson as First Lord, well assured that he would soon be rid of Jellicoe. As the whole Navy was to learn when the 'Geddes Axe' was applied to reducing the Navy List after the war, no man could be more ruthless towards those who had earned the Nation's gratitude.

At was, therefore, the pliant Wemyss who savoured the fruits of the victory for which Jellicoe had hesitated to lay the sure foundations. 'I know,' wrote the Civil Lord, Lord Lytton, 'that our ultimate salvation was due to the anti-submarine organization set up by Jellicoe.' But not until May 1918 was it so effective that, for the first time since February 1917, the tonnage of new British ships exceeded the tonnage lost by enemy action. As important, because the convoy system compelled the U-boats to seek their prey where Allied forces were already concentrated, the number sunk in 1917–

18 was as high as 132.* This raised the total to nearly half of those in service during the war, and to a rate of loss in both craft and crews that Germany could ill afford.

The convoy system did not, however, diminish the need for other measures. On the contrary, two in particular were intensified. From the first months of the war Britain augmented her conventional minefields in the Heligoland Bight and its approaches, which were designed to trap surface craft, with others laid at a depth where they were a danger to submarines that attempted to pass them submerged. But although some U-boats fell victims to this hazard, it was not an effective deterrent to their leaving and returning to German ports. When the North Sea was their principal operational area this was not of great importance: the Grand Fleet had an adequate destroyer force for its protection. But the onset of unrestricted U-boat warfare posed the need to provide barriers against such craft reaching the shipping lanes off the western coasts of the British Isles, both north-about and through the Straits of Dover. For the former, a deep mine barrage from the Orkneys to Norway was the only solution, but this had to await the USA's entry into the war. To cover a distance of nearly 250 miles was a project of such magnitude that although the first of more than 70,000 mines was shipped across the Atlantic in January 1918, the Northern Barrage was not completed by November. So its efficacy was never proved. (Nor was a similar barrage which the British Navy attempted to lay between the west coast of Scotland and Iceland in the Second World War, because this more difficult task was abandoned as an unjustified waste of limited resources before it could be finished.)

The Dover Straits were a different story. Indicator nets of light wire were laid there in January 1915. When fouled by a submarine, these fired carbide flares as a signal to watching patrol craft, whose weapons included controlled mines. And U32's report of her near-destruction by this obstacle on 6 April alarmed the Admiralstab into denying this route to their U-boats. Thenceforward their journeys to and from the Irish Sea north-about were lengthened by 1,400 miles, which cut their time on patrol by seven days. The Admiralty was, however, unaware of this ban: they noted only that the indicator nets accounted for very few U-boats. So Admiral

*By the end of the war 285 aeroplanes, 291 seaplanes and flying-boats, and 103 airships were employed on anti-U-boat duties in Home waters alone in addition to a multitude of surface craft, and these machines played an indispensable part in the protection of merchant shipping.

Bacon, commanding the Dover Patrol, tried to reinforce them with a more solid obstruction of heavy nets, such as protected the entrance to Scapa Flow. But the difficulties of laying these across 20 miles of gale- and tide-swept waters proved insurmountable.

This failure was not, however, of importance until December 1916 when, coincident with the decision to begin the second unrestricted U-boat campaign, the *Admiralstab* withdrew their ban on the Dover route. Moreover, to help U-boats through the Straits, they sent large torpedoboats to wreak havoc among the patrolling trawlers. Bacon responded by reinforcing these with his destroyers, which led to several spirited actions, such as one described by Commander E. R. G. R. Evans of the *Broke*:

> On the night of 20 April 1917, the *Swift* and *Broke* were fortunate enough to meet six modern torpedoboats within seven miles of Dover. Nothing could have suited us better because the *Broke*'s four 4-inch guns were equal to the broadside of any German, and the *Swift*'s 6-inch gun was a nasty thing to come up against. Seeing gun flashes shortly after midnight, we followed the *Swift* at full speed towards them. As the *Broke* opened fire, one of her torpedoes struck an enemy torpedoboat amidships. We then swung round to ram the next one, crashing into the port side of *G42* abreast her after funnel. As the bow swung round we carried her bodily along on our ram, pouring a deadly fire into her terrorized crew. Many clambered on to our forecastle, only to meet with instant death from our well-armed seamen and stokers. When we eventually broke clear, we left *G42* a sinking, blazing wreck. Later we tried to ram another enemy vessel, but missed astern owing to an explosion in a boiler-room. The *Broke* had 57 casualties, including 21 killed. We picked up 140 Germans to whom, when I later visited the mess-deck, I found our men giving a fried egg and bacon breakfast.

In April 1918, this and similar fights were transcended by another exploit, to be described by Churchill as 'the finest feat of arms' in the Great War, and an episode unsurpassed in the history of the Royal Navy'. The torpedoboats that raided the Dover Patrol, and the U-boats which passed through the Straits to attack shipping in the Channel and South-Western Approaches, were fortunate in having Bruges for their base. Six miles inland, nothing could attack them there, except aircraft against whose 100-lb bombs they were easily given concrete shelters. But if denied this port they would have to fall back to the distant Ems or Heligoland. So, as early as

November 1916, Asquith told General Sir William Robertson, Chief of the Imperial General Staff: 'There is no operation of war to which the War Committee attach greater importance than the deprivation to the enemy of Ostend and Zeebrugge' — the ports at which the two canals leading to Bruges entered the sea. And Jellicoe's pessimistic declaration to the War Committee in June 1917, that unless these ports were denied to the enemy the Allies would lose the war, was enough for Lloyd George to accept the heavy casualties which were expected of Haig's plan for capturing them. But this was foredoomed to failure: deprived of French support by the mutinies that afflicted their armies, then handicapped by exceptionally wet weather, the British advance was stopped in July by the battles of Messines and Third Ypres, and finally floundered in the tragedy of Passchendaele in November.

Meantime, Bacon evolved enormous concrete towers which were to be sunk at intervals across the Straits, so that these could be so well illuminated by flares and searchlights that U-boats would be compelled to make the passage submerged by night as well as day, and be trapped in the deep minefields. (The one tower completed by November 1918 has now served for nearly 50 years the peaceful purpose of marking the Nab shoal at the entrance to Spithead.) More important, Bacon saw in Tyrwhitt's rejected suggestion for an amphibious assault on the mole at Zeebrugge, as the prelude to a military advance on Antwerp, a possible way to block the canals. Jellicoe agreed and authorized its execution, but he did not show sufficient enthusiasm for such an admittedly hazardous operation to satisfy his Director of Plans, Rear-Admiral Roger Keyes (already noted for his part in the Heligoland Bight action, and for his conviction, when serving as Chief of Staff to de Robeck, that the Navy alone could force the Dardanelles). And knowing Keyes's exceptional aptitude for such a venture, one of Wemyss's first acts, on succeeding Jellicoe, was to appoint him to relieve Bacon at Dover.

There, in the first six weeks of 1918, Keyes was much more than a new broom that swept vigorously into every corner of the already established defences. Since Bruges was the base for three flotillas of torpedoboats and as many as 30 U-boats, he and his staff, notably Commander A. F. B. Carpenter, produced detailed plans for an operation with a threefold aim: to block the Bruges canal at Zeebrugge, to block Ostend harbour, and to inflict as much damage as possible on both these ports. Two months of intensive preparations followed. A special force of 82 officers and 1,698 men, all of them volunteers, many from the Grand Fleet, was given special training:

they included 30 officers and 660 other ranks of the Royal Marines. And a small armada of vessels was assembled at an anchorage in the Thames estuary where they were invisible from the shore. Including Tyrwhitt's Harwich Force, which was to cover the operation against any interference by German units coming down from the north, they numbered:

Monitors	8	Motor launches (MLs)	62
Old cruisers	6	Coastal motorboats (CMBs)	24
Light cruisers	8	Submarines	2
Destroyers	52	Ferry boats	2

and 1 picket boat

Many of these had to be specially adapted for the role they were required to play. The 6-inch armament of the cruiser *Vindictive*, of 5,750 tons, completed in 1899, was augmented with an 11-inch howitzer, flame-throwers and Stokes mortars, and a dozen long-hinged brows were fitted on her port side. The *Brilliant*, *Iphigenia*, *Intrepid*, *Sirius* and *Thetis*, cruisers of 3,600 tons built as far back as 1890–4, were each filled with 1,500 tons of concrete, and equipped with electrically fired scuttling charges. The small and likewise obsolescent submarines *C1* and *C3* carried large charges of explosives in their forward compartments. And the upper works of the *Iris II* and *Daffodil*, which had been withdrawn from their daily task of ferrying the people of Liverpool and Birkenhead across the Mersey, were protected with mattresses and bullet-proof plating.

By 7 April all was ready. Four days later the force sailed. The approach went well: at 2300 Commodore H. Lynes, with the ships destined for Ostend, parted company, whilst the remainder, led by Keyes in the destroyer *Warwick*, continued towards Zeebrugge. An hour later both ports were subjected to a heavy bombardment by aircraft and the monitors' guns. The noise drowned the roar from the engines of the CMBs as they closed the shore at high speed to lay a heavy smoke screen devised by Wing-Commander F. A. Brock of the RNAS. Unfortunately, the wind, needed to ensure that this screen cloaked the final approach of the force, suddenly shifted and began to blow it away. This left Keyes with no prudent alternative to cancelling the attack; and despite the difficulty of reversing the course of so many darkened ships, all returned safely to the Swin, with the single exception of *CMB33* which had the misfortune to ground on an offshore shoal, and was captured by the enemy.

Nor was this Keyes's only disappointment. No sooner had he

sailed his force for the second time, on 13 April, than the wind freshened to a gale and he was again compelled to signal the recall, and face the fact that ten days must now elapse before the tides would be suitable for another try. The delay could have been fatal. From *CMB33* Admiral Ludwig von Schröder, commander of the Flanders naval forces and of the *Marinekorps* of German naval reservists who manned the coast defences, obtained a copy of Keyes's operation orders. To quote the German official historian:

> Whilst the hostile activity on the night of 11th–12th April was not out of the ordinary, the orders found in *CMB33* called for special attention. A heightened degree of combat readiness was ordered for the coastline – but this measure was not transmitted to the mole battery at Zeebrugge, nor to the torpedoboats berthed alongside the mole –

an error that was to be as fortunate for Keyes as the young captain of *CMB33*'s disregard of his explicit instructions against carrying any written orders onboard might have been disastrous.

The British armada left the Swin for the third time on the afternoon of 22 April. Shortly before dusk Keyes was reminded that this was the eve of St George's Day and signalled four inspiring words to his ships: 'St George for England'. From Carpenter, to whom Keyes had given the honour of commanding the *Vindictive*, came the apt reply: 'May we give the dragon's tail a damned good twist.' The passage was otherwise uneventful, except for the parting of submarine *C1*'s tow-rope which was to prevent her reaching her destination, and an engine breakdown in one of the MLs which was unable to take off surplus stokers from the *Intrepid*, as was done with the other expendable cruisers. And shortly after 2300 Lynes again led his ships away towards Ostend.

At Zeebrugge the sentries at the guns on the extension at the seaward end of the two-mile-long mole,

> being accustomed to nightly air raids, saw no reason to increase the state of alertness when they first heard the sound of engines around 2330. But when this did not diminish, star-shell were fired which revealed a fog developing in the west. An alert was then ordered for the entire coastline [protected by batteries mounting 225 guns of which 136 were of 6-inch up to 15-inch calibre] just as the monitors *Erebus* and *Terror* began bombarding Zeebrugge with their 15-inch guns. The fog was too dense to be pierced by the searchlights on the mole, and the numerous

small craft that were glimpsed through it vanished before the mole battery could open fire – until at 2350, the *Vindictive* suddenly appeared out of the fog, only 1,500 yards away.

And in the five minutes that it took her to reach the protection of the mole's high outer wall, German guns decimated the naval and marine storming parties that were standing ready on her upper deck and superstructure, killing their commanders, Captain H. C. Halahan and Lieutenant-Colonel B. N. Elliot. This barrage, to which the *Vindictive*'s weapons, directed by Commander E. O. B. S. Osborne, immediately replied, also wrecked eight of her special brows and damaged two more. But it did not prevent Carpenter placing his ship alongside the mole just one minute after the scheduled hour of midnight, where the bows of the *Daffodil*, Lieutenant H. Campbell, held her until her special anchors could be secured.

'The attack on the mole,' wrote Keyes, 'was intended to distract the enemy's attention. Its objectives were, firstly, the capture of the 5·9-inch mole battery which was a serious menace to the blockships and, secondly, to do as much damage to the material on the mole as time permitted.' So, over the two remaining brows went the three companies of the naval storming party, led by Lieutenant-Commander B. F. Adams of the battlecruiser *Princess Royal*, first to make the *Vindictive* fast, then to wreck the battery. Unfortunately, in the dark inferno of shot and shell, Carpenter had been unable to place his ship nearer than some two hundred yards to the west of this objective. Adams and his men were, therefore, subjected to heavy machine-gun fire from the fortified zone at the end of the mole, which delayed their advance along the parapet until they had insufficient time to do more than destroy the control position at the battery's shore end. For the same reason, coupled with the difficulty which Commander V. Gibbs experienced in keeping the *Iris II* in her berth ahead of the *Vindictive* for long enough to land her company of the storming party, the marines, whom Major B. G. Weller led across the cruiser's surging brows, to drop by ropes and scaling ladders to the floor of the mole, were held up by stiff opposition from the *Marinekorps* defenders – even though these numbered only 100 officers and men because the 200 manning the seaplane base near the railway viaduct remained in their bomb-proof shelter to which, as was usual with the almost nightly air raids, they had withdrawn at the first alarm. So did the crews of the seven torpedo-boats berthed alongside the mole, until their officers persuaded them

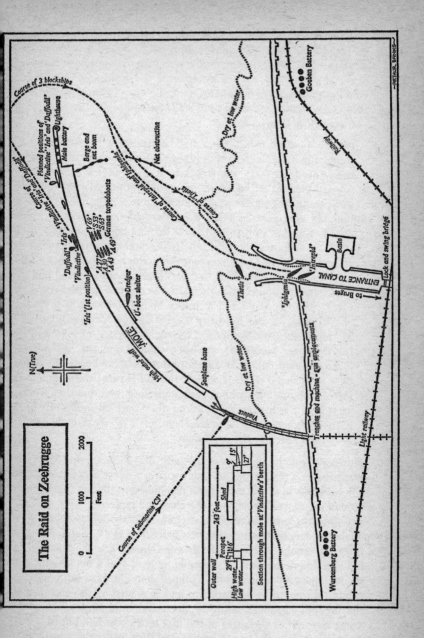

The Raid on Zeebrugge

N (True)

0   1000   2000
         Feet

Course of 3 blockships

Planned positions of "Vindictive," "Iris" and "Daffodil"

Lighthouse

Mole battery

Barge and net boom

Net obstruction

Course of "Warwick" and "Phoebe"

Course of "Iris"

"Daffodil" "Iris"

"Vindictive"

V.69
S.53
S.63
G.49 German torpedoboats
A.27
A.30
A.43

"Iris" (1st position)

Dredger
U-boat shelter

Course and "Daffodil"

"Vindictive" "Iris"

Fifth outer mole

MOLE

Seaplane base

Dry at low water

Viaduct

Railway

Dry at low water

Basin

"Intrepid"

ENTRANCE TO CANAL

Lock and swing bridge

to Bruges

"Iphigenia"

"Thetis"

Trenches and machine-gun emplacements

Light railway

Goeben Battery

Wurtemberg Battery

Course of Submarine "C3"

Outer wall

243 feet

Parapet

Shed

High water
Low water

29'
11.6'

9'   15'
12'

Section through mole at "Vindictive's" berth

—ARTHUR BANKS.

to return to their ships, just in time to forestall a gallant attempt by Lieutenant C. D. R. Lamplough to seize *S53* with a handful of marines. The delay was, however, enough to prevent the naval demolition company, under Lieutenant C. C. Dickinson of the battleship *Resolution*, from advancing along the mole to destroy its works before the *Vindictive*'s siren sounded the recall.

Long before this, in order to

prevent reinforcements from the land passing on to the mole, submarine *C3*, Lieutenant R. D. Sandford, sighted the viaduct right ahead. At 0015 she struck it at right angles between two rows of piers at 9½ knots, riding up on to the horizontal girders, and penetrating as far as her conning tower. The crew lowered the skiff: the fuses were then ignited and the submarine abandoned: the skiff's propeller having been damaged, oars had to be used. Immediately the skiff left, two searchlights were switched on and fire opened with machine-guns, rifles and pom-poms. The boat was holed many times, but was kept afloat by special pumps. The charge exploded when the skiff was but two or three hundred yards from the viaduct. The picket boat [which made a voyage of 170 miles to and from the Belgian coast under the command of Lieutenant-Commander F. H. Sandford, much of it in tow of the destroyer *Moorsom*] was then sighted and the skiff's crew taken onboard. Mr. R. D. Sandford describes the behaviour of his crew as splendid. To this modest praise I [Keyes] would add that the officers and men who eagerly undertook such hazards are deserving of the highest recognition: they were all well aware that if their means of rescue failed them, as it nearly did, they must have been killed by the explosion.

This breached the viaduct for a length of 120 feet – but the Germans did not realize this in time to stop a bicycle company, that was hurrying on to the mole, from plunging into the sea that swirled around the twisted remains of the piers and girders.

Coincident with Sandford's exploit, whose success made *C1*'s mishap of no consequence, the first blockship, HMS *Thetis*, emerged from the smoke screen. Under heavy German fire she steamed at full speed past the head of the mole, only to foul a net obstruction on its landward side, which stopped her engines. In a sinking condition she swung to starboard and grounded by the entrance to the dredged channel leading to the canal. And there, instead of going right up to the gates of the first lock as he had hoped – perhaps into it since the keeper had opened them under the illusion that the approaching ship was a friendly one – Commander Ralph Sneyd had to blow her scuttling charges. He and a steaming party of some 50 officers and men then abandoned ship into their one remaining cutter from which they were rescued by a waiting ML.

If the *Thetis*'s attempt at blocking the canal was in one sense a failure, in another it served the good purpose of drawing much of the fire of the mole and coastal batteries from the two ships that were following her. Thus protected, Lieutenant Stuart Bonham-Carter was able to take the *Intrepid* into the canal where he blew her scuttling charges, then embarked with as many as 86 officers and men, instead of the intended 53, in *ML282*. And following the *Intrepid* came her sister-ship, the *Iphigenia*, which Lieutenant E. W. Billyard-Leake, after first ramming an obstructing dredger, was likewise able to place across the canal before blowing the scuttling charges. He and his crew made their escape, first by cutter, then (because the ML detailed for this role was damaged) in *ML282*, whose young captain, Lieutenant P. T. Dean, RNVR, was willing to attempt the return journey with the best part of 150 survivors onboard.

With all three blockships sunk well inside the planned hour, there was no reason for Carpenter to delay recalling the storming parties later than 0100. By 15 minutes past that hour the *Vindictive* had re-embarked the survivors, including the wounded (except for 1 officer and 14 men who failed to reach the brows in time and were made prisoners-of-war), and was on a course for home. Half an hour later Keyes in the *Warwick* led the destroyers *North Star* and *Phoebe* in an attack on the German torpedoboats. One of their torpedoes struck the mole extension, another sank the dredger *Hessen*, which was insufficient compensation for the loss of the *North Star* to the German batteries. She was, however, the only sizeable British ship sunk in the raid, other than those that were expendable. The British casualties totalled 214 killed and 383 wounded, but the decorations awarded numbered as many as 11 VCs, 21 DSOs, 29 DSCs, 16 CGMs and 143 DSMs. And these figures speak more eloquently than any words for Keyes's near-genius in conceiving such a unique operation, for the meticulous way in which it was planned and prepared, and for the fantastic skill and courage with which it was carried out against tremendous odds.

Keyes believed the Zeebrugge raid to have been 'completely successful in attaining its first and most important object: the entrance to the Bruges ship canal was blocked'. But he also had to report:

I regret that the effort to block Ostend did not succeed. The *Brilliant*, Commander A. R. Godsal, with the *Sirius*, Lieutenant-Commander H. N. M. Hardy, in her wake, did not sight the buoy [marking the channel into Ostend harbour] in its charted position at midnight, as was expected. When the Ostend piers should have been seen, breakers were observed on the *Brilliant*'s starboard bow, and although her helm was put to starboard, she grounded. The *Sirius* immediately put her helm hard over and her engines full astern, but being already badly damaged by gunfire, she did not answer her helm and collided with the *Brilliant*'s port quarter. Both being then fast ashore, one with her port engine immovable, the other in a sinking condition, they were blown up where they were stranded. The rescue of their crews by MLs which had been standing by under heavy fire, was carried out in a most gallant manner. Their Lordships will share our disappointment at the defeat of our plans by the legitimate ruse of the enemy in shifting the Stroom Bank buoy, unknown to us, to a new position about 2,400 yards to the east of the canal entrance.

Keyes might be disappointed, but he was anything but disheartened. He immediately planned another raid on Ostend, using the *Vindictive* and *Sappho* as blockships, the latter being a sister-ship of the *Thetis*. These were ready to sail as soon as the afternoon of 9 May, but shortly after leaving the Swin the *Sappho* dropped astern with an engine defect. However, Keyes, who was again leading the covering force in the *Warwick*, and Lynes, who was likewise directing the raid itself from the flotilla leader *Faulknor*, determined to go on. And at 0130 next morning the heavy guns of four monitors began the attack with a bombardment directed at the coastal batteries, whilst MLs and CMBs laid an offshore smoke screen whose density was reinforced by a sea mist. Before she could gain its cover, the *Vindictive*, now commanded by Godsal of the ill-fated *Brilliant*, was sighted by two patrolling German torpedoboats. But these not only failed to attempt an attack on the approaching blockship, but were themselves involved in a disabling collision.

Unaware of this incident, Godsal steamed on. This time he was successful in finding the channel into Ostend harbour. He also manœuvred his ship safely through the barrage of fire which the German batteries brought to bear as she emerged through the smoke. Unfortunately, he was killed as the *Vindictive* was steaming in between the two piers, just after he had given a helm order designed to keep her in mid-channel. Before Lieutenant Victor Crutchley could assume command in his place, the blockship was hard aground against the eastern pier, where she had to be scuttled even though she was not obstructing the channel. All who remained of the *Vindictive*'s crew were then rescued by an ML, though this was not the end of their night's adventures. Because the ML had been damaged and was in danger of sinking, Crutchley and his men were taken off by the *Warwick*; and on her way back to Dover, Keyes's flagship struck a mine aft and had to be towed home by two of her consorts.

The decorations awarded for gallantry in this raid included a VC for Crutchley. But for Keyes it spelled failure: to quote the German official historian, 'the location of the *Vindictive* in no way interfered with the use of Ostend'. So, with characteristic determination, the Admiral planned a further sortie for which, in addition to the *Sappho*, he proposed to use the small pre-dreadnought *Swiftsure* as a blockship. But (to quote the same German source) 'this third operation was not carried out for reasons that are not known'. In fact, the Admiralty withheld approval when they learned that, for a further raid on Ostend to be of any use, another would also have to be made on Zeebrugge.

Understandably [wrote the German historian], the English initially considered the operation against Zeebrugge a complete success. And from Admiral von Schröder's inspection of the mole and locks on the following morning, with the two blockships lying in the narrow channel, it appeared that the enemy had struck a powerful blow at the conduct of the U-boat war. The entrance was blocked at low water, so that U-boats at sea were advised to return via Ostend. Very shortly, however, the actual situation proved to be completely different. As early as noon on 24 April, four small torpedoboats passed out of the Zeebrugge locks at high water. On the next day, 25 April, a further six torpedoboats sailed without difficulty. And on the same day, *UB16* passed both out and in. True, the big U-boats and larger torpedoboats were, for a short time, ordered to leave and return via Ostend. But at a conference called to discuss raising the blockships, it was decided instead to deepen and widen the fairway to east and west of the sunken ships by dredging. And the fairway to the west of the sterns of the two blockships was soon restored to a depth of 12 feet at low water, and after 14 May it was completely open for all submarines and torpedoboats.

The German historian continues with this tribute:

The English attack on Zeebrugge is a model of a meticulously planned, magnificently prepared and boldly executed attempt to eliminate a strongly defended enemy base by blocking it from the sea. The leadership was in the hands of a battle-proven, experienced and determined Admiral. Officers and men were specially selected, trained to perfection for their special tasks, and filled with aggressive spirit. Preparations had been conceived and carried out to the smallest detail, and stringent secrecy skilfully maintained. Better prospects for success could hardly have occurred – yet it was a failure. The *Vindictive*'s berthing at the wrong place alongside the mole, the destruction of most of her brows, and the casualties among the leaders of her storming parties could not be compensated for, however great the offensive spirit. This and other deviations from a minutely prepared and practised plan had such a marked influence on the overall result that all gallantry was in vain, and the goal of blocking the canal was not achieved.

This verdict is more objective than that of most British writers who have been as prone to acclaim Zeebrugge as a glorious success as others have treated Dunkirk (1940) as a British victory. Yet those who lost their lives in this raid did not give them in vain; nor was Keyes wrong, when he was later awarded a peerage, to take the title of Baron Keyes of Zeebrugge and Dover. On the contrary, the mole at Zeebrugge rightly bears to this day a plaque marking the spot where the *Vindictive* berthed in the early hours of St George's Day, 1918. For, although the canal was only partially blocked for a few short weeks, the news that the Royal Navy had carried out this direct assault on an enemy-held port, coming as it did shortly after German troops had broken through the British line at St Quentin (21 March), proved an inspiration that upheld the Allies' flagging spirits until they launched their successful counter-attack at Château-Thierry (18 June), which was the curtain-raiser to five months of unbroken victory that ended with the armistice in November. Contrariwise, in Germany, where the Grand Fleet's blockade had brought morale to a low ebb, the news came as a stunning blow. Ludendorff's complaints that the coastal defence batteries had signally failed to prevent the blockships entering Ostend and Zeebrugge harbours were bitter. As strong was von Schröder's riposte:

There is no infallible defensive measure against ruthlessly prosecuted blocking attempts undertaken under cover of night and fog. The English may be expected to continue their attempts to render the Flanders bases useless for the U-boat war. Aside from stepped-up bombardments and air attacks, we will have to expect more blocking attempts. Landings on a large scale, which might be significant for the fighting on land, are out of the question, but surprise assaults may occur at any time. Should the Army consider it necessary to prevent these, the entire coastline will have to be manned by a continuous line of infantry, requiring three to four times the forces used heretofore.

Although these were not available, much effort was expended against further British raids. More guns were added to the coastal batteries; the defences on the mole were strengthened; a torpedo-boat was berthed alongside the mole extension with her tubes manned ready to sink an approaching blockship; further minefields were laid to seaward; and the approaches to Zeebrugge and Ostend were constantly patrolled by torpedoboats and minesweepers.

By this time, however, there was no need for the Royal Navy to repeat such costly raids: the convoy system had won the long-drawn battle against the U-boats. The Allies had made their command of the sea as effective below the surface as it was above. But the Kaiser's attempt to set Britain's sea power at nought had come too near success for the Germans to believe their defiance of the accepted rules of war to be no better than a gambler's fatal throw. Pressed by the Allies after signing the Treaty of Versailles, they arraigned a mere five of their many U-boat captains as war criminals. The Supreme Court at Leipzig went so far as to sentence two to four years' imprisonment: they had sunk a hospital ship and then tried to obliterate all traces of their deed by destroying her survivor-laden boats. But of the other three, one was acquitted and two received sentences of no more than six to ten months' imprisonment. As Stephen Roskill has justly written: 'Such was the paltry outcome of the first attempt to bring home to the German people the inhumanity displayed by some members of their armed forces in war.'

The consequences were far-reaching. In contravention of a peace treaty that forbade the inclusion of a single submarine in Germany's small post-war Fleet, a secret U-boat design section was soon established at the Hague under cover of a Dutch firm. Admiral

Raeder, on becoming C-in-C of the German Navy in 1928, ordered two experimental boats to be built, the first of 750 tons in Spain, the second of 250 tons in Finland. The latter became the prototype for 24 U-boats to be prefabricated in 1934 ready for rapid assembly as soon as the Anglo-German Naval Agreement was signed a year later. By 3 September 1939 nearly 50 U-boats were in commission and as many under construction. Thus prepared, Nazi Germany unleashed unrestricted U-boat warfare on the first day of the Second World War, by sinking the liner *Athenia*, and thereafter devoted most of her naval effort to a second attempt to cut Britain's jugular vein.

Fortunately, the Admiralty had learned the lesson of 1917: the convoy system was begun without delay in September 1939 (but not by the USA when she entered the war, so that shipping running up and down her east coast suffered near-catastrophic losses in the months that followed December 1941). Even so, it was not until the spring of 1943, after the Allies had lost more than half a million tons of shipping in only 20 days that the tide was turned, and the way was clear for the Battle of the Atlantic to be won by the destruction of 785 out of Germany's total force of more than 1,000 U-boats.

Today, Britain and Germany are allied members of NATO. But unrestricted submarine warfare came too near success in two world wars for the lesson to be ignored by another renascent naval power. The USSR has built up, and now maintains in peace, a force of more than 400 submarines. Have the NATO powers the ships and aircraft to counter such a threat to their seaborne trade? And if that threat should become a reality, will convoys prove to be the most effective defence? Or will the concentrations of shipping which these involve be too vulnerable to annihilation by nuclear weapons?

It will be best if these questions are not put to the test of a third world war.

EPILOGUE

15

Death of a Fleet

---

*Von Hipper's last sortie in October 1918 – The scuttling of the
High Seas Fleet in June 1919*

> When Jellicoe assumed the name of Viscount Scapa (*sic*),
> there was a good deal of scoffing that an admiral should
> take the name of a desolate place where his fleet had re-
> mained at anchor almost continuously for four years. And
> yet by those four years the English Fleet exerted that
> decisive pressure which ended in our whole fighting Fleet
> being led to this same Scapa Flow where it now lies on
> the sea bottom. What a triumph for the 'Viscount of
> Scapa'!
>
> > *Commander von Hase*

Though it passed unrecognized at the time, the Allies' victory in
the long-drawn battle against the U-boats was the beginning
of the end. Germany had no other weapon with which to dispute
command of the sea, no other way in which to disrupt the flow of
supplies across the Channel and Atlantic, nor to prevent the Allied
armies in France being reinforced by a million fresh US troops. Foch
was enabled to do more than halt Ludendorff's spring offensive
short of the gates of Paris: he followed up with a crushing riposte
on the Marne. On 8 August, Haig's men, who had been fighting
'with their backs to the wall', advanced nine miles – 'the black day
of the German Army'; four weeks later Ludendorff's troops were
retreating all along the Western Front.

Germany's allies fared no better: by the middle of September
General Franchet d'Espérey had breached the Macedonian front and
was threatening Sofia, impelling the Bulgarians to ask for an
armistice, which was granted on the 30th. With the way opened
for the Allies to by-pass the Dardanelles, and her armies reeling

back from Allenby's offensive in Palestine, Turkey made a like request to save Constantinople. By this time Germany was menaced by a greater danger than the defeat of her armies in the West. Brought near to starvation by the Grand Fleet's blockade, the German people were raising the red flag of revolt against a war that subjected them to so much suffering. To avert a tragedy similar to that to which Russia had succumbed, the Kaiser appointed a new Chancellor, Prince Max of Baden, with authority to seek an armistice. But on 5 October President Wilson answered to the effect that negotiations were impossible so long as U-boats were sinking passenger ships.

Scheer, who had moved to Berlin early in August on von Holtzendorff's retirement, went farther than accepting this limitation. Regarding it as equivalent to abandoning unrestricted warfare by his U-boats, he recalled them to Germany on 21 October. This freed them, for the first time since 1916, to support a sortie by the High Seas Fleet which 'must be thrown into the scales: it is a matter of honour for the Navy to have done its utmost in the last battle' – which could affect the armistice negotiations, just as the Dutch raid on the Medway had done at Breda in 1667. Having accepted his high office on condition that the three parts of the naval high command were amalgamated into a *Seekriegsleitung*, where he would have unfettered responsibility for naval operations comparable with that of the British First Sea Lord, Scheer had no need to seek the approval of the Kaiser or the Chancellor before authorizing von Hipper, his natural successor as C-in-C High Seas Fleet, to plan this desperate venture. Two groups of light cruisers, accompanied by torpedoboats, would carry out simultaneous dawn raids on Allied trade, one along the Flanders coast, the other in the Thames Estuary. Both were to be covered by 18 battleships, five battlecruisers, and six flotillas of torpedoboats, a massive force with which Hipper hoped to bring the Grand Fleet to action off Terschelling later that day. To help achieve this, he would deploy seven zeppelins to report Beatty's progress south; light cruisers would lay mines across the British line of advance; and, further to reduce the British superiority, U-boats would patrol off the Firth of Forth and elsewhere in the North Sea, with orders to use their torpedoes at every warship sighted.

The U-boats were the first to sail: 25 began leaving German ports on 25 October. Three days later, *U78* was torpedoed by the British submarine *G2*. *UB116* was another that was destined never to return, for reasons worth telling in greater detail. A 519-ton boat, armed with five 19·7-inch tubes, she carried her normal crew of 26 officers and men (*not* a volunteer crew of officers only, as some authorities have erroneously stated) under the command of Lieutenant H. J. Emsmann when she left Heligoland with orders to attempt an operation such as had only been tried once before – by Lieutenant-Commander von Hennig's *U18* in November 1914 (see p 134). *UB116* was 'to attack the English Battle Fleet in Scapa Flow, regardless of the risk involved, during the night of 28–29 October, otherwise on 29–30, in order to weaken the enemy as much as possible before the decisive battle'. Why the Leader of Submarines issued such an order is obscure: it was well known that the Grand Fleet had moved to Rosyth in April. But this mistake was not so disastrous as another paragraph in Commodore Michelsen's instructions: Emsmann was advised to enter the Flow by Hoxa Sound, because U-boats passing through the Pentland Firth had reported this to be in regular use by British vessels so that, unlike the other entrances, it would not be blocked by nets, mines or other obstacles.

This assumed that the British had abandoned a once-common method of defending a harbour entrance, lines of moored mines that could be fired electrically from the shore, but which were only of use against a vessel that was seen to cross them, and identified as an enemy. In fact, British scientists had overcome this deficiency: by 1918 the mines moored across Hoxa Sound had been augmented by long loops of cable on the sea bed, in which a crossing vessel induced an electric current sufficient to deflect a galvanometer needle in an observation hut ashore. So when, at 2221 on the night of 28 October, hydrophones on Stanger Head picked up the sounds of approaching engines, and no friendly vessel was expected, a possible U-boat was reported, and the loop minefields activated. Emsmann saw the searchlights on each side of Hoxa switched on and start sweeping: nonetheless, in the confident belief that he could not be detected so long as he remained submerged, he continued his approach. And he was not seen until 2330 when he surfaced momentarily to check his position, by which time he was very near to the entrance and heading straight for it. But two minutes later the magnetism in *UB116*'s hull moved the galvanometer needles on Flotta, the mines across Hoxa Sound were fired, and when the sound of their detonation had died away, there was nothing to be heard from the listening hydrophones. Daylight revealed patches of oil on the surface; depth charges released wreckage and a German naval watchcoat; and divers identified the crushed and flooded remains of Emsmann's first and last command.

The other 23 U-boats returned to Germany, but without firing their torpedoes at the Grand Fleet. Although Scheer and von Hipper tried to conceal their plans under the guise of a fleet exercise, they could not blind the Admiralty's intelligence sources. Their suspicions were roused by the cessation of U-boat attacks on shipping, and Beatty was warned that he might be required to put to sea. By 27 October they knew that U-boats were concentrated to seaward of the Firth of Forth and spread across the Grand Fleet's likely course if it moved south. Twenty-four hours later, Beatty was told that an attempt to draw the Grand Fleet out might be made next day. The Admiralty could not, however, divine the High Seas Fleet's objective, to which they added the incorrect appreciation that von Hipper would not risk a fleet action when an armistice was being negotiated. But these shortcomings were of small importance: the Grand Fleet was not required to leave harbour. As the German C-in-C ordered his ships, assembled in the Jade, to raise steam late on 29 October, several of their crews refused to obey their officers: demoralized by the same seeds of unrest as those to which they had fallen prey in 1917, they had no intention of being sacrificed in battle when the end of the war was near. When this disaffection spread to more ships next day, von Hipper was faced with a mutiny which compelled him to cancel the sortie, and disperse his squadrons to other ports where hundreds of ratings were marched ashore under arrest. His attempts to restore discipline were only partially successful before the armistice was signed, and the red flag of revolution replaced the Imperial naval ensign.

But what if the High Seas Fleet had sailed for this 'death battle'? The Grand Fleet and the Harwich Force would have been ordered to sea: even if the Admiralty had failed to detect von Hipper's initial move at daybreak on the 30th, they must have risen to the bait on the 31st, the raids by his light forces on shipping off the Flanders coast and in the Thames Estuary. As the Grand Fleet came south, some of the waiting U-boats would have attacked it; but there is no reason why they would have been more successful than in August 1916, that they would have damaged or sunk more than a handful of British capital ships or cruisers. Even if German mines had done as much, Beatty would have had twice the number of von Hipper's battleships and battlecruisers. And with this superiority; with ships whose magazines were no longer vulnerable to cordite flash and filled with effective armour-piercing shell; with admirals and captains who knew that they were expected to seize every opening that the enemy offered; with officers and men imbued with a confidence denied to their enemies; who can doubt that the Grand Fleet would have gained an annihilating victory ... *if* the two Battle Fleets had come to grips. The weather, always fickle in the North Sea, might have intervened. Von Hipper, for all the courage he had shown at Jutland, might have flinched from such unequal combat. The Admiralty, or Beatty, might have hesitated to hazard the Grand Fleet so far south in the North Sea as Terschelling (though von Hipper's orders allowed for this to the extent that, if the Battle Fleets failed to meet by the evening of 1 November, his torpedoboat flotillas were to go north and attack that night, whilst his waiting U-boats would have a further chance against what was left of the Grand Fleet as it returned to harbour). This great 'battle that never was' might, then, have been no more than a series of clashes between the Harwich Force and German light forces raiding the Flanders coast and the Thames Estuary. Be this as it may, it is impossible to believe that von Hipper would have achieved a tithe of what de Ruyter did in 1667, when he raided the Medway because Charles II was so unwise as to pay off his Fleet before the end of the Second Dutch War; for on 30 October 1918, the British Fleet was at a peak of efficiency, the mightiest naval force the world had known.

Honour, nonetheless, to Scheer and von Hipper for intending to hazard the High Seas Fleet in this way: though compelled soon afterwards to submit to internment at Scapa Flow, the German ships deserved a better grave than the one to which they went some eight months later. From the end of November 1918 until midsummer 1919 the pride of the Imperial German Navy rusted at their anchors in the gale-swept waters of the Orkney Islands: 11 dreadnought battleships, five battlecruisers, eight light cruisers, and 50 torpedoboats. Of the 400 officers and men needed to steam each capital ship to Scapa Flow, half were soon returned to Germany, and likewise with the smaller vessels. Those who remained were under Rear-Admiral von Reuter's command; he was responsible for complying with the armistice terms and with Beatty's orders. The British admirals who took it in turns to ensure this for a month at a time had an unenviable task. Beatty and Wemyss wanted the High Seas Fleet to be *surrendered*: others on the Supreme War Council argued that a demand so drastic must await a peace treaty; that, until then, Germany's principal warships could only be *interned* in an Allied port. No one foresaw that so long would elapse before the Allies agreed on peace terms. For all this time the Scapa guardships – a battle squadron, a flotilla of destroyers and patrolling trawlers – were in a position to foil any attempt by the German ships to escape to neutral Norway. They could also prevent their crews from leaving their ships. But they could not ensure compliance with Article XXXI of the armistice terms, 'no destruction of ships ... to be permitted', because von Reuter had to be allowed to visit them if he was to maintain his authority; and British guards could not be placed onboard the German vessels unless they committed a breach of the armistice terms.

However, as each month passed, such treachery seemed more and more unlikely. Von Reuter, who added poor health to the humiliation of defeat, appeared willing to cooperate with his gaolers. Moreover, his men were seldom far from mutiny: indeed, he had so much trouble with the crew of the *Friedrich der Grosse* that he was allowed to transfer his flag to the *Emden*. Except for this, nothing of note occurred up to the end of March 1919, when Beatty's flag was struck, the Grand Fleet ceased to exist, and responsibility for the interned German ships passed to the newly formed Atlantic Fleet, under Madden's command. And everything remained quiet after the arrival of the 1st BS, composed of the five 'Revenges', in the middle of May, until the last day of that month, when the German ships contravened Beatty's orders by hoisting the Imperial naval ensign to mark the anniversary of Jutland.

There is no reason to doubt von Reuter's denial of responsibility for this gesture of defiance, not least because many of his ships also hoisted the red flag. That he turned it to his own advantage is another matter. Until then he had always insisted that he needed a minimum of 200 officers and men onboard each of his capital ships to keep them in good order, which neither Beatty nor Madden felt able to deny him whilst they remained German property. Now, von Reuter suggested that further trouble might be obviated by cutting each caretaker crew to 120; and no one suspected his willingness to allow more than 2,000 to leave Scapa for Germany in the middle of June. No one realized that because the Allies had at last agreed on peace terms which included the *surrender* of his fleet, von Reuter no longer needed to keep his ships in running order. Moreover, his officers and men had completed preparations for an act of immolation for which it was best that only an essential few remained.

On board the *Revenge*, Vice-Admiral Sydney Fremantle was informed that the Treaty would be signed at Versailles on 21 June. He made plans to seize the German ships at the time the armistice ended, possibly against opposition: he had no authority to board them earlier. But because he foresaw the possibility that the Ger-

mans might forestall him by taking some action in contravention
of Article XXXI of the armistice terms, he decided that his squadron
ought to remain in harbour all that day. He signalled Madden for
approval to defer the practice torpedo attacks which his destroyer
flotilla had been ordered to carry out on the 1st BS. But, despite the
reasons given by the 'man on the spot', the C-in-C did not agree.

The conflict between Fremantle's responsibilities and his orders
was, however, seemingly resolved on the evening of the 20th. He
learned – and at once sent word to von Reuter – that the armistice
was to be extended for 48 hours. Since the 23rd was now the crucial
day, he no longer hesitated to take the 1st BS out into the Pentland
Firth on the 21st. The first torpedo attack was finished by noon. At
that hour the five battleships were some eight miles from the Orkneys, waiting for the nine destroyers to recover their torpedoes and
prepare for another attack in the afternoon. It was never carried out:
a few minutes after 1200 Fremantle received an urgent signal from
the Orkney naval base which impelled him to order his whole force
back to the Flow: 'German ships sinking. Some already sunk.'

'It was unthinkable to surrender defenceless ships to the enemy,'
wrote von Reuter afterwards. 'We officers were bound by a decision
of the All Highest to destroy them.' Since the Kaiser had abdicated
over six months before, it is more pertinent to enquire whether von
Reuter was acting on the orders of his Government. Berlin denied
this: 'scuttling was carried out without the knowledge or wish of
any German civil authority'. There is, however, evidence that they
gave the Admiral the latitude to do what he did. As it became clear
that a peace treaty involving surrender would soon be signed, his
officers prepared their ships for scuttling by opening inlets such as
condenser doors and submerged torpedo tubes, and ensuring that
neither these nor watertight doors and hatches could be closed again.
And on the 17th von Reuter issued orders that scuttling was to take
place at 1000 on 21 June, before the armistice expired, so as to forestall British boarding parties. Having thus decided to contravene
Article XXXI and so, in effect, to commit an act of war, he saw no
reason to change his plans when he learned that the armistice was
to be extended; he would gain the additional advantage of the absence of Fremantle's guardships. The Orkney islanders who chanced
to be watching the tideswept waters of Scapa Flow that morning saw
every German warship again hoist the Imperial naval ensign in
defiance of Beatty's order, though an hour or more elapsed before
anyone realized that the ships were going down by the head or
stern, or had an abnormal list to port or starboard. All, that is, ex-

cept for the *Emden*: von Reuter feared that the British drifter, which was berthed alongside to act as a link between him and Fremantle, would give the alarm in time for effective counteraction to be taken. As it was, no word reached the British Admiral before noon, by which hour most of the German ships were low in the water, or heeled near to capsizing. The few small British vessels that remained in the Flow could do nothing except pick up such Germans as jumped overboard, and order the rest to remain onboard until they were taken off under guard. A few shots were fired to enforce this, killing the captain of the *Markgraf*, and causing 22 other casualties; but no one else suffered, contrary to von Reuter's subsequent charge of 'ferocity and inhumanity'. 'Since feeling against Germany ran high in the British Navy,' wrote Captain Swabey of the *Revenge*, 'this speaks well for the discipline of men who had waited for over four years to play their part, and had been denied it because the German Fleet would not come out and accept battle.'

It was 1400 when Fremantle's force re-entered Scapa Flow and anchored near the sinking ships. Strong armed parties were immediately sent to close their underwater inlets, hatches and doors, and to try to beach them. But in all but a handful, this task was too difficult: the Germans had made their preparations with characteristic thoroughness. As Swabey wrote: 'We could get nothing out of the *Baden*'s crew as to the position of the seacocks which had been opened. And it is not difficult to imagine what it was like down in the bowels of a strange ship, minutely subdivided, as all German ships are, with no light except for a hand torch, knowing that she was sinking, and that at any moment she might heel over and go to the bottom.' The *Baden* was, however, the one capital ship to be saved, together with the light cruisers *Emden*, *Frankfurt* and *Nürnberg*, and half the torpedoboats. All the rest had sunk to the bottom by 1600.

This treacherous breach of the armistice – as Fremantle castigated it before ordering von Reuter, together with his officers and men, to be treated as prisoners of war – incited disapproval in Britain and among the Allies. Those who knew nothing of Madden's refusal to allow the torpedo practice to be deferred, criticized Fremantle for taking his force to sea on the 21st. But he could not have circumvented von Reuter's action, even if he had remained in harbour, though he might have beached a larger number of German ships before they sank. The Admiralty placed the responsibility squarely on the Supreme War Council for refusing to accept the British view that the ships should be surrendered under the armistice terms, instead of being interned with their crews onboard. But Wemyss wrote in his diary, 'I look upon the sinking as a real blessing. It disposes of the thorny question of the distribution of the German ships. I suppose there will be an outcry at the beginning, but when the facts become known, everybody will probably think, like me, "thank the Lord".' The surrendered ships were to have been divided amongst the Allies in proportion to the losses they had suffered during the war: but none needed more than a tithe of them: their Navies were already big enough. And the Scapa scuttle allowed a more useful penalty to be exacted from Germany: she was required to surrender five more light cruisers to France and Italy, and 'a large quantity of naval material such as floating docks, cranes, etc', which served the Royal Navy well in the Second World War.

The end of the High Seas Fleet is soon told. Of the beached ships, the *Baden* and *Nürnberg* were handed over to Britain, the *Emden* to France, the *Frankfurt* to the USA, where none survived for more than a handful of years. Of the scuttled vessels, five torpedoboats and one light cruiser were raised and scrapped at Scapa. Between 1924 and 1933, Messrs Cox and Danks lifted five capital ships, one light cruiser and no fewer than 26 torpedoboats, which were towed to Rosyth for breaking up. Metal Industries continued this, the biggest salvage operation ever undertaken. The *Derfflinger* was lifted from 20 fathoms in the spring of 1939, but by then another war with Germany was so imminent that no dock could be spared to take her upturned hull. She stayed at Scapa for the next seven years, when she was towed round to the Clyde to be broken up at Roseneath. The hulls of the dreadnoughts and four light cruisers remained beneath the waters of the Flow until after the Second World War.

Such was the squalid end of the Kaiser's Fleet that challenged Jellicoe and Beatty 30 years before: as Hitler said to Grand Admiral Raeder, who was on von Hipper's staff at Jutland: 'The scuttling of the fleet at Scapa Flow does not redound to the credit of the German Navy'. For the ships that composed the Grand Fleet, there was a more honourable end. Most were sacrificed to the twin gods of economy and disarmament in the decade that followed the Treaty of Versailles, but ten battleships of the 'Queen Elizabeth' and 'Royal Sovereign' classes, the battlecruisers *Repulse* and *Renown*, and the aircraft carrier *Furious*, together with the *Courageous* and *Glorious* likewise converted, formed the hard core of Britain's Fleet up to 1939. As many as a score of 'C' and 'D' class light cruisers, nearly 50 'V' and 'W' class destroyers, and a dozen of the smaller 'S' and 'T' class, remained in service for as long. All these fired their guns in anger again in 1939, and in the next six years played no small part in the destruction of the Navies of the Nazis and Japan, and in securing the surrender of Mussolini's Fleet. Assuredly these ships, some veterans of Jutland, served Britain well; and none more than the *Warspite*. The great guns of this charmed survivor of Hellfire Corner on 31 May 1916, turned the scales for the Allied armies at Salerno in September 1943; and in 1946, defiant to the last, she chose a rocky cove in Cornwall for her grave instead of submission to the shipbreaker's hammer.

But sea wars and sea battles are not won by ships alone. More depends on the men who man them, the captains who command them and the admirals who lead them. Versailles ended the naval career of the two great German admirals of the First World War, both Scheer and von Hipper retiring from public life, the former to die in 1928 when he was about to visit England as Jellicoe's guest, the latter in 1932. Von Tirpitz continued to strut the political stage in the Reichstag from 1924 to 1928, where he was chiefly responsible for persuading von Hindenburg to accept the presidency; but he, too, was dead before Hitler seized power and ordered the rebuilding of Germany's Fleet in a second attempt to seize Britannia's trident.

On the British side, both Beresford, the true begetter of the Grand Fleet, and Fisher, its incomparable architect, died before the ink was dry at Versailles, the first in 1919, the second in 1920. Jellicoe made a world tour of the Dominions and produced a report strongly recommending a two-ocean Imperial Navy, but this was largely ignored in Ottawa, Canberra and Whitehall, to the British Commonwealth's subsequent irrecoverable cost; he then served as Governor-General of New Zealand. From November 1919, when he succeeded Wemyss as First Sea Lord, until 1927, Beatty fought the hardest battle of his life, to maintain the strength of the British Navy against the apathy of a war-weary, impoverished nation. He live long enough to insist, though suffering from influenza, on walking behind Jellicoe's coffin in 1935; four months later he, too, was honoured with a funeral in St Paul's. None can deny these four, Beresford and Fisher, Jellicoe and Beatty, chief credit for the humiliating end of the High Seas Fleet at Scapa Flow.

And their legacy was not what Fisher called 'the tragedy' of Jutland, but a Navy freed of its chains, one which showed all the old Nelsonic skill when it was again called upon to defend Britain's moat in 1939, with Dudley Pound of the *Colossus* at the Admiralty's helm. Henry Harwood did not hesitate to match the *Exeter*, *Ajax* and

Achilles against the more powerful *Graf Spee*. Jack Tovey of the *Onslow*, now in command of the Home Fleet, brought the *Bismarck* to bay. Andrew Cunningham, with a Mediterranean Fleet that had been schooled by Chatfield of the *Lion* and W. W. Fisher of the *St Vincent* to fight a night action, showed the old aggressive spirit against a stronger enemy, destroying much of it at Taranto and Matapan. Bruce Fraser hunted and sank the *Scharnhorst*. Percy Noble and Max Horton achieved victory in the longest and fiercest battles of all, against Doenitz's U-boats. Above all, the British Navy and Mercantile Marine were used to transport large armies overseas whereby, first in North Africa, next in Sicily and Italy, and finally across the Channel, Germany's second attempt to conquer Europe was decisively defeated.

Jellicoe paid this tribute in one of his Jutland Dispatches:

Sir David Beatty showed his fine qualities of gallant leadership, firm determination and correct strategic insight. He appreciated the situation at once on sighting first the enemy's light forces, then his battlecruisers, and finally his Battle Fleet. I can fully sympathize with his feelings when the evening mist and failing light robbed the fleet of that complete victory for which he had manœuvred, and for which the vessels in company with him had striven so hard. The services rendered by him, not only on this, but on two previous occasions have been of the very greatest value.

Twenty years later Beatty wrote in *The Times*:

Jellicoe epitomized all the highest ideals for which the British Navy stands. The country owes a deep debt of gratitude to him for the valiant work he did during the war. He was an upright man and a model of integrity in everything he undertook. The tradition of the British Navy meant a great deal to him, and he was an admiral who made that tradition even more glorious.

The Nation delivered its verdict in 1948 in the words of the Duke of Gloucester when he unveiled bronze busts of both these admirals:

Together they led the Royal Navy through the last crisis of the long centuries when sea power depended upon ships and seamen alone. Their names bridge the gulf between the classic tradition of Trafalgar and the onset of total war. They were buried in St Paul's Cathedral twelve years ago; but it is right that we should do them this final honour in Trafalgar Square, beside the monument of our greatest seaman, on the anniversary of his greatest victory.

Jellicoe and Beatty may not merit columns as high as Nelson's but they well earned niches where,

> *On such the cryptic sightless eye is cast*
> *Of one with neither words nor time to spare,*
> *Only too thankful both have joined at last*
> *His lonely vigil in Trafalgar Square.*

Since then the tide of British sea power, which came to full flood in 1805 and remained high through the two world wars of this century, has ebbed away. In the 50 years that have elapsed since 1918, in the 23 years that have passed since 1945, the British people have been gripped by the creeping paralysis of craven fear of being great. We have lost our faith in a Fleet that, as it once destroyed the malevolent genius of Napoleon, so in our own time set at naught the ambitions of the Kaiser and of Hitler. We have allowed its strength to decline until it ranks a poor third in the navies of the world. Maybe the tide will turn, as most tides do. It *must* turn if Britain is to survive because, as Churchill said with all the percipience of his youth as long ago as 1901: 'The whole course of our history, the geography of our country, all the evidence proclaim beyond a doubt that Britain's power and prosperity depend on the economic command of markets and the Navy's command of the seas.'

But if this cannot be so in my lifetime – and I make no apologies for ending on a personal note – then I am glad that my earliest memory is of the mighty fleet of dreadnoughts that gathered at Spithead in July 1914; and that almost 30 years later 'I was there' in August 1943 to see the Italian Battle Fleet brought to anchor under the guns of the fortress of Malta. For the White Ensign under which I had the honour to serve for 35 years is not, nor has ever been, a brutal symbol of armed might. The sight of that flag waving in the breeze evokes more than memories of Sturdee at the Falklands, of Jellicoe and Beatty at Jutland, of Keyes at Zeebrugge. The Navy that flies it will always be remembered for having kept the peace of the world for as long as a hundred years. And for its chivalry and humanity to all nations both in peace and in war, in victory and in defeat, that Navy's ensign is still, and always will be saluted with a kind of international pride by many more than those who go down to the sea in ships and have their business in great waters.

Select Bibliography

Admiralty, *Jutland Despatches*
  Narrative of the Battle of Jutland
  Record of the Battle of Jutland (prepared by Captain J. E. T. Harper)
Alexander, R., *The Cruise of the Raider 'Wolf'*
Altham, Captain E. A., *Jellicoe*
Aspinall-Oglander, C. F., *Gallipoli*
  Roger Keyes
Bacon, Admiral Sir R. H., *The Life of Lord Fisher of Kilverstone*
  The Life of John Rushworth Earl Jellicoe
Bacon, Sir Reginald and McMurtrie, F. E., *Modern Naval Strategy*
Barnett, Corelli, *The Swordbearers*
Bennett, Geoffrey, *Coronel and the Falklands*
  The Battle of Jutland
Bingham, Commander the Hon H., *Falklands, Jutland and the Bight*
Brodie, Admiral C. G., *Forlorn Hope, 1915*
Busch, F. O., *Admiral Graf Spees Sieg und Untergang*
Bush, Eric, *Bless Our Ship*
Campbell, G., *My Mystery Ships*
Carpenter, Captain A. F. B., *The Blocking of Zeebrugge*
Chalmers, Rear-Admiral W. S., *The Life and Letters of David Beatty, Admiral of the Fleet*
Chatfield, Admiral of the Fleet, Lord, *The Navy and Defence*
Chatterton, E. Keble, *Danger Zone: The Story of the Queenstown Command*
Churchill, Winston S., *The World Crisis, 1914–1918*
Cooper, Commander H. Spencer, *The Battle of the Falkland Islands*
Corbett, Julian, and Newbolt, Henry, *Naval Operations, 1914–1918*
Creswell, Captain John, *Naval Warfare*
Cunningham, Admiral of the Fleet Viscount, of Hyndhope, *A Sailor's Odyssey*
Dawson, R. M., *Winston Churchill at the Admiralty*
Delage, E., *La Guerre sous les Mers*
Dewar, Vice-Admiral K. G. B., *The Navy from Within*
Dick, Admiral C., *The Cruiser Squadron, its Formation, Victory and End*
Dreyer, Admiral Sir Frederic, *The Sea Heritage*
Edwards, Lieutenant-Commander Kenneth, *We Dive at Dawn*
Falls, Cyril, *The First World War*

Fawcett, H. W., and Hooper, G. W. W., *The Fighting at Jutland*
Fayle, C. E., *Seaborne Trade, 1914–1918*
Fremantle, Admiral Sir Sydney, *My Naval Career, 1880–1928*
Frost, Commander H., USN, *The Battle of Jutland*
Frothingham, *The Naval History of the World War*
Gibson, Langhorne, and Harper, Vice Admiral J. E. T., *The Riddle of Jutland*
Gibson, R. H., and Prendergast, Maurice, *The German Submarine War, 1914–1918*
Goodenough, Admiral Sir William, *A Rough Record*
Grant, Robert, *U-boats Destroyed*
Gröner, *Die Deutschen Kriegsschiffe, 1815–1936*
Guépratte, Admiral, *L'expédition des Dardanelles*
Hamilton, General Sir Ian, *Gallipoli Diary*
Hankey, Lord, *The Supreme Command, 1914–18*
Harper, Vice-Admiral J. E. T., *The Truth about Jutland*
Hartz, H. von Waldeyer, *Von Tsingtau zu den Falkland Inseln*
Hase, Commander G. von, *Kiel and Jutland*
Hickling, Vice-Admiral Harold, *Saltwater Admiral*
Higgins, Trumbull, *Winston Churchill and the Dardanelles*
Hirst, Paymaster-Commander Lloyd, *Coronel and After*
Hoehling, A. A., *Lonely Command: The Story of the 'Emden'*
Horn, Daniel, *War, Mutiny and Revolution in the German Navy*
Hurd, A., *The Merchant Navy, 1914–18*
Irving, J., *Coronel and Falklands*
James, Robert Rhodes, *Gallipoli*
James, Admiral Sir William, *The Eyes of the Navy*
    A Great Seaman: The Life of Admiral of the Fleet Sir Henry Oliver
Jameson, Rear-Admiral Sir William, *The Fleet that Jack Built*
Jellicoe, Admiral Viscount John R., *The Grand Fleet, 1914–16: Its Creation, Development and Work*
    The Crisis of the Naval War
    The Submarine Peril
Jose, A. W., *Official History of Australia in the War of 1914–18, Vol IX, The Royal Australian Navy*
Joseph, Franz, Oberleutnant Prince von Hohenzollern, *Emden*
Kemp, Lieutenant-Commander P. K., *The Papers of Admiral Sir John Fisher* (Navy Records Society)
    H.M. Submarines
Keyes, Admiral Sir Roger, *Naval Memoirs*
King-Hall, Commander Sir Stephen, *My Naval Life*
    A Naval Lieutenant (under pseudonym 'Etienne')
Kirchoff, Vice-Admiral Hermann, *Maximilian Graf von Spee*
Laar, C., *Die Grauen Wölfe des Grafen Spee*
McGuire, F. M., *The Royal Australian Navy*
Macintyre, Captain Donald, *Jutland*
Magnus, Philip, *Kitchener: Portrait of an Imperialist*

Marder, A. J., *Fear God and Dread Nought*
  From the Dreadnought to Scapa Flow
  Portrait of an Admiral
Middlemas, Keith, *Command the Far Seas*
Milne, Admiral Sir Berkeley, *The Flight of the 'Goeben' and 'Breslau'*
Moorehead, Alan, *Gallipoli*
Mücke, Hellmuth von, *Emden-Ayesha*
Mühlmann, C., *Der Kampf um die Dardanellen*
Newbolt, Sir H., *Submarine and Anti-Submarine*
North, John, *Gallipoli, the Fading Vision*
Padfield, Peter, *Aim Straight*
Pastfield, The Rev. J. L., *New Light on Jutland*
Patterson, A. Temple, *The Jellicoe Papers* (Navy Records Society)
Pitt, Barrie, *Coronel and Falklands*
  Zeebrugge
Pochhammer, Hans, *Before Jutland: Admiral Spee's Last Voyage*
Raeder, E., and others, *Der Krieg zur See, 1914–18*
Reuter, L. von, *Scapa Flow*
Richmond, Admiral Sir Herbert, *National Policy and Naval Strength*
Robinson, Douglas, *The Zeppelin in Combat*
Roskill, Stephen, *The Strategy of Sea Power*
Sanders, Liman von, *Five Years in Turkey*
Scheer, Admiral Reinhard, *Germany's High Seas Fleet in the World War*
Schneider, H., *Die Letzte Fahrt des Kleinen Kreuzer 'Dresden'*
Schoen, Walter von, *Kreuzerkriegführen*
Schoultz, Commodore G. von, *With the British Battle Fleet: War Recollections of a Russian Naval Officer*
Scott, Admiral Sir Percy, *Fifty Years in the Royal Navy*
Seymour, Lady, *Commander Ralph Seymour*
Shankland, Peter, and Hunter, Anthony, *Dardanelles Patrol*
Sims, Admiral W. S., USN, *Victory at Sea*
Siney, Marion, *The Allied Blockade of Germany, 1914–16*
Stoker, Captain H. G., *Straws in the Wind*
'Taffrail', *Swept Channels*
Thomazi, *La guerre navale aux Dardanelles*
Tirpitz, Grand Admiral von, *My Memoirs*
Verner, Commander R., *The Battlecruisers in the Action off the Falkland Islands*
Waldeyer-Hartz, Hugo von, *Admiral von Hipper*
Weizsacker, Ernst von, *Memoirs*
Wemyss, Lady W., *Life and Letters of Lord Wester-Wemyss*
Wester-Wemyss, Admiral of the Fleet Lord, *The Navy in the Dardanelles Campaign*
Woodward, C. L., *Great Britain and the German Navy*
Wyllie, W. L., and Wren, M. F., *Sea Fights of the Great War*
Young, Filson, *With the Battlecruisers*

Index

The numerals in **heavy type** refer to the figure numbers of the illustrations

PERSONS

With a few exceptions these are given the highest rank and title which they attained at the time of the events chronicled in this book

BRITISH AND ALLIED SHIPS

Vessels *other than* British are distinguished by suffixes, viz: (F), French; (J), Japanese; (R), Russian; (US), United States. Destroyers which took part in the battle of Jutland, but which are mentioned by name only in Appendix F (pp. 194–9), are *not* included

GERMAN AND ALLIED SHIPS

Vessels other than German are distinguished by the suffix (T), Turkish. Different ships bearing the same name are distinguished by the suffixes (1) or (2)

Grand Strategy Series

GALLIPOLI (Illus)   75p

Robert Rhodes James

In the annals of war, the battlefields of the Gallipoli campaign stand for a breathtaking combination of heroism, muddle, endurance, incompetence and sacrifice.

This classic study re-examines the complex political, strategical and tactical aspects of the Dardanelles adventure that became one of the most inspiring, infuriating and heart-breaking of all the Allied campaigns in the Great War.

Robert Rhodes James has sifted through diaries and letters, documents published and unpublished, of those who fought at Gallipoli to show how the spirit of fighting men triumphed over every disaster as their high hopes were drowned in blood.

'Full, satisfying, authentic . . . much to say on the merits of both commanders and troops' – *Daily Telegraph*

'Grandly retold with many a look from the Turkish side of the hill' – *Sunday Times*

Grand Strategy Series

THE BOMBER OFFENSIVE (Illus)   75p

Anthony Verrier

Lancasters, Halifaxes, Stirlings, Liberators and Fortresses ... the names of the big bombers conjure up recollections of the thousand-bomber raids over Germany that were such a crucial factor in the strategy of the Second World War.

Anthony Verrier's book is a highly readable and impressively expert tribute to the aircraft and the men who flew them, allied to an arresting analysis of the development of air bombing strategy that culminated in the Anglo-American offensive in Europe through the later years of the war.